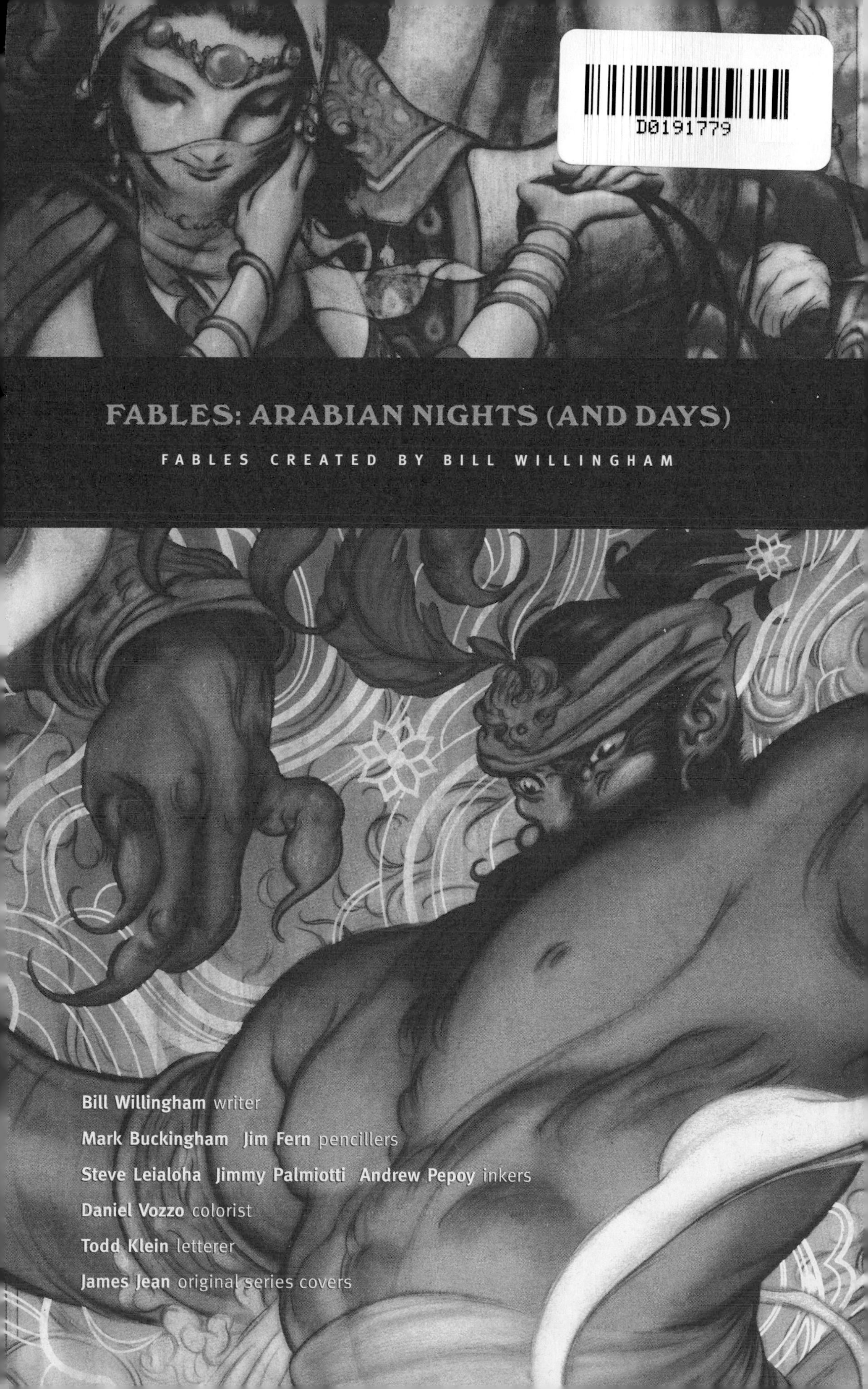

FABLES: ARABIAN NIGHTS (AND DAYS)

FABLES CREATED BY BILL WILLINGHAM

Bill Willingham writer
Mark Buckingham Jim Fern pencillers
Steve Leialoha Jimmy Palmiotti Andrew Pepoy inkers
Daniel Vozzo colorist
Todd Klein letterer
James Jean original series covers

*I would like to dedicate this one to
the whole team on FABLES who make
working on this comic a monthly
pleasure. Most especially to Bill and
Shelly for wanting me to be a part of
FABLES from the very beginning.*

*This one's also for Irma, without whom I
would never have made it through the
Arabian Deadline nights and days.*

— Mark Buckingham

*This collection is dedicated with
admiration to Sir Richard Burton
(the explorer and scholar, not the one
who married Liz Taylor all those times).*

— Bill Willingham

FABLES: ARABIAN NIGHTS (AND DAYS)

Published by DC Comics. Cover and compilation
Copyright © 2006 DC Comics.
All Rights Reserved.

Originally published in single magazine form
as FABLES 42-47. Copyright © 2005, 2006
Bill Willingham and DC Comics. All Rights
Reserved. All characters, their distinctive
likenesses and related elements featured in this
publication are trademarks of Bill Willingham.
VERTIGO is a trademark of DC Comics.
The stories, characters and incidents featured
in this publication are entirely fictional.
DC Comics does not read or accept unsolicited
submissions of ideas, stories or artwork.

DC Comics, 4000 Warner Blvd., Burbank, CA 91522
A Warner Bros. Entertainment Company.
Printed in Canada. Seventh Printing.
ISBN: 978-1-4012-1000-7

SUSTAINABLE FORESTRY INITIATIVE
Certified Chain of Custody
Promoting Sustainable Forestry
www.sfiprogram.org
SFI-00507
This label only applies to the text section.

Library of Congress Cataloging-in-Publication
Data

Willingham, Bill.
  Fables. Vol. 7, Arabian nights (and days) / Bill
Willingham, Mark Buckingham, Steve Leialoha,
Jim Fern, Jimmy Palmiotti, Andrew Pepoy.
    p. cm.
  "Originally published in single magazine form
as Fables 42-47."
  ISBN 978-1-4012-1000-7 (alk. paper)
  1. Legends--Adaptations--Comic books, strips,
etc. 2. Graphic novels. I. Buckingham, Mark. II.
Leialoha, Steve. III. Fern, Jim. IV. Palmiotti,
Jimmy. V. Pepoy, Andrew. VI. Title. VII. Title:
Arabian nights (and days).
  PN6727.W52F388 2012
  741.5'973–dc23
                                    2012038985

Table of Contents

WHO'S WHO IN FABLETOWN

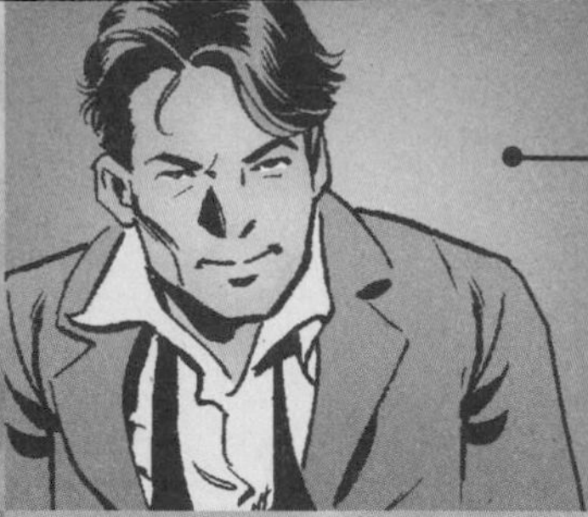

PRINCE CHARMING

He's the new mayor of Fabletown, and he's discovered that having the job isn't nearly as much fun as getting the job.

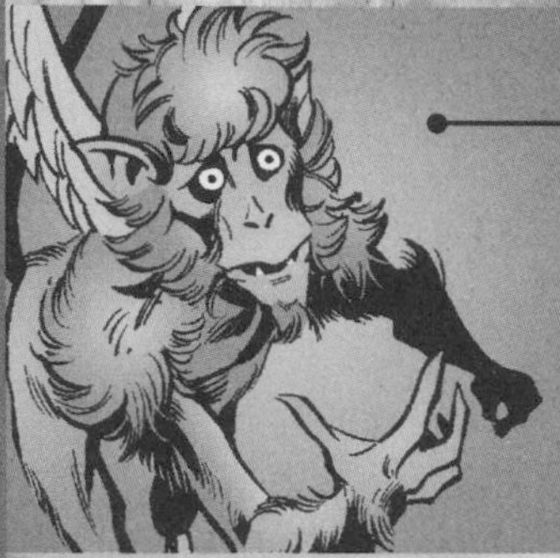

BUFKIN

A flying monkey who works in the Business Office and is easily overlooked.

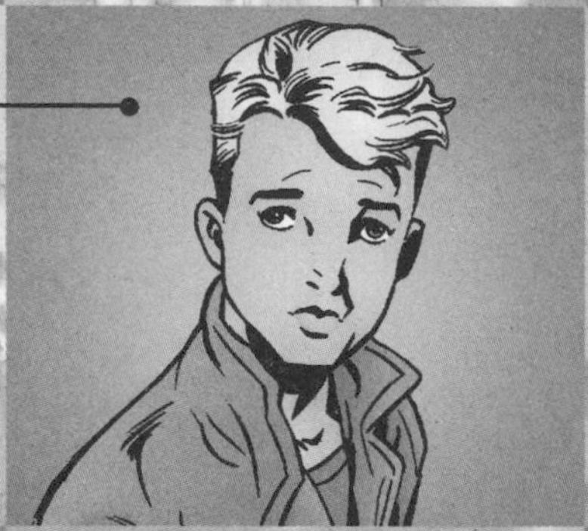

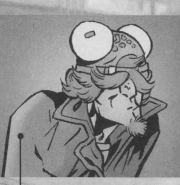

BOY BLUE

A former swashbuckling hero who would much rather be a file clerk. He's doing time in Fabletown's jail for stealing valuable magic items for his recent trip of revenge and rescue back to the Homelands.

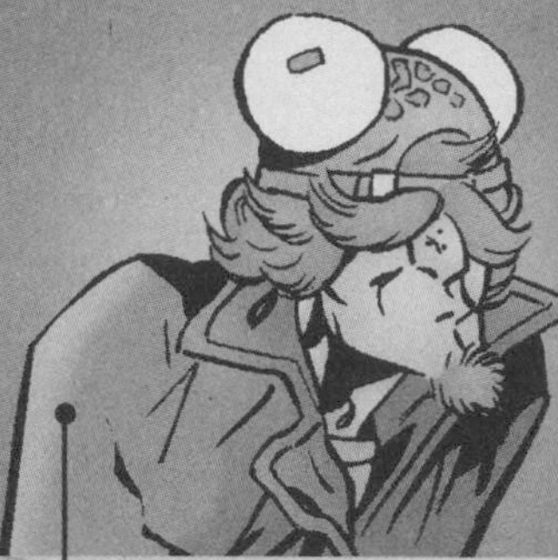

FLYCATCHER

The Frog Prince of old and now the Woodland Building's more-or-less-permanent janitor and maintenance man.

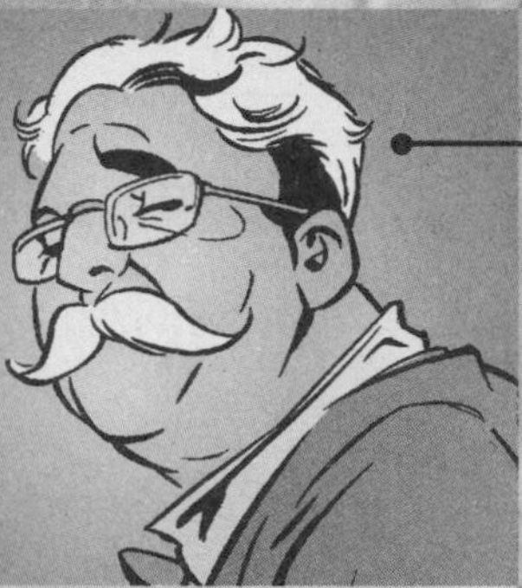

KING COLE

He was the mayor of Fabletown until Prince Charming booted him out of office. Since then he hasn't been seen much.

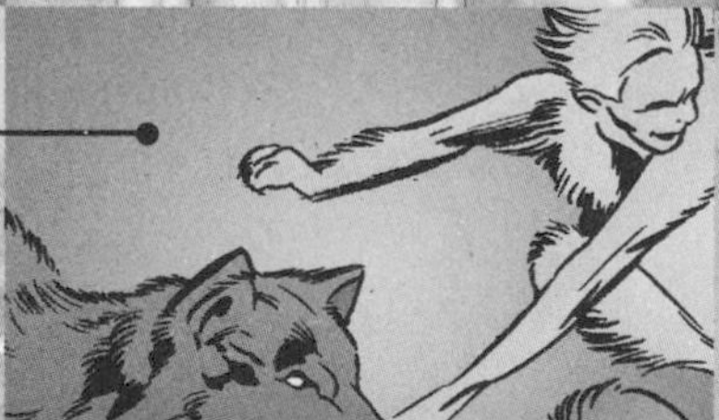

THE CUBS

The six rambunctious babies of Snow and Bigby who can look human sometimes and turn into wolves at other times and have a bad habit of flying off when they shouldn't.

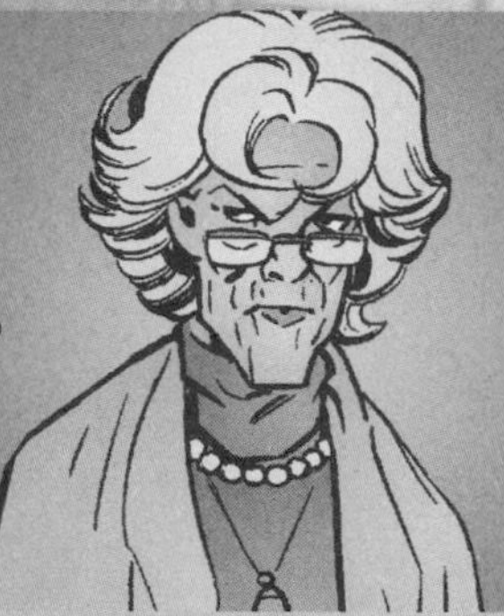

FRAU TOTENKINDER

The Black Forest witch who used to liv in a gingerbread house. She's wiser and more deadly than she looks.

MR. NORTH

He's the living embodiment of the North Wind. He's also Bigby Wolf's estranged father. He's been living at the Farm lately to spend time with his new pack of grandkids.

THE STORY SO FAR

Things have been fairly peaceful of late in Fabletown. Prince Charming's new regime is still running the government, but not very well by most Fables' standards. Boy Blue is back from his adventures in the Homelands, bringing much vital intelligence about the Adversary, along with the real (we're pretty sure this time) Red Riding Hood.

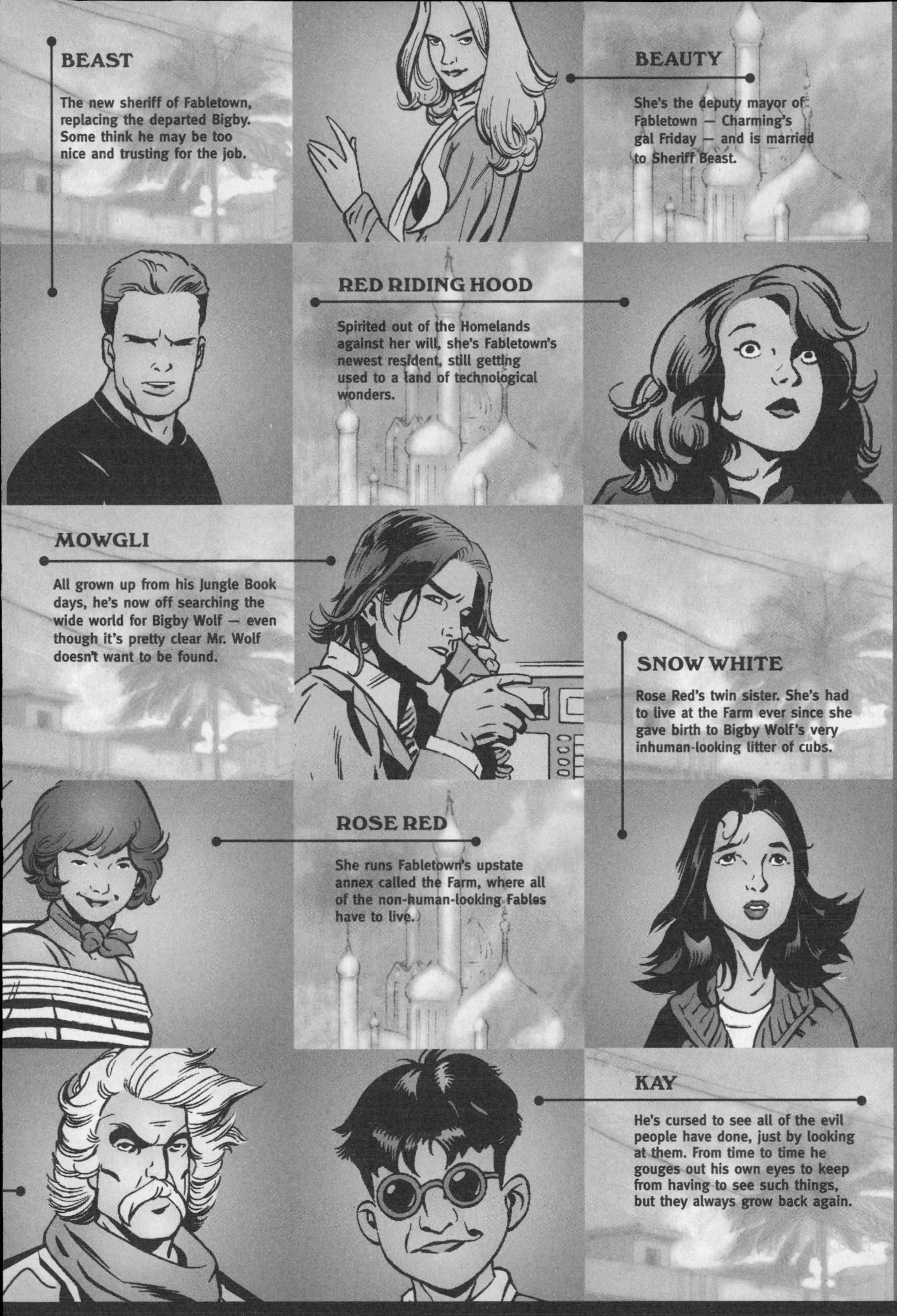
BEAST
The new sheriff of Fabletown, replacing the departed Bigby. Some think he may be too nice and trusting for the job.
BEAUTY
She's the deputy mayor of Fabletown — Charming's gal Friday — and is married to Sheriff Beast.
RED RIDING HOOD
Spirited out of the Homelands against her will, she's Fabletown's newest resident, still getting used to a land of technological wonders.
MOWGLI
All grown up from his Jungle Book days, he's now off searching the wide world for Bigby Wolf — even though it's pretty clear Mr. Wolf doesn't want to be found.
SNOW WHITE
Rose Red's twin sister. She's had to live at the Farm ever since she gave birth to Bigby Wolf's very inhuman-looking litter of cubs.
ROSE RED
She runs Fabletown's upstate annex called the Farm, where all of the non-human-looking Fables have to live.
KAY
He's cursed to see all of the evil people have done, just by looking at them. From time to time he gouges out his own eyes to keep from having to see such things, but they always grow back again.

Bigby Wolf is still living somewhere away from Fabletown and Snow White is still living up at the Farm, where she's raising her six children (by Bigby) with the help of her sister, Rose Red, and Bigby's father, the North Wind.
But recently it was learned that the Adversary has invaded the Arabian Fables' worlds...

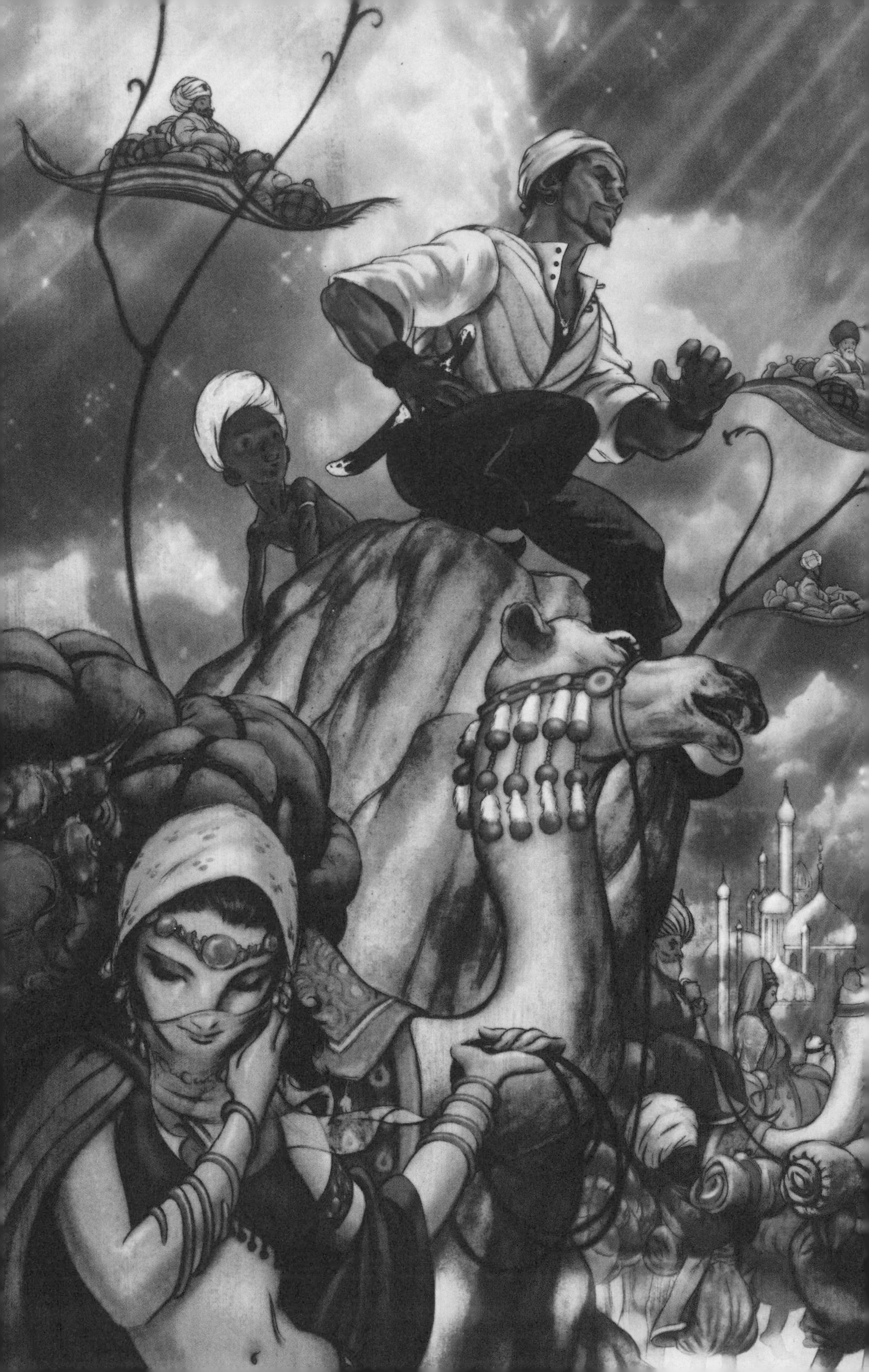

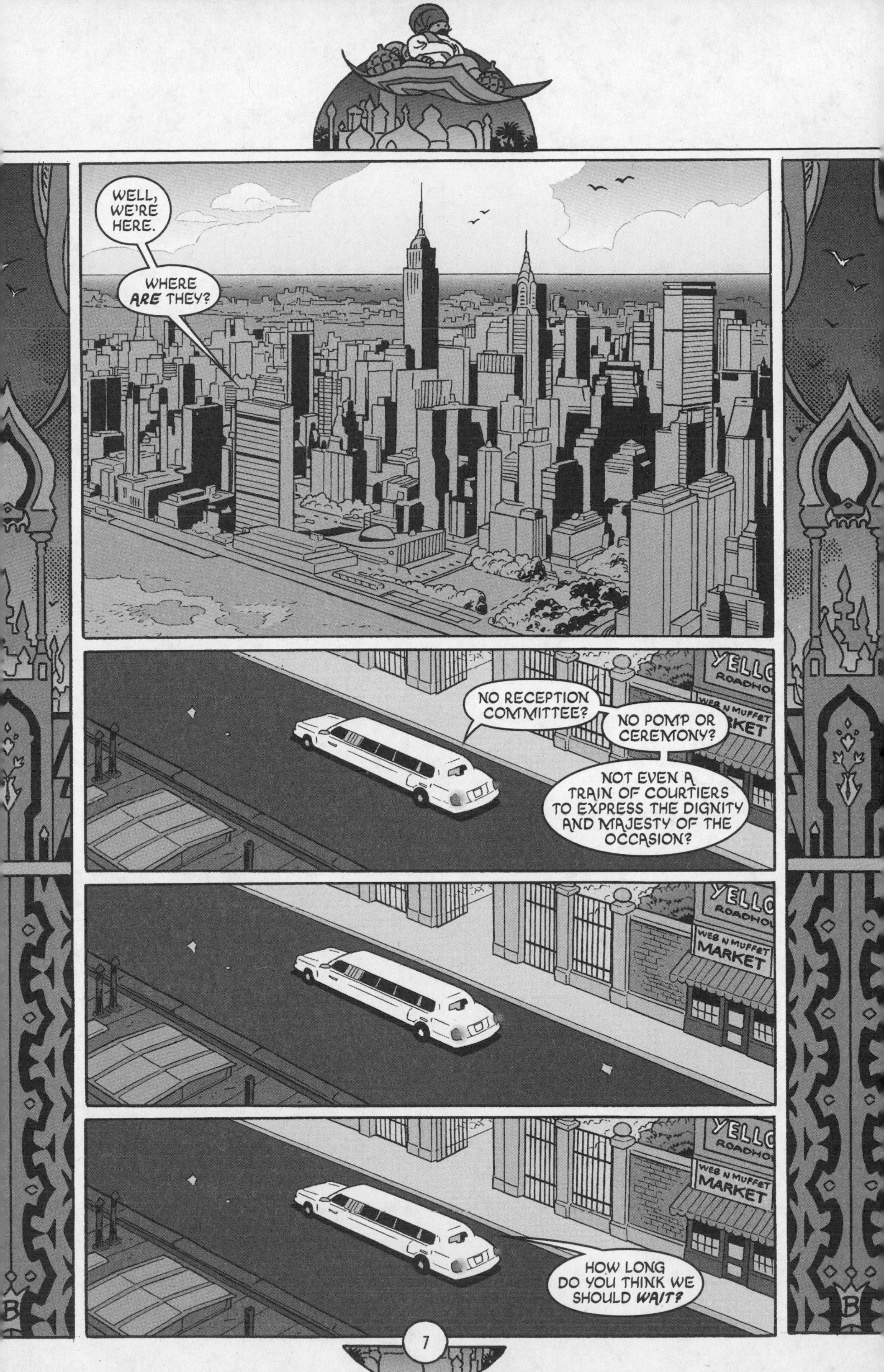
WELL, WE'RE HERE.
WHERE ARE THEY?
NO RECEPTION COMMITTEE?
NO POMP OR CEREMONY?
NOT EVEN A TRAIN OF COURTIERS TO EXPRESS THE DIGNITY AND MAJESTY OF THE OCCASION?
HOW LONG DO YOU THINK WE SHOULD WAIT?

BROKEN ENGLISH

Chapter ONE of Arabian Nights (and Days)

YAWN
YYYRRRRRRRR

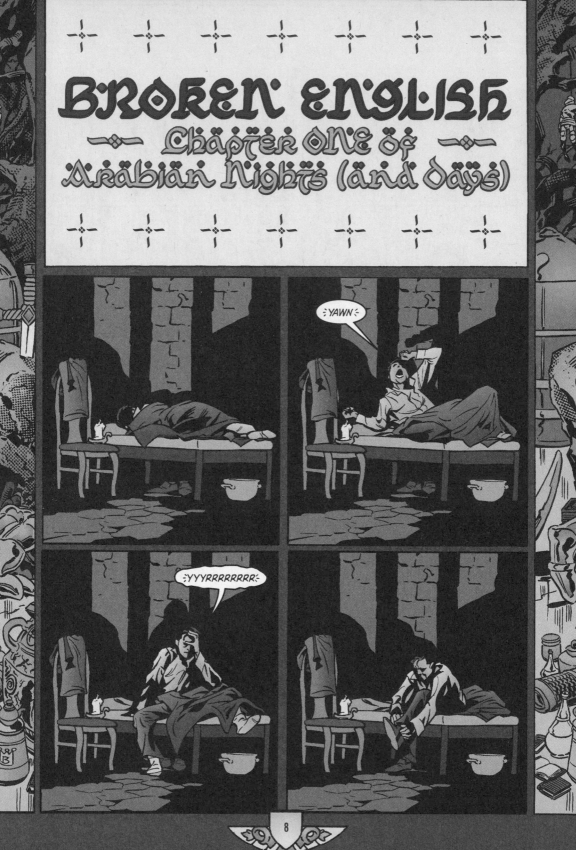

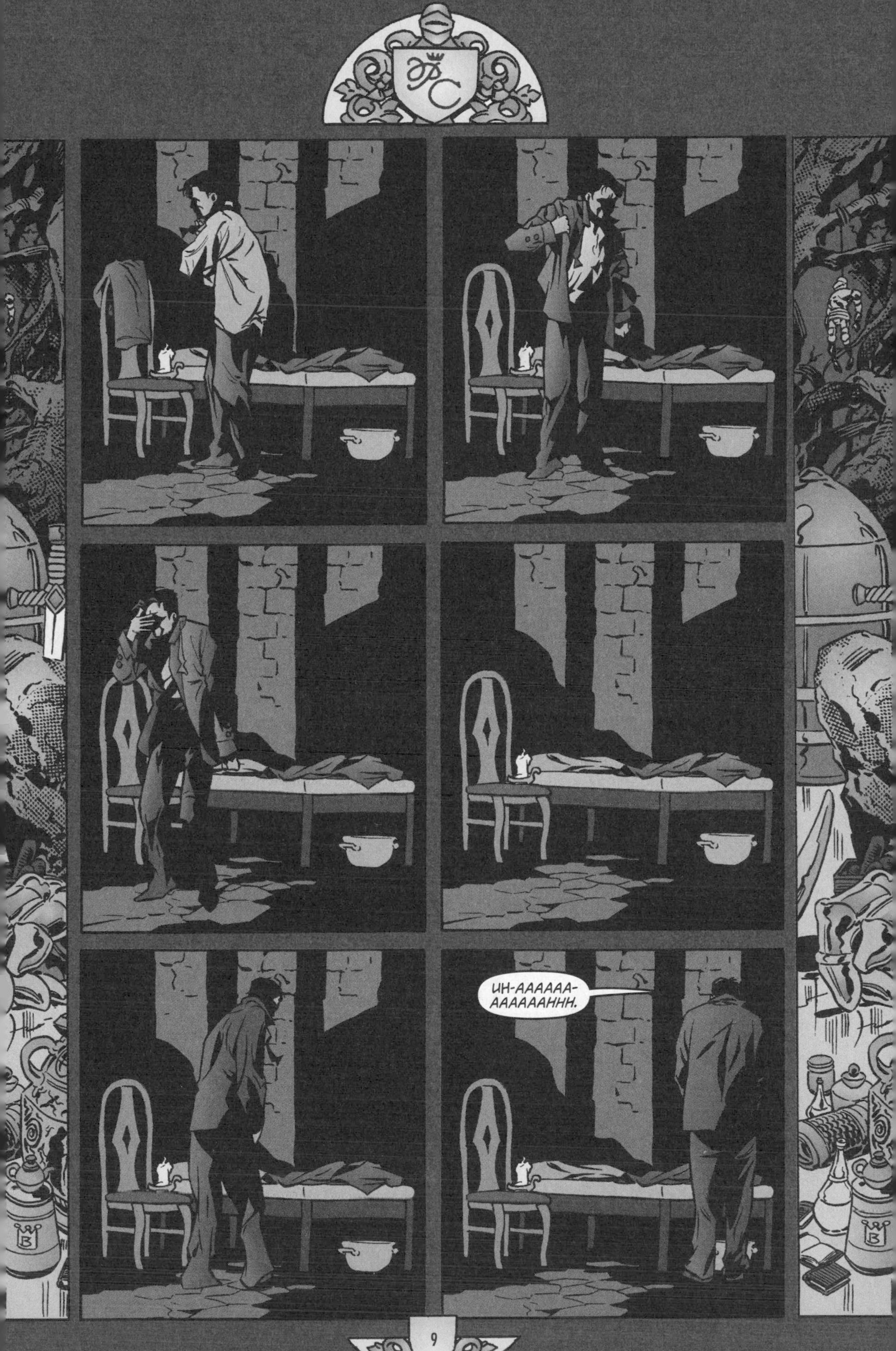
UH-AAAAAA-
AAAAAAAHHH.

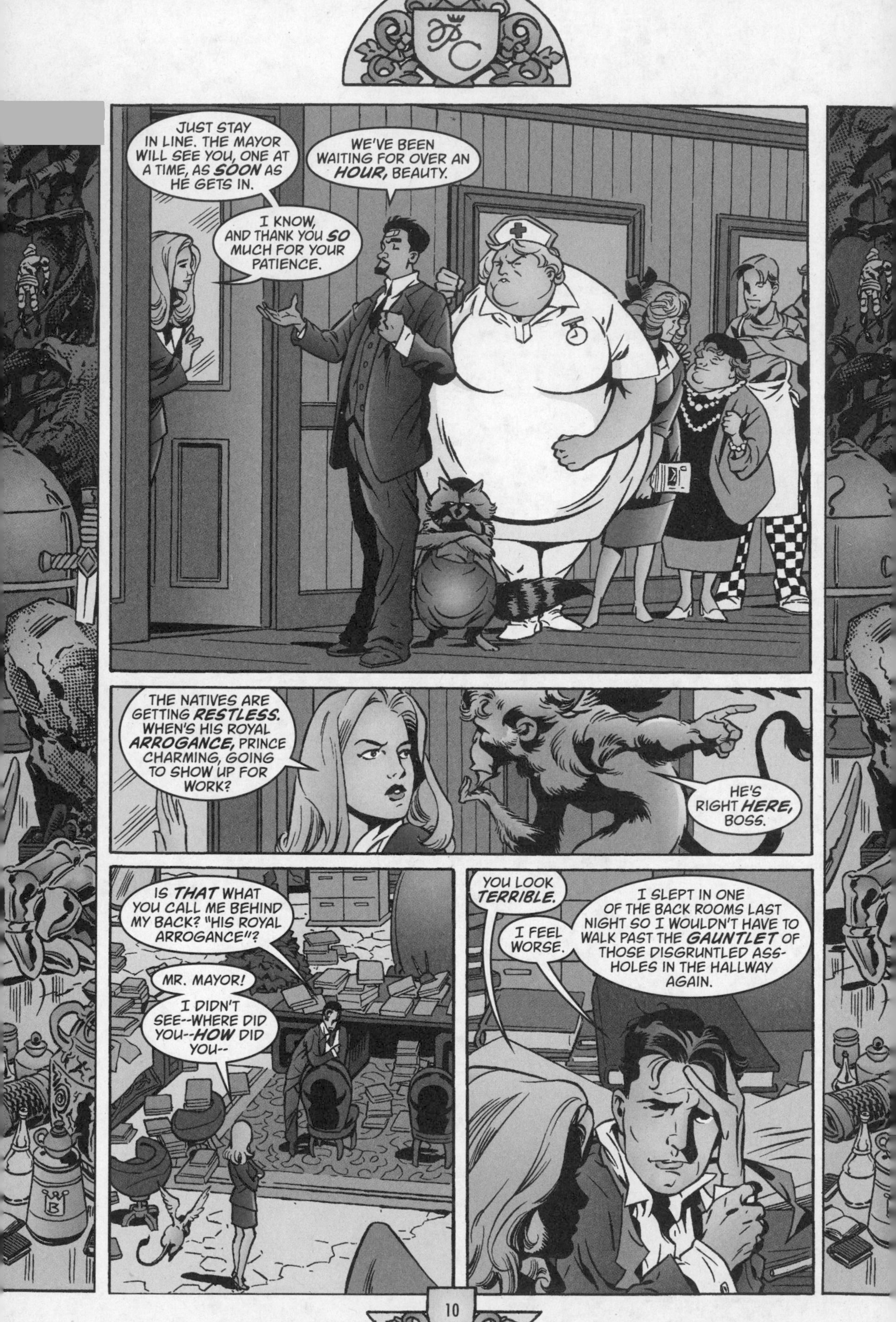
JUST STAY IN LINE. THE MAYOR WILL SEE YOU, ONE AT A TIME, AS SOON AS HE GETS IN.
WE'VE BEEN WAITING FOR OVER AN HOUR, BEAUTY.
I KNOW, AND THANK YOU SO MUCH FOR YOUR PATIENCE.
THE NATIVES ARE GETTING RESTLESS. WHEN'S HIS ROYAL ARROGANCE, PRINCE CHARMING, GOING TO SHOW UP FOR WORK?
HE'S RIGHT HERE, BOSS.
IS THAT WHAT YOU CALL ME BEHIND MY BACK? "HIS ROYAL ARROGANCE"?
MR. MAYOR!
I DIDN'T SEE--WHERE DID YOU--HOW DID YOU--
YOU LOOK TERRIBLE.
I FEEL WORSE.
I SLEPT IN ONE OF THE BACK ROOMS LAST NIGHT SO I WOULDN'T HAVE TO WALK PAST THE GAUNTLET OF THOSE DISGRUNTLED ASS-HOLES IN THE HALLWAY AGAIN.

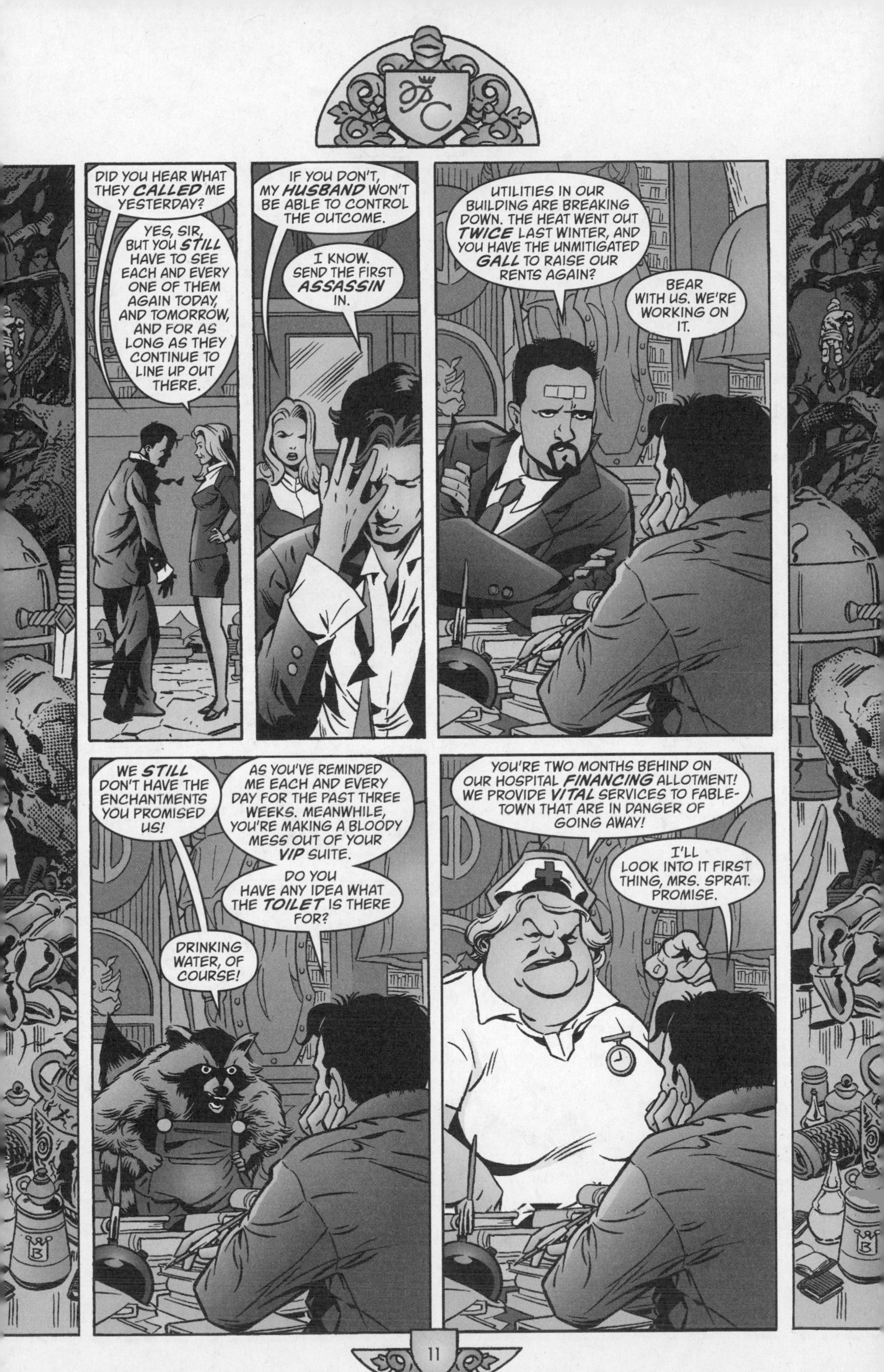
DID YOU HEAR WHAT THEY CALLED ME YESTERDAY?
YES, SIR, BUT YOU STILL HAVE TO SEE EACH AND EVERY ONE OF THEM AGAIN TODAY, AND TOMORROW, AND FOR AS LONG AS THEY CONTINUE TO LINE UP OUT THERE.
IF YOU DON'T, MY HUSBAND WON'T BE ABLE TO CONTROL THE OUTCOME.
I KNOW. SEND THE FIRST ASSASSIN IN.
UTILITIES IN OUR BUILDING ARE BREAKING DOWN. THE HEAT WENT OUT TWICE LAST WINTER, AND YOU HAVE THE UNMITIGATED GALL TO RAISE OUR RENTS AGAIN?
BEAR WITH US. WE'RE WORKING ON IT.
WE STILL DON'T HAVE THE ENCHANTMENTS YOU PROMISED US!
AS YOU'VE REMINDED ME EACH AND EVERY DAY FOR THE PAST THREE WEEKS. MEANWHILE, YOU'RE MAKING A BLOODY MESS OUT OF YOUR VIP SUITE.
DO YOU HAVE ANY IDEA WHAT THE TOILET IS THERE FOR?
DRINKING WATER, OF COURSE!
YOU'RE TWO MONTHS BEHIND ON OUR HOSPITAL FINANCING ALLOTMENT! WE PROVIDE VITAL SERVICES TO FABLE-TOWN THAT ARE IN DANGER OF GOING AWAY!
I'LL LOOK INTO IT FIRST THING, MRS. SPRAT. PROMISE.

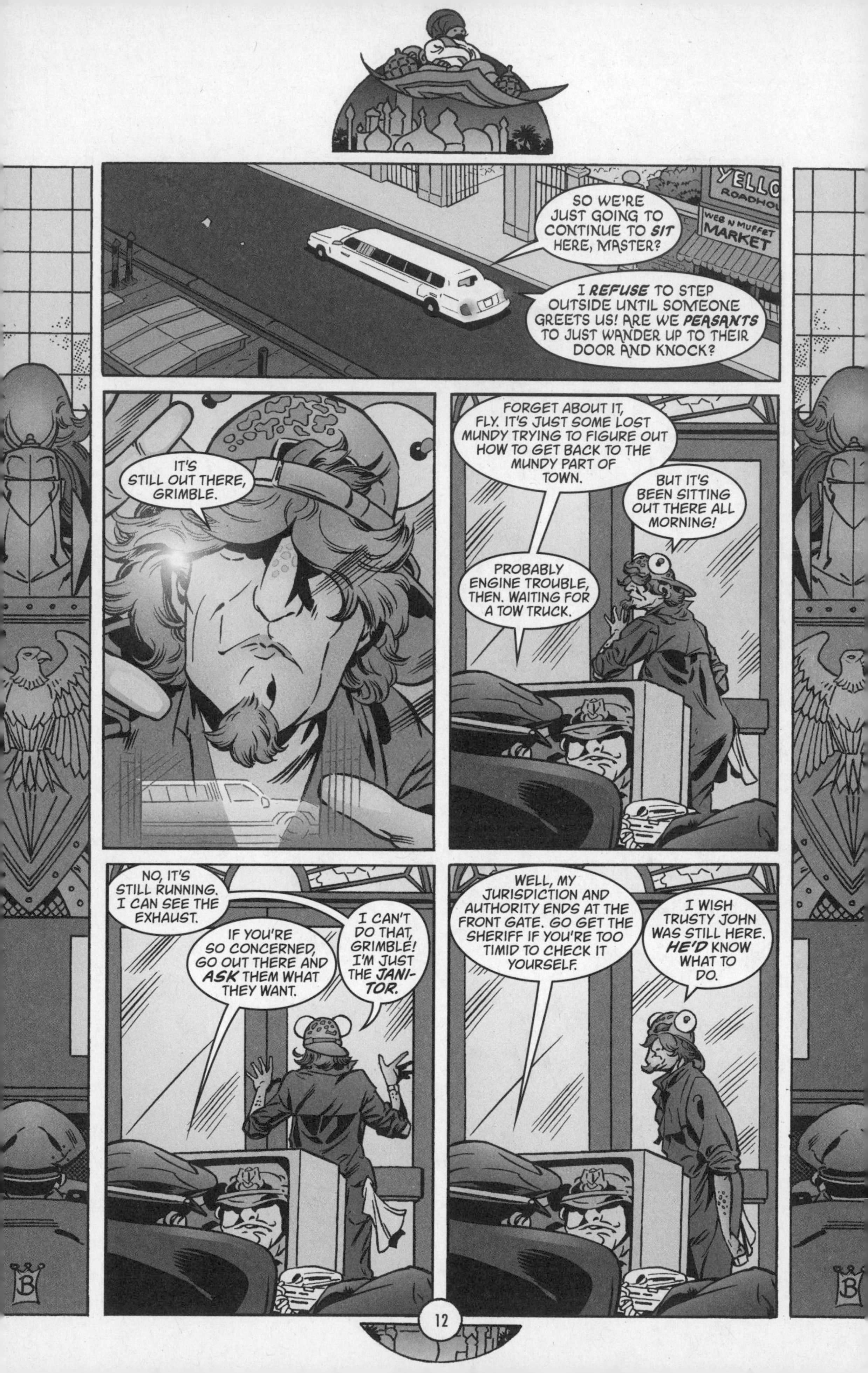

YELLO
ROADHOU
WEB N MUFFET
MARKET
SO WE'RE JUST GOING TO CONTINUE TO SIT HERE, MASTER?
I REFUSE TO STEP OUTSIDE UNTIL SOMEONE GREETS US! ARE WE PEASANTS TO JUST WANDER UP TO THEIR DOOR AND KNOCK?
IT'S STILL OUT THERE, GRIMBLE.
FORGET ABOUT IT, FLY. IT'S JUST SOME LOST MUNDY TRYING TO FIGURE OUT HOW TO GET BACK TO THE MUNDY PART OF TOWN.
BUT IT'S BEEN SITTING OUT THERE ALL MORNING!
PROBABLY ENGINE TROUBLE, THEN. WAITING FOR A TOW TRUCK.
NO, IT'S STILL RUNNING. I CAN SEE THE EXHAUST.
IF YOU'RE SO CONCERNED, GO OUT THERE AND ASK THEM WHAT THEY WANT.
I CAN'T DO THAT, GRIMBLE! I'M JUST THE JANITOR.
WELL, MY JURISDICTION AND AUTHORITY ENDS AT THE FRONT GATE. GO GET THE SHERIFF IF YOU'RE TOO TIMID TO CHECK IT YOURSELF.
I WISH TRUSTY JOHN WAS STILL HERE. HE'D KNOW WHAT TO DO.

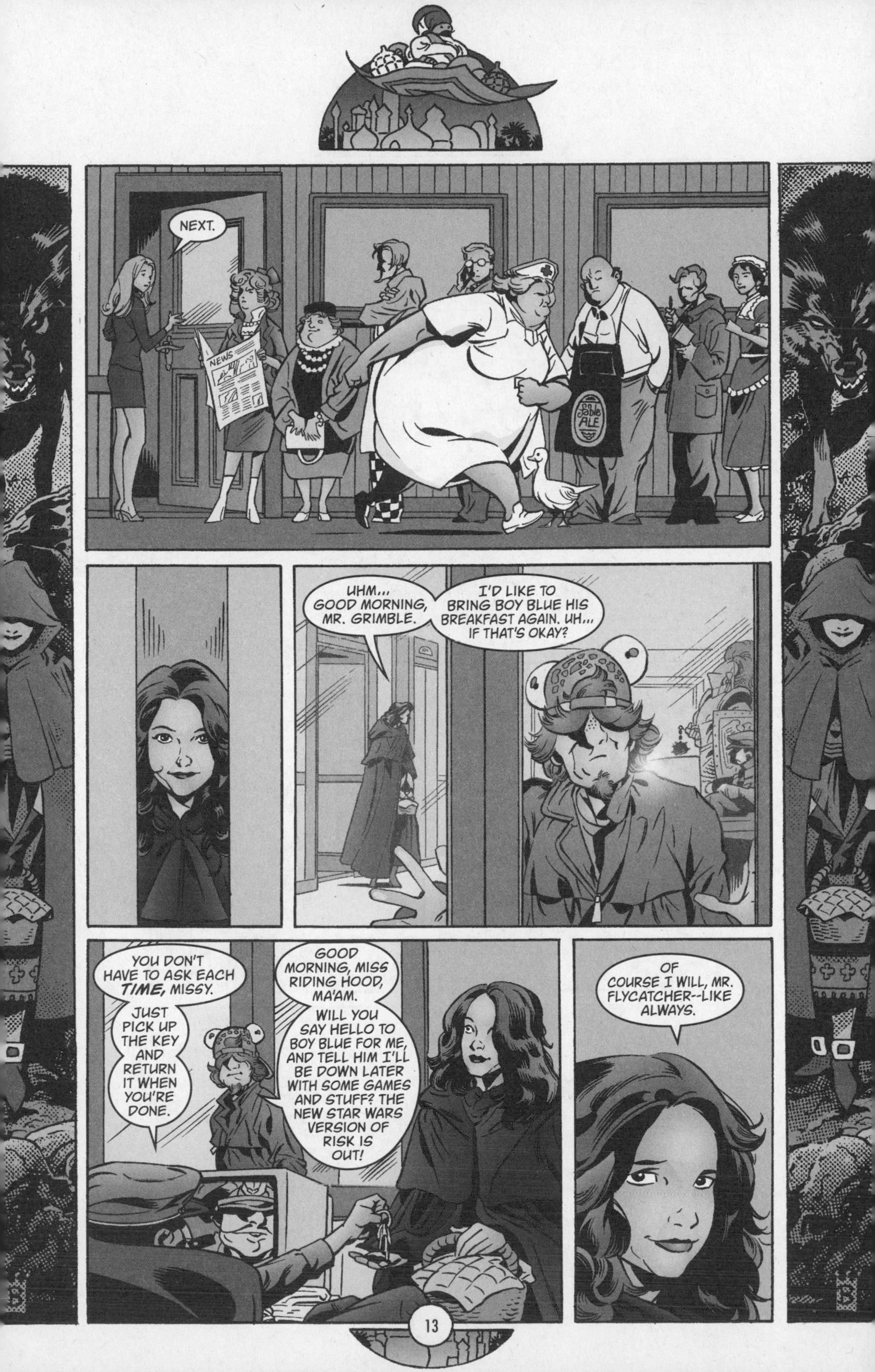
NEXT.
NEWS
Sable ALE
UHM... GOOD MORNING, MR. GRIMBLE.
I'D LIKE TO BRING BOY BLUE HIS BREAKFAST AGAIN. UH... IF THAT'S OKAY?
YOU DON'T HAVE TO ASK EACH *TIME,* MISSY.
JUST PICK UP THE KEY AND RETURN IT WHEN YOU'RE DONE.
GOOD MORNING, MISS RIDING HOOD, MA'AM.
WILL YOU SAY HELLO TO BOY BLUE FOR ME, AND TELL HIM I'LL BE DOWN LATER WITH SOME GAMES AND STUFF? THE NEW STAR WARS VERSION OF RISK IS OUT!
OF COURSE I WILL, MR. FLYCATCHER--LIKE ALWAYS.

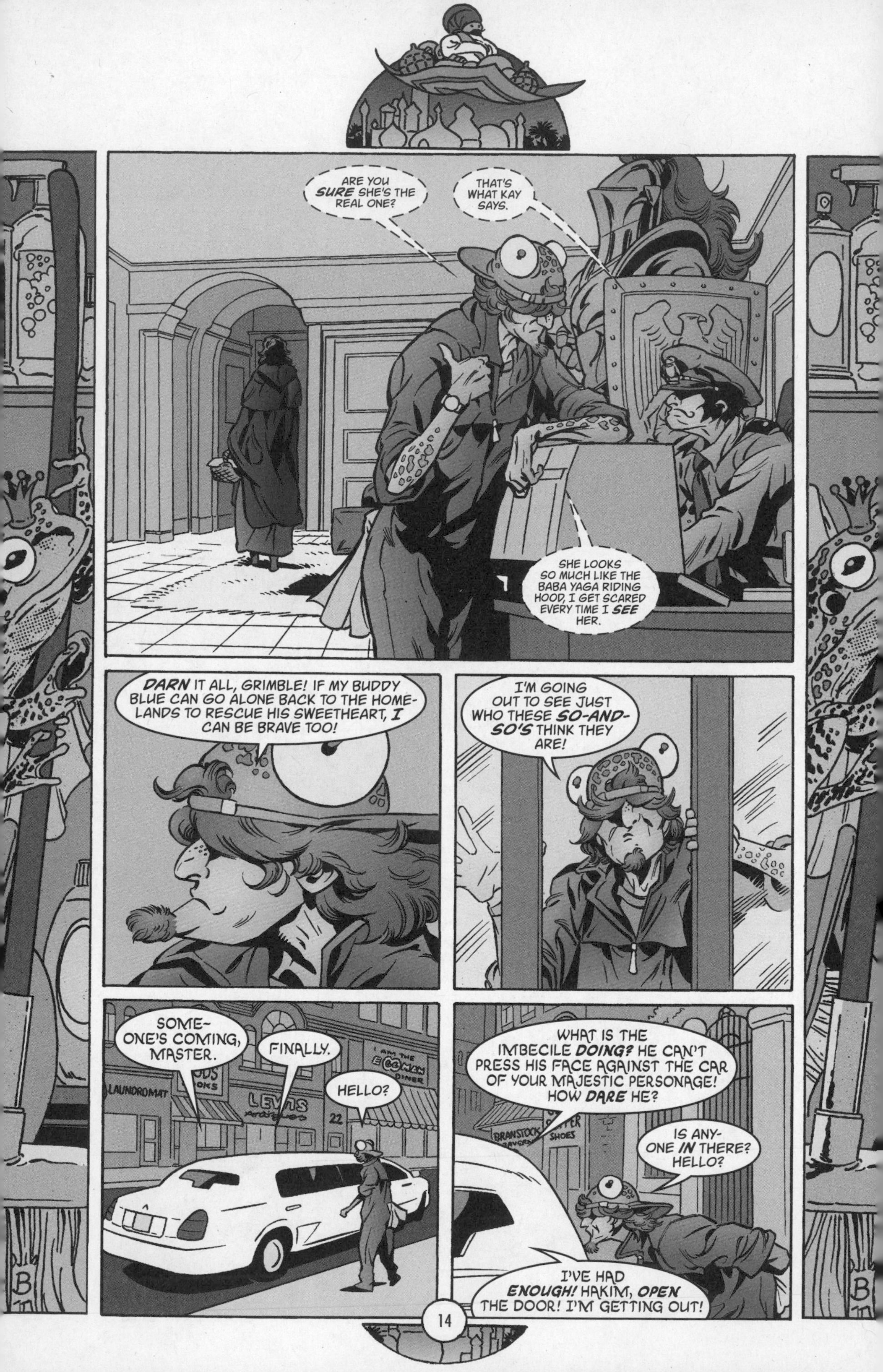
ARE YOU SURE SHE'S THE REAL ONE?
THAT'S WHAT KAY SAYS.
SHE LOOKS SO MUCH LIKE THE BABA YAGA RIDING HOOD, I GET SCARED EVERY TIME I SEE HER.
DARN IT ALL, GRIMBLE! IF MY BUDDY BLUE CAN GO ALONE BACK TO THE HOME-LANDS TO RESCUE HIS SWEETHEART, I CAN BE BRAVE TOO!
I'M GOING OUT TO SEE JUST WHO THESE SO-AND-SO'S THINK THEY ARE!
SOME-ONE'S COMING, MASTER.
FINALLY.
HELLO?
LAUNDROMAT
LEVITS
I AM THE EGGMAN DINER
22
WHAT IS THE IMBECILE DOING? HE CAN'T PRESS HIS FACE AGAINST THE CAR OF YOUR MAJESTIC PERSONAGE! HOW DARE HE?
BRANSTOCK
SHOES
IS ANY-ONE IN THERE? HELLO?
I'VE HAD ENOUGH! HAKIM, OPEN THE DOOR! I'M GETTING OUT!

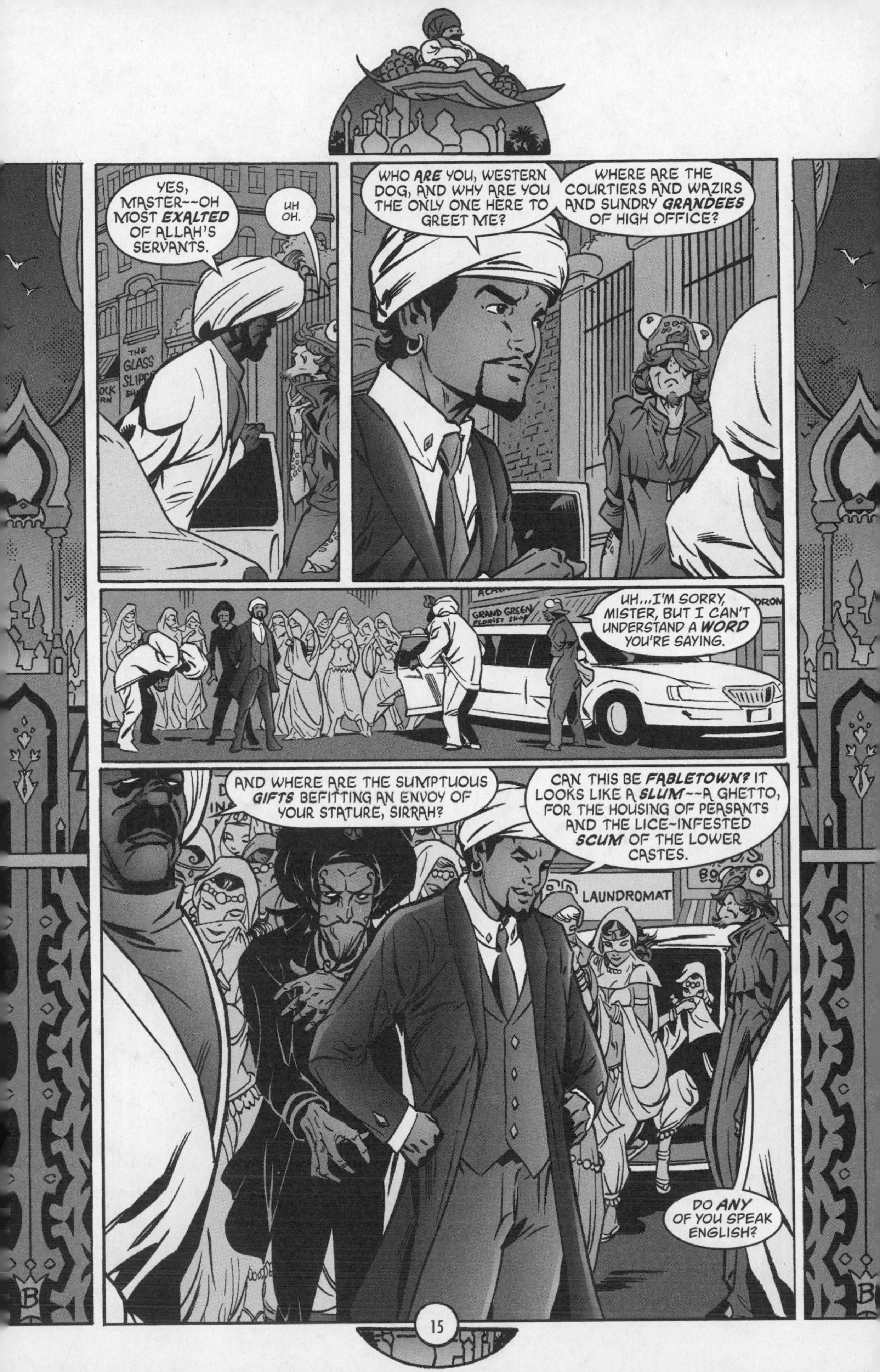
YES, MASTER--OH MOST EXALTED OF ALLAH'S SERVANTS.
UH OH.
THE GLASS SLIPP
WHO ARE YOU, WESTERN DOG, AND WHY ARE YOU THE ONLY ONE HERE TO GREET ME?
WHERE ARE THE COURTIERS AND WAZIRS AND SUNDRY GRANDEES OF HIGH OFFICE?
GRAND GREEN FLORIST SHOP
UH...I'M SORRY, MISTER, BUT I CAN'T UNDERSTAND A WORD YOU'RE SAYING.
AND WHERE ARE THE SUMPTUOUS GIFTS BEFITTING AN ENVOY OF YOUR STATURE, SIRRAH?
CAN THIS BE FABLETOWN? IT LOOKS LIKE A SLUM--A GHETTO, FOR THE HOUSING OF PEASANTS AND THE LICE-INFESTED SCUM OF THE LOWER CASTES.
LAUNDROMAT
DO ANY OF YOU SPEAK ENGLISH?

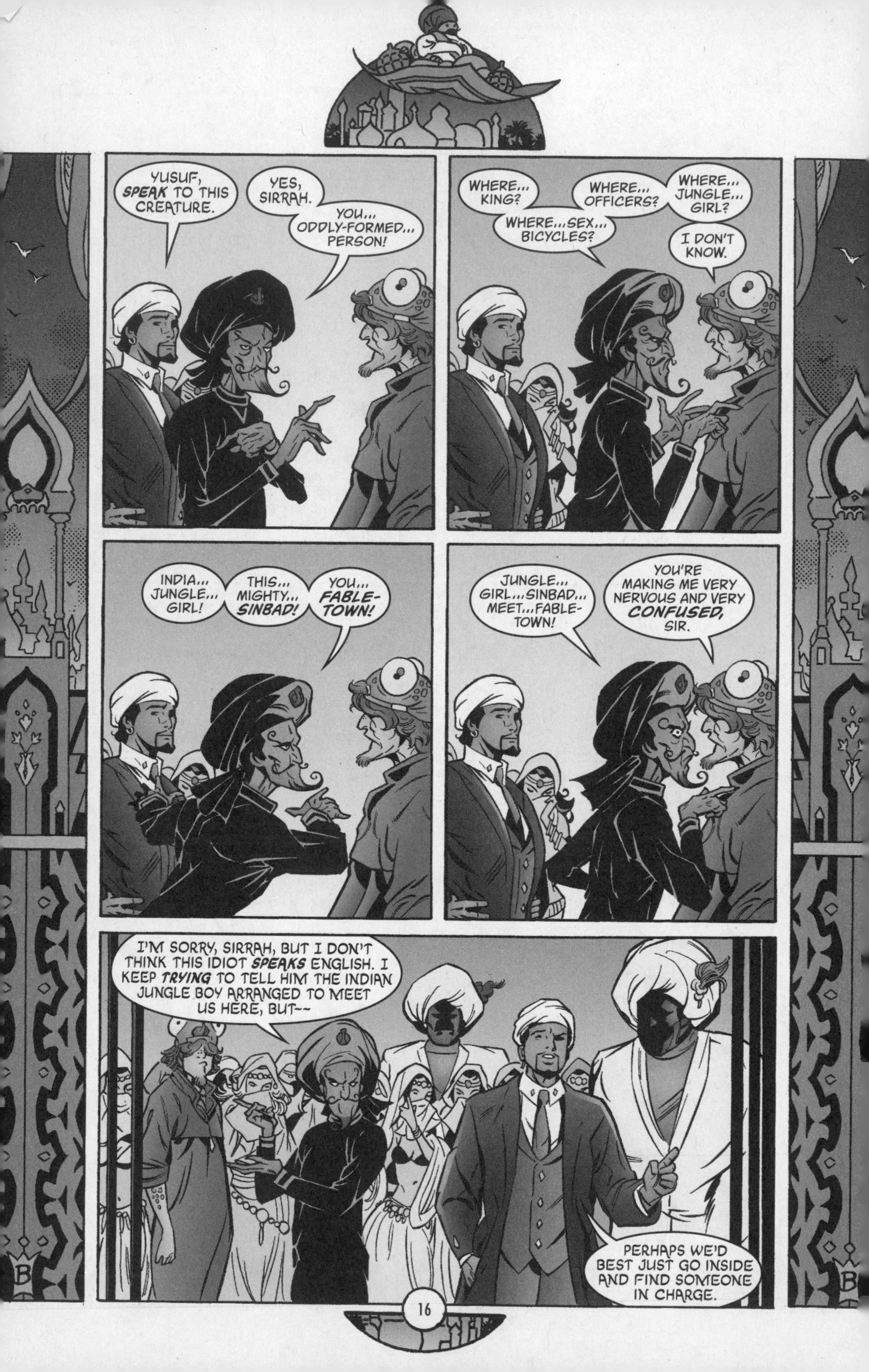
YUSUF, SPEAK TO THIS CREATURE.
YES, SIRRAH.
YOU... ODDLY-FORMED... PERSON!
WHERE... KING?
WHERE... OFFICERS?
WHERE... JUNGLE... GIRL?
WHERE...SEX... BICYCLES?
I DON'T KNOW.
INDIA... JUNGLE... GIRL!
THIS... MIGHTY... SINBAD!
YOU... FABLE-TOWN!
JUNGLE... GIRL...SINBAD... MEET...FABLE-TOWN!
YOU'RE MAKING ME VERY NERVOUS AND VERY CONFUSED, SIR.
I'M SORRY, SIRRAH, BUT I DON'T THINK THIS IDIOT SPEAKS ENGLISH. I KEEP TRYING TO TELL HIM THE INDIAN JUNGLE BOY ARRANGED TO MEET US HERE, BUT--
PERHAPS WE'D BEST JUST GO INSIDE AND FIND SOMEONE IN CHARGE.

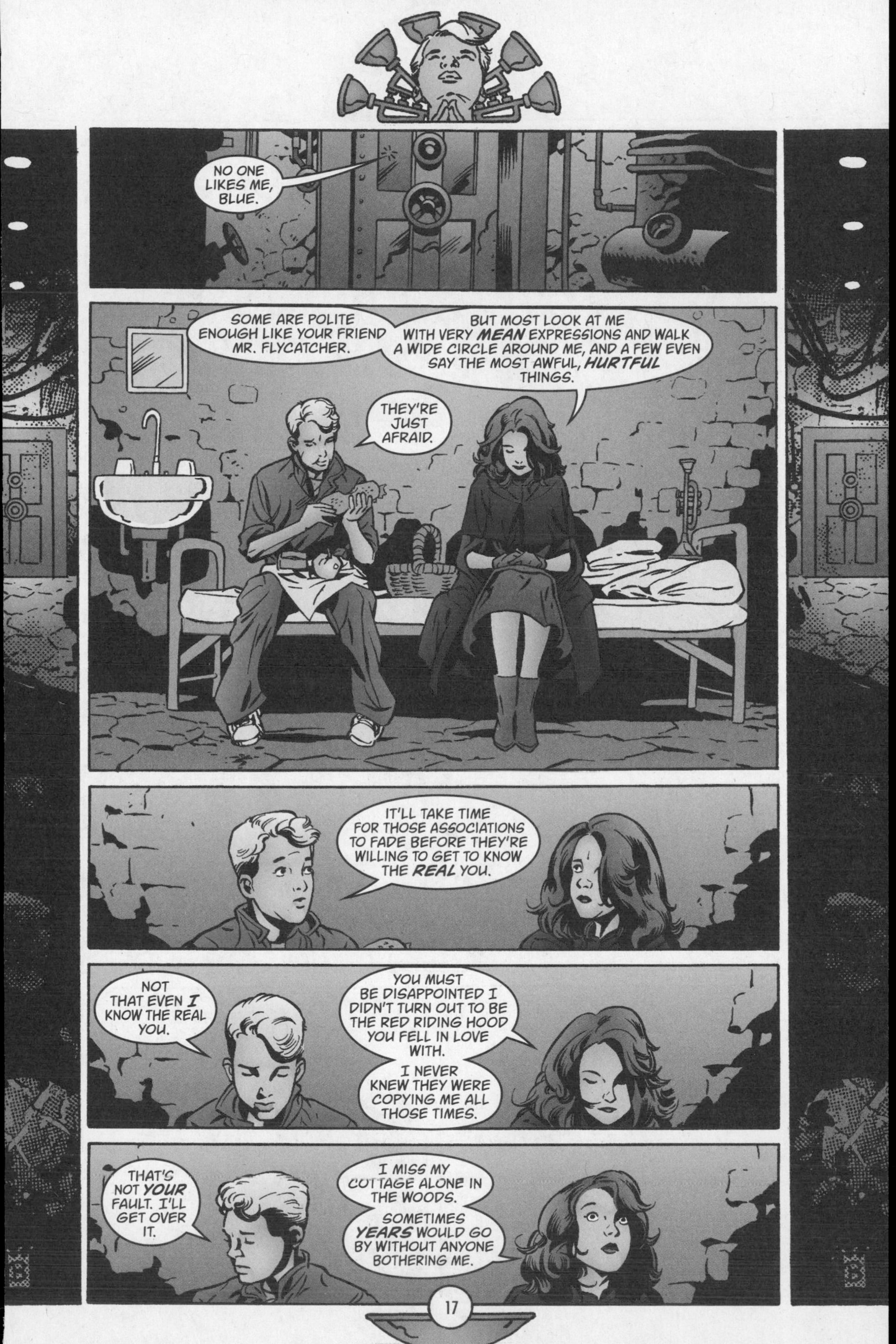
NO ONE LIKES ME, BLUE.
SOME ARE POLITE ENOUGH LIKE YOUR FRIEND MR. FLYCATCHER.
BUT MOST LOOK AT ME WITH VERY MEAN EXPRESSIONS AND WALK A WIDE CIRCLE AROUND ME, AND A FEW EVEN SAY THE MOST AWFUL, HURTFUL THINGS.
THEY'RE JUST AFRAID.
IT'LL TAKE TIME FOR THOSE ASSOCIATIONS TO FADE BEFORE THEY'RE WILLING TO GET TO KNOW THE REAL YOU.
NOT THAT EVEN I KNOW THE REAL YOU.
YOU MUST BE DISAPPOINTED I DIDN'T TURN OUT TO BE THE RED RIDING HOOD YOU FELL IN LOVE WITH.
I NEVER KNEW THEY WERE COPYING ME ALL THOSE TIMES.
THAT'S NOT YOUR FAULT. I'LL GET OVER IT.
I MISS MY COTTAGE ALONE IN THE WOODS.
SOMETIMES YEARS WOULD GO BY WITHOUT ANYONE BOTHERING ME.

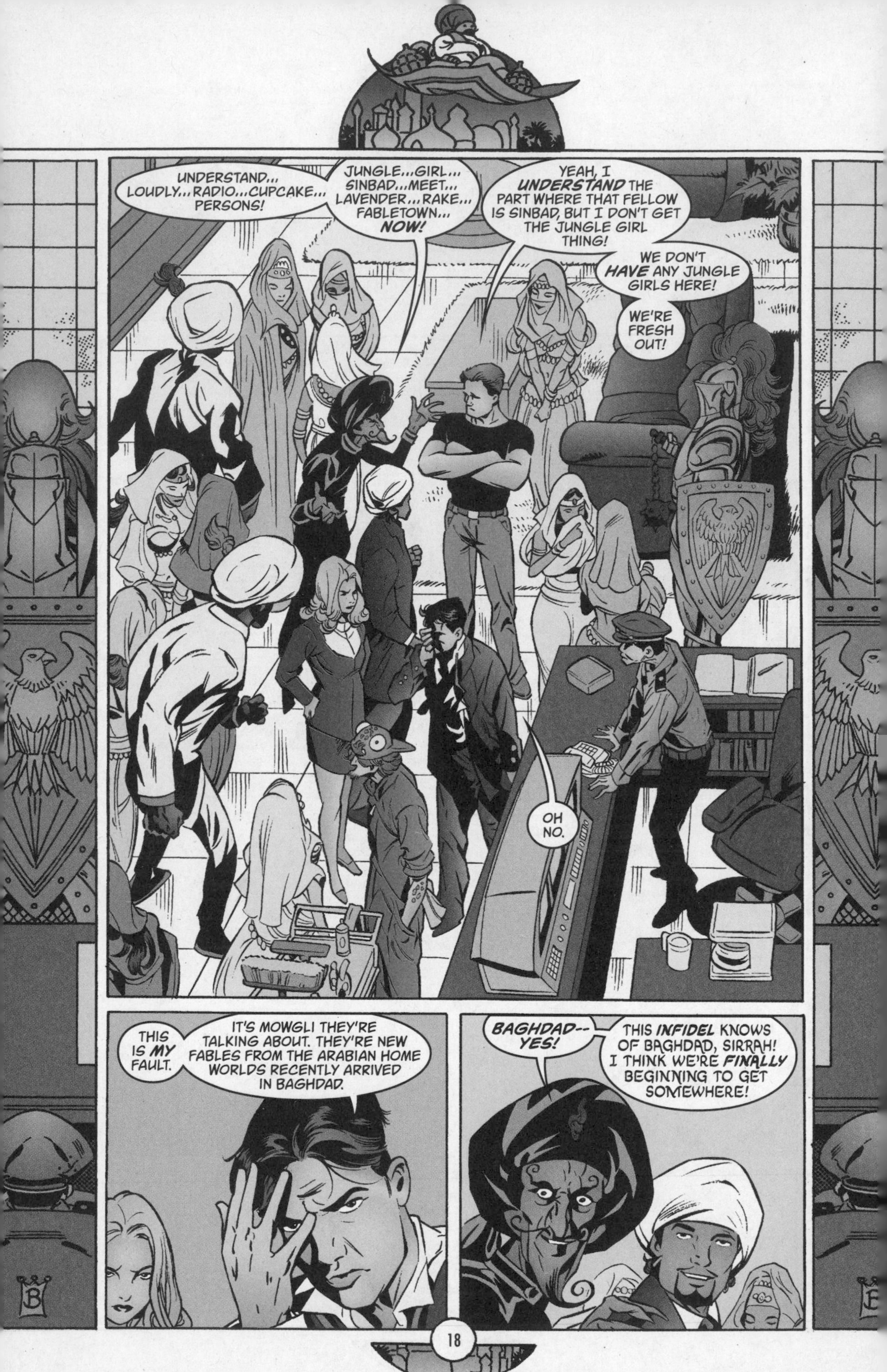
UNDERSTAND... LOUDLY... RADIO... CUPCAKE... PERSONS!
JUNGLE... GIRL... SINBAD... MEET... LAVENDER... RAKE... FABLETOWN... NOW!
YEAH, I UNDERSTAND THE PART WHERE THAT FELLOW IS SINBAD, BUT I DON'T GET THE JUNGLE GIRL THING!
WE DON'T HAVE ANY JUNGLE GIRLS HERE!
WE'RE FRESH OUT!
OH NO.
THIS IS MY FAULT.
IT'S MOWGLI THEY'RE TALKING ABOUT. THEY'RE NEW FABLES FROM THE ARABIAN HOME WORLDS RECENTLY ARRIVED IN BAGHDAD.
BAGHDAD-- YES!
THIS INFIDEL KNOWS OF BAGHDAD, SIRRAH! I THINK WE'RE FINALLY BEGINNING TO GET SOMEWHERE!

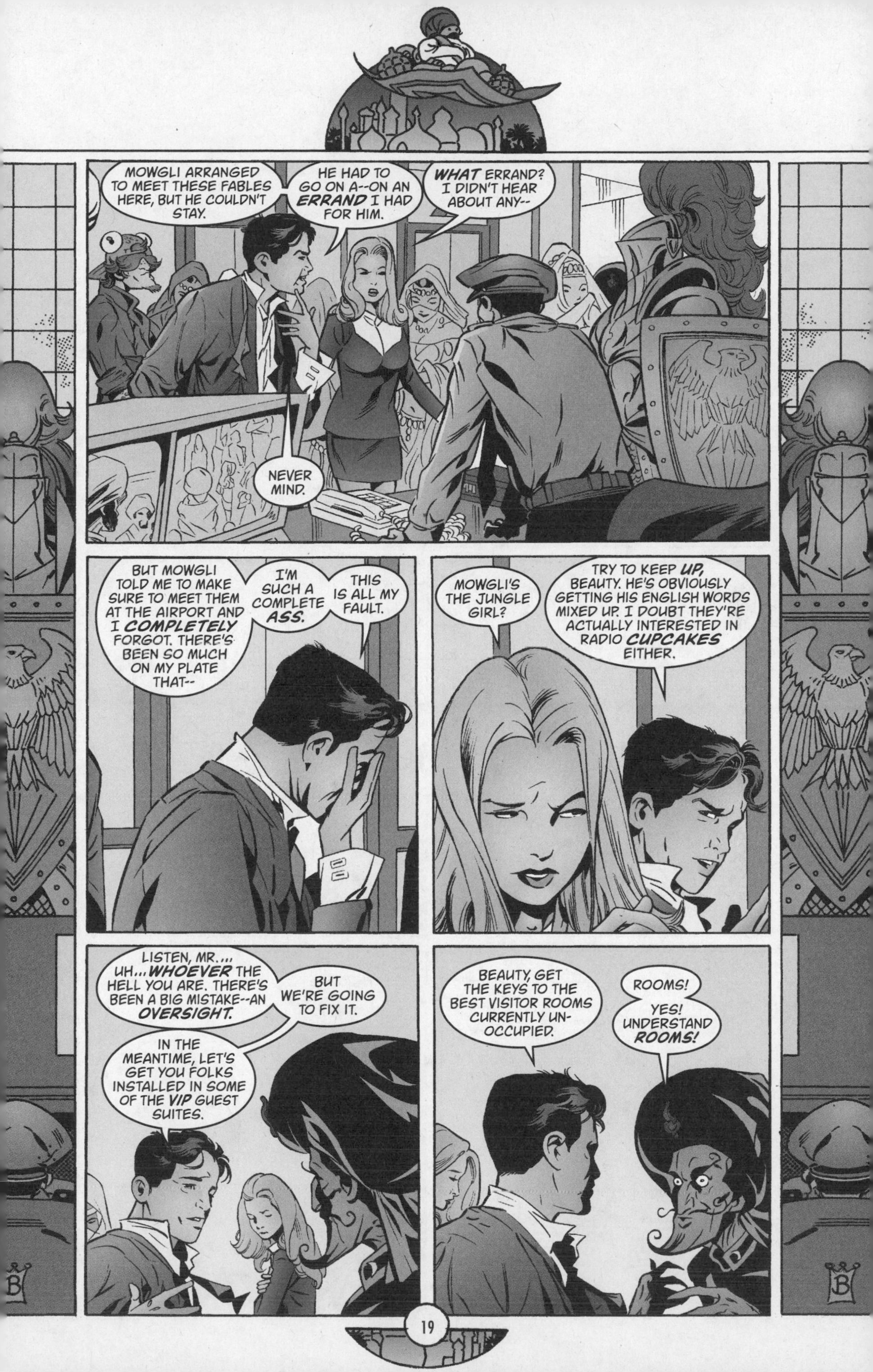

MOWGLI ARRANGED TO MEET THESE FABLES HERE, BUT HE COULDN'T STAY.
HE HAD TO GO ON A--ON AN ERRAND I HAD FOR HIM.
WHAT ERRAND? I DIDN'T HEAR ABOUT ANY--
NEVER MIND.
BUT MOWGLI TOLD ME TO MAKE SURE TO MEET THEM AT THE AIRPORT AND I COMPLETELY FORGOT. THERE'S BEEN SO MUCH ON MY PLATE THAT--
I'M SUCH A COMPLETE ASS.
THIS IS ALL MY FAULT.
MOWGLI'S THE JUNGLE GIRL?
TRY TO KEEP UP, BEAUTY. HE'S OBVIOUSLY GETTING HIS ENGLISH WORDS MIXED UP. I DOUBT THEY'RE ACTUALLY INTERESTED IN RADIO CUPCAKES EITHER.
LISTEN, MR.... UH...WHOEVER THE HELL YOU ARE. THERE'S BEEN A BIG MISTAKE--AN OVERSIGHT.
BUT WE'RE GOING TO FIX IT.
IN THE MEANTIME, LET'S GET YOU FOLKS INSTALLED IN SOME OF THE VIP GUEST SUITES.
BEAUTY, GET THE KEYS TO THE BEST VISITOR ROOMS CURRENTLY UN-OCCUPIED.
ROOMS!
YES! UNDERSTAND ROOMS!

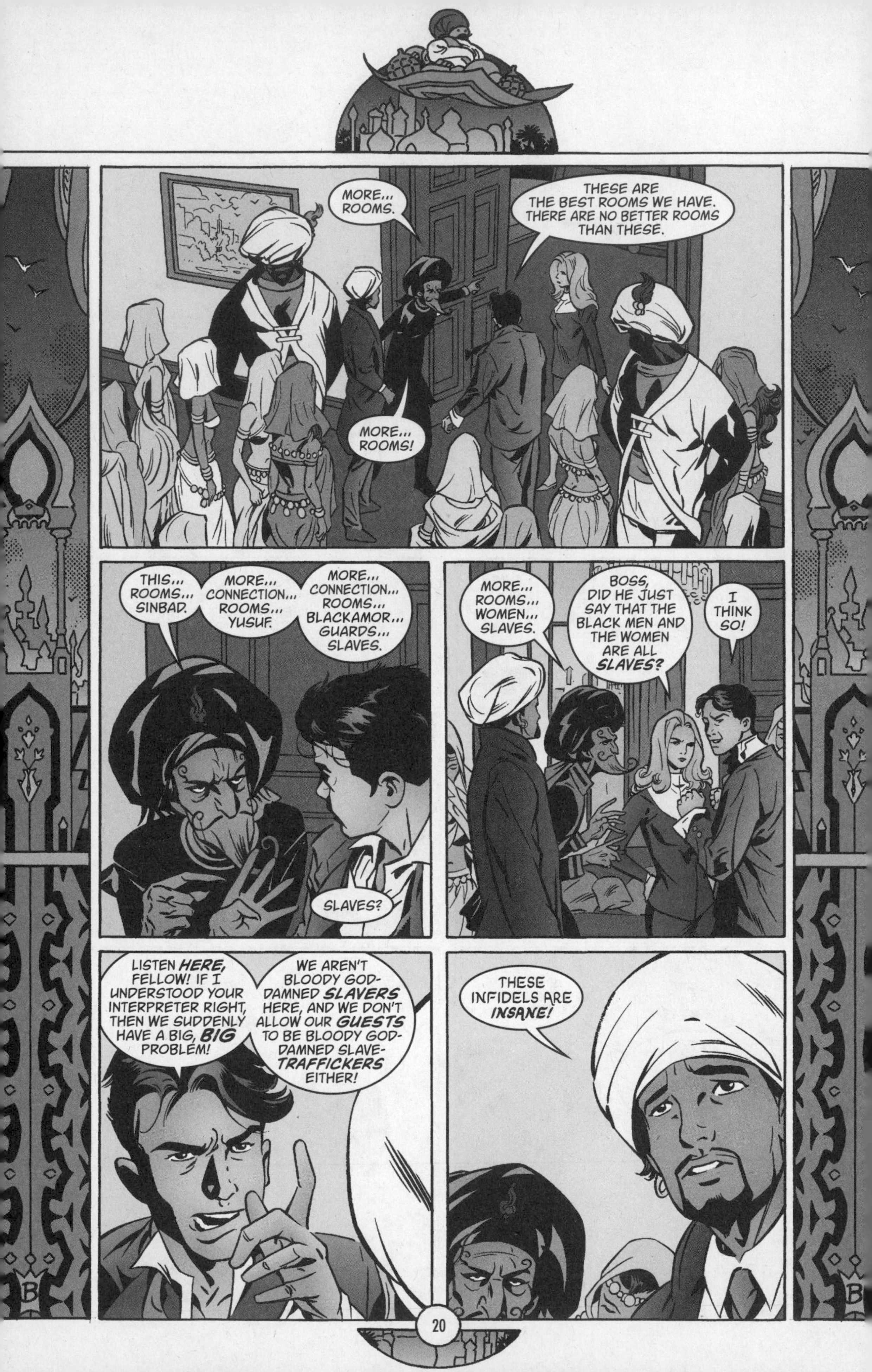
MORE... ROOMS.
THESE ARE THE BEST ROOMS WE HAVE. THERE ARE NO BETTER ROOMS THAN THESE.
MORE... ROOMS!
THIS... ROOMS... SINBAD.
MORE... CONNECTION... ROOMS... YUSUF.
MORE... CONNECTION... ROOMS... BLACKAMOR... GUARDS... SLAVES.
SLAVES?
MORE... ROOMS... WOMEN... SLAVES.
BOSS, DID HE JUST SAY THAT THE BLACK MEN AND THE WOMEN ARE ALL SLAVES?
I THINK SO!
LISTEN HERE, FELLOW! IF I UNDERSTOOD YOUR INTERPRETER RIGHT, THEN WE SUDDENLY HAVE A BIG, BIG PROBLEM!
WE AREN'T BLOODY GOD-DAMNED SLAVERS HERE, AND WE DON'T ALLOW OUR GUESTS TO BE BLOODY GOD-DAMNED SLAVE-TRAFFICKERS EITHER!
THESE INFIDELS ARE INSANE!

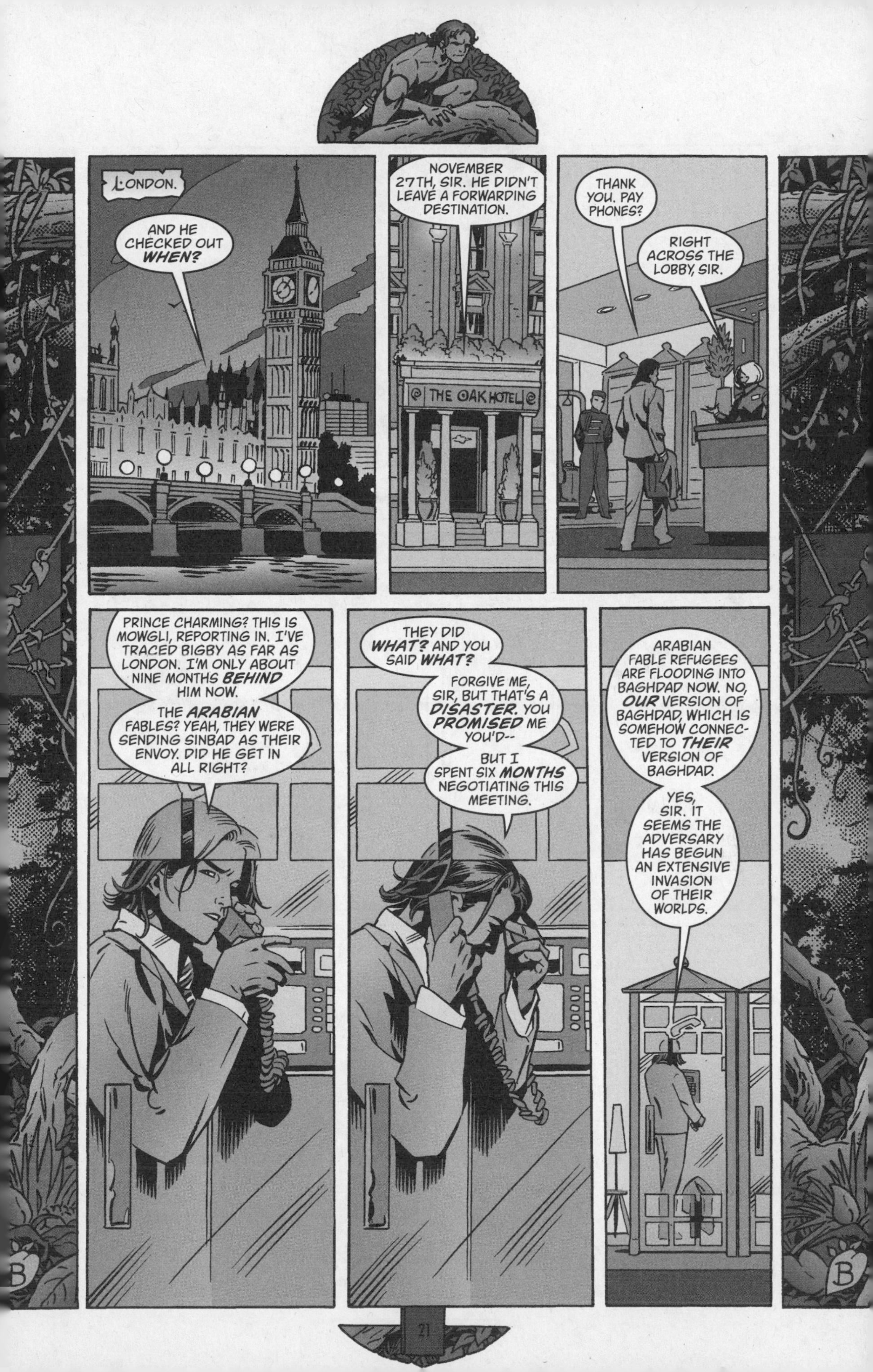

LONDON.
AND HE CHECKED OUT WHEN?
NOVEMBER 27TH, SIR. HE DIDN'T LEAVE A FORWARDING DESTINATION.
THE OAK HOTEL
THANK YOU. PAY PHONES?
RIGHT ACROSS THE LOBBY, SIR.
PRINCE CHARMING? THIS IS MOWGLI, REPORTING IN. I'VE TRACED BIGBY AS FAR AS LONDON. I'M ONLY ABOUT NINE MONTHS BEHIND HIM NOW.
THE ARABIAN FABLES? YEAH, THEY WERE SENDING SINBAD AS THEIR ENVOY. DID HE GET IN ALL RIGHT?
THEY DID WHAT? AND YOU SAID WHAT?
FORGIVE ME, SIR, BUT THAT'S A DISASTER. YOU PROMISED ME YOU'D--
BUT I SPENT SIX MONTHS NEGOTIATING THIS MEETING.
ARABIAN FABLE REFUGEES ARE FLOODING INTO BAGHDAD NOW. NO, OUR VERSION OF BAGHDAD, WHICH IS SOMEHOW CONNECTED TO THEIR VERSION OF BAGHDAD.
YES, SIR. IT SEEMS THE ADVERSARY HAS BEGUN AN EXTENSIVE INVASION OF THEIR WORLDS.

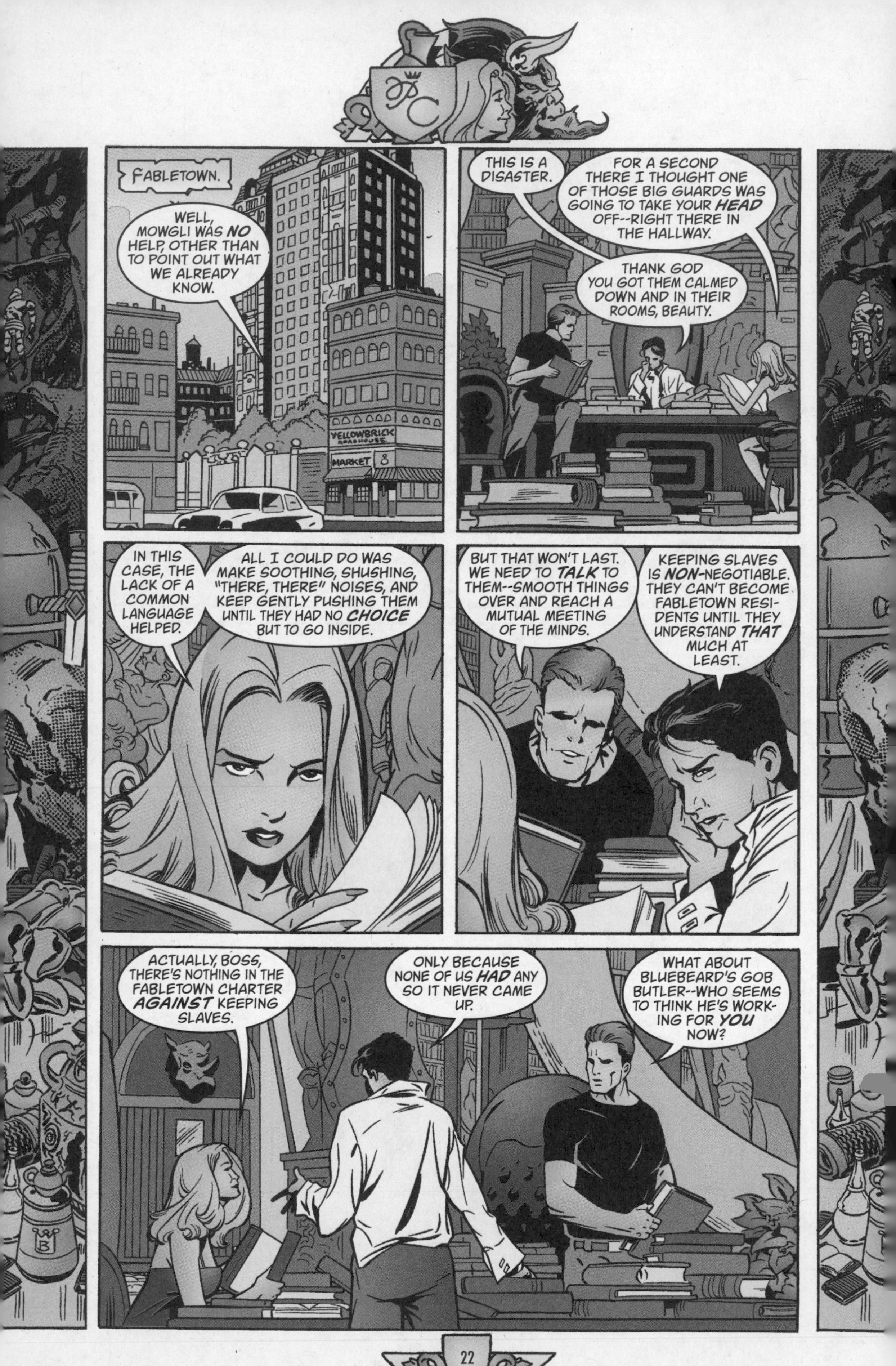
FABLETOWN.
WELL, MOWGLI WAS NO HELP, OTHER THAN TO POINT OUT WHAT WE ALREADY KNOW.
YELLOWBRICK ROADHOUSE
MARKET
THIS IS A DISASTER.
FOR A SECOND THERE I THOUGHT ONE OF THOSE BIG GUARDS WAS GOING TO TAKE YOUR HEAD OFF--RIGHT THERE IN THE HALLWAY.
THANK GOD YOU GOT THEM CALMED DOWN AND IN THEIR ROOMS, BEAUTY.
IN THIS CASE, THE LACK OF A COMMON LANGUAGE HELPED.
ALL I COULD DO WAS MAKE SOOTHING, SHUSHING, "THERE, THERE" NOISES, AND KEEP GENTLY PUSHING THEM UNTIL THEY HAD NO CHOICE BUT TO GO INSIDE.
BUT THAT WON'T LAST. WE NEED TO TALK TO THEM--SMOOTH THINGS OVER AND REACH A MUTUAL MEETING OF THE MINDS.
KEEPING SLAVES IS NON-NEGOTIABLE. THEY CAN'T BECOME FABLETOWN RESIDENTS UNTIL THEY UNDERSTAND THAT MUCH AT LEAST.
ACTUALLY, BOSS, THERE'S NOTHING IN THE FABLETOWN CHARTER AGAINST KEEPING SLAVES.
ONLY BECAUSE NONE OF US HAD ANY SO IT NEVER CAME UP.
WHAT ABOUT BLUEBEARD'S GOB BUTLER--WHO SEEMS TO THINK HE'S WORKING FOR YOU NOW?

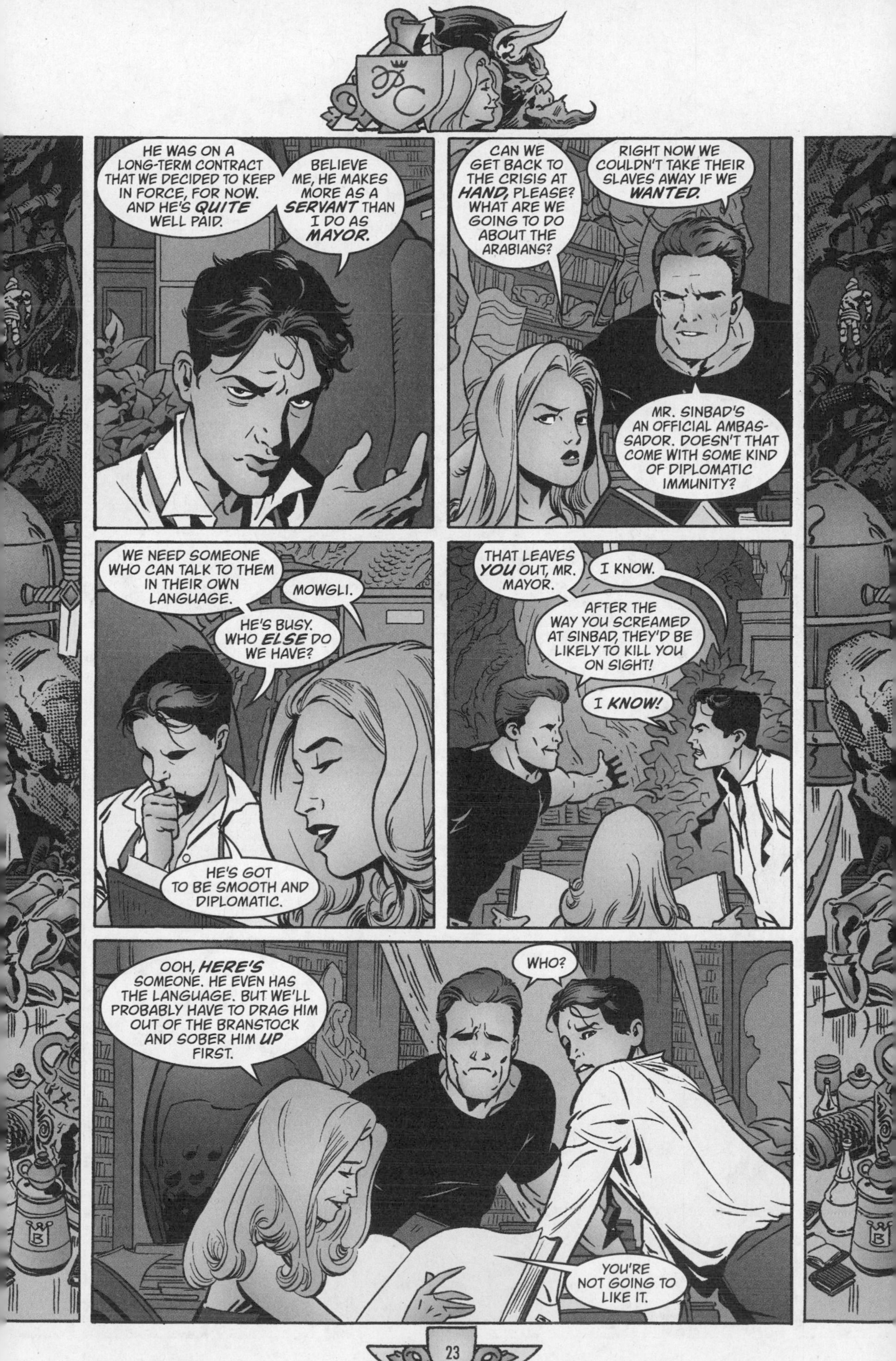
HE WAS ON A LONG-TERM CONTRACT THAT WE DECIDED TO KEEP IN FORCE, FOR NOW. AND HE'S QUITE WELL PAID.
BELIEVE ME, HE MAKES MORE AS A SERVANT THAN I DO AS MAYOR.
CAN WE GET BACK TO THE CRISIS AT HAND, PLEASE? WHAT ARE WE GOING TO DO ABOUT THE ARABIANS?
RIGHT NOW WE COULDN'T TAKE THEIR SLAVES AWAY IF WE WANTED.
MR. SINBAD'S AN OFFICIAL AMBASSADOR. DOESN'T THAT COME WITH SOME KIND OF DIPLOMATIC IMMUNITY?
WE NEED SOMEONE WHO CAN TALK TO THEM IN THEIR OWN LANGUAGE.
MOWGLI.
HE'S BUSY. WHO ELSE DO WE HAVE?
HE'S GOT TO BE SMOOTH AND DIPLOMATIC.
THAT LEAVES YOU OUT, MR. MAYOR.
I KNOW.
AFTER THE WAY YOU SCREAMED AT SINBAD, THEY'D BE LIKELY TO KILL YOU ON SIGHT!
I KNOW!
OOH, HERE'S SOMEONE. HE EVEN HAS THE LANGUAGE. BUT WE'LL PROBABLY HAVE TO DRAG HIM OUT OF THE BRANSTOCK AND SOBER HIM UP FIRST.
WHO?
YOU'RE NOT GOING TO LIKE IT.

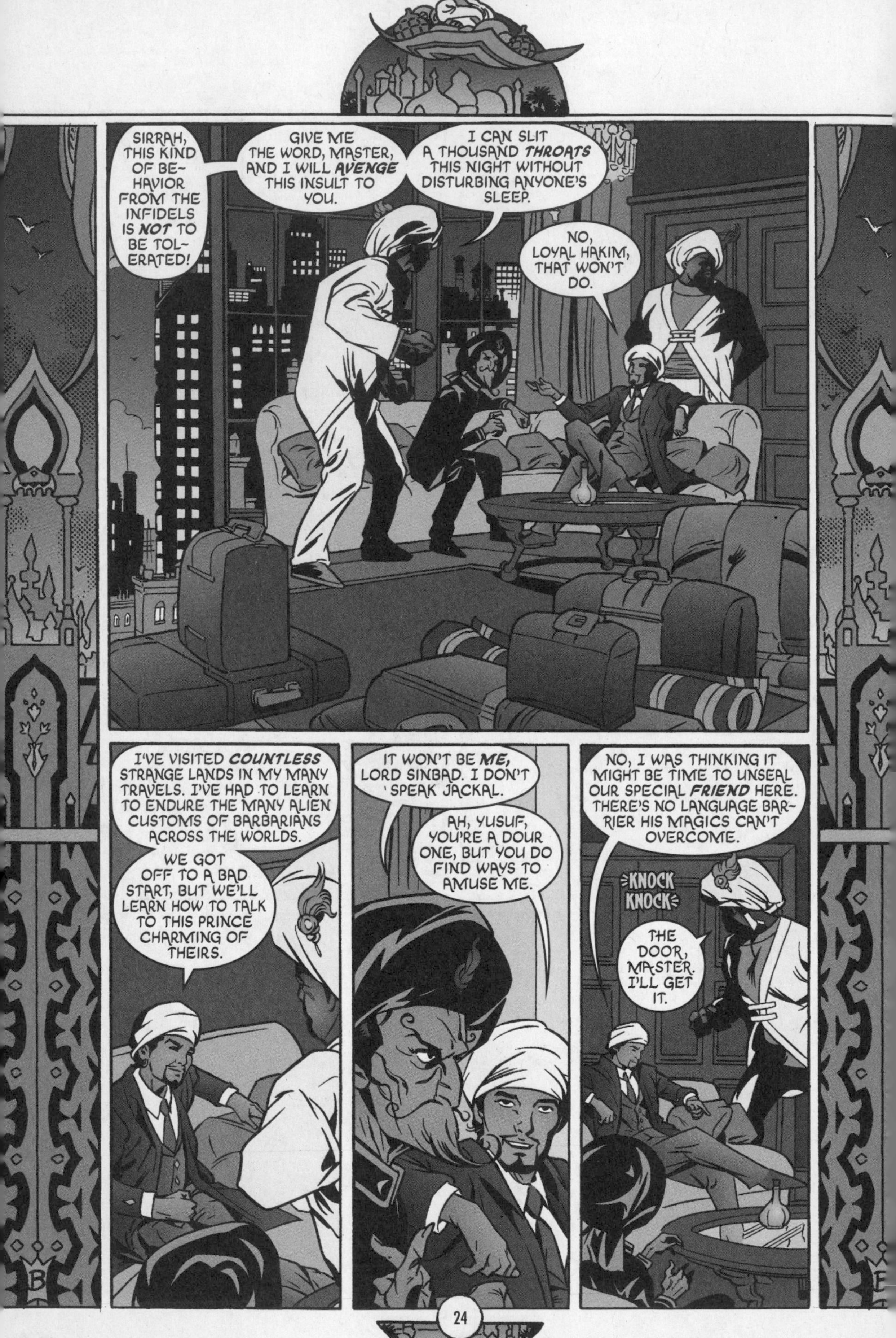

SIRRAH, THIS KIND OF BE-HAVIOR FROM THE INFIDELS IS NOT TO BE TOL-ERATED!
GIVE ME THE WORD, MASTER, AND I WILL AVENGE THIS INSULT TO YOU.
I CAN SLIT A THOUSAND THROATS THIS NIGHT WITHOUT DISTURBING ANYONE'S SLEEP.
NO, LOYAL HAKIM, THAT WON'T DO.
I'VE VISITED COUNTLESS STRANGE LANDS IN MY MANY TRAVELS. I'VE HAD TO LEARN TO ENDURE THE MANY ALIEN CUSTOMS OF BARBARIANS ACROSS THE WORLDS.
WE GOT OFF TO A BAD START, BUT WE'LL LEARN HOW TO TALK TO THIS PRINCE CHARMING OF THEIRS.
IT WON'T BE ME, LORD SINBAD. I DON'T SPEAK JACKAL.
AH, YUSUF, YOU'RE A DOUR ONE, BUT YOU DO FIND WAYS TO AMUSE ME.
NO, I WAS THINKING IT MIGHT BE TIME TO UNSEAL OUR SPECIAL FRIEND HERE. THERE'S NO LANGUAGE BAR-RIER HIS MAGICS CAN'T OVERCOME.
KNOCK KNOCK
THE DOOR, MASTER. I'LL GET IT.

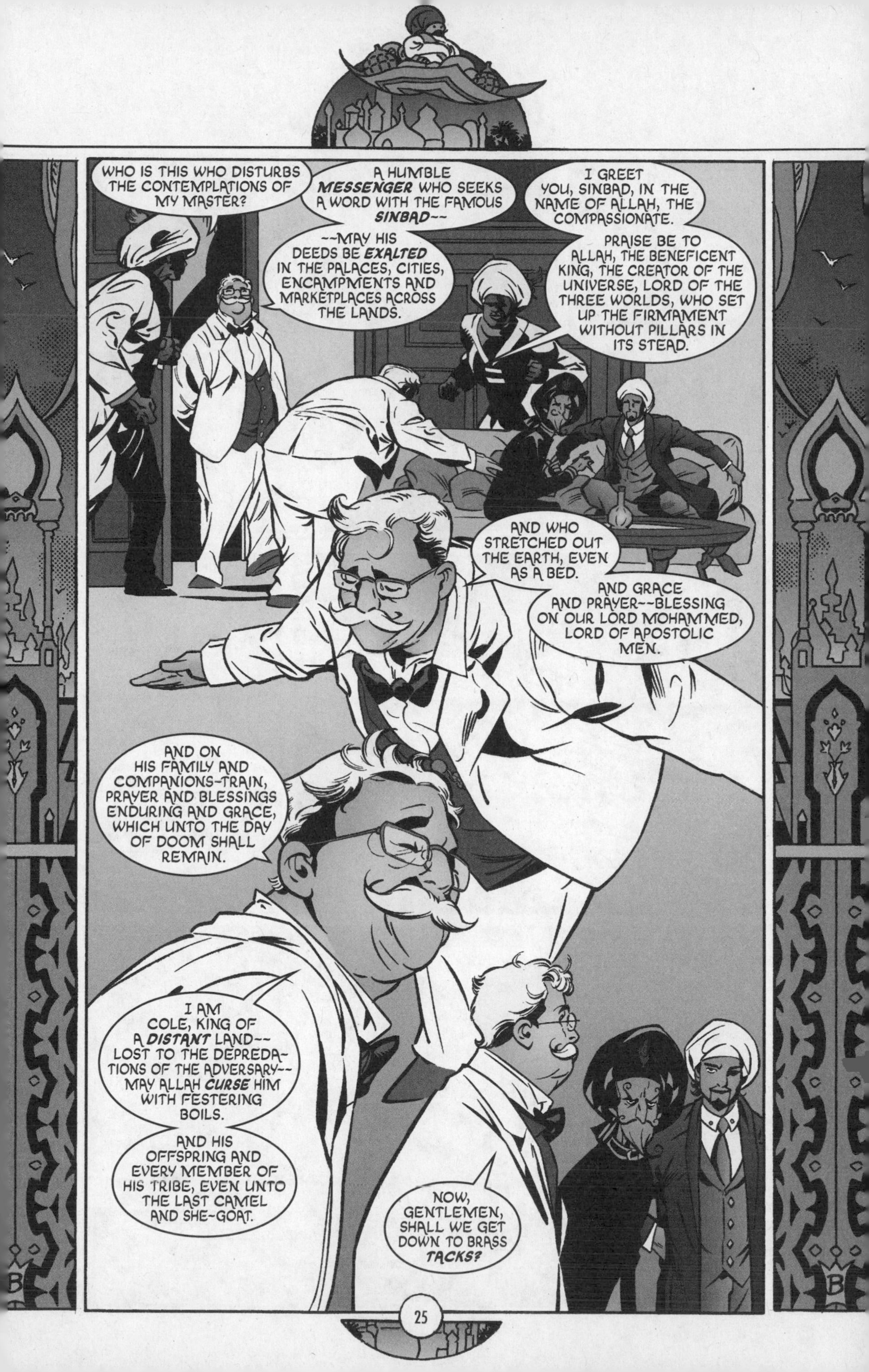
WHO IS THIS WHO DISTURBS THE CONTEMPLATIONS OF MY MASTER?
A HUMBLE MESSENGER WHO SEEKS A WORD WITH THE FAMOUS SINBAD--
--MAY HIS DEEDS BE EXALTED IN THE PALACES, CITIES, ENCAMPMENTS AND MARKETPLACES ACROSS THE LANDS.
I GREET YOU, SINBAD, IN THE NAME OF ALLAH, THE COMPASSIONATE.
PRAISE BE TO ALLAH, THE BENEFICENT KING, THE CREATOR OF THE UNIVERSE, LORD OF THE THREE WORLDS, WHO SET UP THE FIRMAMENT WITHOUT PILLARS IN ITS STEAD.
AND WHO STRETCHED OUT THE EARTH, EVEN AS A BED.
AND GRACE AND PRAYER--BLESSING ON OUR LORD MOHAMMED, LORD OF APOSTOLIC MEN.
AND ON HIS FAMILY AND COMPANIONS-TRAIN, PRAYER AND BLESSINGS ENDURING AND GRACE, WHICH UNTO THE DAY OF DOOM SHALL REMAIN.
I AM COLE, KING OF A DISTANT LAND--LOST TO THE DEPREDATIONS OF THE ADVERSARY--MAY ALLAH CURSE HIM WITH FESTERING BOILS.
AND HIS OFFSPRING AND EVERY MEMBER OF HIS TRIBE, EVEN UNTO THE LAST CAMEL AND SHE-GOAT.
NOW, GENTLEMEN, SHALL WE GET DOWN TO BRASS TACKS?

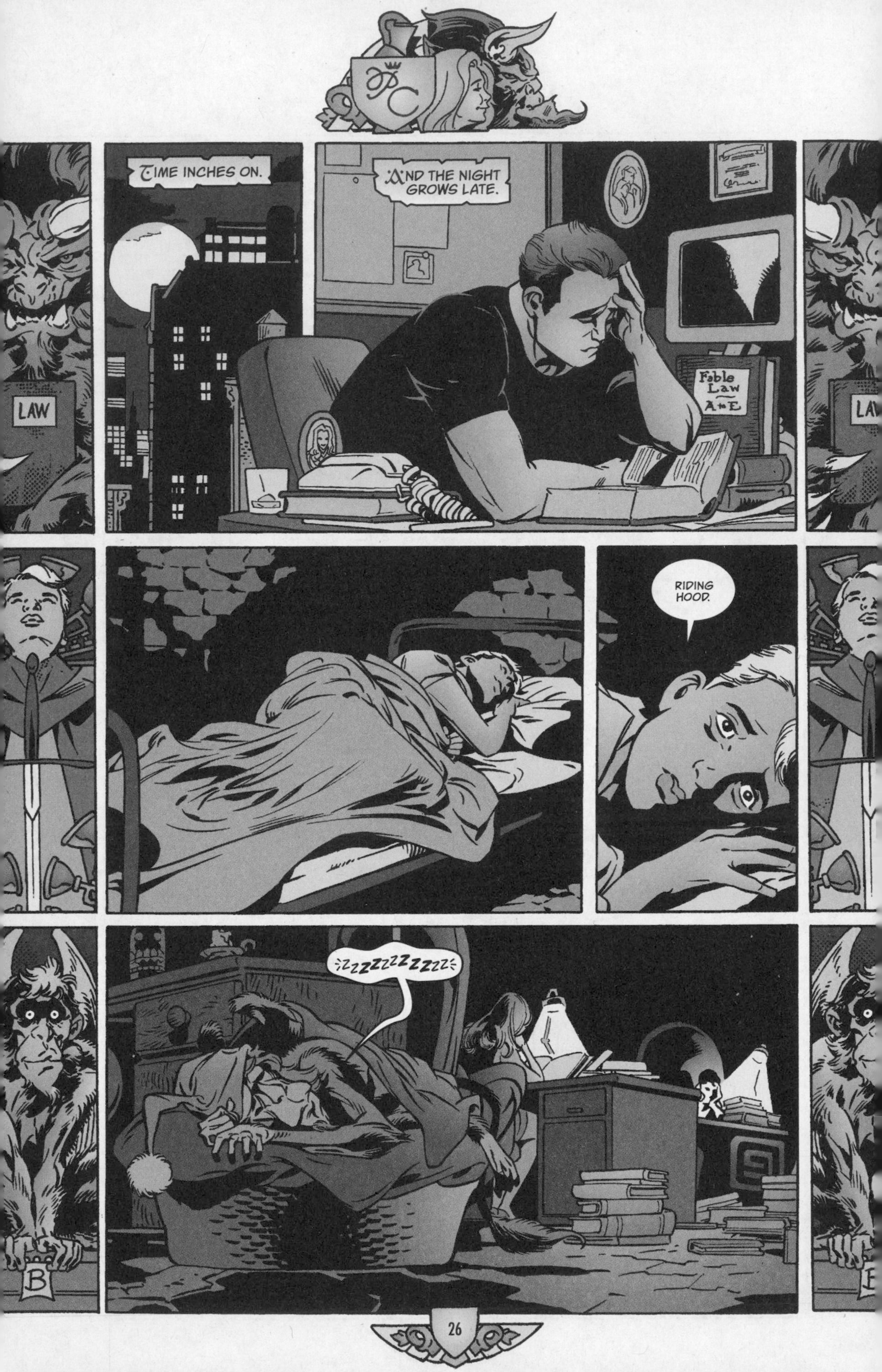
TIME INCHES ON.
AND THE NIGHT GROWS LATE.
Fable Law A to E
LAW
RIDING HOOD.
ZZZZZZZZZZZ

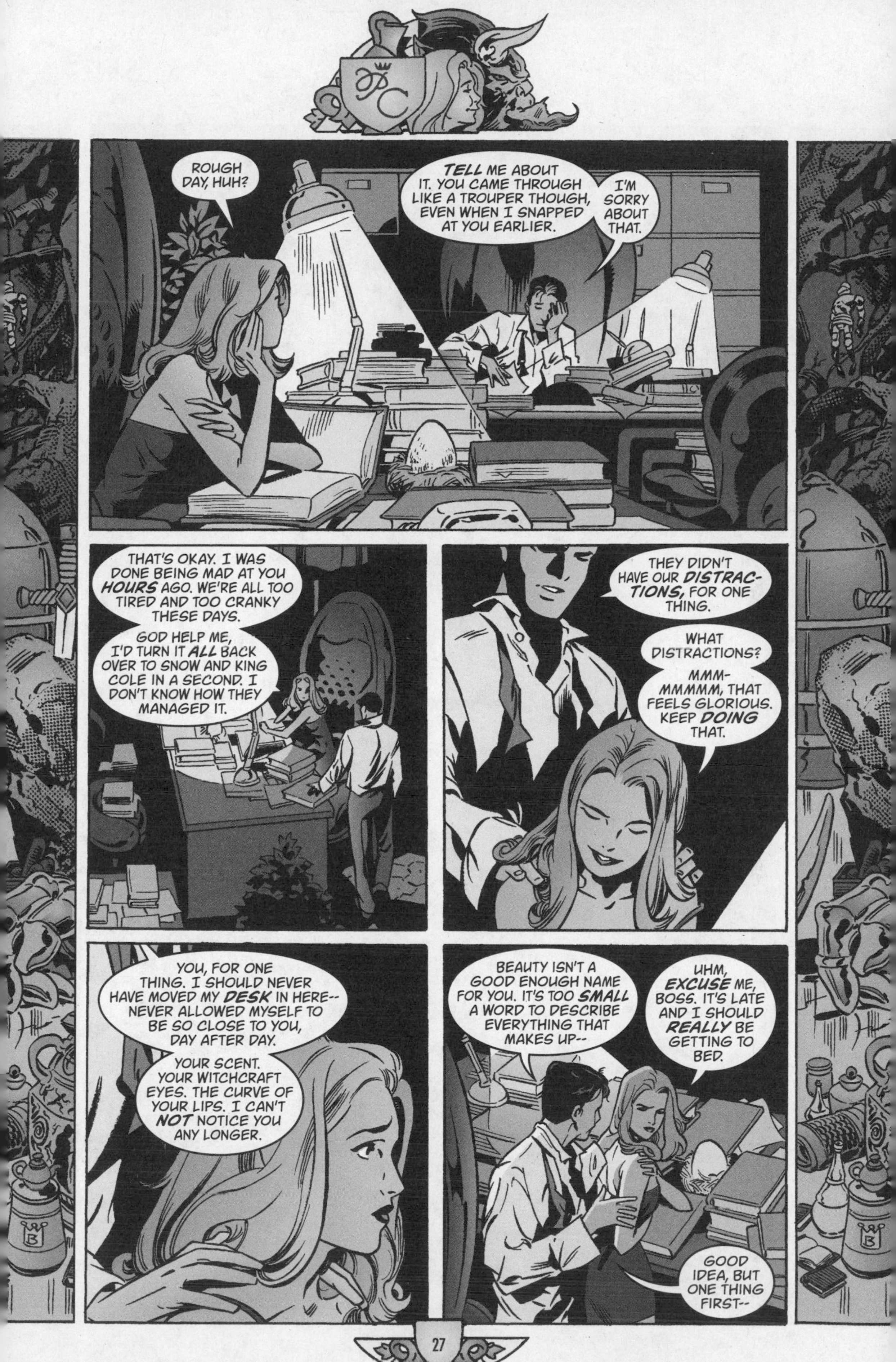

ROUGH DAY, HUH?
TELL ME ABOUT IT. YOU CAME THROUGH LIKE A TROUPER THOUGH, EVEN WHEN I SNAPPED AT YOU EARLIER.
I'M SORRY ABOUT THAT.
THAT'S OKAY. I WAS DONE BEING MAD AT YOU HOURS AGO. WE'RE ALL TOO TIRED AND TOO CRANKY THESE DAYS.
GOD HELP ME, I'D TURN IT ALL BACK OVER TO SNOW AND KING COLE IN A SECOND. I DON'T KNOW HOW THEY MANAGED IT.
THEY DIDN'T HAVE OUR DISTRACTIONS, FOR ONE THING.
WHAT DISTRACTIONS?
MMM-MMMMM, THAT FEELS GLORIOUS. KEEP DOING THAT.
YOU, FOR ONE THING. I SHOULD NEVER HAVE MOVED MY DESK IN HERE--NEVER ALLOWED MYSELF TO BE SO CLOSE TO YOU, DAY AFTER DAY.
YOUR SCENT. YOUR WITCHCRAFT EYES. THE CURVE OF YOUR LIPS. I CAN'T NOT NOTICE YOU ANY LONGER.
BEAUTY ISN'T A GOOD ENOUGH NAME FOR YOU. IT'S TOO SMALL A WORD TO DESCRIBE EVERYTHING THAT MAKES UP--
UHM, EXCUSE ME, BOSS. IT'S LATE AND I SHOULD REALLY BE GETTING TO BED.
GOOD IDEA, BUT ONE THING FIRST--

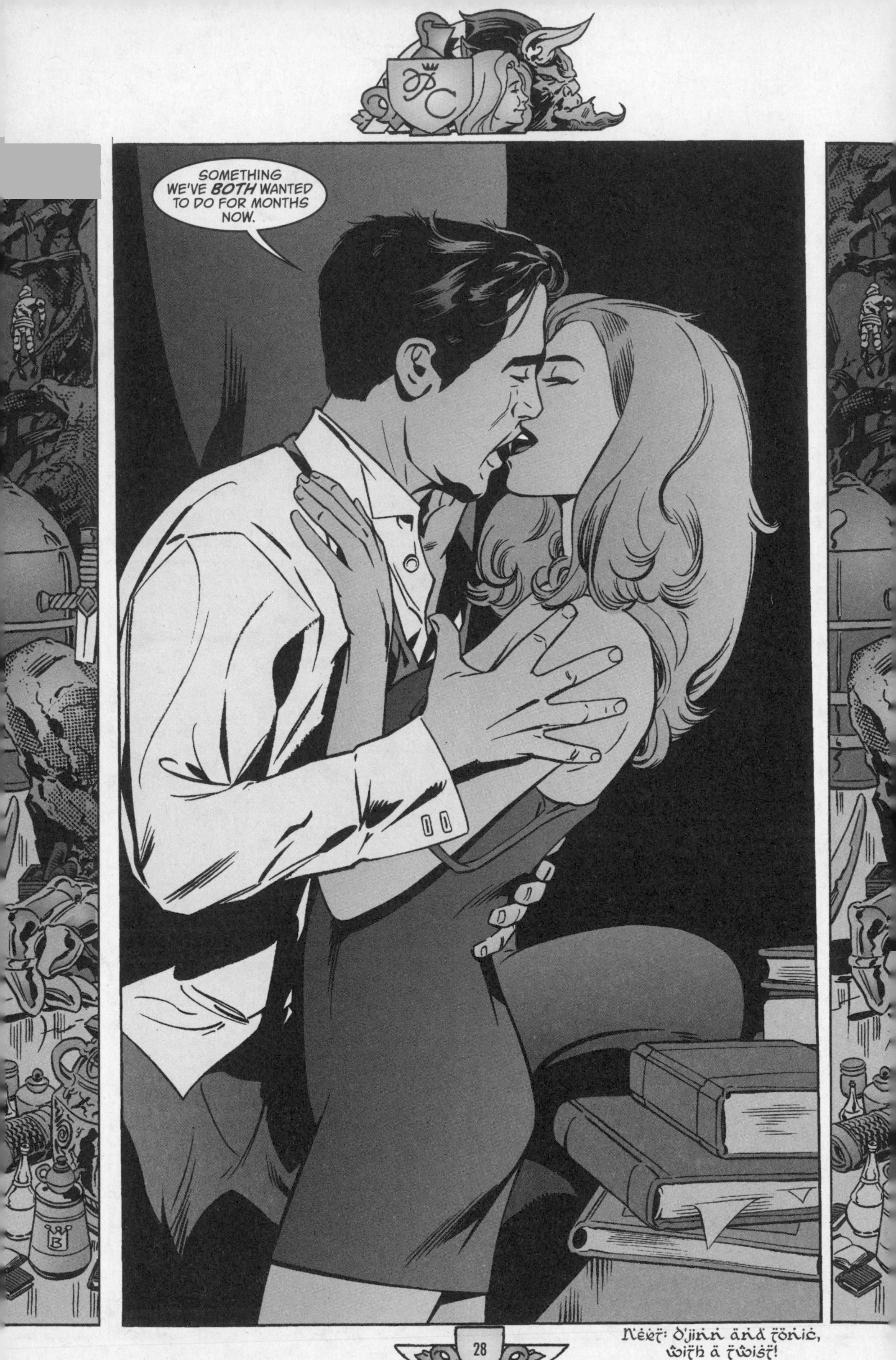
SOMETHING WE'VE **BOTH** WANTED TO DO FOR MONTHS NOW.

Next: D'jinn and Tonic, with a Twist!

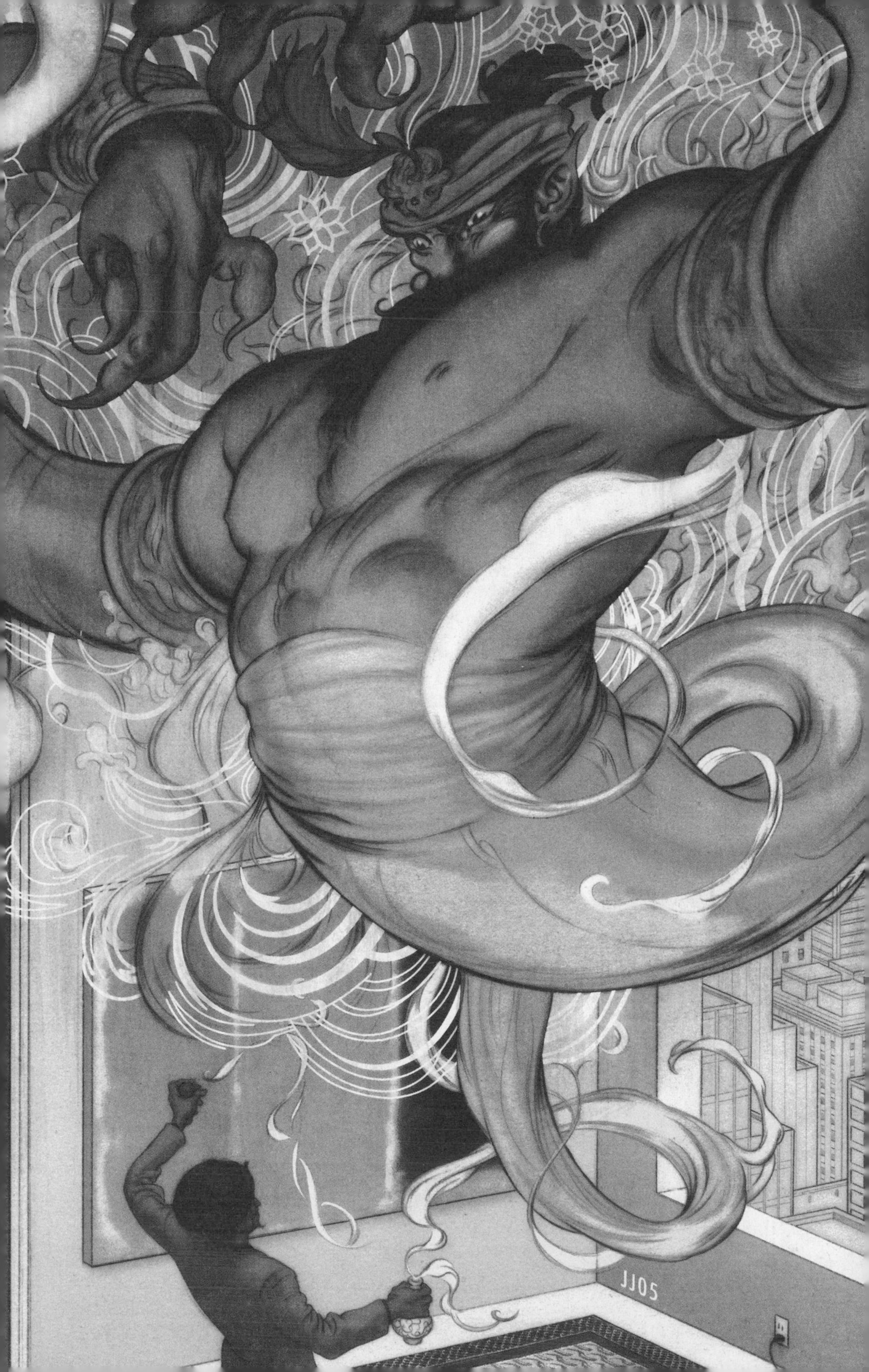
JJ05

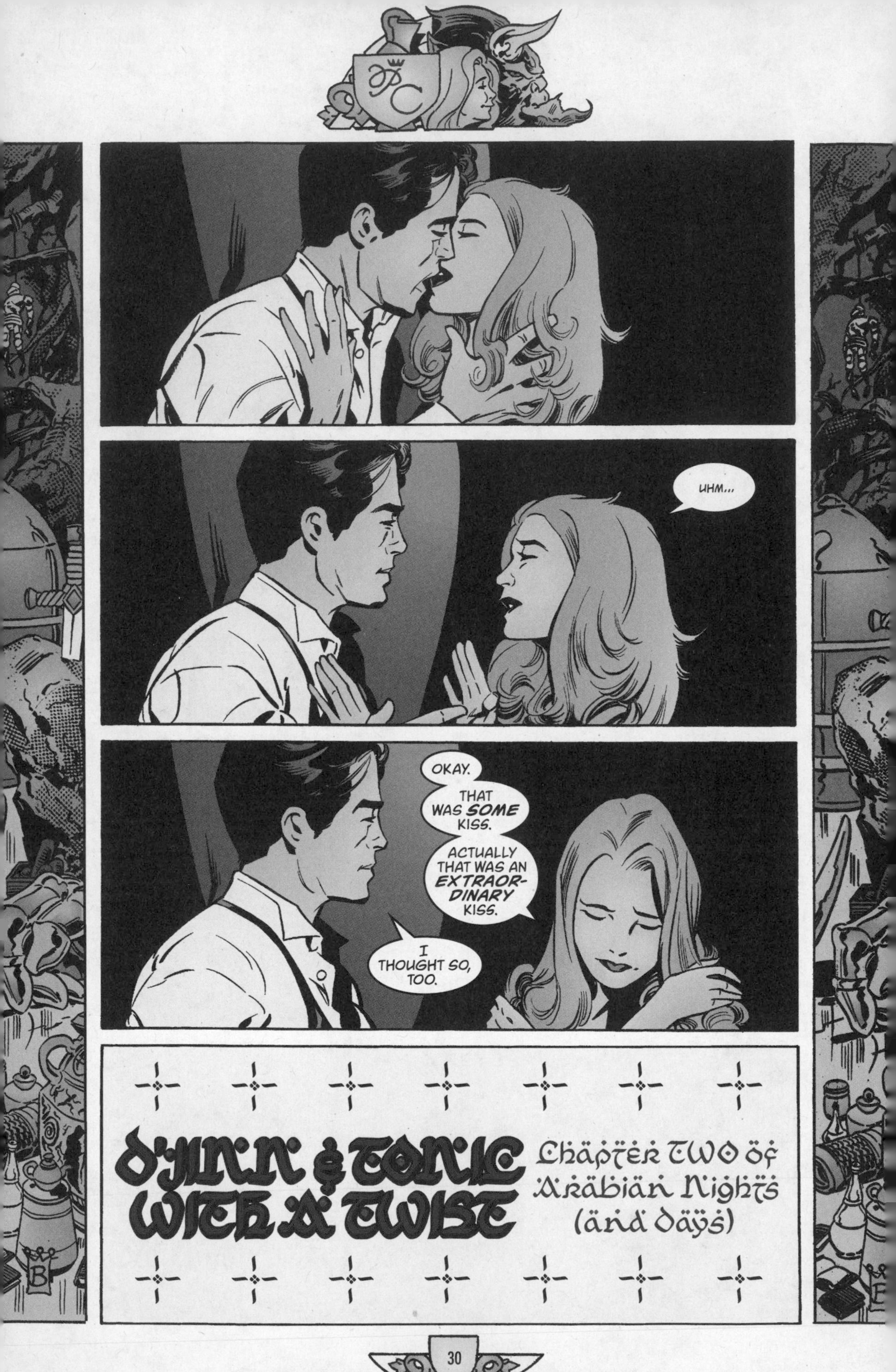

UHM...
OKAY.
THAT WAS SOME KISS.
ACTUALLY THAT WAS AN EXTRAORDINARY KISS.
I THOUGHT SO, TOO.
D'JINN & TONIC WITH A TWIST
Chapter TWO of Arabian Nights (and days)

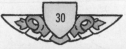

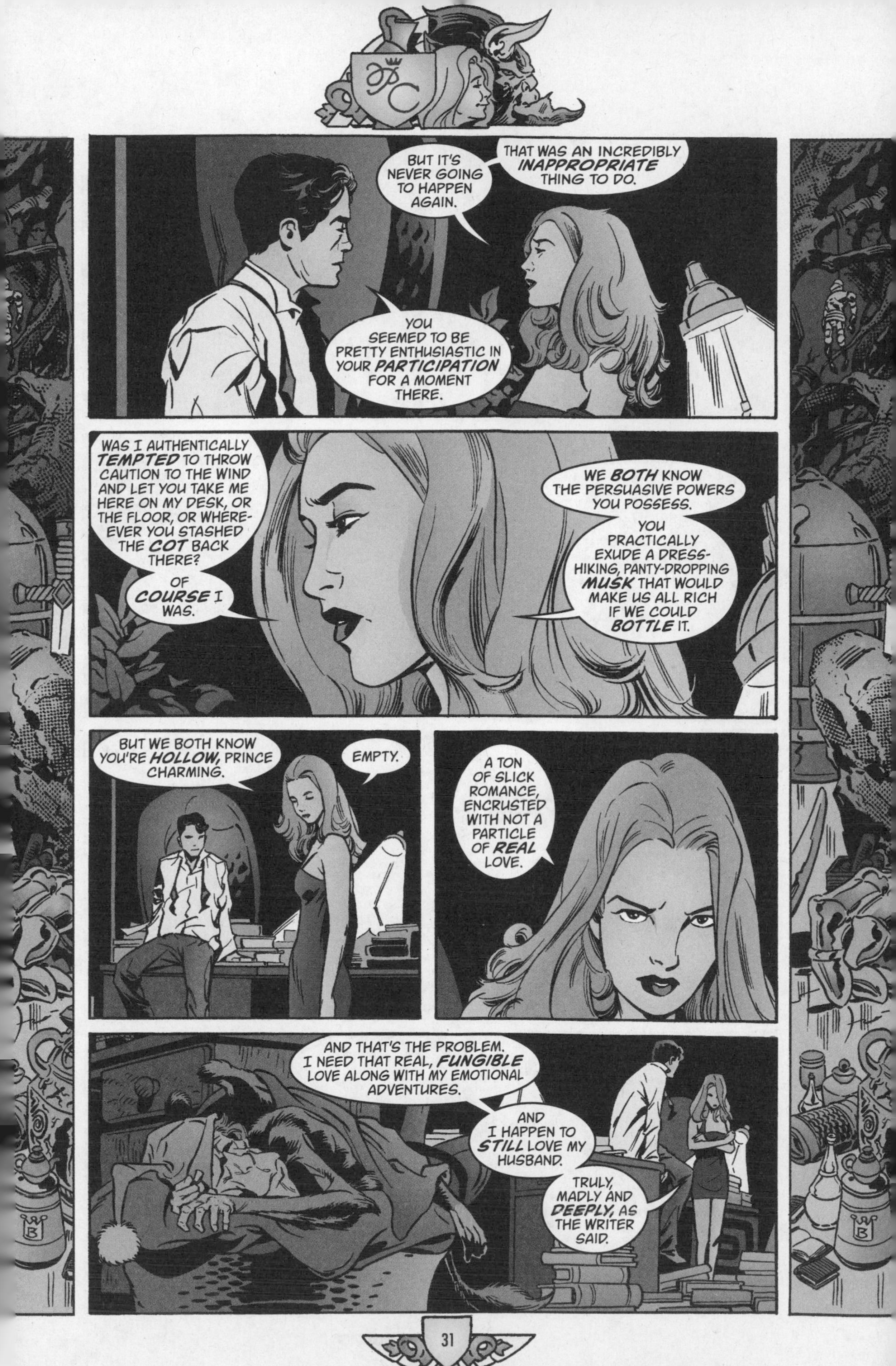
THAT WAS AN INCREDIBLY INAPPROPRIATE THING TO DO.
BUT IT'S NEVER GOING TO HAPPEN AGAIN.
YOU SEEMED TO BE PRETTY ENTHUSIASTIC IN YOUR PARTICIPATION FOR A MOMENT THERE.
WAS I AUTHENTICALLY TEMPTED TO THROW CAUTION TO THE WIND AND LET YOU TAKE ME HERE ON MY DESK, OR THE FLOOR, OR WHERE-EVER YOU STASHED THE COT BACK THERE?
OF COURSE I WAS.
WE BOTH KNOW THE PERSUASIVE POWERS YOU POSSESS.
YOU PRACTICALLY EXUDE A DRESS-HIKING, PANTY-DROPPING MUSK THAT WOULD MAKE US ALL RICH IF WE COULD BOTTLE IT.
BUT WE BOTH KNOW YOU'RE HOLLOW, PRINCE CHARMING.
EMPTY.
A TON OF SLICK ROMANCE, ENCRUSTED WITH NOT A PARTICLE OF REAL LOVE.
AND THAT'S THE PROBLEM. I NEED THAT REAL, FUNGIBLE LOVE ALONG WITH MY EMOTIONAL ADVENTURES.
AND I HAPPEN TO STILL LOVE MY HUSBAND.
TRULY, MADLY AND DEEPLY, AS THE WRITER SAID.

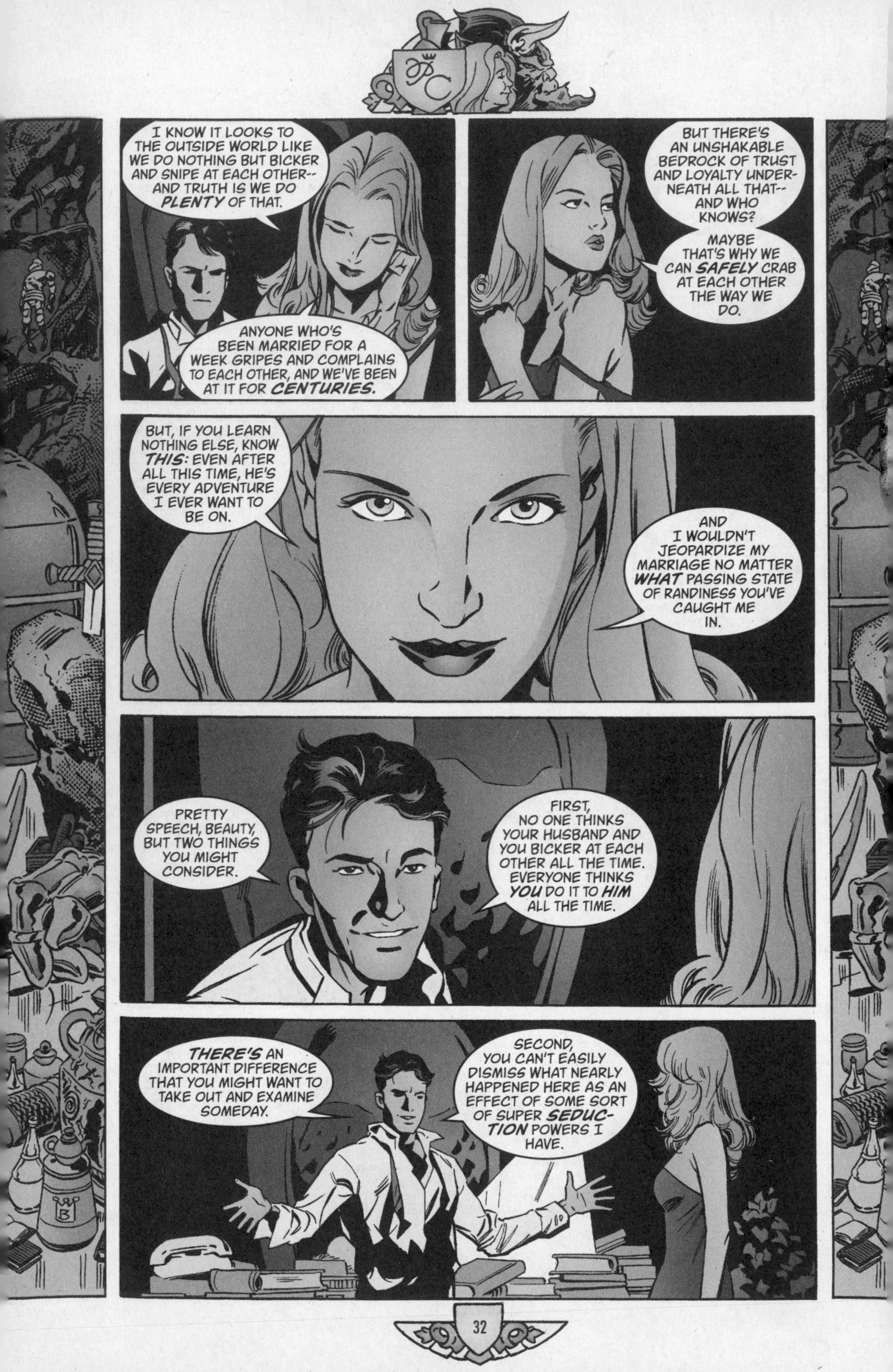

I KNOW IT LOOKS TO THE OUTSIDE WORLD LIKE WE DO NOTHING BUT BICKER AND SNIPE AT EACH OTHER-- AND TRUTH IS WE DO PLENTY OF THAT.
ANYONE WHO'S BEEN MARRIED FOR A WEEK GRIPES AND COMPLAINS TO EACH OTHER, AND WE'VE BEEN AT IT FOR CENTURIES.
BUT THERE'S AN UNSHAKABLE BEDROCK OF TRUST AND LOYALTY UNDER-NEATH ALL THAT-- AND WHO KNOWS?
MAYBE THAT'S WHY WE CAN SAFELY CRAB AT EACH OTHER THE WAY WE DO.
BUT, IF YOU LEARN NOTHING ELSE, KNOW THIS: EVEN AFTER ALL THIS TIME, HE'S EVERY ADVENTURE I EVER WANT TO BE ON.
AND I WOULDN'T JEOPARDIZE MY MARRIAGE NO MATTER WHAT PASSING STATE OF RANDINESS YOU'VE CAUGHT ME IN.
PRETTY SPEECH, BEAUTY, BUT TWO THINGS YOU MIGHT CONSIDER.
FIRST, NO ONE THINKS YOUR HUSBAND AND YOU BICKER AT EACH OTHER ALL THE TIME. EVERYONE THINKS YOU DO IT TO HIM ALL THE TIME.
SECOND, YOU CAN'T EASILY DISMISS WHAT NEARLY HAPPENED HERE AS AN EFFECT OF SOME SORT OF SUPER SEDUC-TION POWERS I HAVE.
THERE'S AN IMPORTANT DIFFERENCE THAT YOU MIGHT WANT TO TAKE OUT AND EXAMINE SOMEDAY.

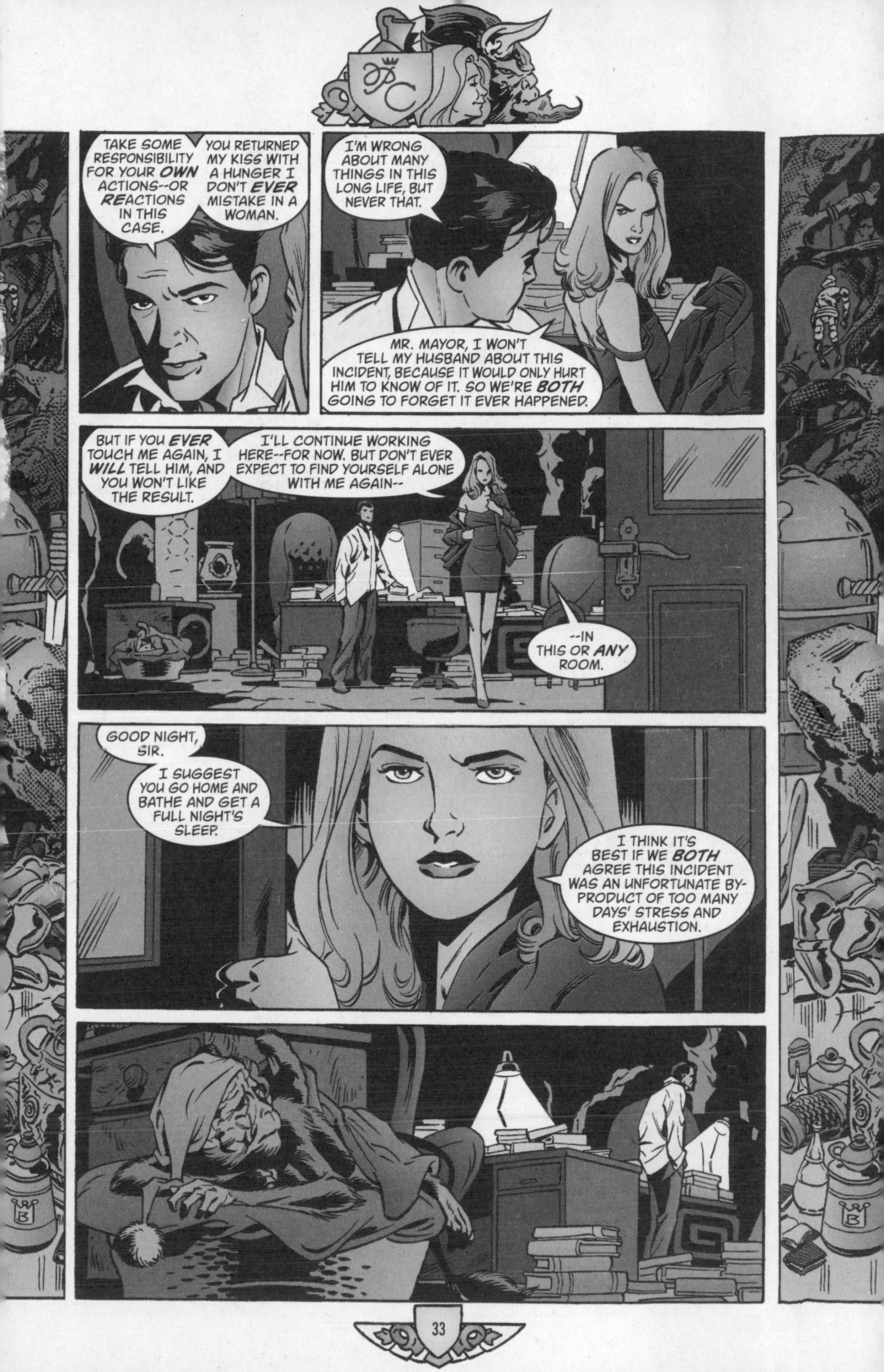
TAKE SOME RESPONSIBILITY FOR YOUR **OWN** ACTIONS--OR **RE**ACTIONS IN THIS CASE.
YOU RETURNED MY KISS WITH A HUNGER I DON'T **EVER** MISTAKE IN A WOMAN.
I'M WRONG ABOUT MANY THINGS IN THIS LONG LIFE, BUT NEVER THAT.
MR. MAYOR, I WON'T TELL MY HUSBAND ABOUT THIS INCIDENT, BECAUSE IT WOULD ONLY HURT HIM TO KNOW OF IT. SO WE'RE **BOTH** GOING TO FORGET IT EVER HAPPENED.
BUT IF YOU **EVER** TOUCH ME AGAIN, I **WILL** TELL HIM, AND YOU WON'T LIKE THE RESULT.
I'LL CONTINUE WORKING HERE--FOR NOW. BUT DON'T EVER EXPECT TO FIND YOURSELF ALONE WITH ME AGAIN--
--IN THIS OR **ANY** ROOM.
GOOD NIGHT, SIR.
I SUGGEST YOU GO HOME AND BATHE AND GET A FULL NIGHT'S SLEEP.
I THINK IT'S BEST IF WE **BOTH** AGREE THIS INCIDENT WAS AN UNFORTUNATE BY-PRODUCT OF TOO MANY DAYS' STRESS AND EXHAUSTION.

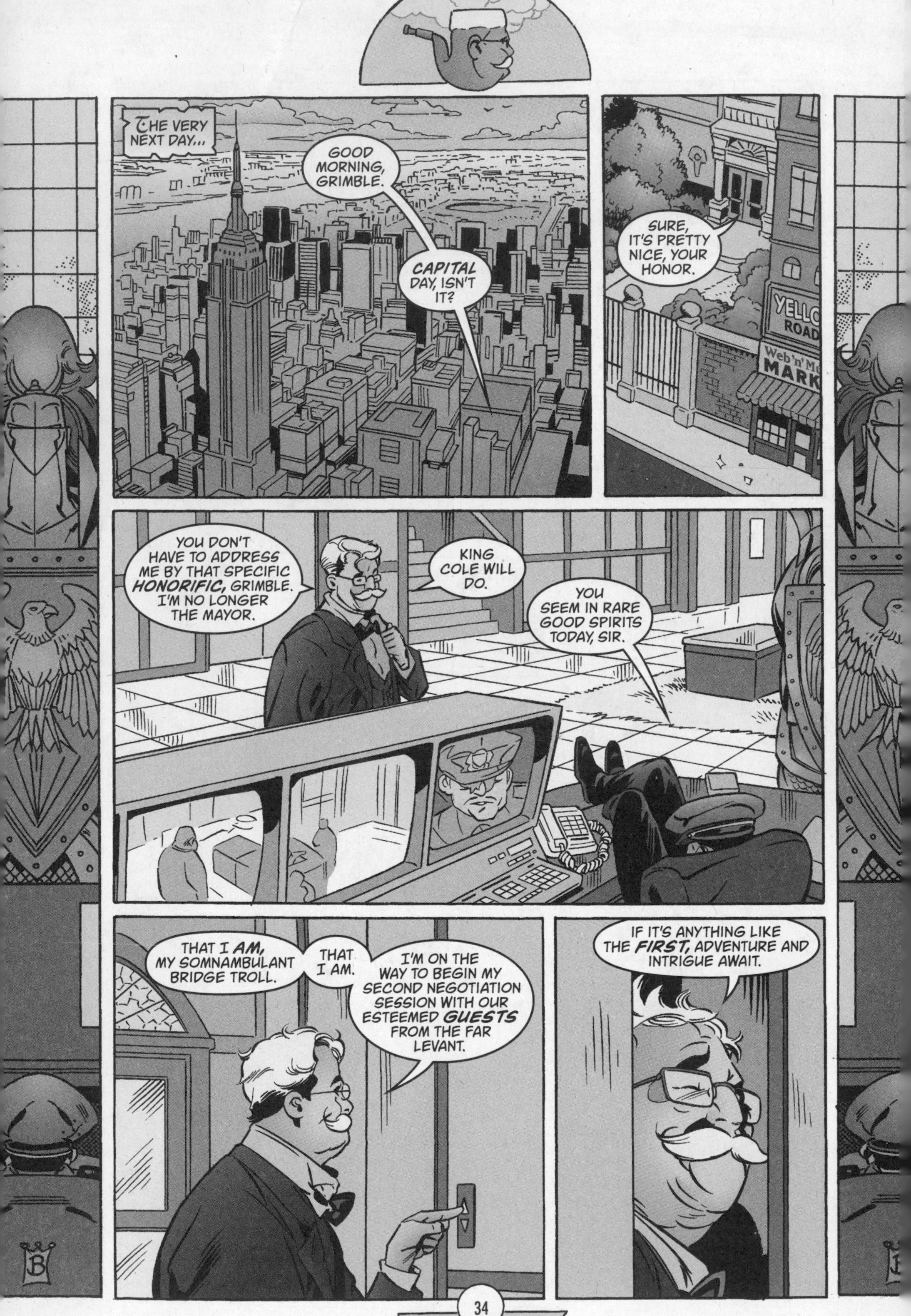
THE VERY NEXT DAY...
GOOD MORNING, GRIMBLE.
CAPITAL DAY, ISN'T IT?
SURE, IT'S PRETTY NICE, YOUR HONOR.
YELLO
ROAD
Web'n'M
MARK
YOU DON'T HAVE TO ADDRESS ME BY THAT SPECIFIC HONORIFIC, GRIMBLE. I'M NO LONGER THE MAYOR.
KING COLE WILL DO.
YOU SEEM IN RARE GOOD SPIRITS TODAY, SIR.
THAT I AM, MY SOMNAMBULANT BRIDGE TROLL.
THAT I AM.
I'M ON THE WAY TO BEGIN MY SECOND NEGOTIATION SESSION WITH OUR ESTEEMED GUESTS FROM THE FAR LEVANT.
IF IT'S ANYTHING LIKE THE FIRST, ADVENTURE AND INTRIGUE AWAIT.

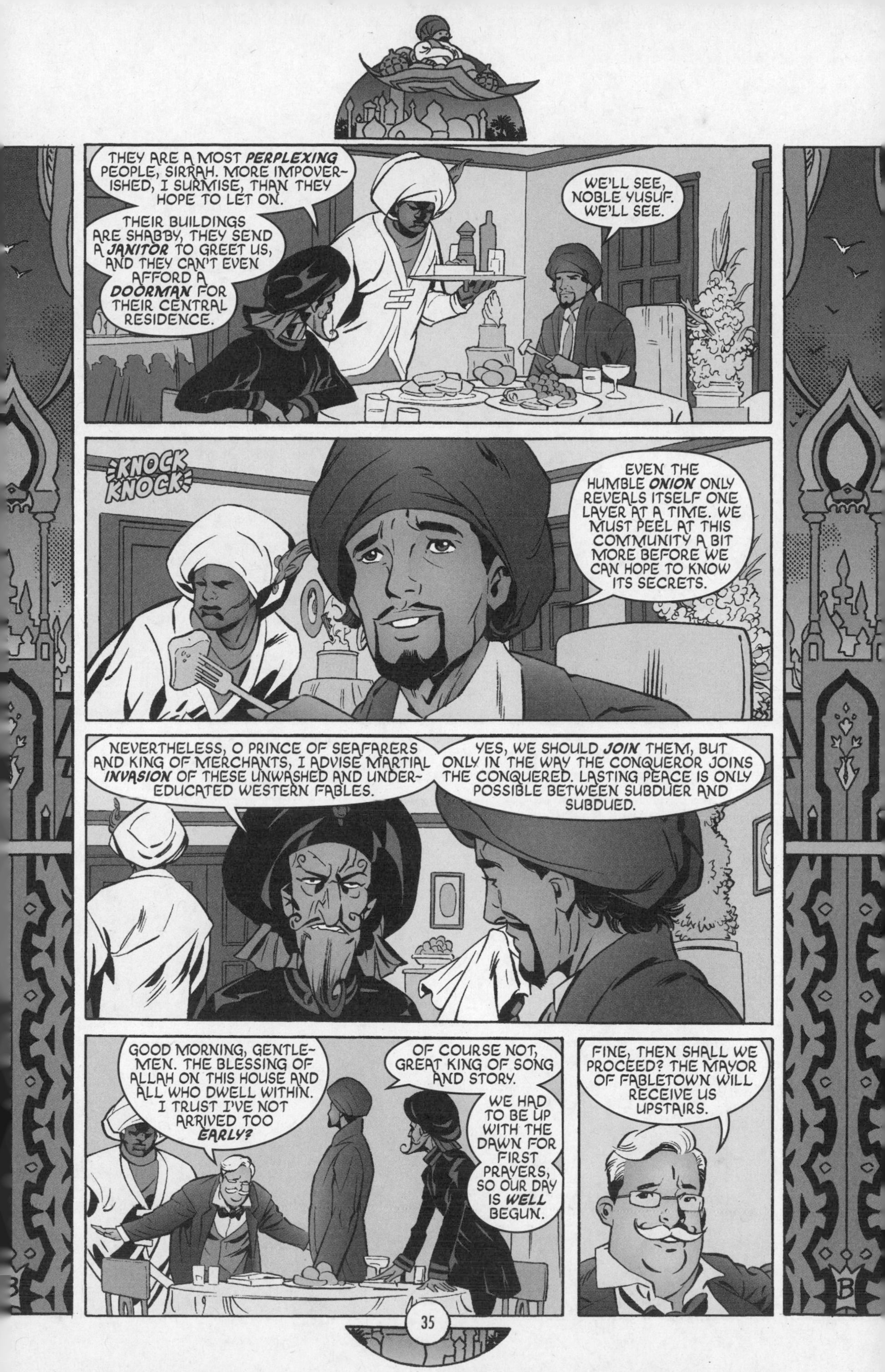
THEY ARE A MOST PERPLEXING PEOPLE, SIRRAH. MORE IMPOVER-ISHED, I SURMISE, THAN THEY HOPE TO LET ON.
THEIR BUILDINGS ARE SHABBY, THEY SEND A JANITOR TO GREET US, AND THEY CAN'T EVEN AFFORD A DOORMAN FOR THEIR CENTRAL RESIDENCE.
WE'LL SEE, NOBLE YUSUF. WE'LL SEE.
KNOCK KNOCK
EVEN THE HUMBLE ONION ONLY REVEALS ITSELF ONE LAYER AT A TIME. WE MUST PEEL AT THIS COMMUNITY A BIT MORE BEFORE WE CAN HOPE TO KNOW ITS SECRETS.
NEVERTHELESS, O PRINCE OF SEAFARERS AND KING OF MERCHANTS, I ADVISE MARTIAL INVASION OF THESE UNWASHED AND UNDER-EDUCATED WESTERN FABLES.
YES, WE SHOULD JOIN THEM, BUT ONLY IN THE WAY THE CONQUEROR JOINS THE CONQUERED. LASTING PEACE IS ONLY POSSIBLE BETWEEN SUBDUER AND SUBDUED.
GOOD MORNING, GENTLE-MEN. THE BLESSING OF ALLAH ON THIS HOUSE AND ALL WHO DWELL WITHIN. I TRUST I'VE NOT ARRIVED TOO EARLY?
OF COURSE NOT, GREAT KING OF SONG AND STORY.
WE HAD TO BE UP WITH THE DAWN FOR FIRST PRAYERS, SO OUR DAY IS WELL BEGUN.
FINE, THEN SHALL WE PROCEED? THE MAYOR OF FABLETOWN WILL RECEIVE US UPSTAIRS.

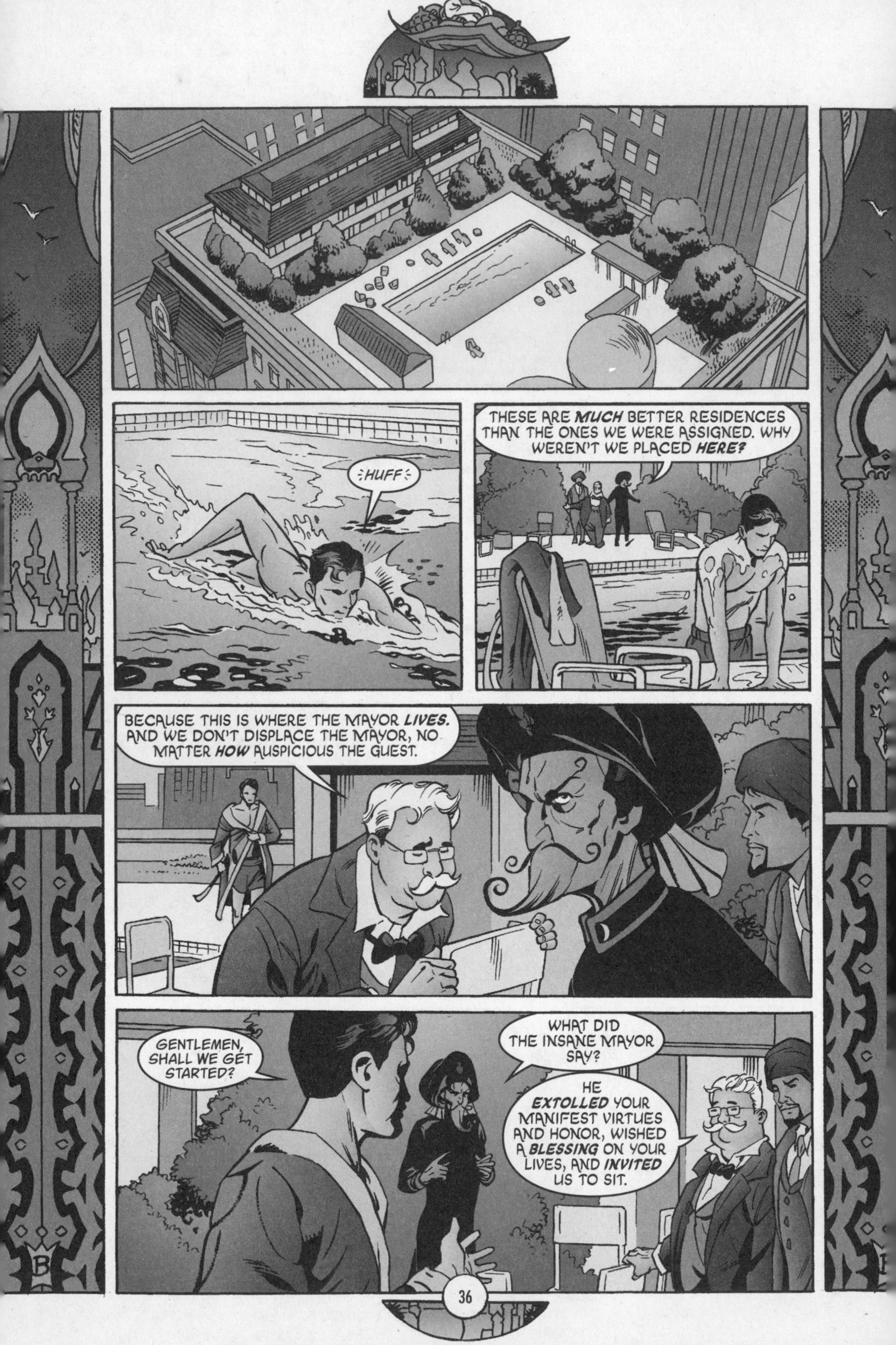
HUFF
THESE ARE MUCH BETTER RESIDENCES THAN THE ONES WE WERE ASSIGNED. WHY WEREN'T WE PLACED HERE?
BECAUSE THIS IS WHERE THE MAYOR LIVES. AND WE DON'T DISPLACE THE MAYOR, NO MATTER HOW AUSPICIOUS THE GUEST.
GENTLEMEN, SHALL WE GET STARTED?
WHAT DID THE INSANE MAYOR SAY?
HE EXTOLLED YOUR MANIFEST VIRTUES AND HONOR, WISHED A BLESSING ON YOUR LIVES, AND INVITED US TO SIT.

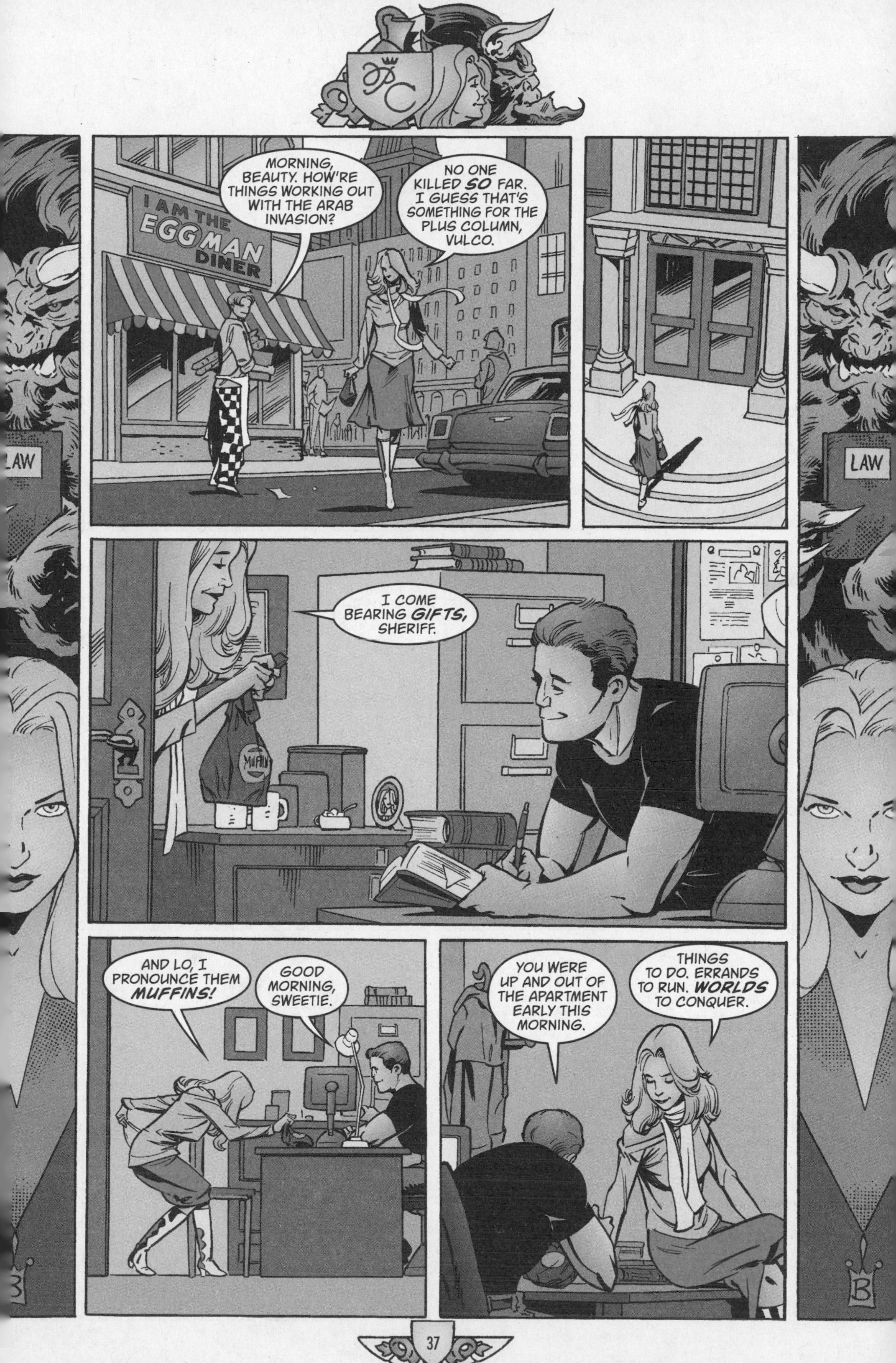
I AM THE EGGMAN DINER
MORNING, BEAUTY. HOW'RE THINGS WORKING OUT WITH THE ARAB INVASION?
NO ONE KILLED SO FAR. I GUESS THAT'S SOMETHING FOR THE PLUS COLUMN, VULCO.
LAW
I COME BEARING GIFTS, SHERIFF.
MUFFINS
AND LO, I PRONOUNCE THEM MUFFINS!
GOOD MORNING, SWEETIE.
YOU WERE UP AND OUT OF THE APARTMENT EARLY THIS MORNING.
THINGS TO DO. ERRANDS TO RUN. WORLDS TO CONQUER.

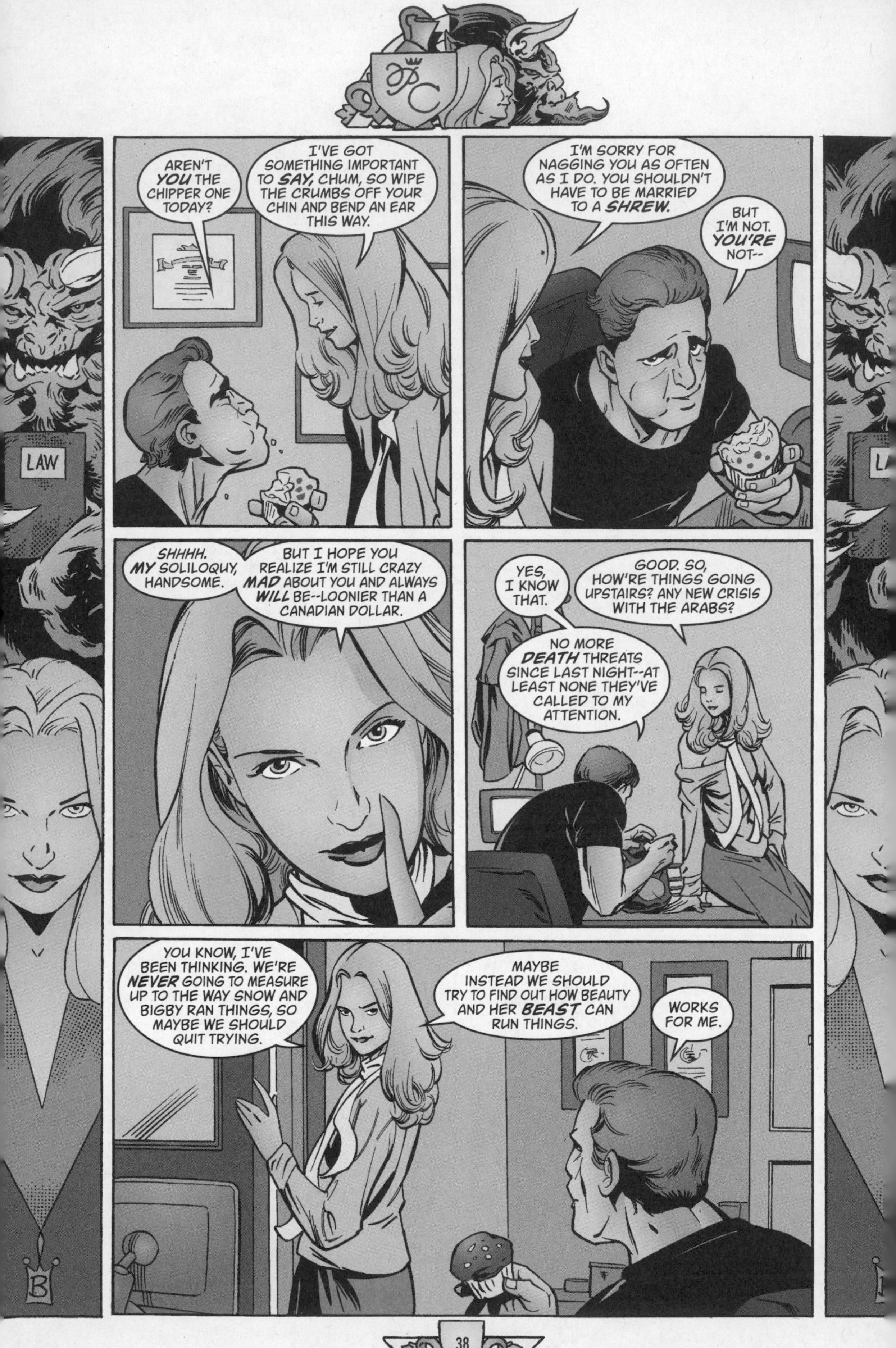
AREN'T YOU THE CHIPPER ONE TODAY?
I'VE GOT SOMETHING IMPORTANT TO SAY, CHUM, SO WIPE THE CRUMBS OFF YOUR CHIN AND BEND AN EAR THIS WAY.
LAW
I'M SORRY FOR NAGGING YOU AS OFTEN AS I DO. YOU SHOULDN'T HAVE TO BE MARRIED TO A SHREW.
BUT I'M NOT. YOU'RE NOT--
SHHHH. MY SOLILOQUY, HANDSOME.
BUT I HOPE YOU REALIZE I'M STILL CRAZY MAD ABOUT YOU AND ALWAYS WILL BE--LOONIER THAN A CANADIAN DOLLAR.
YES, I KNOW THAT.
GOOD. SO, HOW'RE THINGS GOING UPSTAIRS? ANY NEW CRISIS WITH THE ARABS?
NO MORE DEATH THREATS SINCE LAST NIGHT--AT LEAST NONE THEY'VE CALLED TO MY ATTENTION.
YOU KNOW, I'VE BEEN THINKING. WE'RE NEVER GOING TO MEASURE UP TO THE WAY SNOW AND BIGBY RAN THINGS, SO MAYBE WE SHOULD QUIT TRYING.
MAYBE INSTEAD WE SHOULD TRY TO FIND OUT HOW BEAUTY AND HER BEAST CAN RUN THINGS.
WORKS FOR ME.

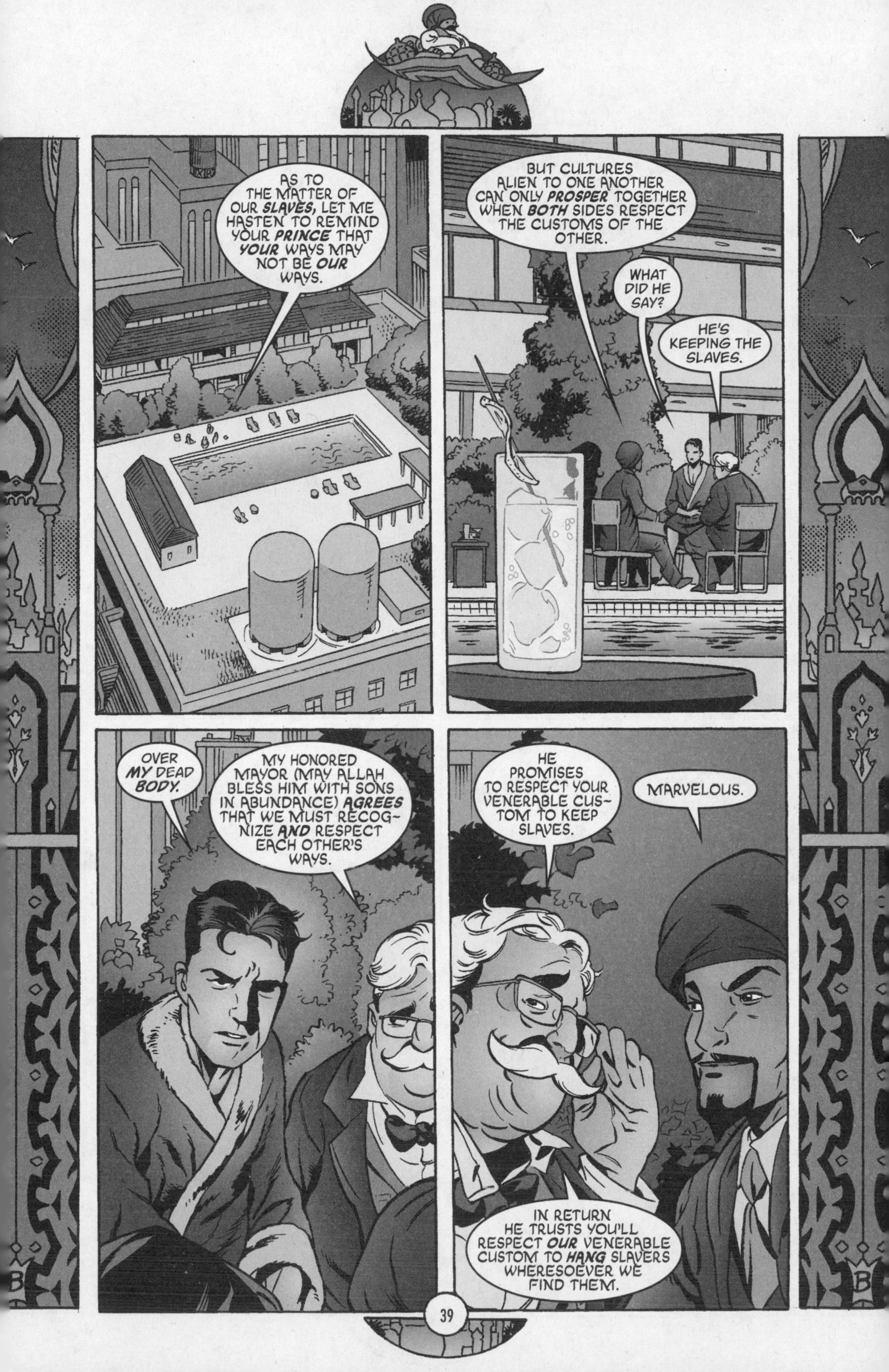
AS TO THE MATTER OF OUR SLAVES, LET ME HASTEN TO REMIND YOUR PRINCE THAT YOUR WAYS MAY NOT BE OUR WAYS.
BUT CULTURES ALIEN TO ONE ANOTHER CAN ONLY PROSPER TOGETHER WHEN BOTH SIDES RESPECT THE CUSTOMS OF THE OTHER.
WHAT DID HE SAY?
HE'S KEEPING THE SLAVES.
OVER MY DEAD BODY.
MY HONORED MAYOR (MAY ALLAH BLESS HIM WITH SONS IN ABUNDANCE) AGREES THAT WE MUST RECOG- NIZE AND RESPECT EACH OTHER'S WAYS.
HE PROMISES TO RESPECT YOUR VENERABLE CUS- TOM TO KEEP SLAVES.
MARVELOUS.
IN RETURN HE TRUSTS YOU'LL RESPECT OUR VENERABLE CUSTOM TO HANG SLAVERS WHERESOEVER WE FIND THEM.

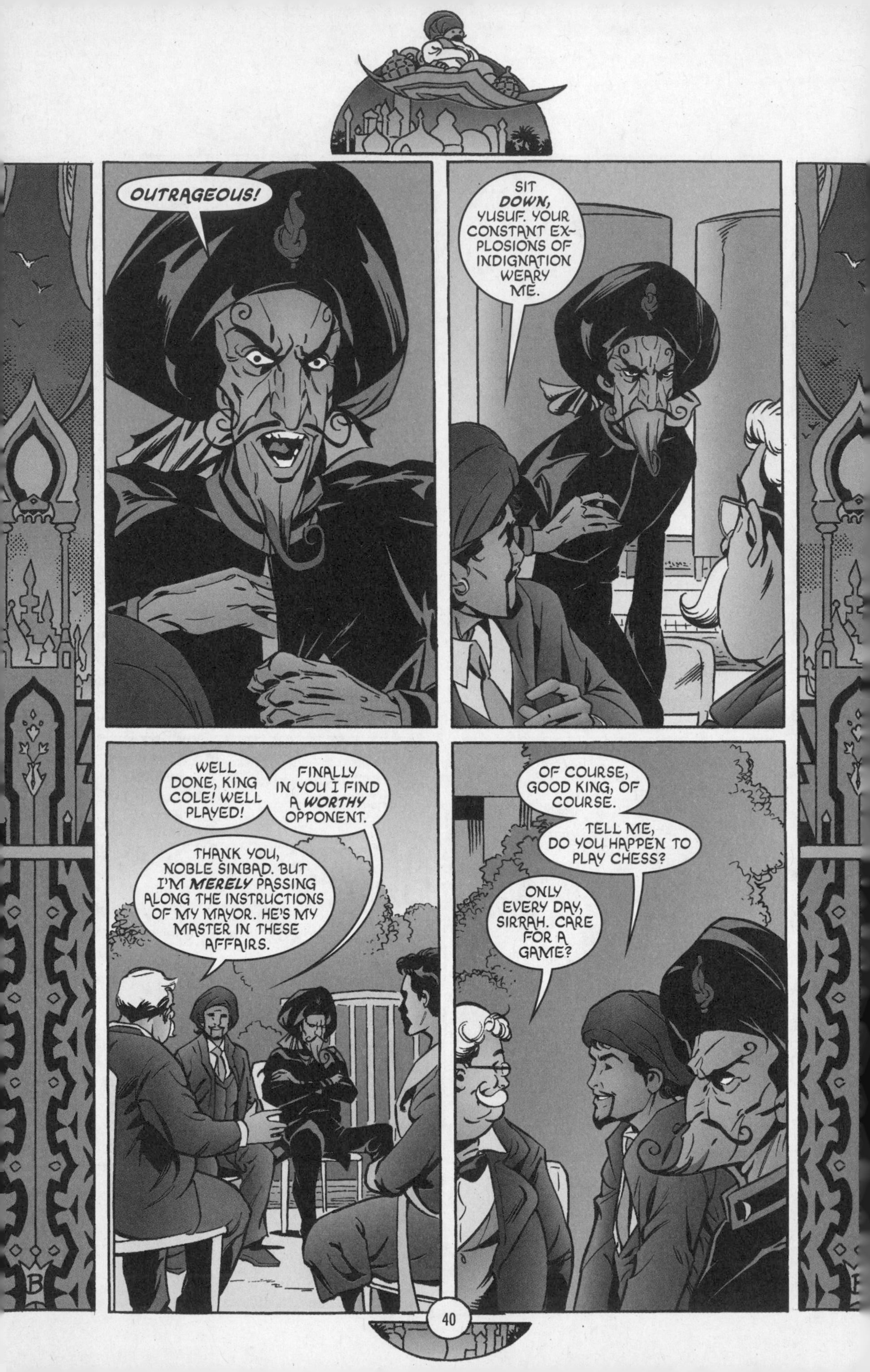

OUTRAGEOUS!
SIT DOWN, YUSUF. YOUR CONSTANT EX-PLOSIONS OF INDIGNATION WEARY ME.
WELL DONE, KING COLE! WELL PLAYED!
FINALLY IN YOU I FIND A WORTHY OPPONENT.
THANK YOU, NOBLE SINBAD. BUT I'M MERELY PASSING ALONG THE INSTRUCTIONS OF MY MAYOR. HE'S MY MASTER IN THESE AFFAIRS.
OF COURSE, GOOD KING, OF COURSE.
TELL ME, DO YOU HAPPEN TO PLAY CHESS?
ONLY EVERY DAY, SIRRAH. CARE FOR A GAME?

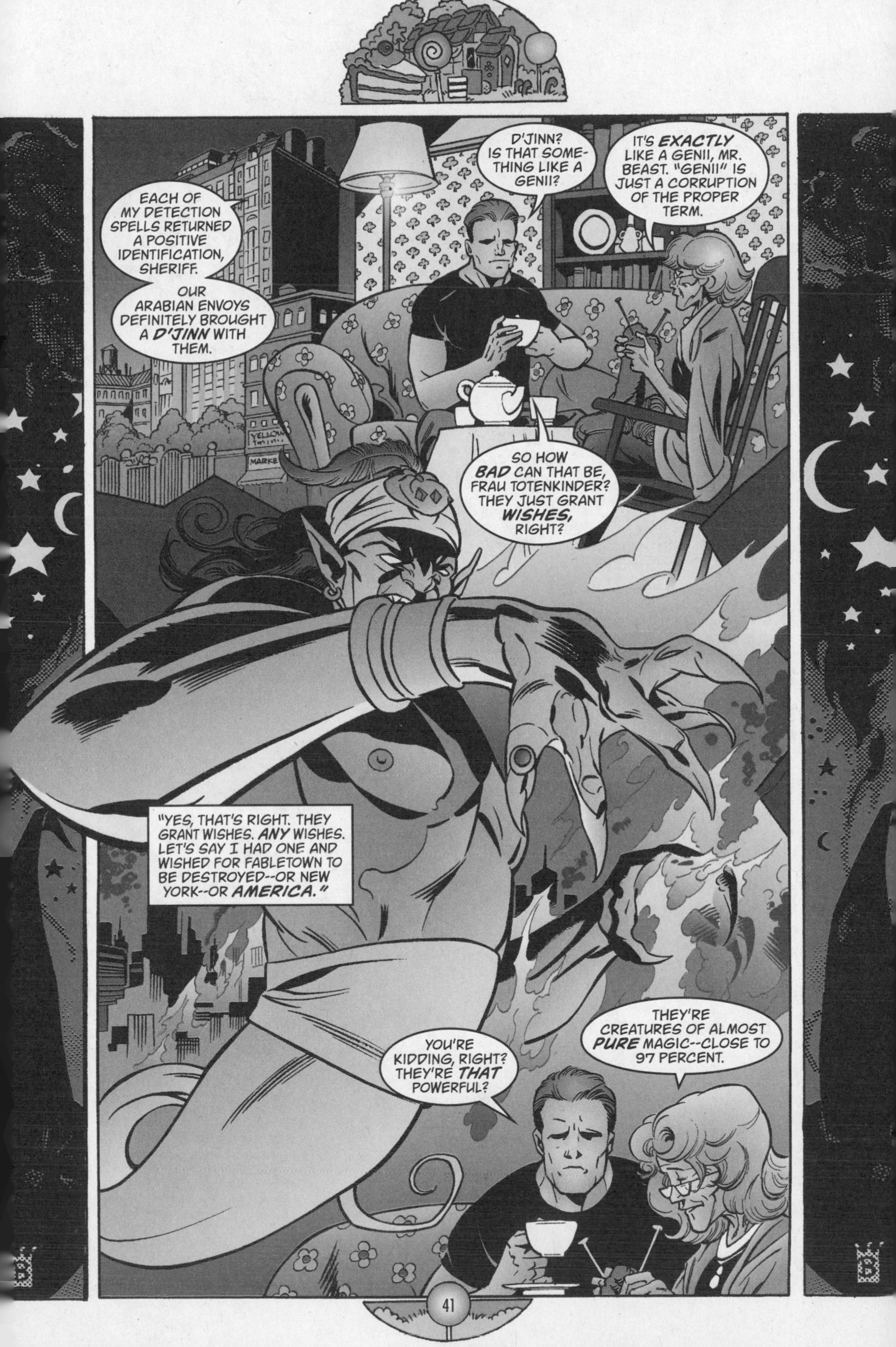

EACH OF MY DETECTION SPELLS RETURNED A POSITIVE IDENTIFICATION, SHERIFF.
OUR ARABIAN ENVOYS DEFINITELY BROUGHT A D'JINN WITH THEM.
D'JINN? IS THAT SOMETHING LIKE A GENII?
IT'S EXACTLY LIKE A GENII, MR. BEAST. "GENII" IS JUST A CORRUPTION OF THE PROPER TERM.
SO HOW BAD CAN THAT BE, FRAU TOTENKINDER? THEY JUST GRANT WISHES, RIGHT?
"YES, THAT'S RIGHT. THEY GRANT WISHES. ANY WISHES. LET'S SAY I HAD ONE AND WISHED FOR FABLETOWN TO BE DESTROYED--OR NEW YORK--OR AMERICA."
YOU'RE KIDDING, RIGHT? THEY'RE THAT POWERFUL?
THEY'RE CREATURES OF ALMOST PURE MAGIC--CLOSE TO 97 PERCENT.

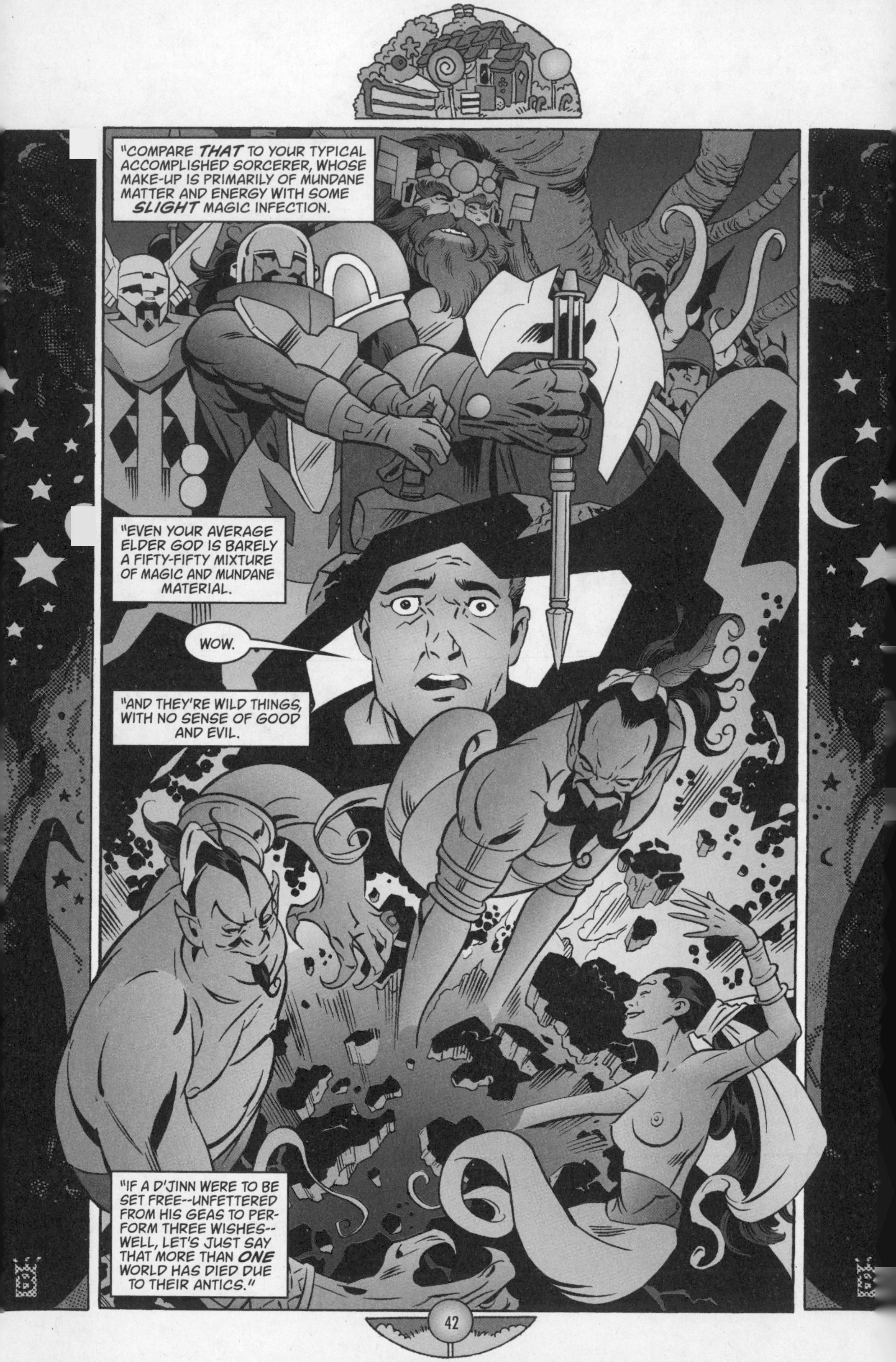
"COMPARE THAT TO YOUR TYPICAL ACCOMPLISHED SORCERER, WHOSE MAKE-UP IS PRIMARILY OF MUNDANE MATTER AND ENERGY WITH SOME SLIGHT MAGIC INFECTION.
"EVEN YOUR AVERAGE ELDER GOD IS BARELY A FIFTY-FIFTY MIXTURE OF MAGIC AND MUNDANE MATERIAL.
WOW.
"AND THEY'RE WILD THINGS, WITH NO SENSE OF GOOD AND EVIL.
"IF A D'JINN WERE TO BE SET FREE--UNFETTERED FROM HIS GEAS TO PERFORM THREE WISHES--WELL, LET'S JUST SAY THAT MORE THAN ONE WORLD HAS DIED DUE TO THEIR ANTICS."

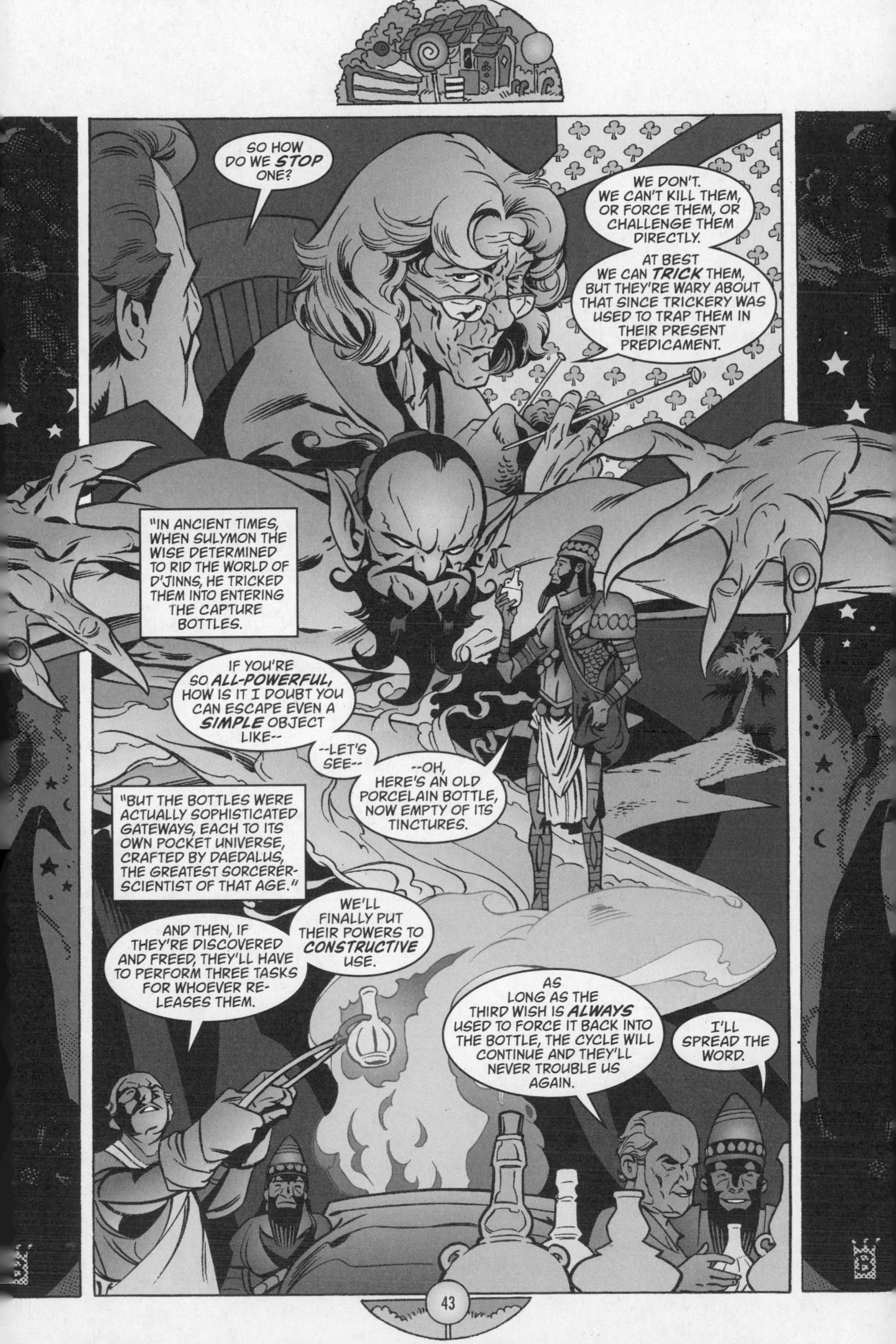

SO HOW DO WE STOP ONE?
WE DON'T. WE CAN'T KILL THEM, OR FORCE THEM, OR CHALLENGE THEM DIRECTLY.
AT BEST WE CAN TRICK THEM, BUT THEY'RE WARY ABOUT THAT SINCE TRICKERY WAS USED TO TRAP THEM IN THEIR PRESENT PREDICAMENT.
"IN ANCIENT TIMES, WHEN SULYMON THE WISE DETERMINED TO RID THE WORLD OF D'JINNS, HE TRICKED THEM INTO ENTERING THE CAPTURE BOTTLES.
IF YOU'RE SO ALL-POWERFUL, HOW IS IT I DOUBT YOU CAN ESCAPE EVEN A SIMPLE OBJECT LIKE--
--LET'S SEE--
--OH, HERE'S AN OLD PORCELAIN BOTTLE, NOW EMPTY OF ITS TINCTURES.
"BUT THE BOTTLES WERE ACTUALLY SOPHISTICATED GATEWAYS, EACH TO ITS OWN POCKET UNIVERSE, CRAFTED BY DAEDALUS, THE GREATEST SORCERER-SCIENTIST OF THAT AGE."
AND THEN, IF THEY'RE DISCOVERED AND FREED, THEY'LL HAVE TO PERFORM THREE TASKS FOR WHOEVER RE-LEASES THEM.
WE'LL FINALLY PUT THEIR POWERS TO CONSTRUCTIVE USE.
AS LONG AS THE THIRD WISH IS ALWAYS USED TO FORCE IT BACK INTO THE BOTTLE, THE CYCLE WILL CONTINUE AND THEY'LL NEVER TROUBLE US AGAIN.
I'LL SPREAD THE WORD.

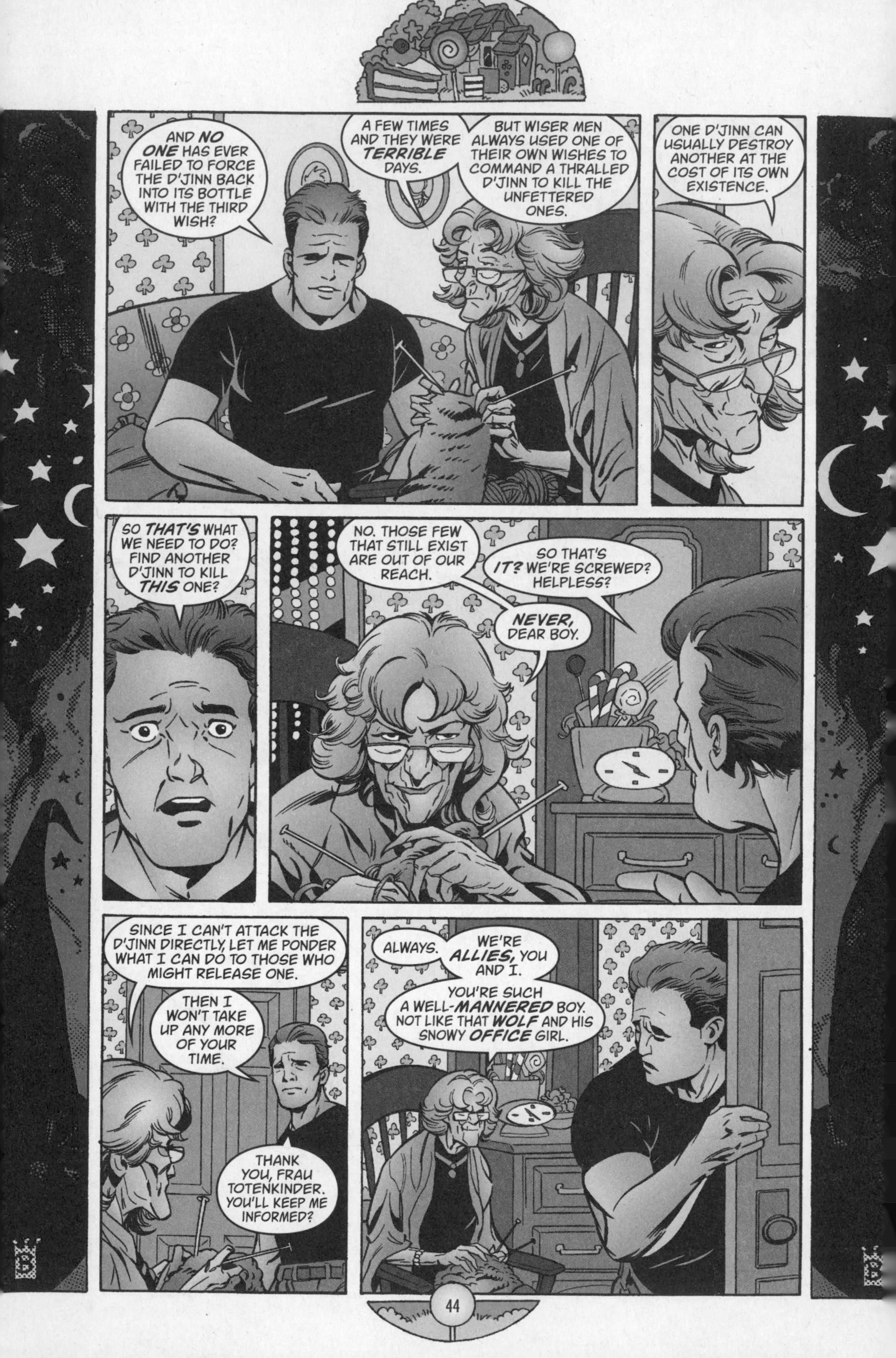
AND NO ONE HAS EVER FAILED TO FORCE THE D'JINN BACK INTO ITS BOTTLE WITH THE THIRD WISH?
A FEW TIMES AND THEY WERE TERRIBLE DAYS.
BUT WISER MEN ALWAYS USED ONE OF THEIR OWN WISHES TO COMMAND A THRALLED D'JINN TO KILL THE UNFETTERED ONES.
ONE D'JINN CAN USUALLY DESTROY ANOTHER AT THE COST OF ITS OWN EXISTENCE.
SO THAT'S WHAT WE NEED TO DO? FIND ANOTHER D'JINN TO KILL THIS ONE?
NO. THOSE FEW THAT STILL EXIST ARE OUT OF OUR REACH.
SO THAT'S IT? WE'RE SCREWED? HELPLESS?
NEVER, DEAR BOY.
SINCE I CAN'T ATTACK THE D'JINN DIRECTLY, LET ME PONDER WHAT I CAN DO TO THOSE WHO MIGHT RELEASE ONE.
THEN I WON'T TAKE UP ANY MORE OF YOUR TIME.
THANK YOU, FRAU TOTENKINDER. YOU'LL KEEP ME INFORMED?
ALWAYS.
WE'RE ALLIES, YOU AND I.
YOU'RE SUCH A WELL-MANNERED BOY. NOT LIKE THAT WOLF AND HIS SNOWY OFFICE GIRL.

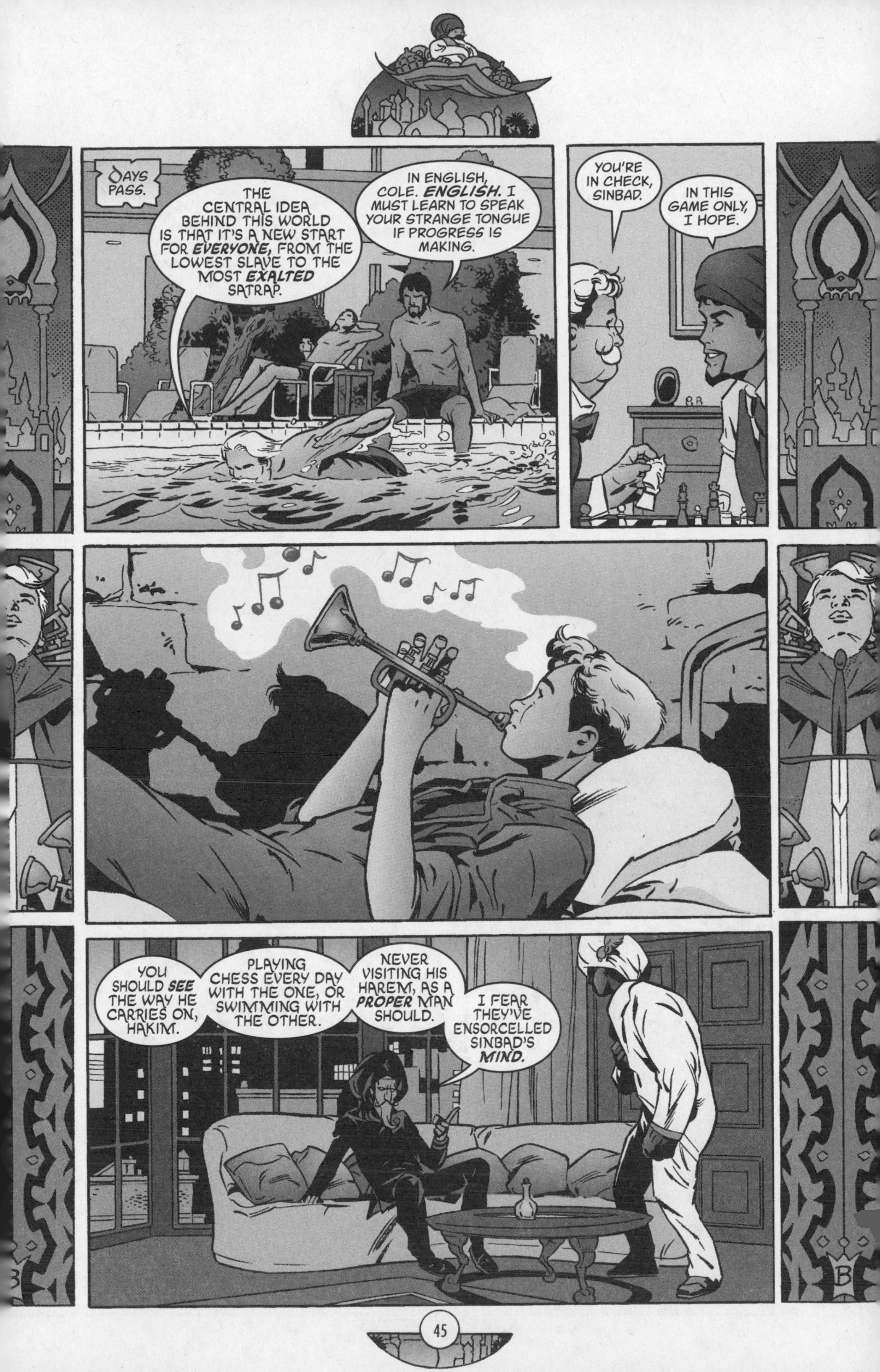
DAYS PASS.
THE CENTRAL IDEA BEHIND THIS WORLD IS THAT IT'S A NEW START FOR EVERYONE, FROM THE LOWEST SLAVE TO THE MOST EXALTED SATRAP.
IN ENGLISH, COLE. ENGLISH. I MUST LEARN TO SPEAK YOUR STRANGE TONGUE IF PROGRESS IS MAKING.
YOU'RE IN CHECK, SINBAD.
IN THIS GAME ONLY, I HOPE.
YOU SHOULD SEE THE WAY HE CARRIES ON, HAKIM.
PLAYING CHESS EVERY DAY WITH THE ONE, OR SWIMMING WITH THE OTHER.
NEVER VISITING HIS HAREM, AS A PROPER MAN SHOULD.
I FEAR THEY'VE ENSORCELLED SINBAD'S MIND.

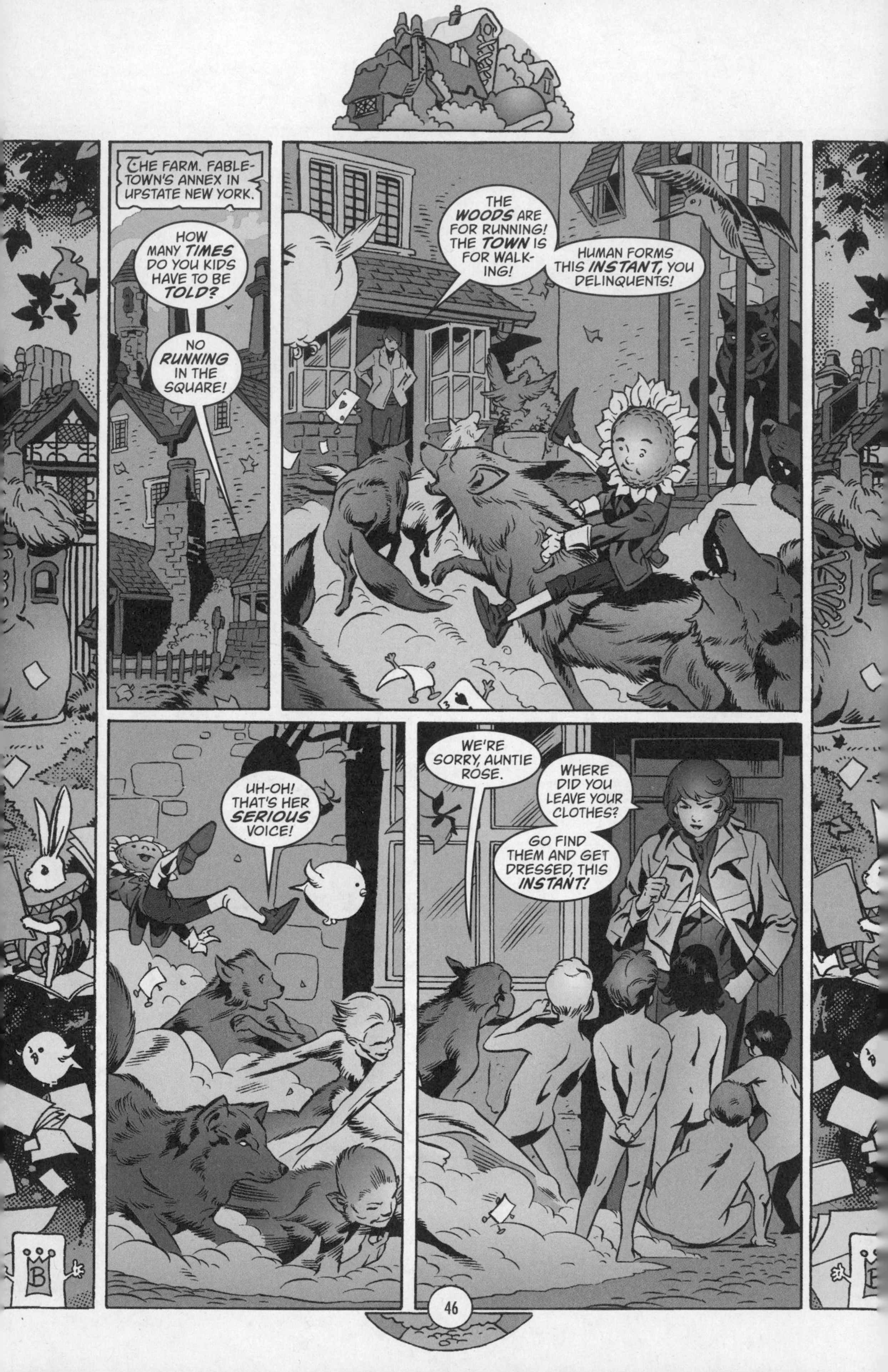
THE FARM. FABLETOWN'S ANNEX IN UPSTATE NEW YORK.
HOW MANY TIMES DO YOU KIDS HAVE TO BE TOLD?
NO RUNNING IN THE SQUARE!
THE WOODS ARE FOR RUNNING! THE TOWN IS FOR WALKING!
HUMAN FORMS THIS INSTANT, YOU DELINQUENTS!
UH-OH! THAT'S HER SERIOUS VOICE!
WE'RE SORRY, AUNTIE ROSE.
WHERE DID YOU LEAVE YOUR CLOTHES?
GO FIND THEM AND GET DRESSED, THIS INSTANT!

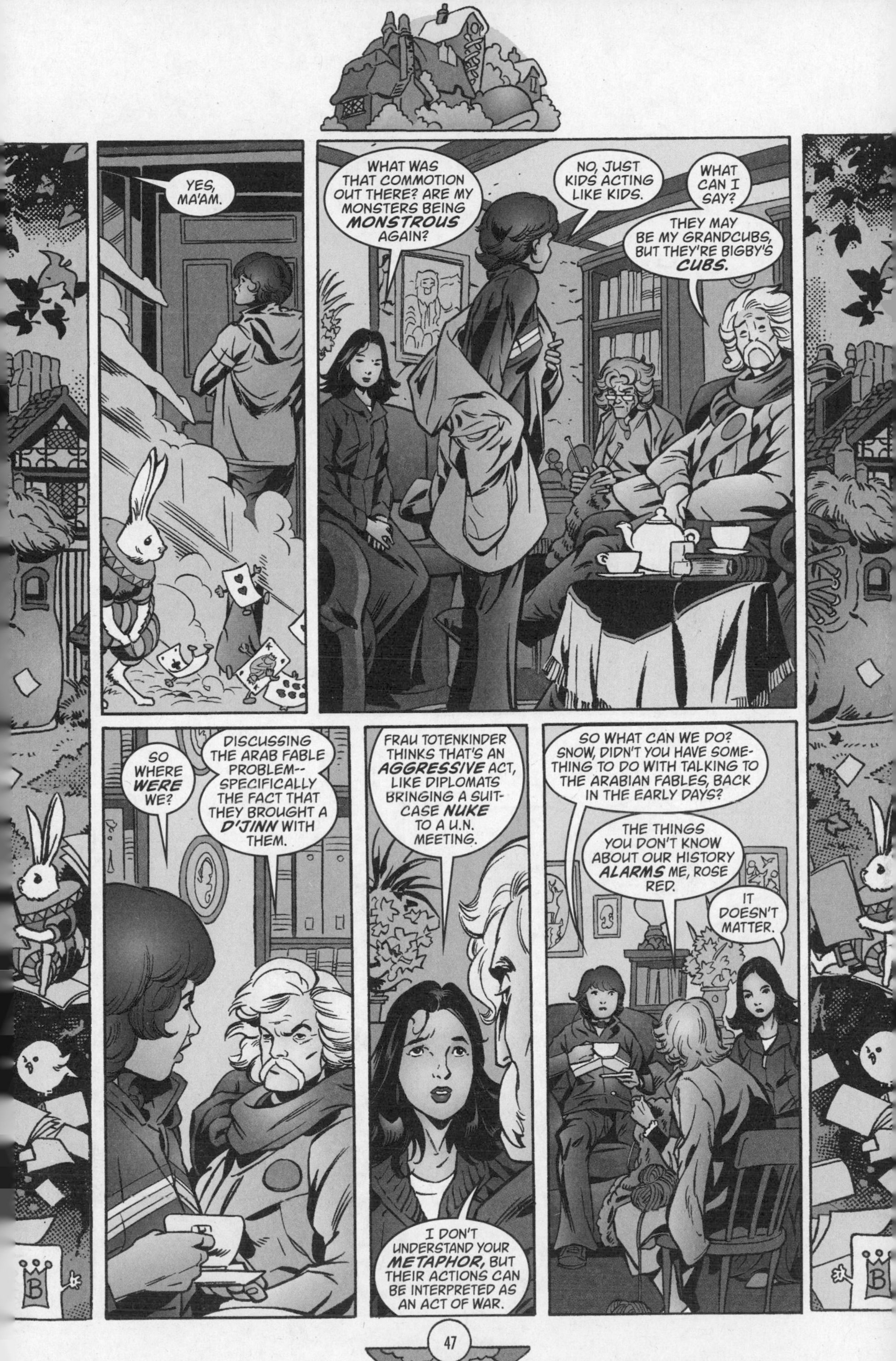
YES, MA'AM.
WHAT WAS THAT COMMOTION OUT THERE? ARE MY MONSTERS BEING MONSTROUS AGAIN?
NO, JUST KIDS ACTING LIKE KIDS.
WHAT CAN I SAY?
THEY MAY BE MY GRANDCUBS, BUT THEY'RE BIGBY'S CUBS.
SO WHERE WERE WE?
DISCUSSING THE ARAB FABLE PROBLEM--SPECIFICALLY THE FACT THAT THEY BROUGHT A D'JINN WITH THEM.
FRAU TOTENKINDER THINKS THAT'S AN AGGRESSIVE ACT, LIKE DIPLOMATS BRINGING A SUITCASE NUKE TO A U.N. MEETING.
I DON'T UNDERSTAND YOUR METAPHOR, BUT THEIR ACTIONS CAN BE INTERPRETED AS AN ACT OF WAR.
SO WHAT CAN WE DO? SNOW, DIDN'T YOU HAVE SOMETHING TO DO WITH TALKING TO THE ARABIAN FABLES, BACK IN THE EARLY DAYS?
THE THINGS YOU DON'T KNOW ABOUT OUR HISTORY ALARMS ME, ROSE RED.
IT DOESN'T MATTER.

I'M NOT IN GOVERNMENT ANY-MORE, AND I DON'T TALK TO *THOSE* PEOPLE.

OOH, I CAN TELL THERE'S A STORY THERE AND I'M GOING TO *DRAG* IT OUT OF YOU SOMEDAY.

PERHAPS. BUT NOT TODAY. WE WERE JUST BEGINNING TO DISCUSS WHAT MR. NORTH MIGHT DO AGAINST A D'JINN.

QUITE A *LOT*, I IMAGINE. HE'S OF THEIR ILK.

REALLY? YOU'RE THAT POWERFUL?

WE ARE RELATED CREATURES--BUT DISTANTLY. WHAT I AM IS THE NORTH WIND IN *ALL* ITS MANIFESTA-TIONS.

IT'S BEEN SOME LONG AGES SINCE I DID BATTLE WITH A D'JINN. I'VE *MISSED* HAVING SUCH CHALLENGES IN MY LIFE.

WAIT A MINUTE! ARE YOU TELLING US YOU CAN--

YOU'RE *THAT* POWER-FUL?

YOU'RE FINALLY CATCHING ON? BETTER LATE THAN NEVER.

THEN WHY DIDN'T YOU *HELP* WHEN WE NEEDED YOU MOST?

WHY DIDN'T YOU STOP THE *ADVERSARY* WHEN HE STARTED *CONQUERING* EVERYTHING?

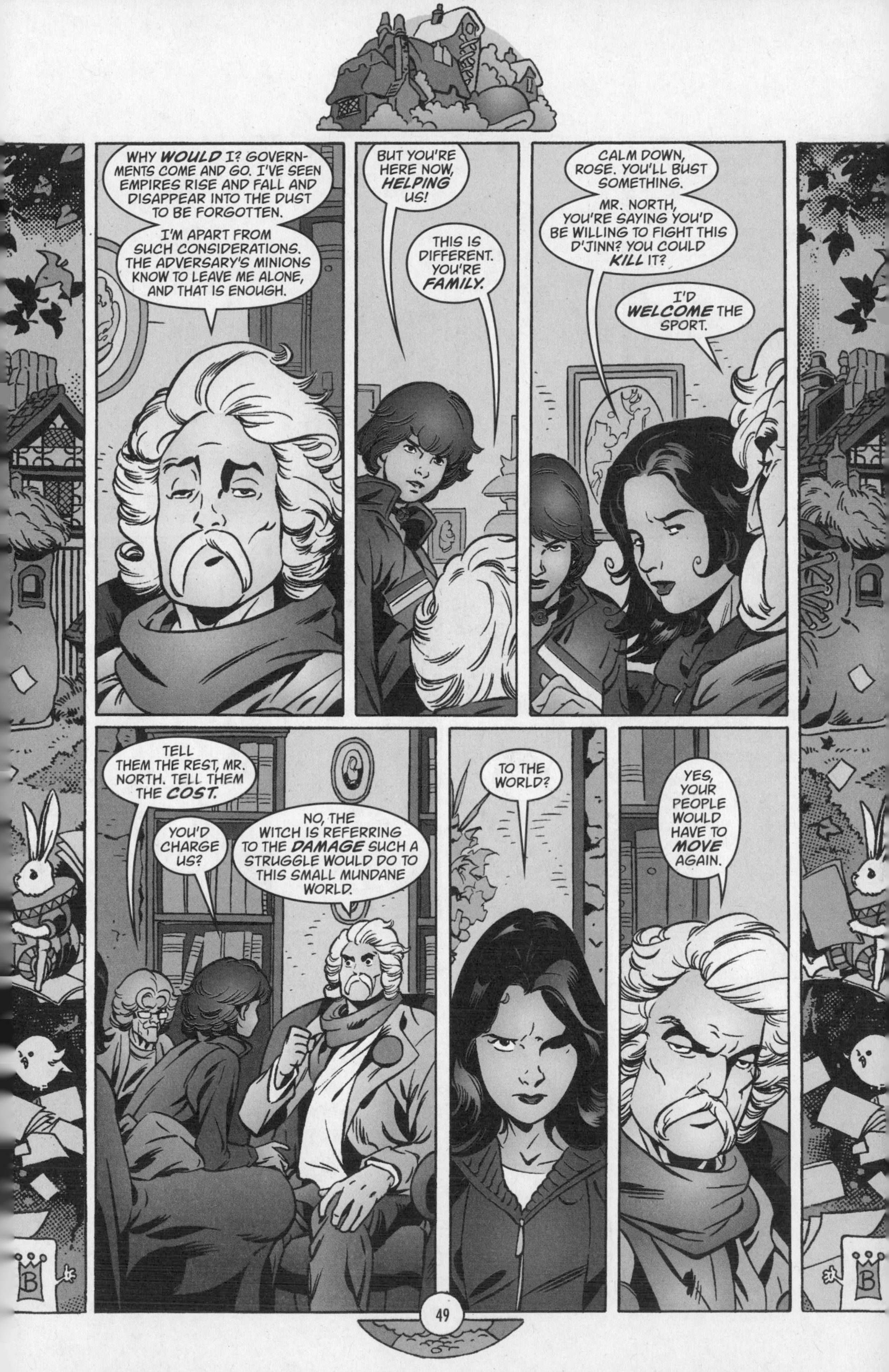

WHY WOULD I? GOVERNMENTS COME AND GO. I'VE SEEN EMPIRES RISE AND FALL AND DISAPPEAR INTO THE DUST TO BE FORGOTTEN.
I'M APART FROM SUCH CONSIDERATIONS. THE ADVERSARY'S MINIONS KNOW TO LEAVE ME ALONE, AND THAT IS ENOUGH.
BUT YOU'RE HERE NOW, HELPING US!
THIS IS DIFFERENT. YOU'RE FAMILY.
CALM DOWN, ROSE. YOU'LL BUST SOMETHING.
MR. NORTH, YOU'RE SAYING YOU'D BE WILLING TO FIGHT THIS D'JINN? YOU COULD KILL IT?
I'D WELCOME THE SPORT.
TELL THEM THE REST, MR. NORTH. TELL THEM THE COST.
YOU'D CHARGE US?
NO, THE WITCH IS REFERRING TO THE DAMAGE SUCH A STRUGGLE WOULD DO TO THIS SMALL MUNDANE WORLD.
TO THE WORLD?
YES, YOUR PEOPLE WOULD HAVE TO MOVE AGAIN.

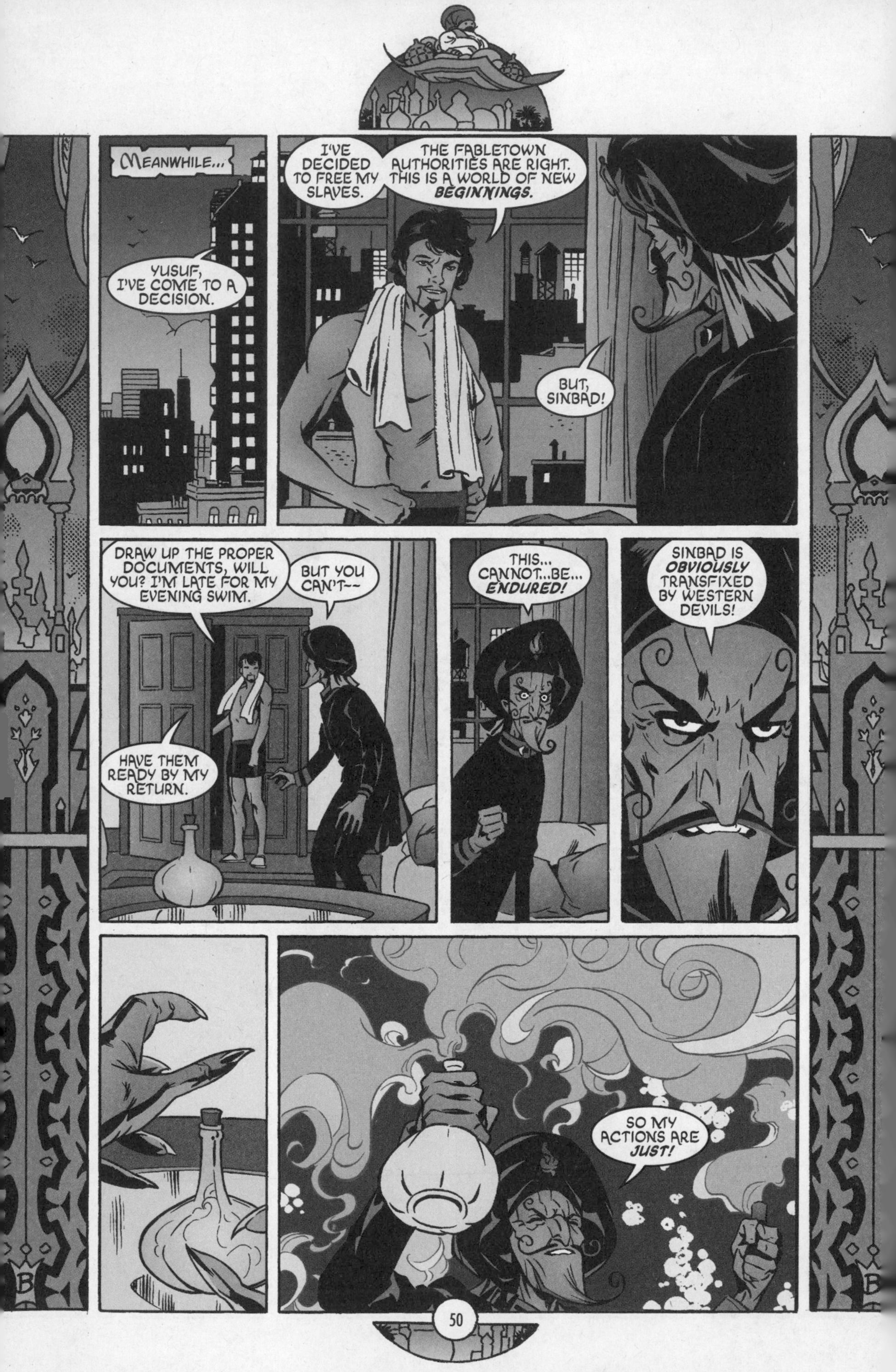
MEANWHILE...
YUSUF, I'VE COME TO A DECISION.
I'VE DECIDED TO FREE MY SLAVES.
THE FABLETOWN AUTHORITIES ARE RIGHT. THIS IS A WORLD OF NEW **BEGINNINGS.**
BUT, SINBAD!
DRAW UP THE PROPER DOCUMENTS, WILL YOU? I'M LATE FOR MY EVENING SWIM.
BUT YOU CAN'T--
HAVE THEM READY BY MY RETURN.
THIS... CANNOT...BE... **ENDURED!**
SINBAD IS **OBVIOUSLY** TRANSFIXED BY WESTERN DEVILS!
SO MY ACTIONS ARE **JUST!**

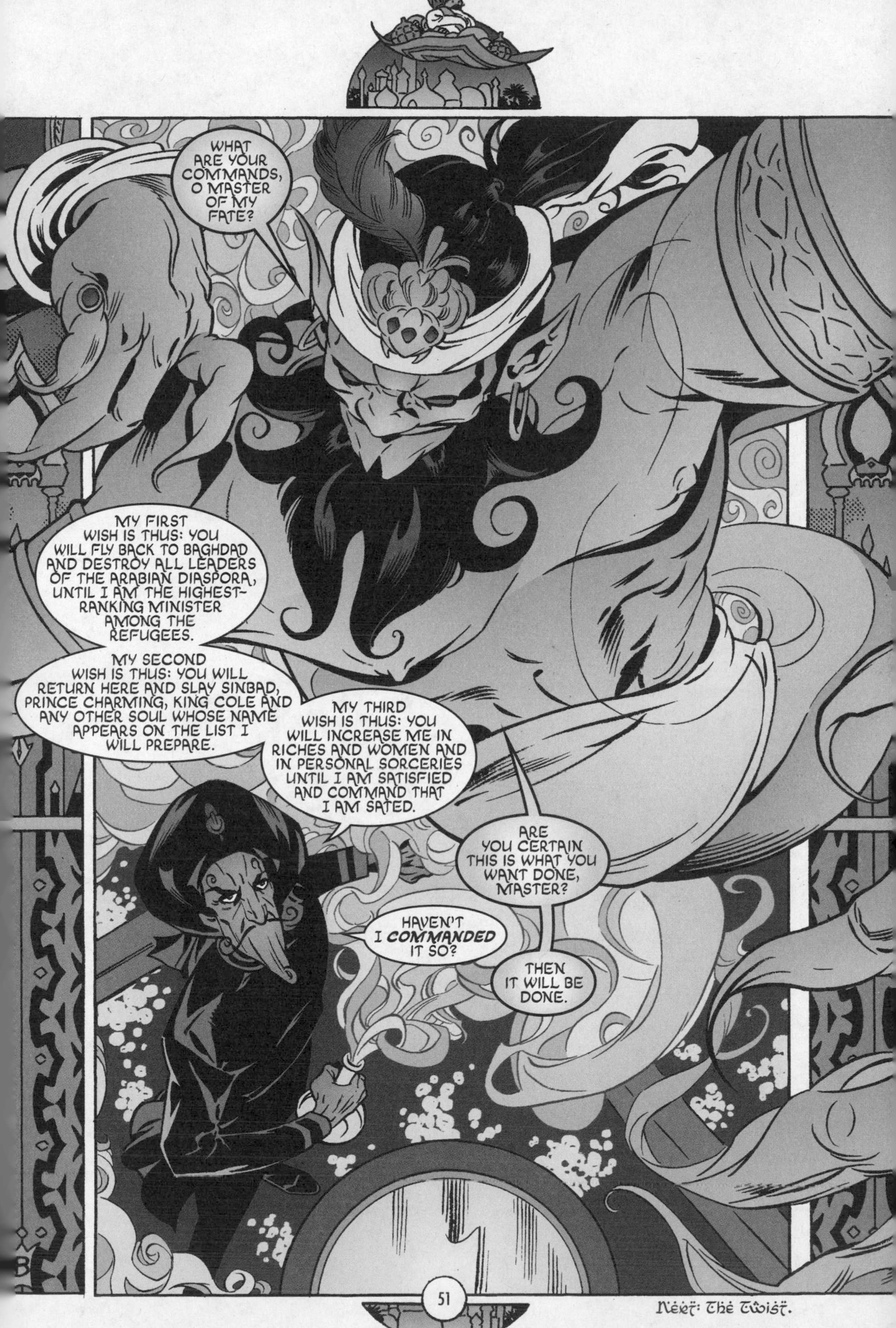
WHAT ARE YOUR COMMANDS, O MASTER OF MY FATE?
MY FIRST WISH IS THUS: YOU WILL FLY BACK TO BAGHDAD AND DESTROY ALL LEADERS OF THE ARABIAN DIASPORA, UNTIL I AM THE HIGHEST-RANKING MINISTER AMONG THE REFUGEES.
MY SECOND WISH IS THUS: YOU WILL RETURN HERE AND SLAY SINBAD, PRINCE CHARMING, KING COLE AND ANY OTHER SOUL WHOSE NAME APPEARS ON THE LIST I WILL PREPARE.
MY THIRD WISH IS THUS: YOU WILL INCREASE ME IN RICHES AND WOMEN AND IN PERSONAL SORCERIES UNTIL I AM SATISFIED AND COMMAND THAT I AM SATED.
ARE YOU CERTAIN THIS IS WHAT YOU WANT DONE, MASTER?
HAVEN'T I ***COMMANDED*** IT SO?
THEN IT WILL BE DONE.

Next: The Twist.

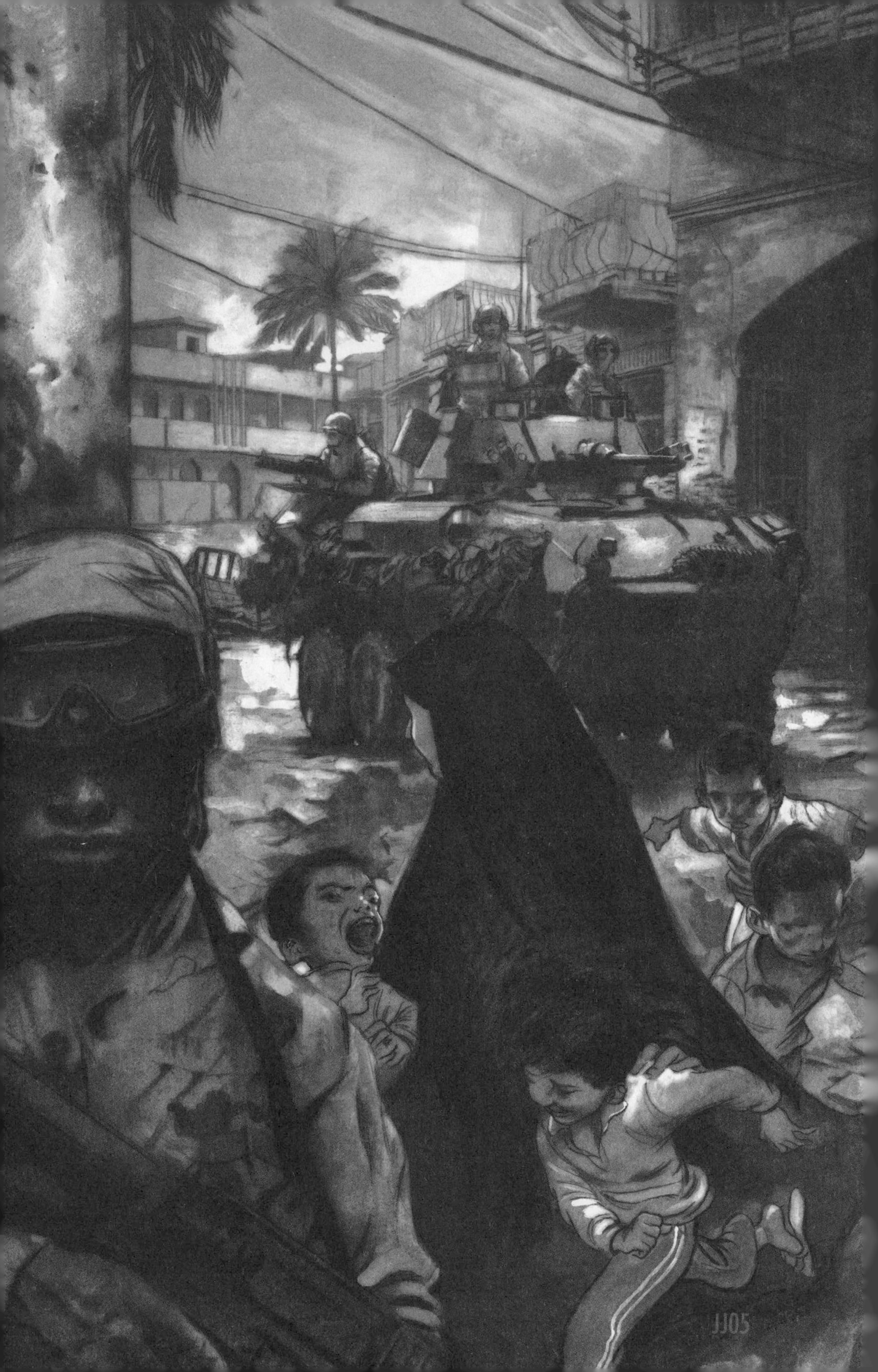
JJ05

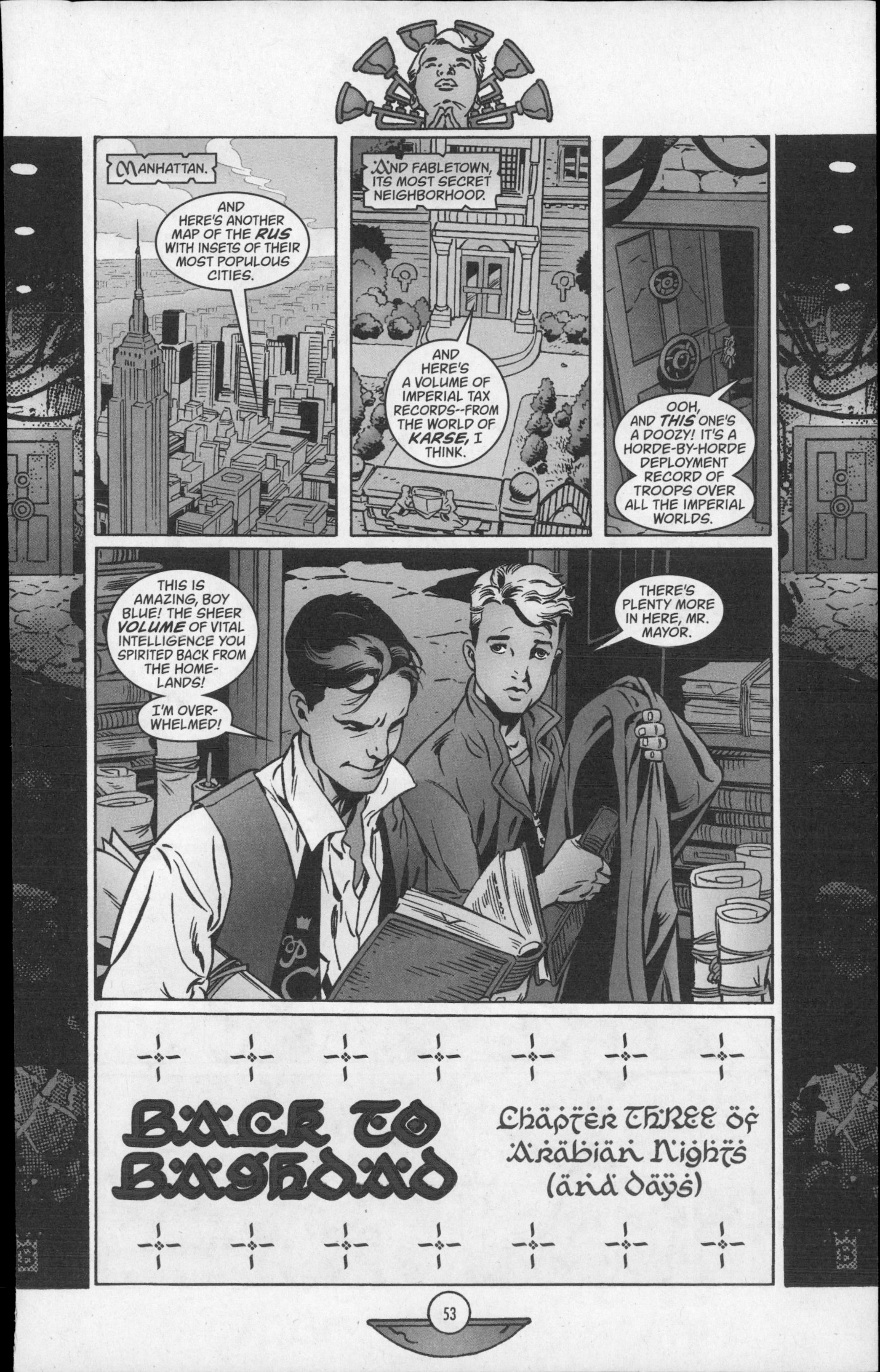
MANHATTAN.
AND HERE'S ANOTHER MAP OF THE RUS WITH INSETS OF THEIR MOST POPULOUS CITIES.
AND FABLETOWN, ITS MOST SECRET NEIGHBORHOOD.
AND HERE'S A VOLUME OF IMPERIAL TAX RECORDS--FROM THE WORLD OF KARSE, I THINK.
OOH, AND THIS ONE'S A DOOZY! IT'S A HORDE-BY-HORDE DEPLOYMENT RECORD OF TROOPS OVER ALL THE IMPERIAL WORLDS.
THIS IS AMAZING, BOY BLUE! THE SHEER VOLUME OF VITAL INTELLIGENCE YOU SPIRITED BACK FROM THE HOME-LANDS!
I'M OVER-WHELMED!
THERE'S PLENTY MORE IN HERE, MR. MAYOR.
BACK TO BAGHDAD
Chapter THREE of Arabian Nights (and days)

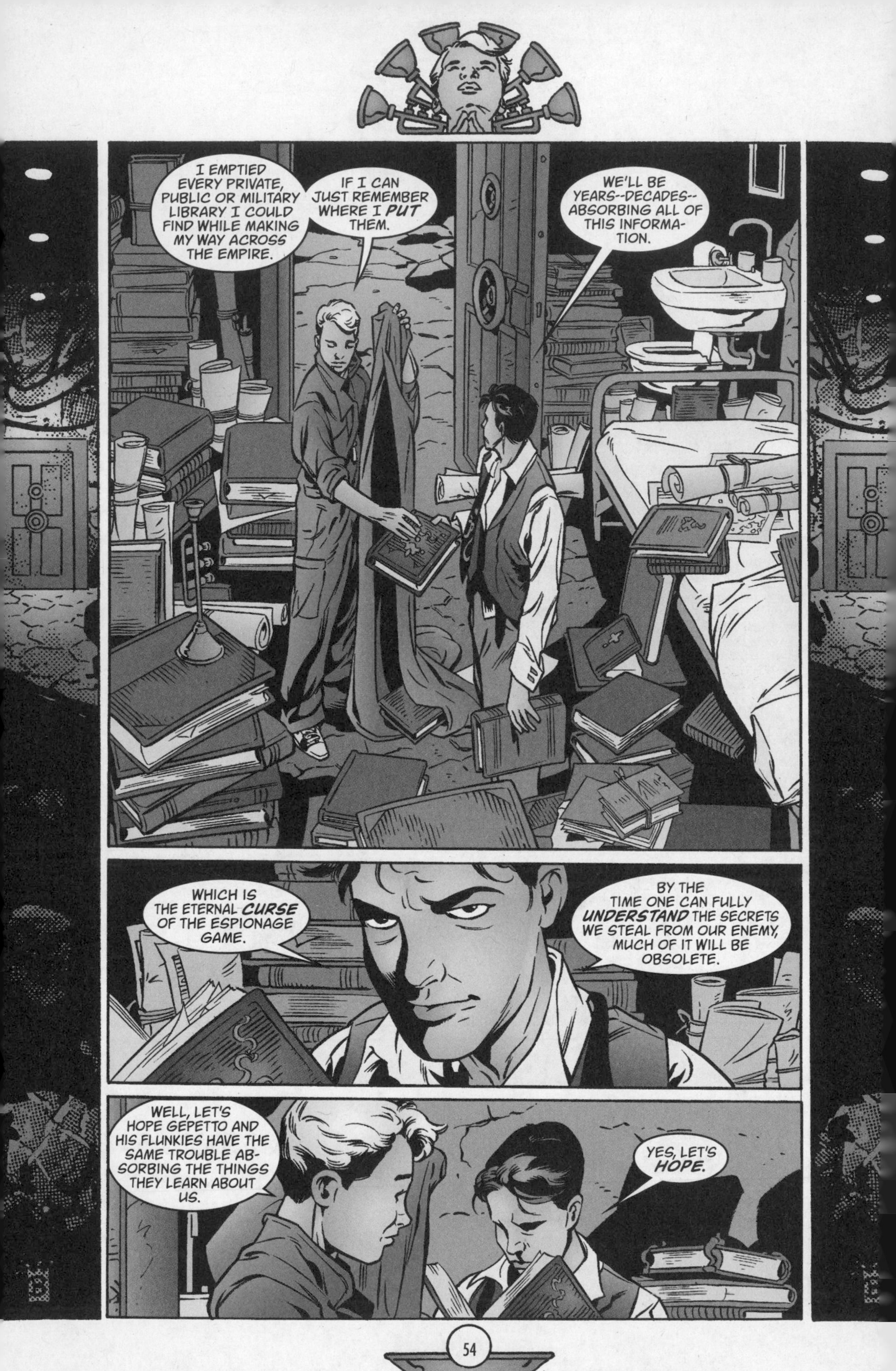
I EMPTIED EVERY PRIVATE, PUBLIC OR MILITARY LIBRARY I COULD FIND WHILE MAKING MY WAY ACROSS THE EMPIRE.
IF I CAN JUST REMEMBER WHERE I PUT THEM.
WE'LL BE YEARS--DECADES--ABSORBING ALL OF THIS INFORMATION.
WHICH IS THE ETERNAL CURSE OF THE ESPIONAGE GAME.
BY THE TIME ONE CAN FULLY UNDERSTAND THE SECRETS WE STEAL FROM OUR ENEMY, MUCH OF IT WILL BE OBSOLETE.
WELL, LET'S HOPE GEPETTO AND HIS FLUNKIES HAVE THE SAME TROUBLE ABSORBING THE THINGS THEY LEARN ABOUT US.
YES, LET'S HOPE.

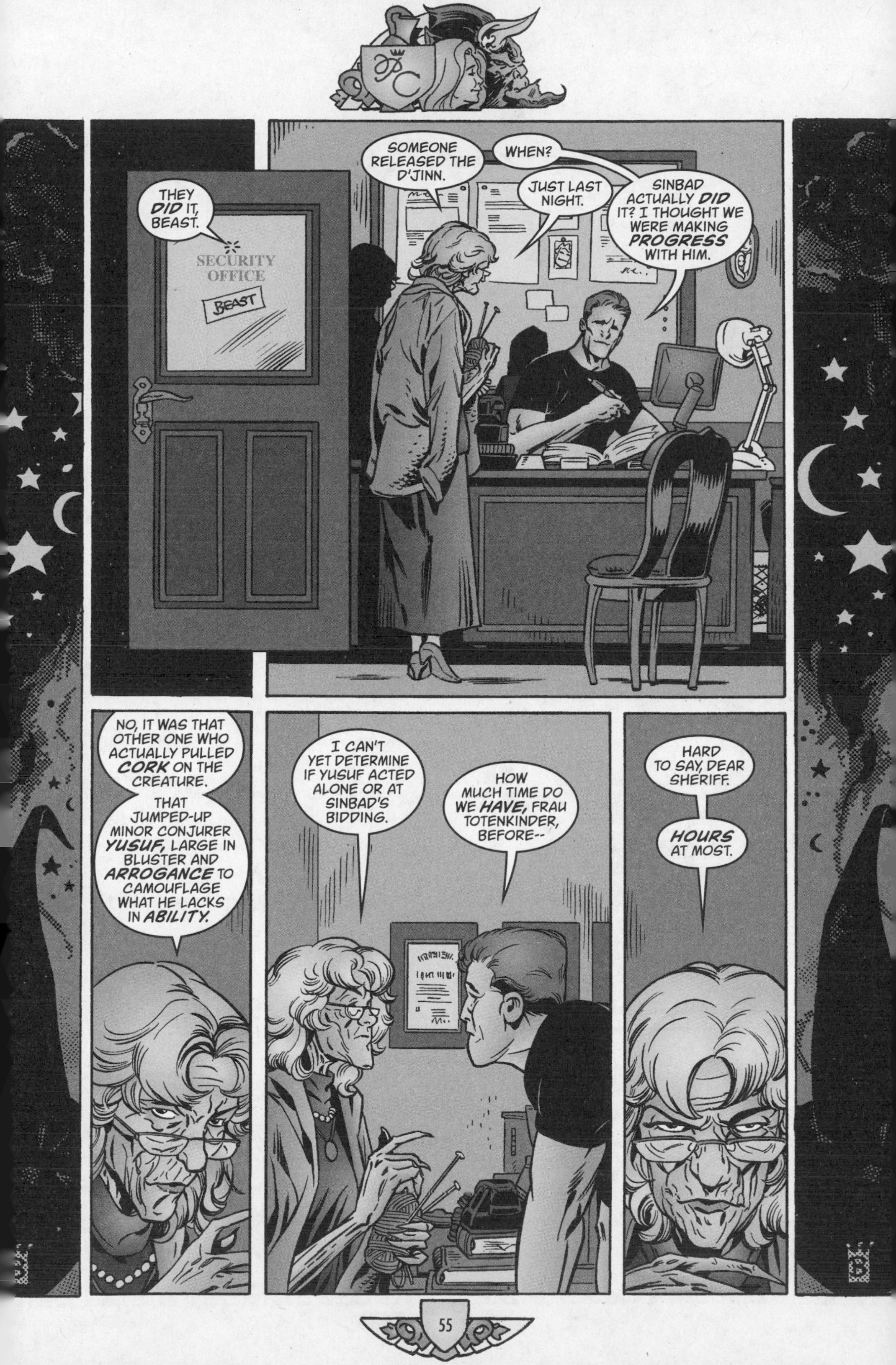

THEY DID IT, BEAST.
SECURITY OFFICE
BEAST
SOMEONE RELEASED THE D'JINN.
WHEN?
JUST LAST NIGHT.
SINBAD ACTUALLY DID IT? I THOUGHT WE WERE MAKING PROGRESS WITH HIM.
NO, IT WAS THAT OTHER ONE WHO ACTUALLY PULLED CORK ON THE CREATURE.
THAT JUMPED-UP MINOR CONJURER YUSUF, LARGE IN BLUSTER AND ARROGANCE TO CAMOUFLAGE WHAT HE LACKS IN ABILITY.
I CAN'T YET DETERMINE IF YUSUF ACTED ALONE OR AT SINBAD'S BIDDING.
HOW MUCH TIME DO WE HAVE, FRAU TOTENKINDER, BEFORE--
HARD TO SAY, DEAR SHERIFF.
HOURS AT MOST.

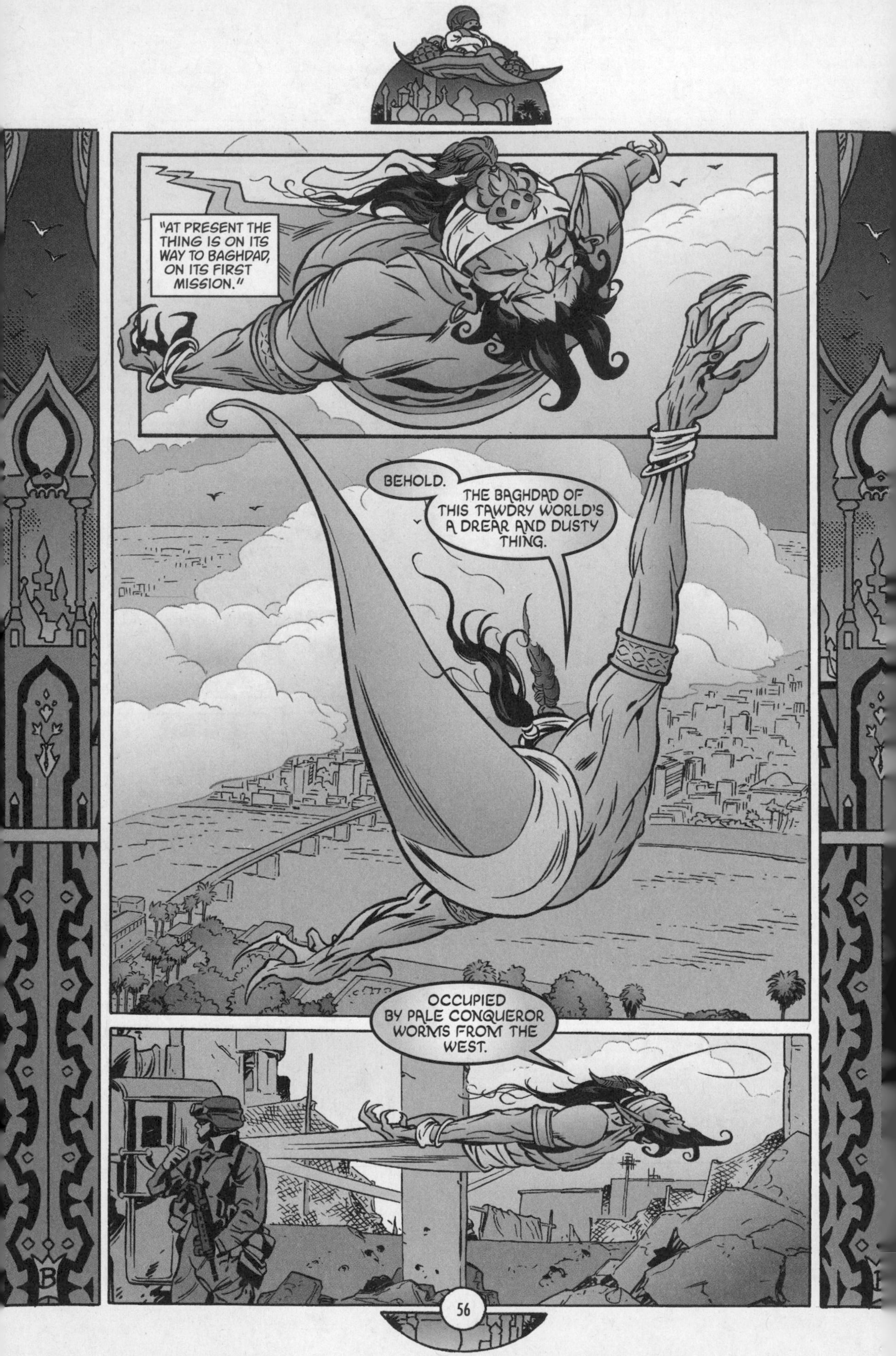
"AT PRESENT THE THING IS ON ITS WAY TO BAGHDAD, ON ITS FIRST MISSION."
BEHOLD.
THE BAGHDAD OF THIS TAWDRY WORLD'S A DREAR AND DUSTY THING.
OCCUPIED BY PALE CONQUEROR WORMS FROM THE WEST.

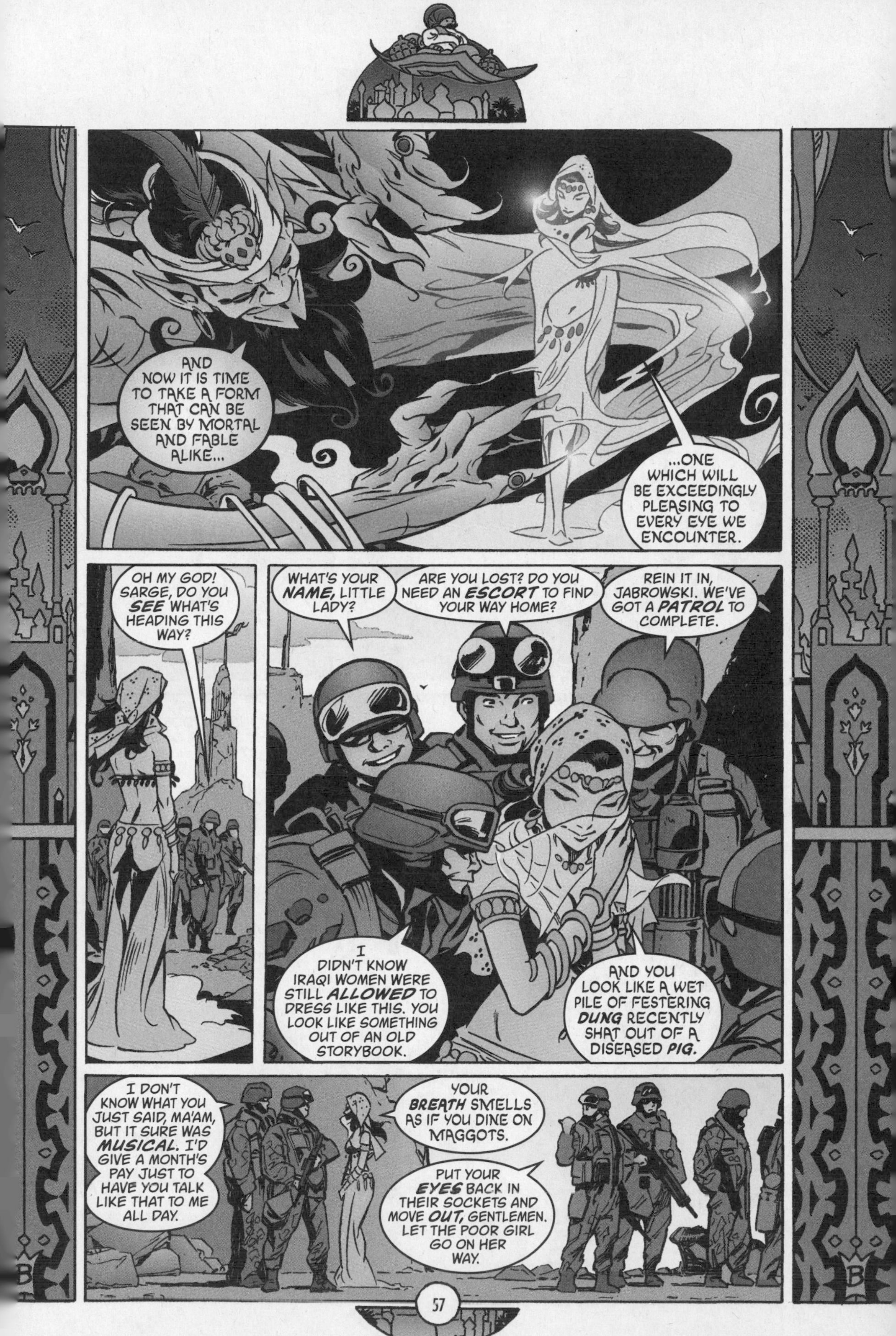
AND NOW IT IS TIME TO TAKE A FORM THAT CAN BE SEEN BY MORTAL AND FABLE ALIKE...
...ONE WHICH WILL BE EXCEEDINGLY PLEASING TO EVERY EYE WE ENCOUNTER.
OH MY GOD! SARGE, DO YOU SEE WHAT'S HEADING THIS WAY?
WHAT'S YOUR NAME, LITTLE LADY?
ARE YOU LOST? DO YOU NEED AN ESCORT TO FIND YOUR WAY HOME?
REIN IT IN, JABROWSKI. WE'VE GOT A PATROL TO COMPLETE.
I DIDN'T KNOW IRAQI WOMEN WERE STILL ALLOWED TO DRESS LIKE THIS. YOU LOOK LIKE SOMETHING OUT OF AN OLD STORYBOOK.
AND YOU LOOK LIKE A WET PILE OF FESTERING DUNG RECENTLY SHAT OUT OF A DISEASED PIG.
I DON'T KNOW WHAT YOU JUST SAID, MA'AM, BUT IT SURE WAS MUSICAL. I'D GIVE A MONTH'S PAY JUST TO HAVE YOU TALK LIKE THAT TO ME ALL DAY.
YOUR BREATH SMELLS AS IF YOU DINE ON MAGGOTS.
PUT YOUR EYES BACK IN THEIR SOCKETS AND MOVE OUT, GENTLEMEN. LET THE POOR GIRL GO ON HER WAY.

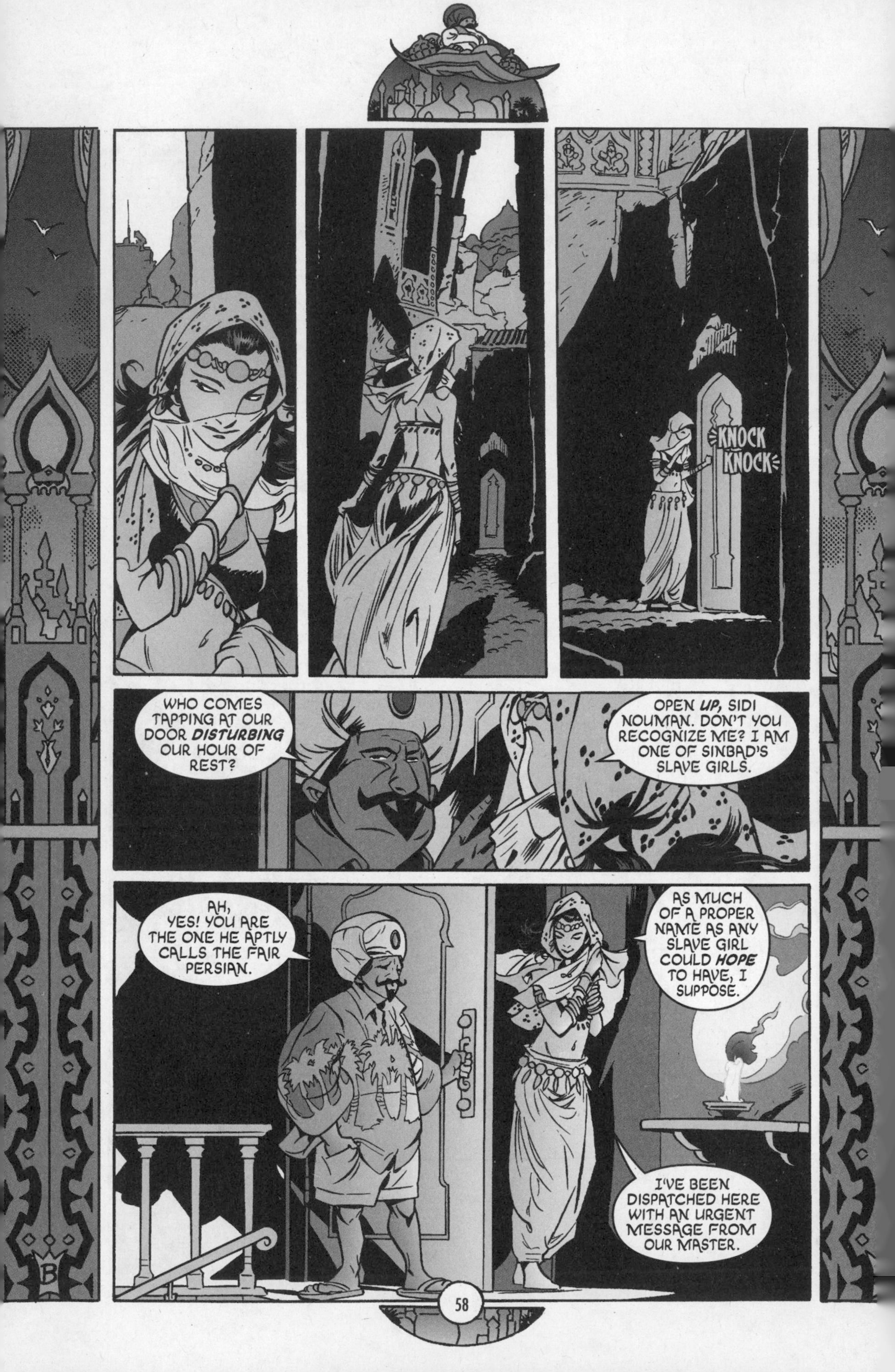

KNOCK KNOCK
WHO COMES TAPPING AT OUR DOOR DISTURBING OUR HOUR OF REST?
OPEN UP, SIDI NOUMAN. DON'T YOU RECOGNIZE ME? I AM ONE OF SINBAD'S SLAVE GIRLS.
AH, YES! YOU ARE THE ONE HE APTLY CALLS THE FAIR PERSIAN.
AS MUCH OF A PROPER NAME AS ANY SLAVE GIRL COULD HOPE TO HAVE, I SUPPOSE.
I'VE BEEN DISPATCHED HERE WITH AN URGENT MESSAGE FROM OUR MASTER.

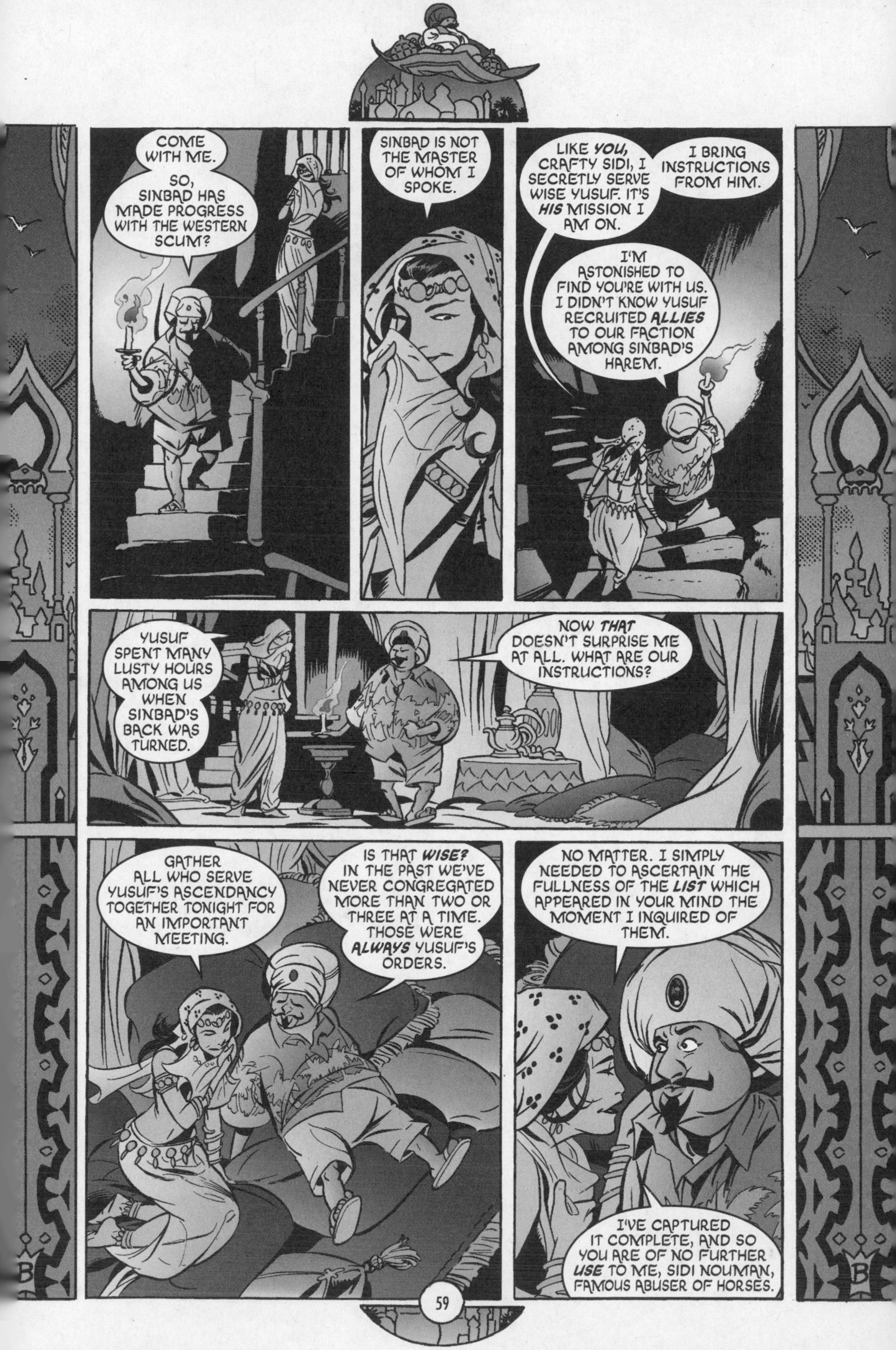
COME WITH ME.
SO, SINBAD HAS MADE PROGRESS WITH THE WESTERN SCUM?
SINBAD IS NOT THE MASTER OF WHOM I SPOKE.
LIKE *YOU,* CRAFTY SIDI, I SECRETLY SERVE WISE YUSUF. IT'S *HIS* MISSION I AM ON.
I BRING INSTRUCTIONS FROM HIM.
I'M ASTONISHED TO FIND YOU'RE WITH US. I DIDN'T KNOW YUSUF RECRUITED *ALLIES* TO OUR FACTION AMONG SINBAD'S HAREM.
YUSUF SPENT MANY LUSTY HOURS AMONG US WHEN SINBAD'S BACK WAS TURNED.
NOW *THAT* DOESN'T SURPRISE ME AT ALL. WHAT ARE OUR INSTRUCTIONS?
GATHER ALL WHO SERVE YUSUF'S ASCENDANCY TOGETHER TONIGHT FOR AN IMPORTANT MEETING.
IS THAT *WISE?* IN THE PAST WE'VE NEVER CONGREGATED MORE THAN TWO OR THREE AT A TIME. THOSE WERE *ALWAYS* YUSUF'S ORDERS.
NO MATTER. I SIMPLY NEEDED TO ASCERTAIN THE FULLNESS OF THE *LIST* WHICH APPEARED IN YOUR MIND THE MOMENT I INQUIRED OF THEM.
I'VE CAPTURED IT COMPLETE, AND SO YOU ARE OF NO FURTHER *USE* TO ME, SIDI NOUMAN, FAMOUS ABUSER OF HORSES.

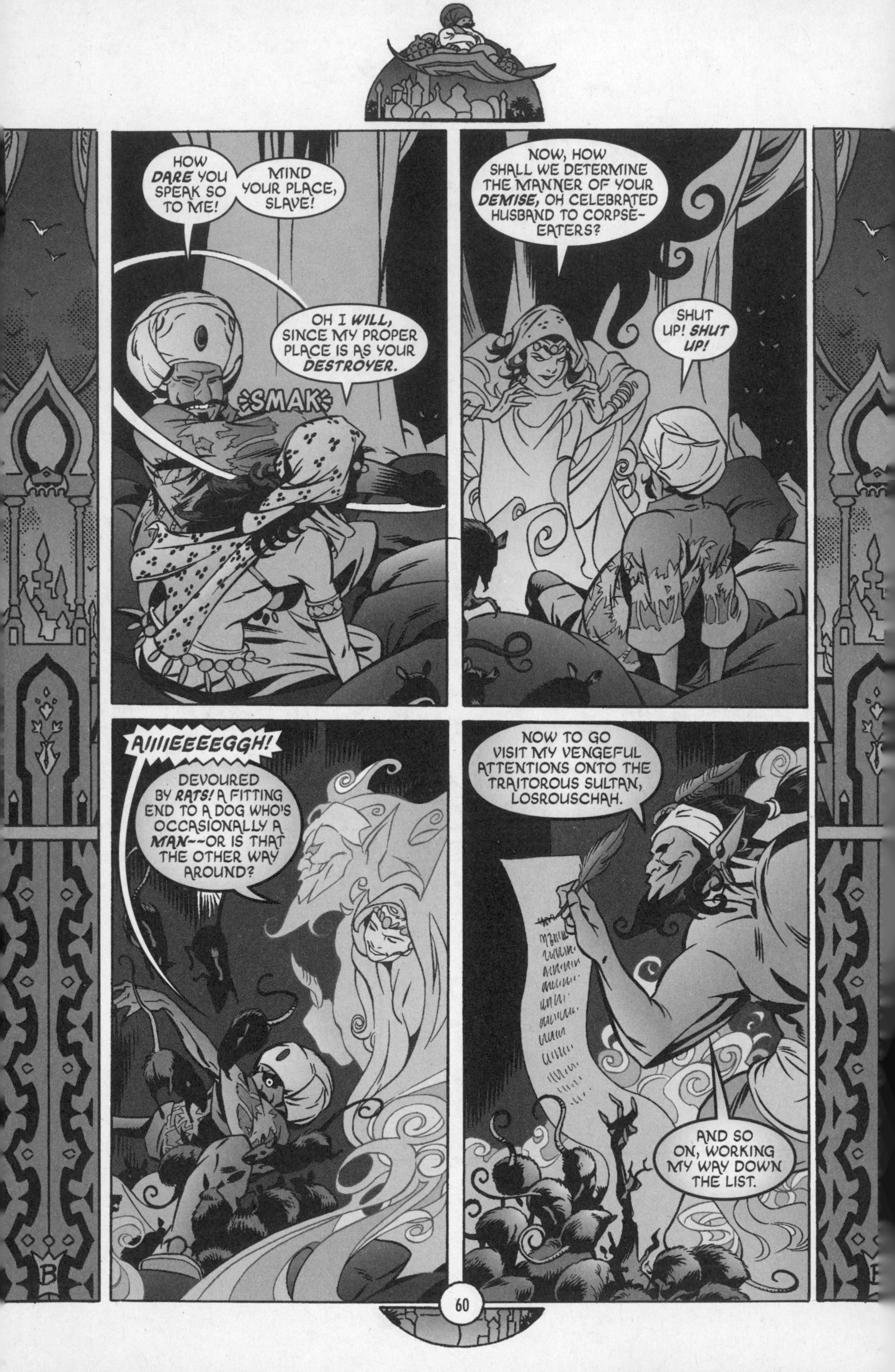
HOW DARE YOU SPEAK SO TO ME!
MIND YOUR PLACE, SLAVE!
OH I WILL, SINCE MY PROPER PLACE IS AS YOUR DESTROYER.
SMAK
NOW, HOW SHALL WE DETERMINE THE MANNER OF YOUR DEMISE, OH CELEBRATED HUSBAND TO CORPSE-EATERS?
SHUT UP! SHUT UP!
AIIIIEEEEEGGH!
DEVOURED BY RATS! A FITTING END TO A DOG WHO'S OCCASIONALLY A MAN--OR IS THAT THE OTHER WAY AROUND?
NOW TO GO VISIT MY VENGEFUL ATTENTIONS ONTO THE TRAITOROUS SULTAN, LOSROUSCHAH.
AND SO ON, WORKING MY WAY DOWN THE LIST.

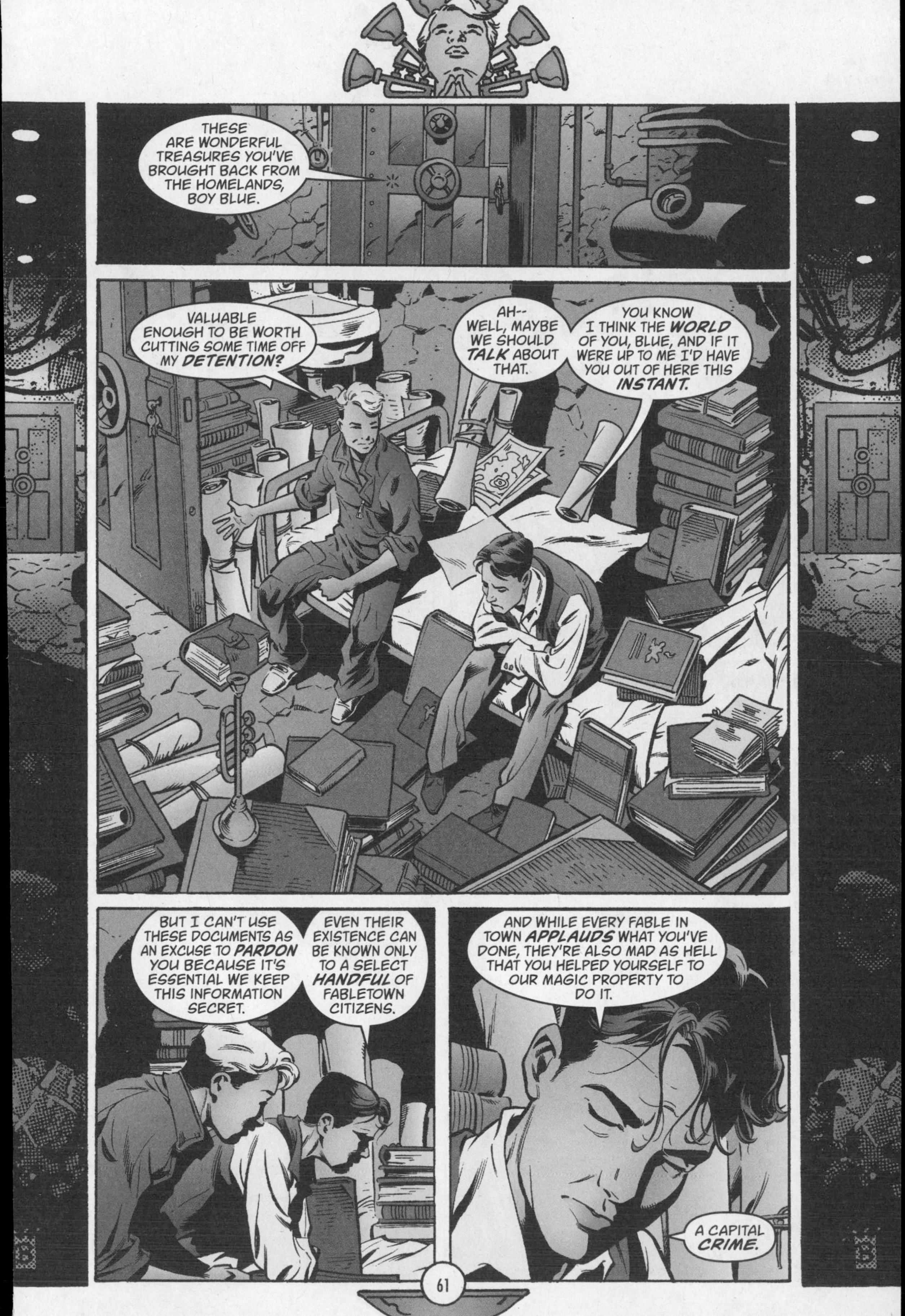
THESE ARE WONDERFUL TREASURES YOU'VE BROUGHT BACK FROM THE HOMELANDS, BOY BLUE.
VALUABLE ENOUGH TO BE WORTH CUTTING SOME TIME OFF MY DETENTION?
AH-- WELL, MAYBE WE SHOULD TALK ABOUT THAT.
YOU KNOW I THINK THE WORLD OF YOU, BLUE, AND IF IT WERE UP TO ME I'D HAVE YOU OUT OF HERE THIS INSTANT.
BUT I CAN'T USE THESE DOCUMENTS AS AN EXCUSE TO PARDON YOU BECAUSE IT'S ESSENTIAL WE KEEP THIS INFORMATION SECRET.
EVEN THEIR EXISTENCE CAN BE KNOWN ONLY TO A SELECT HANDFUL OF FABLETOWN CITIZENS.
AND WHILE EVERY FABLE IN TOWN APPLAUDS WHAT YOU'VE DONE, THEY'RE ALSO MAD AS HELL THAT YOU HELPED YOURSELF TO OUR MAGIC PROPERTY TO DO IT.
A CAPITAL CRIME.

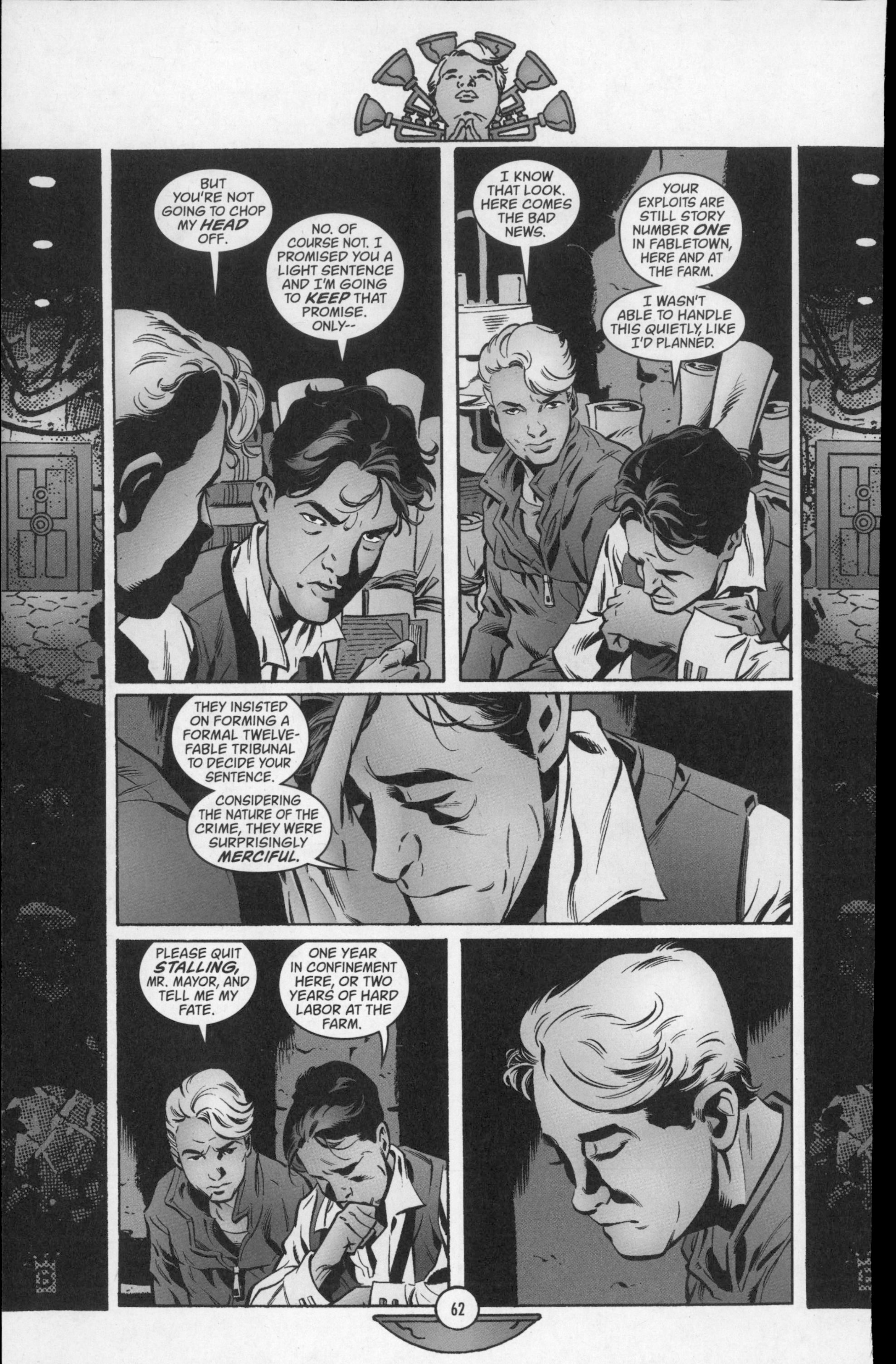
BUT YOU'RE NOT GOING TO CHOP MY HEAD OFF.
NO. OF COURSE NOT. I PROMISED YOU A LIGHT SENTENCE AND I'M GOING TO KEEP THAT PROMISE. ONLY--
I KNOW THAT LOOK. HERE COMES THE BAD NEWS.
YOUR EXPLOITS ARE STILL STORY NUMBER ONE IN FABLETOWN, HERE AND AT THE FARM.
I WASN'T ABLE TO HANDLE THIS QUIETLY, LIKE I'D PLANNED.
THEY INSISTED ON FORMING A FORMAL TWELVE-FABLE TRIBUNAL TO DECIDE YOUR SENTENCE.
CONSIDERING THE NATURE OF THE CRIME, THEY WERE SURPRISINGLY MERCIFUL.
PLEASE QUIT STALLING, MR. MAYOR, AND TELL ME MY FATE.
ONE YEAR IN CONFINEMENT HERE, OR TWO YEARS OF HARD LABOR AT THE FARM.

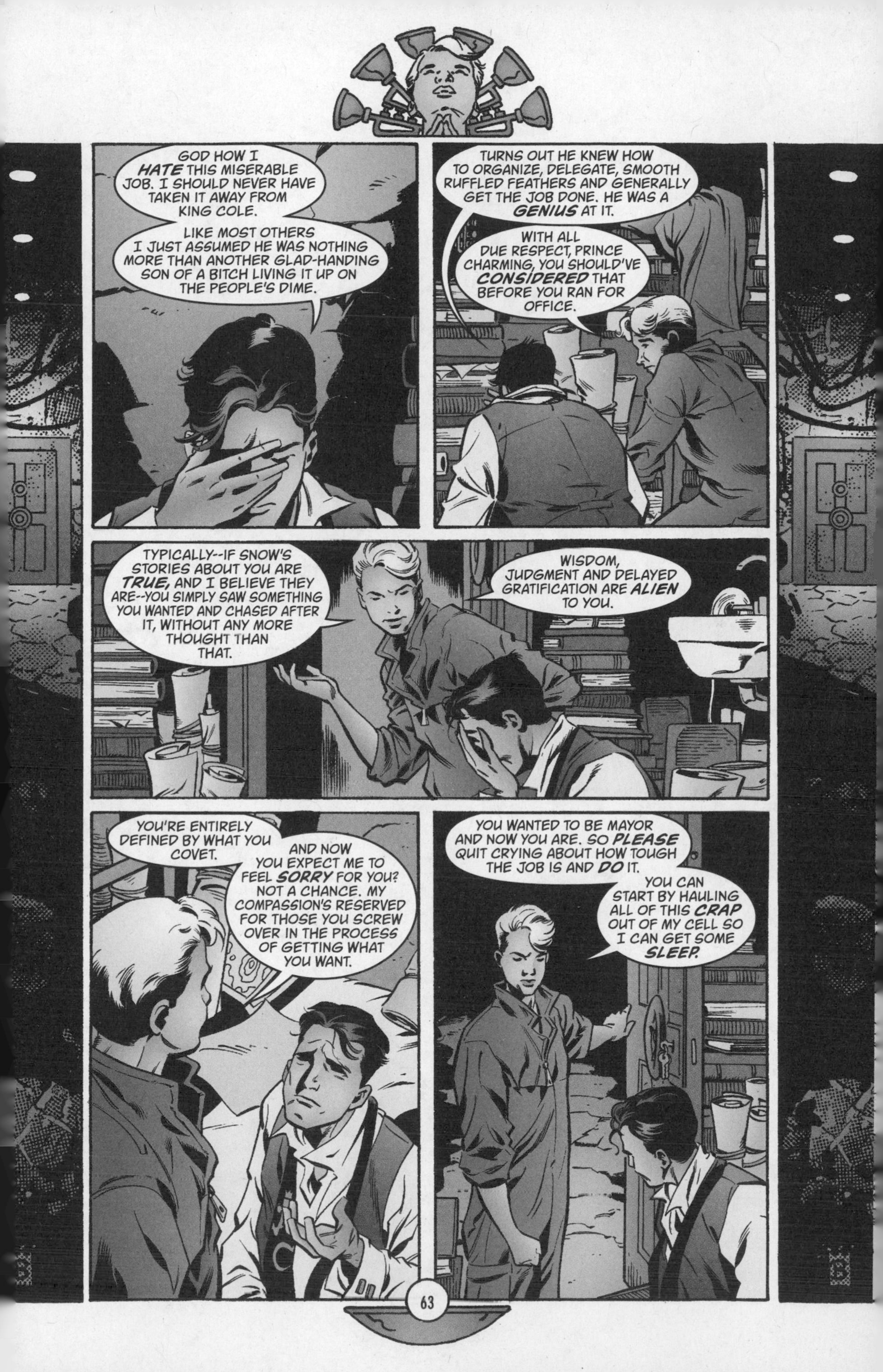
GOD HOW I HATE THIS MISERABLE JOB. I SHOULD NEVER HAVE TAKEN IT AWAY FROM KING COLE.
LIKE MOST OTHERS I JUST ASSUMED HE WAS NOTHING MORE THAN ANOTHER GLAD-HANDING SON OF A BITCH LIVING IT UP ON THE PEOPLE'S DIME.
TURNS OUT HE KNEW HOW TO ORGANIZE, DELEGATE, SMOOTH RUFFLED FEATHERS AND GENERALLY GET THE JOB DONE. HE WAS A GENIUS AT IT.
WITH ALL DUE RESPECT, PRINCE CHARMING, YOU SHOULD'VE CONSIDERED THAT BEFORE YOU RAN FOR OFFICE.
TYPICALLY--IF SNOW'S STORIES ABOUT YOU ARE TRUE, AND I BELIEVE THEY ARE--YOU SIMPLY SAW SOMETHING YOU WANTED AND CHASED AFTER IT, WITHOUT ANY MORE THOUGHT THAN THAT.
WISDOM, JUDGMENT AND DELAYED GRATIFICATION ARE ALIEN TO YOU.
YOU'RE ENTIRELY DEFINED BY WHAT YOU COVET.
AND NOW YOU EXPECT ME TO FEEL SORRY FOR YOU? NOT A CHANCE. MY COMPASSION'S RESERVED FOR THOSE YOU SCREW OVER IN THE PROCESS OF GETTING WHAT YOU WANT.
YOU WANTED TO BE MAYOR AND NOW YOU ARE. SO PLEASE QUIT CRYING ABOUT HOW TOUGH THE JOB IS AND DO IT.
YOU CAN START BY HAULING ALL OF THIS CRAP OUT OF MY CELL SO I CAN GET SOME SLEEP.

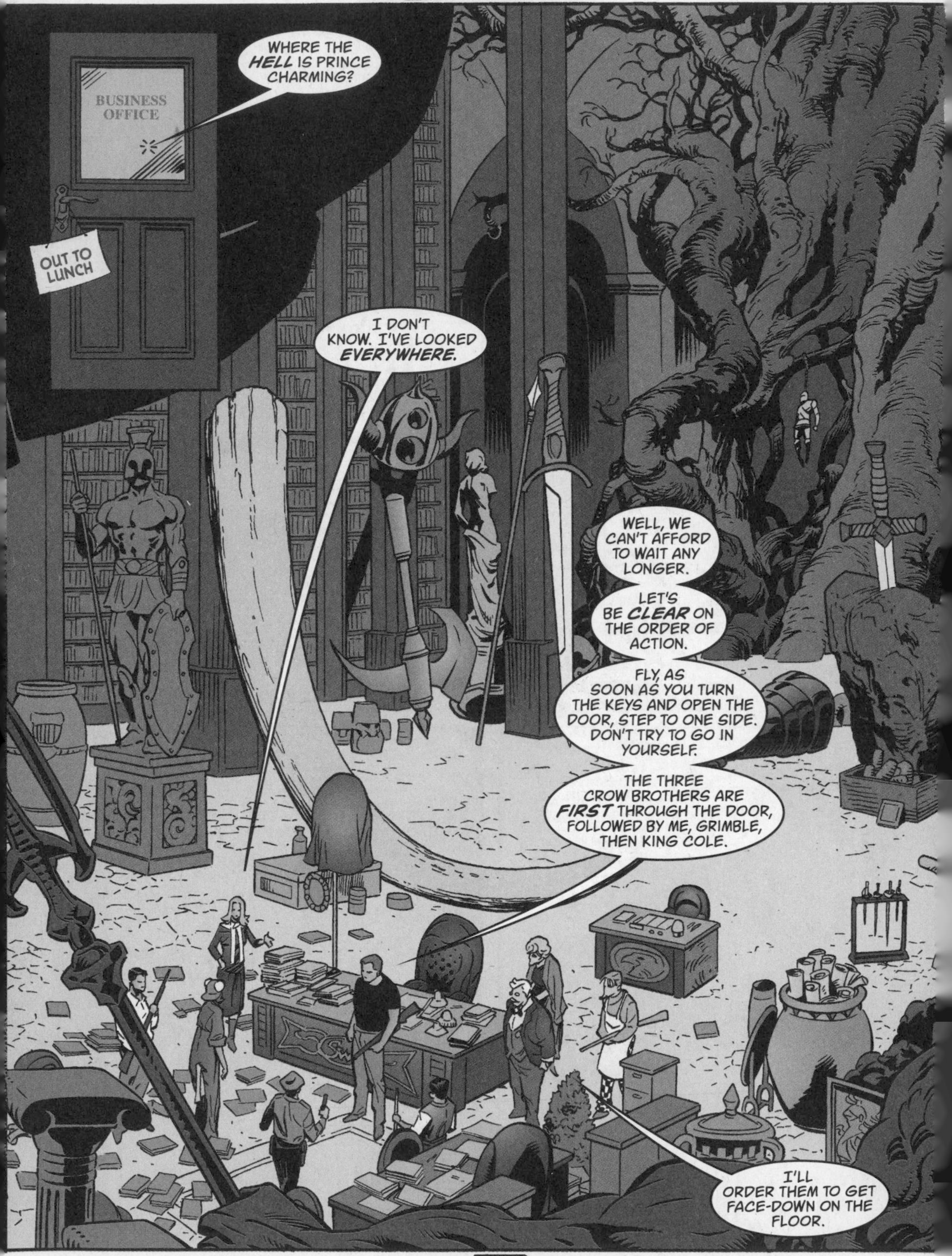

BUSINESS OFFICE
OUT TO LUNCH
WHERE THE HELL IS PRINCE CHARMING?
I DON'T KNOW. I'VE LOOKED EVERYWHERE.
WELL, WE CAN'T AFFORD TO WAIT ANY LONGER.
LET'S BE CLEAR ON THE ORDER OF ACTION.
FLY, AS SOON AS YOU TURN THE KEYS AND OPEN THE DOOR, STEP TO ONE SIDE. DON'T TRY TO GO IN YOURSELF.
THE THREE CROW BROTHERS ARE FIRST THROUGH THE DOOR, FOLLOWED BY ME, GRIMBLE, THEN KING COLE.
I'LL ORDER THEM TO GET FACE-DOWN ON THE FLOOR.

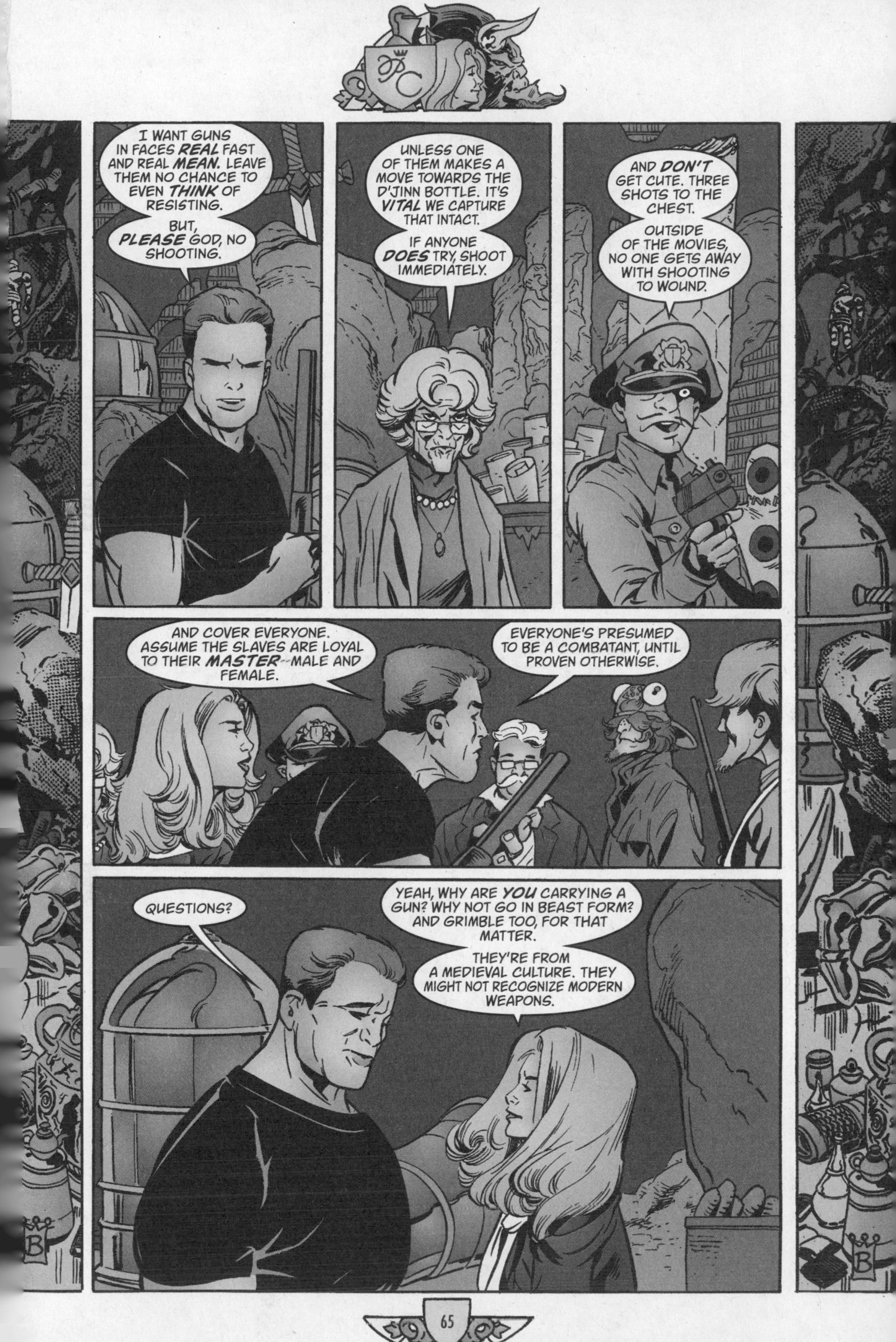
I WANT GUNS IN FACES REAL FAST AND REAL MEAN. LEAVE THEM NO CHANCE TO EVEN THINK OF RESISTING.
BUT, PLEASE GOD, NO SHOOTING.
UNLESS ONE OF THEM MAKES A MOVE TOWARDS THE D'JINN BOTTLE. IT'S VITAL WE CAPTURE THAT INTACT.
IF ANYONE DOES TRY, SHOOT IMMEDIATELY.
AND DON'T GET CUTE. THREE SHOTS TO THE CHEST.
OUTSIDE OF THE MOVIES, NO ONE GETS AWAY WITH SHOOTING TO WOUND.
AND COVER EVERYONE. ASSUME THE SLAVES ARE LOYAL TO THEIR MASTER--MALE AND FEMALE.
EVERYONE'S PRESUMED TO BE A COMBATANT, UNTIL PROVEN OTHERWISE.
QUESTIONS?
YEAH, WHY ARE YOU CARRYING A GUN? WHY NOT GO IN BEAST FORM? AND GRIMBLE TOO, FOR THAT MATTER.
THEY'RE FROM A MEDIEVAL CULTURE. THEY MIGHT NOT RECOGNIZE MODERN WEAPONS.

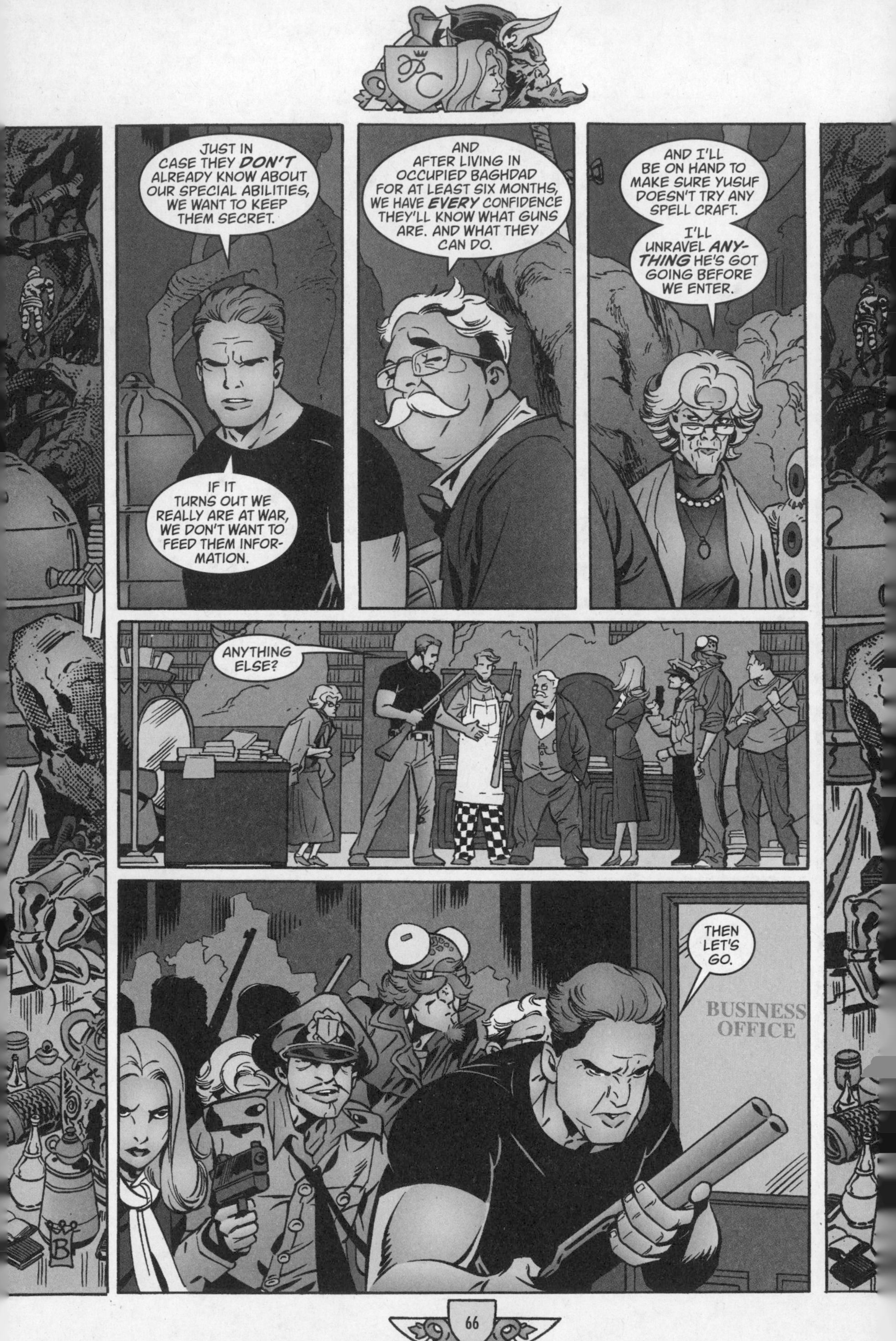

JUST IN CASE THEY DON'T ALREADY KNOW ABOUT OUR SPECIAL ABILITIES, WE WANT TO KEEP THEM SECRET.
IF IT TURNS OUT WE REALLY ARE AT WAR, WE DON'T WANT TO FEED THEM INFORMATION.
AND AFTER LIVING IN OCCUPIED BAGHDAD FOR AT LEAST SIX MONTHS, WE HAVE EVERY CONFIDENCE THEY'LL KNOW WHAT GUNS ARE. AND WHAT THEY CAN DO.
AND I'LL BE ON HAND TO MAKE SURE YUSUF DOESN'T TRY ANY SPELL CRAFT.
I'LL UNRAVEL ANYTHING HE'S GOT GOING BEFORE WE ENTER.
ANYTHING ELSE?
THEN LET'S GO.
BUSINESS OFFICE

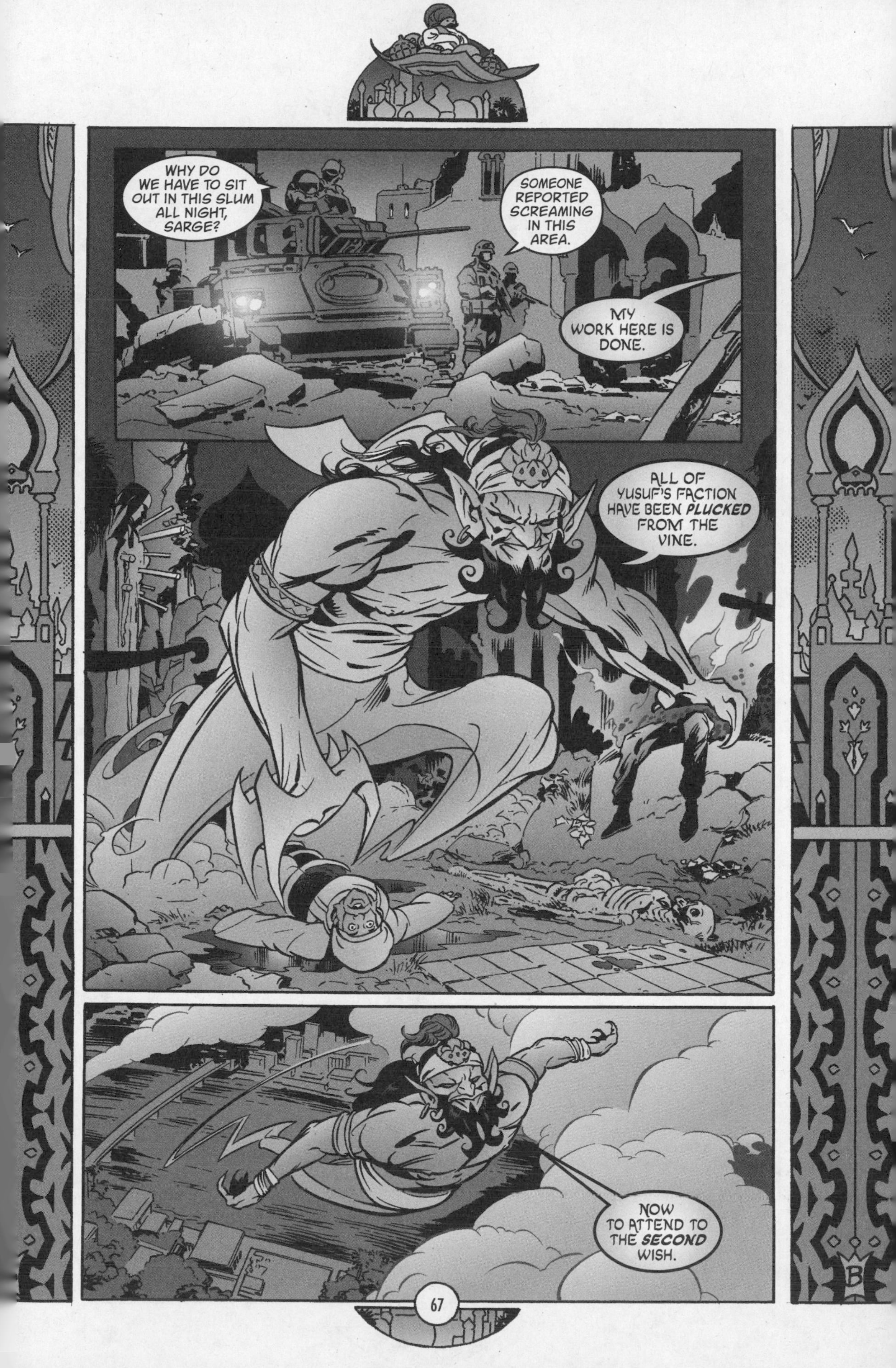
WHY DO WE HAVE TO SIT OUT IN THIS SLUM ALL NIGHT, SARGE?
SOMEONE REPORTED SCREAMING IN THIS AREA.
MY WORK HERE IS DONE.
ALL OF YUSUF'S FACTION HAVE BEEN *PLUCKED* FROM THE VINE.
NOW TO ATTEND TO THE *SECOND* WISH.

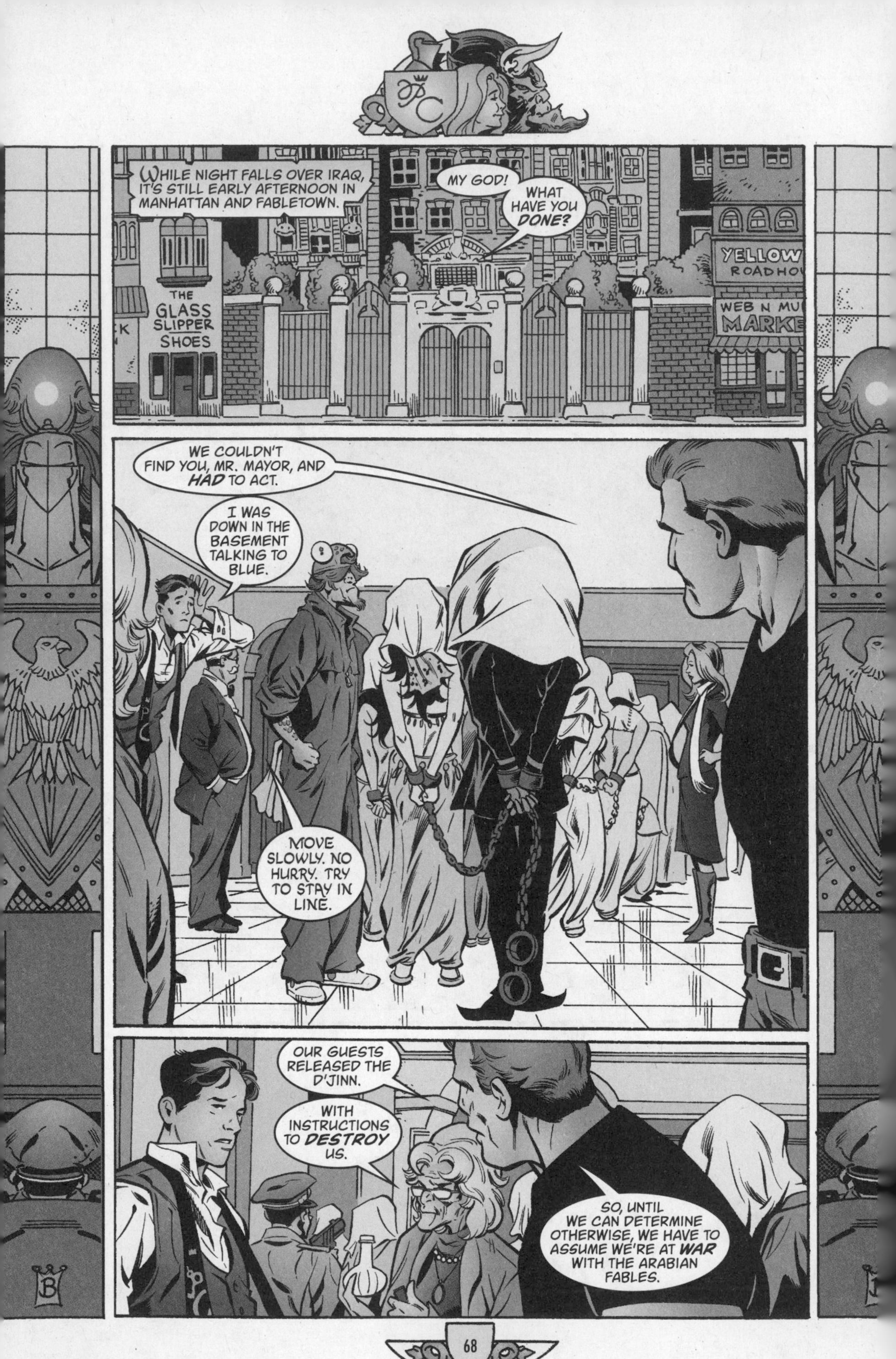
WHILE NIGHT FALLS OVER IRAQ, IT'S STILL EARLY AFTERNOON IN MANHATTAN AND FABLETOWN.
MY GOD!
WHAT HAVE YOU DONE?
THE GLASS SLIPPER SHOES
YELLOW ROADHOU
WEB N MU MARKE
WE COULDN'T FIND YOU, MR. MAYOR, AND HAD TO ACT.
I WAS DOWN IN THE BASEMENT TALKING TO BLUE.
MOVE SLOWLY. NO HURRY. TRY TO STAY IN LINE.
OUR GUESTS RELEASED THE D'JINN.
WITH INSTRUCTIONS TO DESTROY US.
SO, UNTIL WE CAN DETERMINE OTHERWISE, WE HAVE TO ASSUME WE'RE AT WAR WITH THE ARABIAN FABLES.

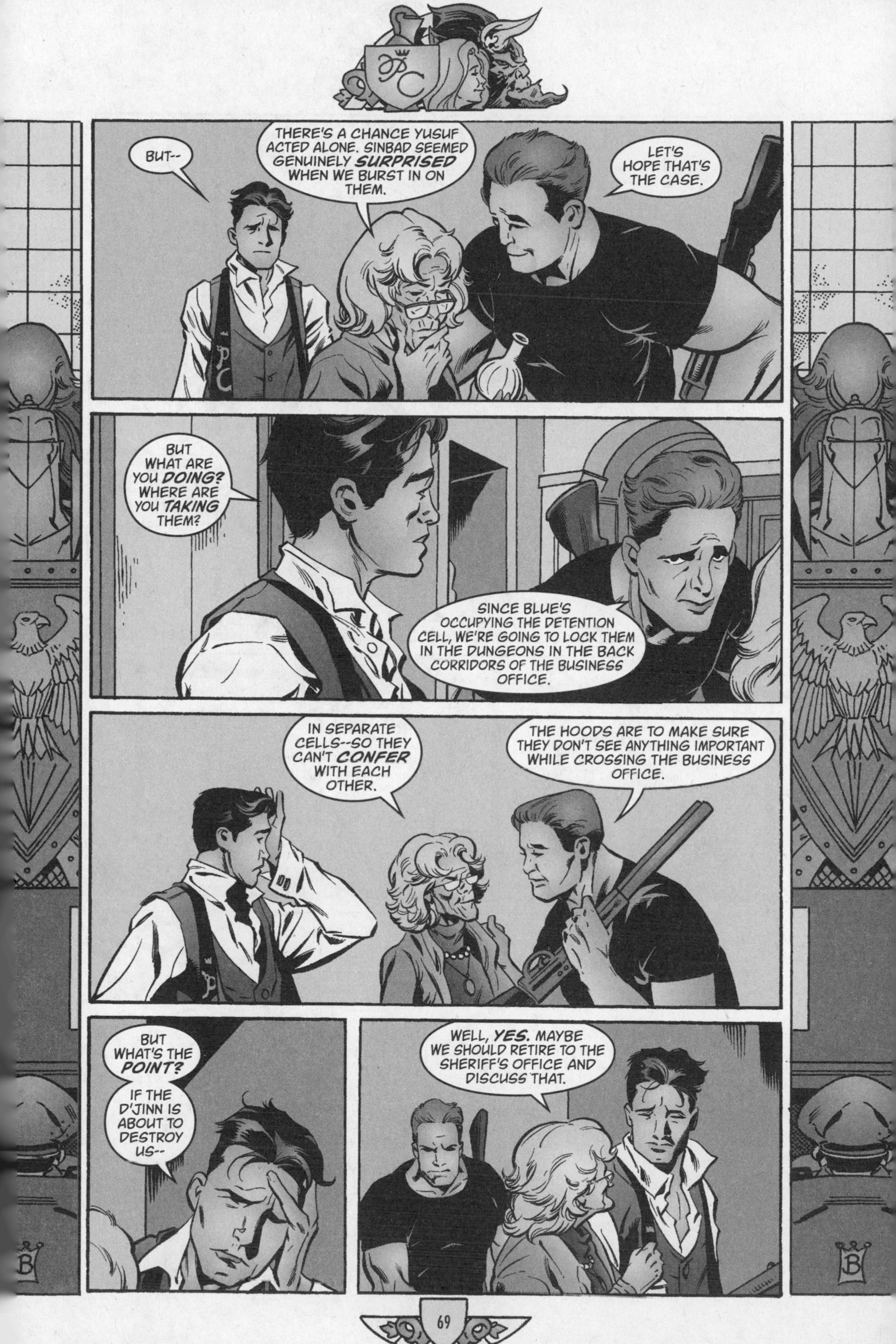
BUT--
THERE'S A CHANCE YUSUF ACTED ALONE. SINBAD SEEMED GENUINELY SURPRISED WHEN WE BURST IN ON THEM.
LET'S HOPE THAT'S THE CASE.
BUT WHAT ARE YOU DOING? WHERE ARE YOU TAKING THEM?
SINCE BLUE'S OCCUPYING THE DETENTION CELL, WE'RE GOING TO LOCK THEM IN THE DUNGEONS IN THE BACK CORRIDORS OF THE BUSINESS OFFICE.
IN SEPARATE CELLS--SO THEY CAN'T CONFER WITH EACH OTHER.
THE HOODS ARE TO MAKE SURE THEY DON'T SEE ANYTHING IMPORTANT WHILE CROSSING THE BUSINESS OFFICE.
BUT WHAT'S THE POINT?
IF THE D'JINN IS ABOUT TO DESTROY US--
WELL, YES. MAYBE WE SHOULD RETIRE TO THE SHERIFF'S OFFICE AND DISCUSS THAT.

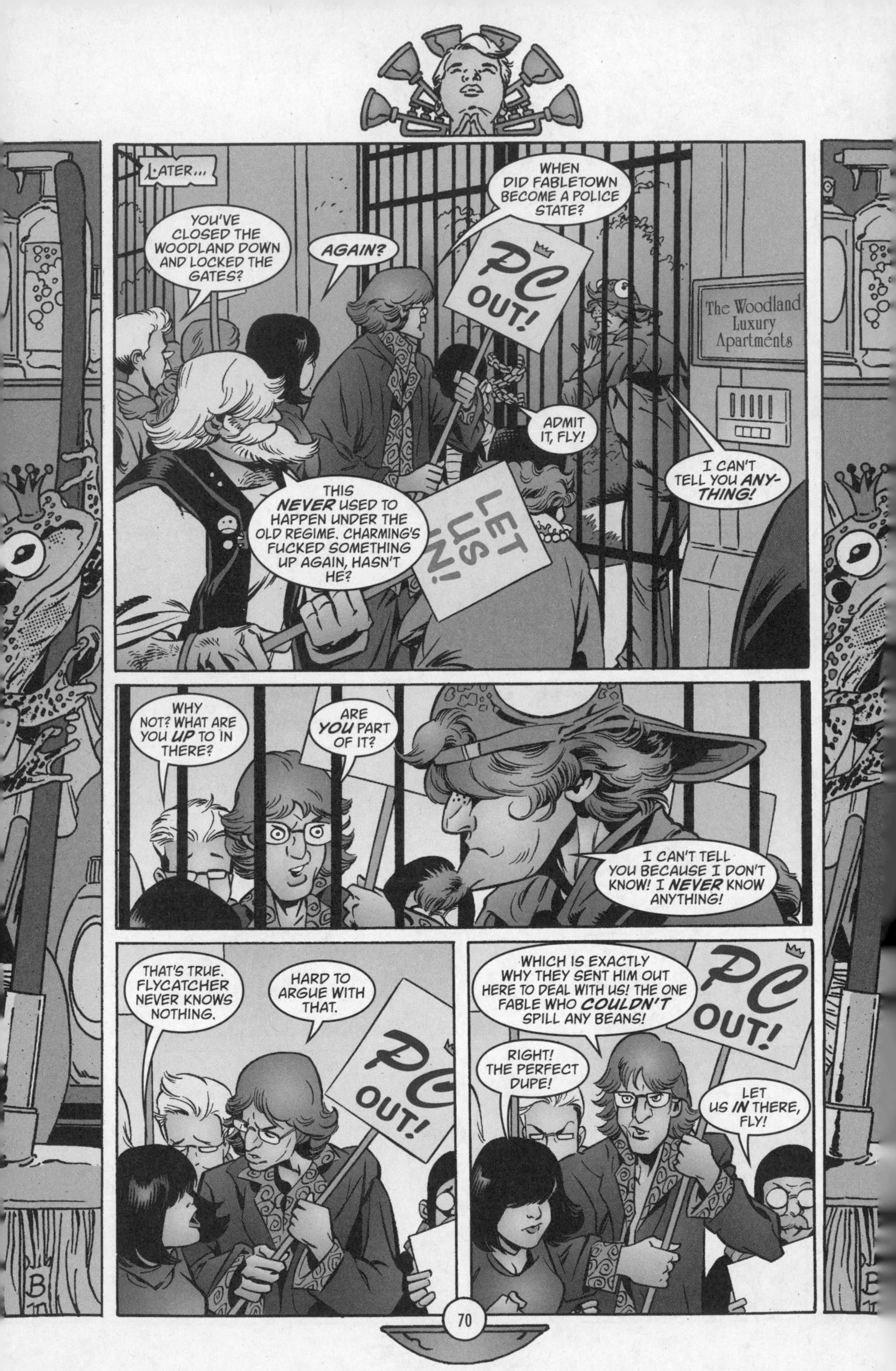

LATER...
YOU'VE CLOSED THE WOODLAND DOWN AND LOCKED THE GATES?
AGAIN?
WHEN DID FABLETOWN BECOME A POLICE STATE?
PC OUT!
The Woodland Luxury Apartments
ADMIT IT, FLY!
THIS NEVER USED TO HAPPEN UNDER THE OLD REGIME. CHARMING'S FUCKED SOMETHING UP AGAIN, HASN'T HE?
LET US IN!
I CAN'T TELL YOU ANY-THING!
WHY NOT? WHAT ARE YOU UP TO IN THERE?
ARE YOU PART OF IT?
I CAN'T TELL YOU BECAUSE I DON'T KNOW! I NEVER KNOW ANYTHING!
THAT'S TRUE. FLYCATCHER NEVER KNOWS NOTHING.
HARD TO ARGUE WITH THAT.
PC OUT!
WHICH IS EXACTLY WHY THEY SENT HIM OUT HERE TO DEAL WITH US! THE ONE FABLE WHO COULDN'T SPILL ANY BEANS!
PC OUT!
RIGHT! THE PERFECT DUPE!
LET US IN THERE, FLY!

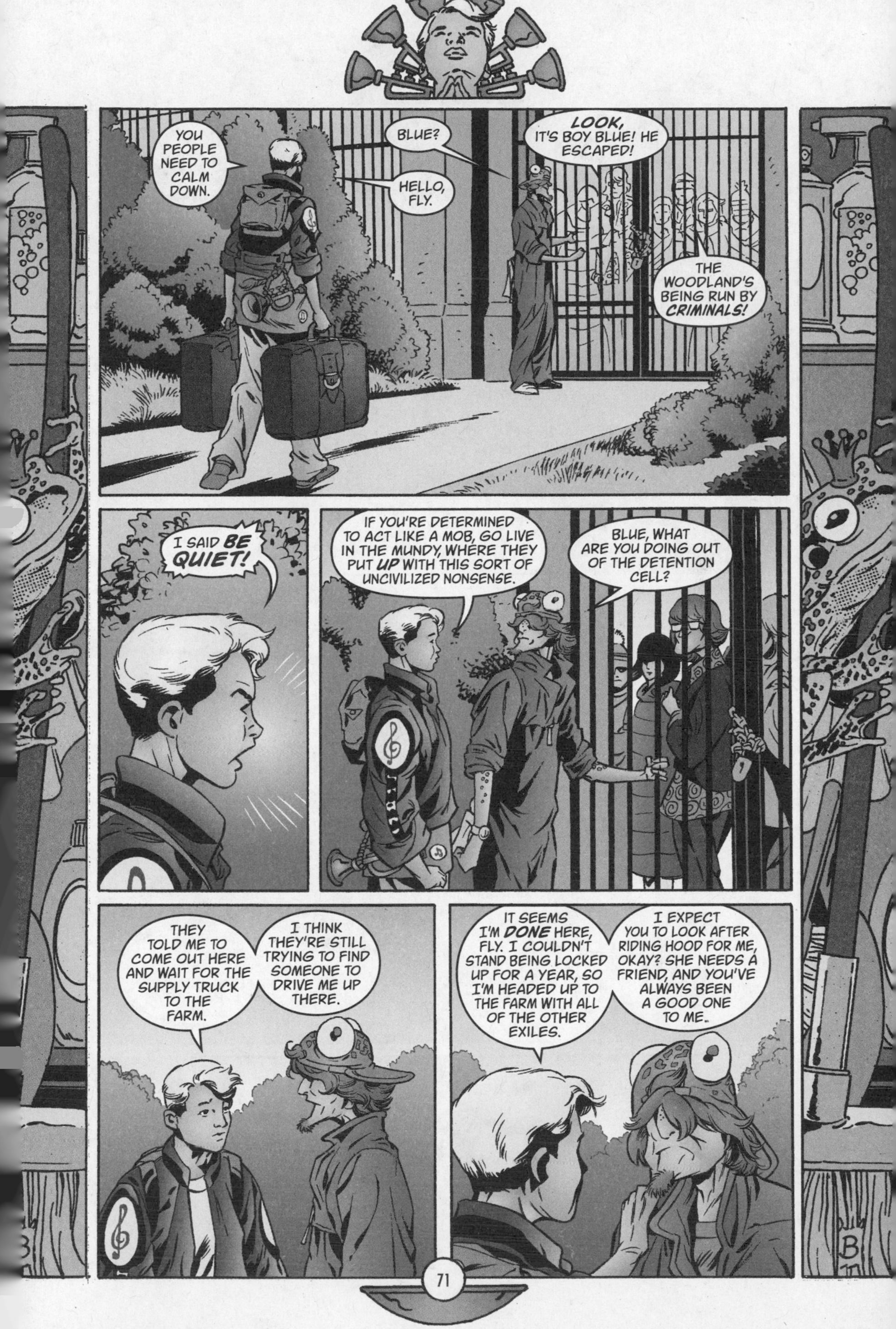
YOU PEOPLE NEED TO CALM DOWN.
BLUE?
HELLO, FLY.
LOOK, IT'S BOY BLUE! HE ESCAPED!
THE WOODLAND'S BEING RUN BY CRIMINALS!
I SAID BE QUIET!
IF YOU'RE DETERMINED TO ACT LIKE A MOB, GO LIVE IN THE MUNDY, WHERE THEY PUT UP WITH THIS SORT OF UNCIVILIZED NONSENSE.
BLUE, WHAT ARE YOU DOING OUT OF THE DETENTION CELL?
THEY TOLD ME TO COME OUT HERE AND WAIT FOR THE SUPPLY TRUCK TO THE FARM.
I THINK THEY'RE STILL TRYING TO FIND SOMEONE TO DRIVE ME UP THERE.
IT SEEMS I'M DONE HERE, FLY. I COULDN'T STAND BEING LOCKED UP FOR A YEAR, SO I'M HEADED UP TO THE FARM WITH ALL OF THE OTHER EXILES.
I EXPECT YOU TO LOOK AFTER RIDING HOOD FOR ME, OKAY? SHE NEEDS A FRIEND, AND YOU'VE ALWAYS BEEN A GOOD ONE TO ME.

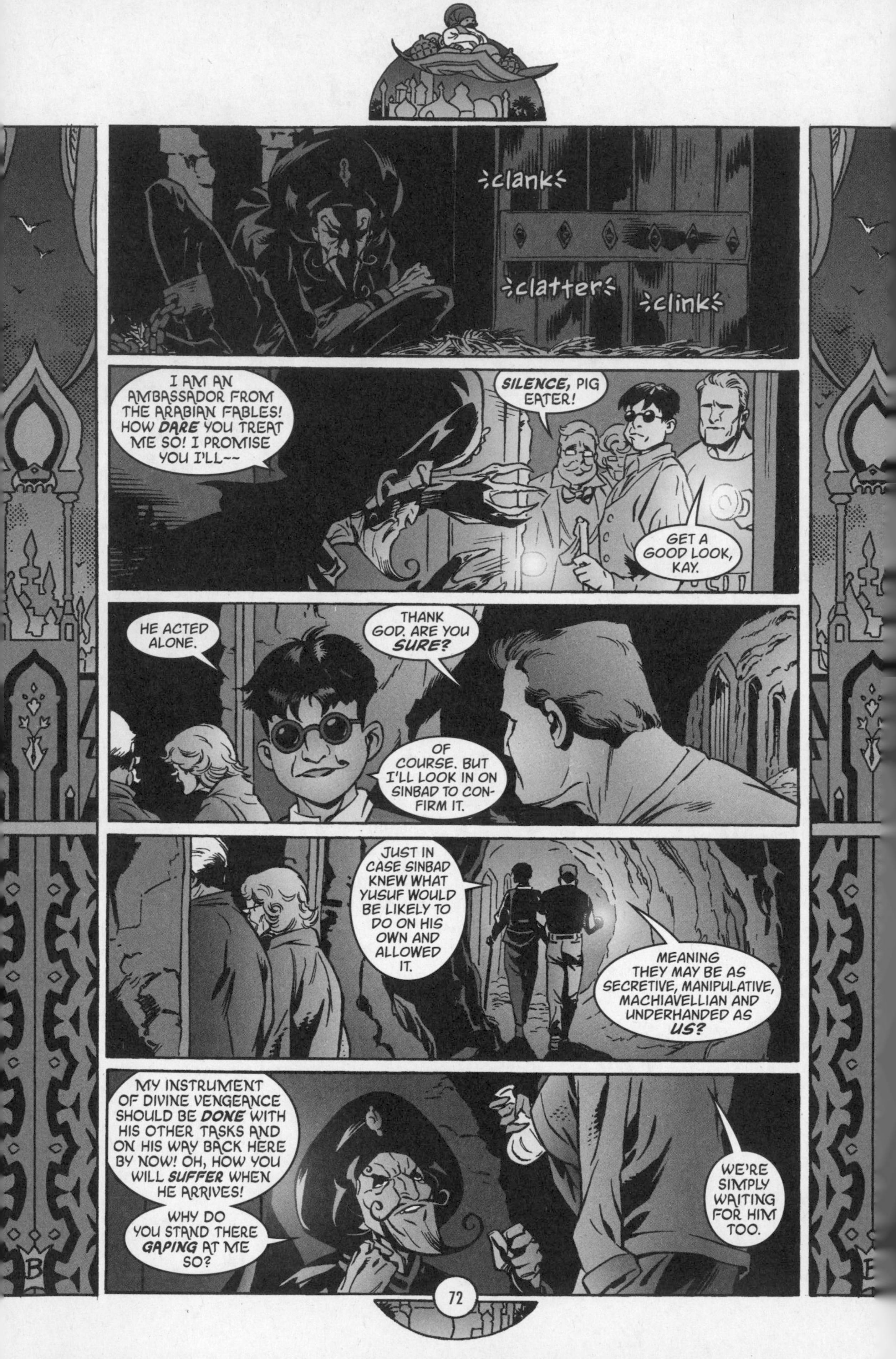
clank
clatter
clink
I AM AN AMBASSADOR FROM THE ARABIAN FABLES! HOW DARE YOU TREAT ME SO! I PROMISE YOU I'LL~~
SILENCE, PIG EATER!
GET A GOOD LOOK, KAY.
HE ACTED ALONE.
THANK GOD. ARE YOU SURE?
OF COURSE. BUT I'LL LOOK IN ON SINBAD TO CONFIRM IT.
JUST IN CASE SINBAD KNEW WHAT YUSUF WOULD BE LIKELY TO DO ON HIS OWN AND ALLOWED IT.
MEANING THEY MAY BE AS SECRETIVE, MANIPULATIVE, MACHIAVELLIAN AND UNDERHANDED AS US?
MY INSTRUMENT OF DIVINE VENGEANCE SHOULD BE DONE WITH HIS OTHER TASKS AND ON HIS WAY BACK HERE BY NOW! OH, HOW YOU WILL SUFFER WHEN HE ARRIVES!
WHY DO YOU STAND THERE GAPING AT ME SO?
WE'RE SIMPLY WAITING FOR HIM TOO.

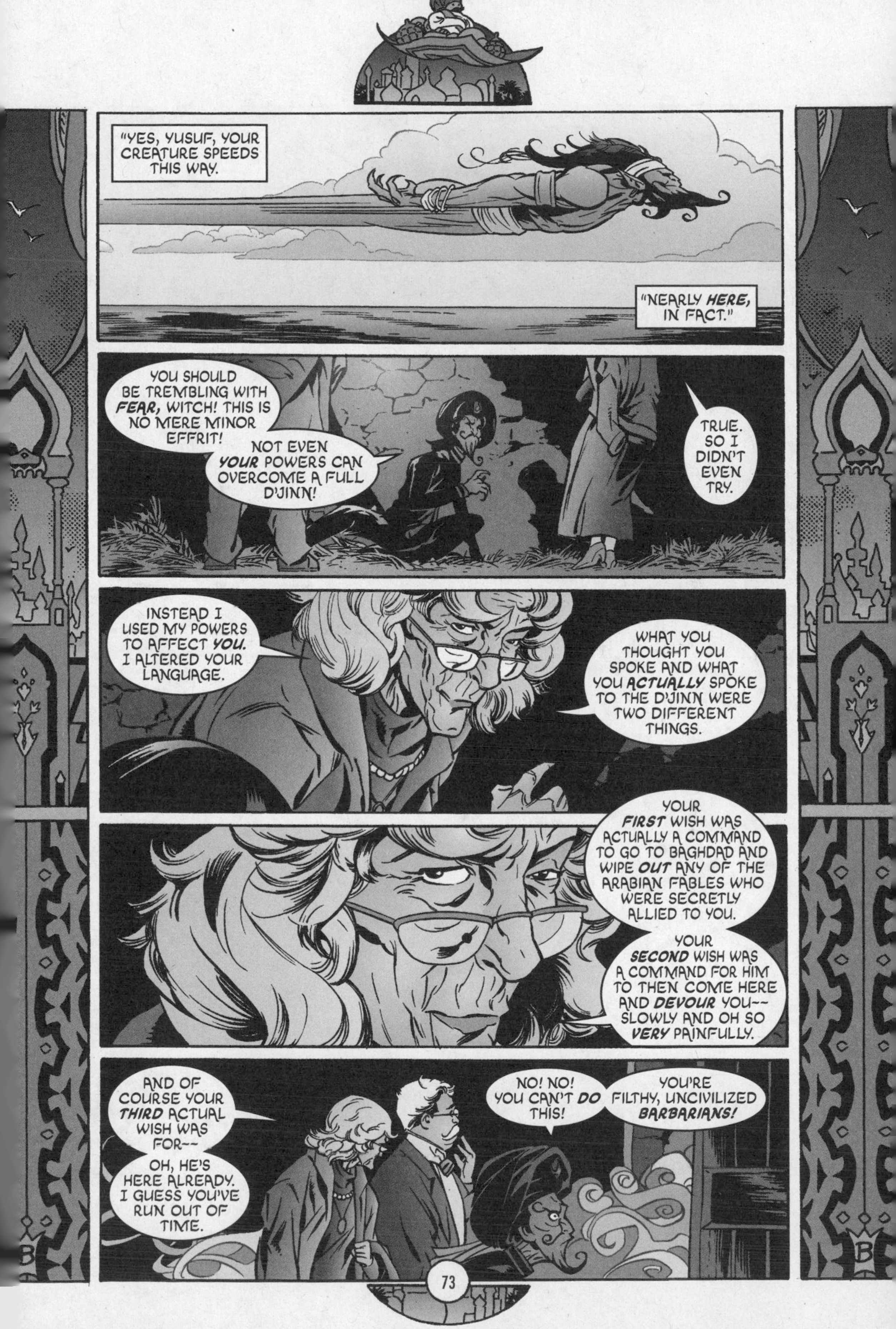

"YES, YUSUF, YOUR CREATURE SPEEDS THIS WAY.
"NEARLY HERE, IN FACT."
YOU SHOULD BE TREMBLING WITH FEAR, WITCH! THIS IS NO MERE MINOR EFFRIT!
NOT EVEN YOUR POWERS CAN OVERCOME A FULL D'JINN!
TRUE. SO I DIDN'T EVEN TRY.
INSTEAD I USED MY POWERS TO AFFECT YOU. I ALTERED YOUR LANGUAGE.
WHAT YOU THOUGHT YOU SPOKE AND WHAT YOU ACTUALLY SPOKE TO THE D'JINN WERE TWO DIFFERENT THINGS.
YOUR FIRST WISH WAS ACTUALLY A COMMAND TO GO TO BAGHDAD AND WIPE OUT ANY OF THE ARABIAN FABLES WHO WERE SECRETLY ALLIED TO YOU.
YOUR SECOND WISH WAS A COMMAND FOR HIM TO THEN COME HERE AND DEVOUR YOU-- SLOWLY AND OH SO VERY PAINFULLY.
AND OF COURSE YOUR THIRD ACTUAL WISH WAS FOR--
OH, HE'S HERE ALREADY. I GUESS YOU'VE RUN OUT OF TIME.
NO! NO! YOU CAN'T DO THIS!
YOU'RE FILTHY, UNCIVILIZED BARBARIANS!

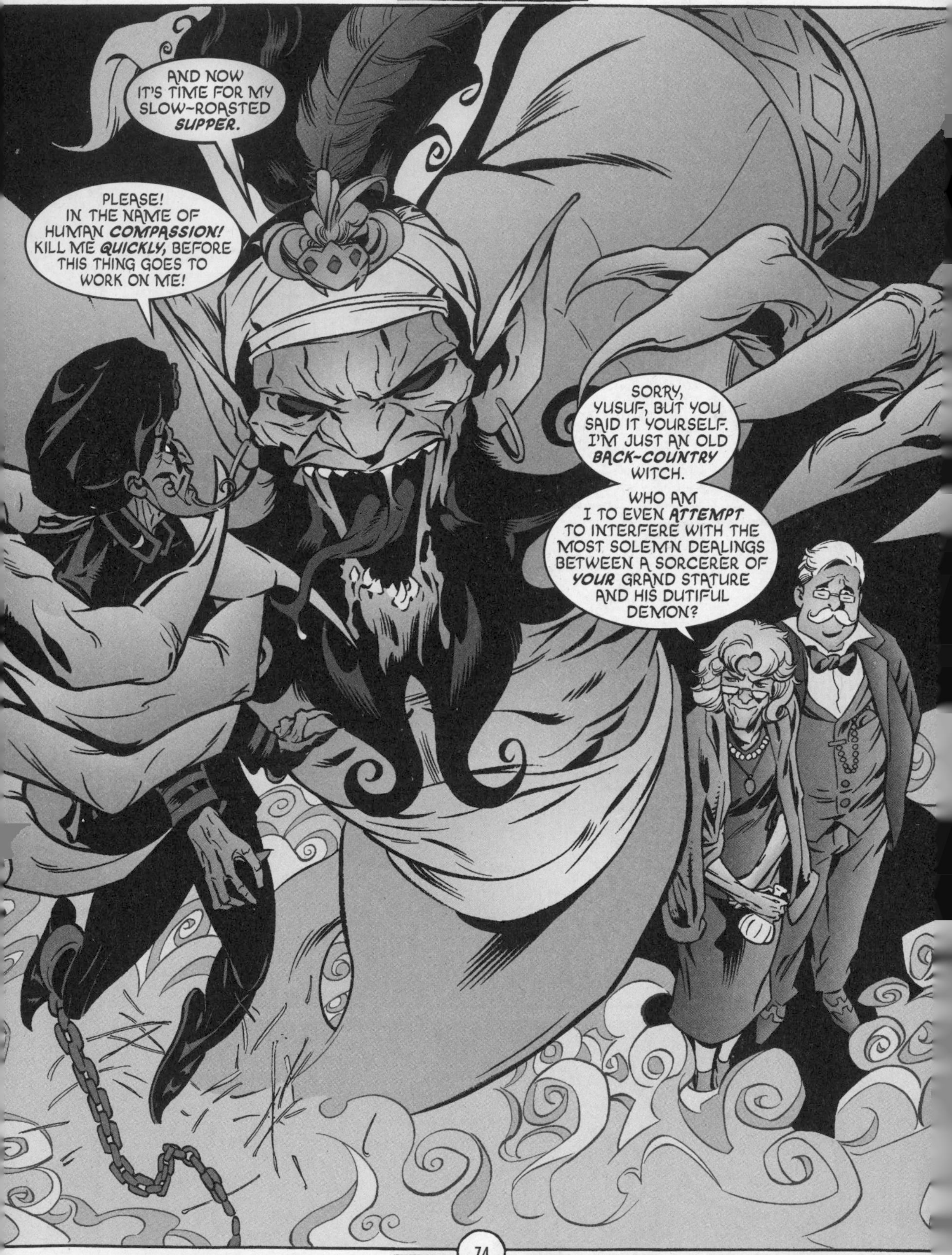
AND NOW IT'S TIME FOR MY SLOW-ROASTED SUPPER.
PLEASE! IN THE NAME OF HUMAN COMPASSION! KILL ME QUICKLY, BEFORE THIS THING GOES TO WORK ON ME!
SORRY, YUSUF, BUT YOU SAID IT YOURSELF. I'M JUST AN OLD BACK-COUNTRY WITCH.
WHO AM I TO EVEN ATTEMPT TO INTERFERE WITH THE MOST SOLEMN DEALINGS BETWEEN A SORCERER OF YOUR GRAND STATURE AND HIS DUTIFUL DEMON?

Next: Sinbäd, Aläddin & Ali Bäbä.

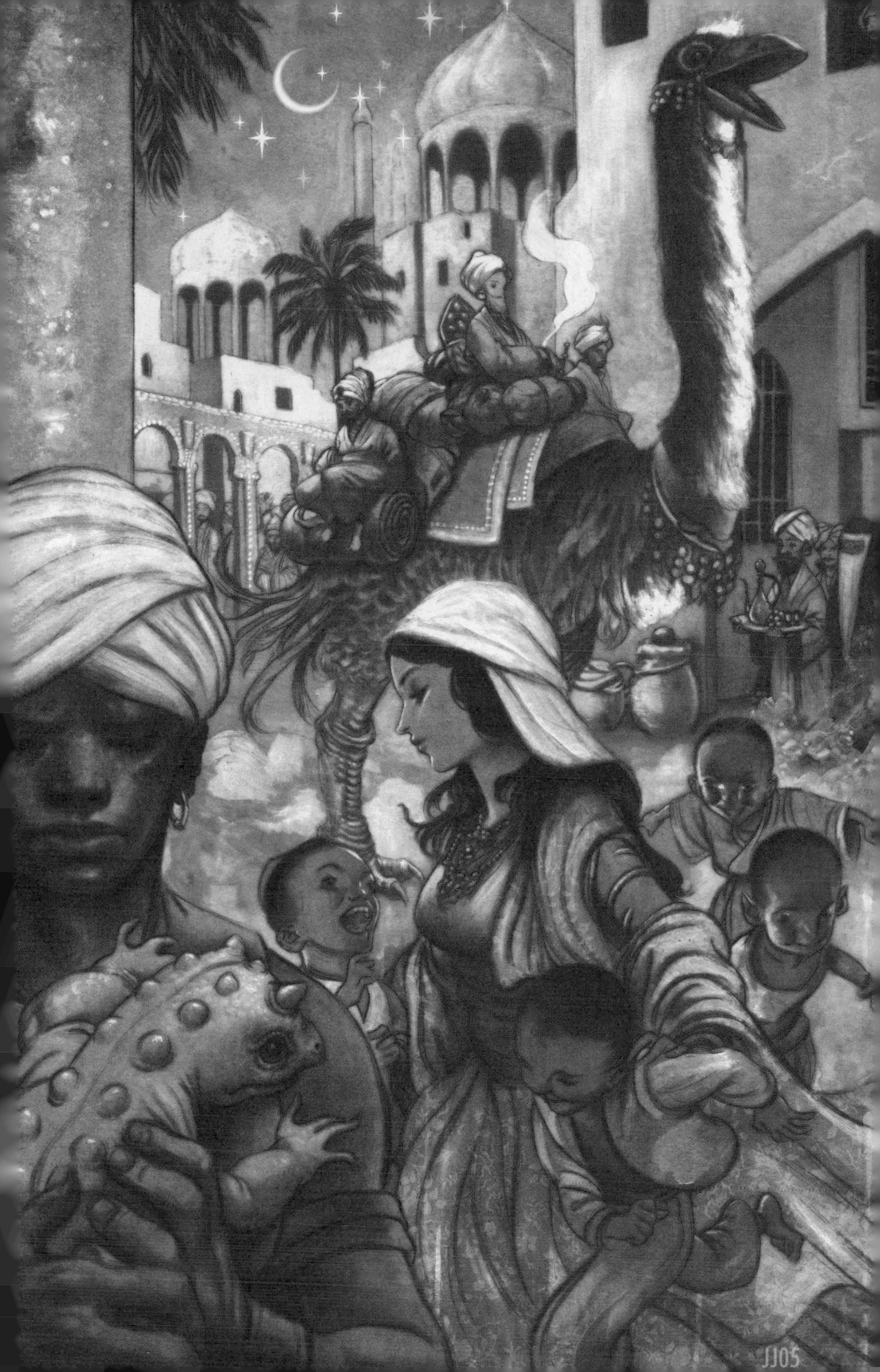
JJ05

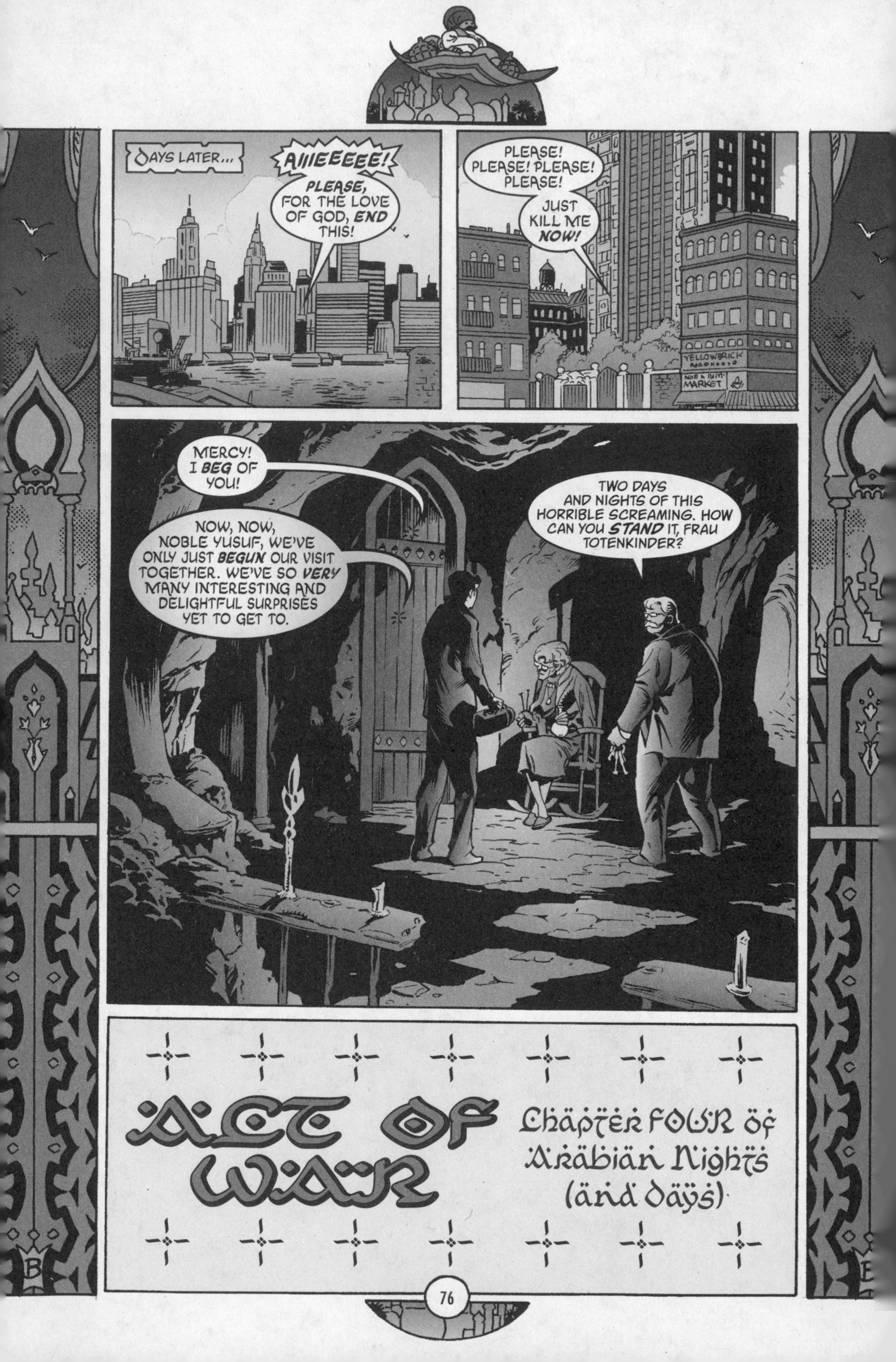
DAYS LATER...
AIIIEEEEE!
PLEASE, FOR THE LOVE OF GOD, END THIS!
PLEASE! PLEASE! PLEASE! PLEASE!
JUST KILL ME NOW!
YELLOWBRICK
MARKET
MERCY! I BEG OF YOU!
NOW, NOW, NOBLE YUSUF, WE'VE ONLY JUST BEGUN OUR VISIT TOGETHER. WE'VE SO VERY MANY INTERESTING AND DELIGHTFUL SURPRISES YET TO GET TO.
TWO DAYS AND NIGHTS OF THIS HORRIBLE SCREAMING. HOW CAN YOU STAND IT, FRAU TOTENKINDER?

ACT OF WAR

Chapter FOUR of Arabian Nights (and Days)

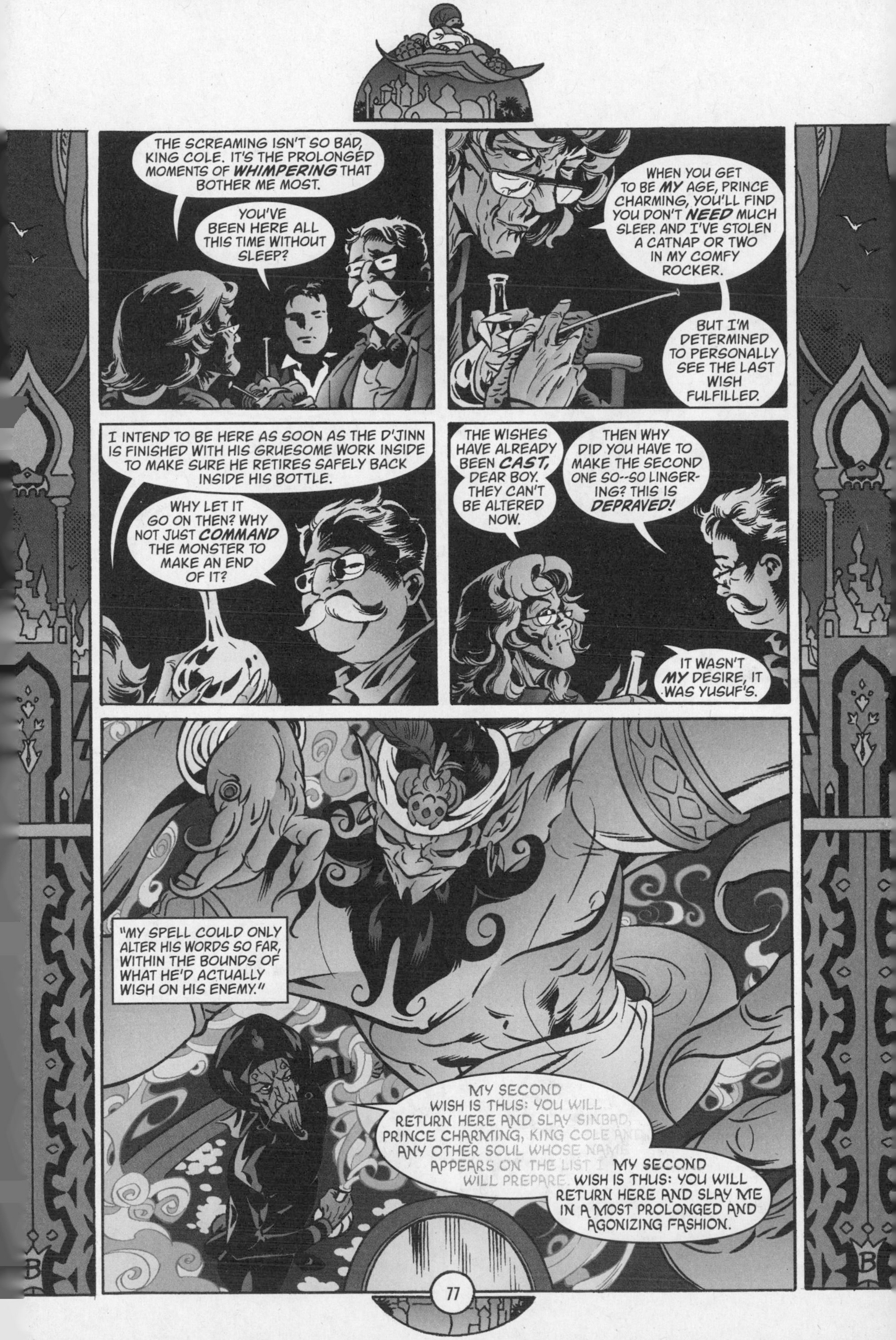
THE SCREAMING ISN'T SO BAD, KING COLE. IT'S THE PROLONGED MOMENTS OF WHIMPERING THAT BOTHER ME MOST.
YOU'VE BEEN HERE ALL THIS TIME WITHOUT SLEEP?
WHEN YOU GET TO BE MY AGE, PRINCE CHARMING, YOU'LL FIND YOU DON'T NEED MUCH SLEEP. AND I'VE STOLEN A CATNAP OR TWO IN MY COMFY ROCKER.
BUT I'M DETERMINED TO PERSONALLY SEE THE LAST WISH FULFILLED.
I INTEND TO BE HERE AS SOON AS THE D'JINN IS FINISHED WITH HIS GRUESOME WORK INSIDE TO MAKE SURE HE RETIRES SAFELY BACK INSIDE HIS BOTTLE.
WHY LET IT GO ON THEN? WHY NOT JUST COMMAND THE MONSTER TO MAKE AN END OF IT?
THE WISHES HAVE ALREADY BEEN CAST, DEAR BOY. THEY CAN'T BE ALTERED NOW.
THEN WHY DID YOU HAVE TO MAKE THE SECOND ONE SO--SO LINGERING? THIS IS DEPRAVED!
IT WASN'T MY DESIRE, IT WAS YUSUF'S.
"MY SPELL COULD ONLY ALTER HIS WORDS SO FAR, WITHIN THE BOUNDS OF WHAT HE'D ACTUALLY WISH ON HIS ENEMY."
MY SECOND WISH IS THUS: YOU WILL RETURN HERE AND SLAY SINBAD, PRINCE CHARMING, KING COLE AND ANY OTHER SOUL WHOSE NAME APPEARS ON THE LIST I WILL PREPARE.
MY SECOND WISH IS THUS: YOU WILL RETURN HERE AND SLAY ME IN A MOST PROLONGED AND AGONIZING FASHION.

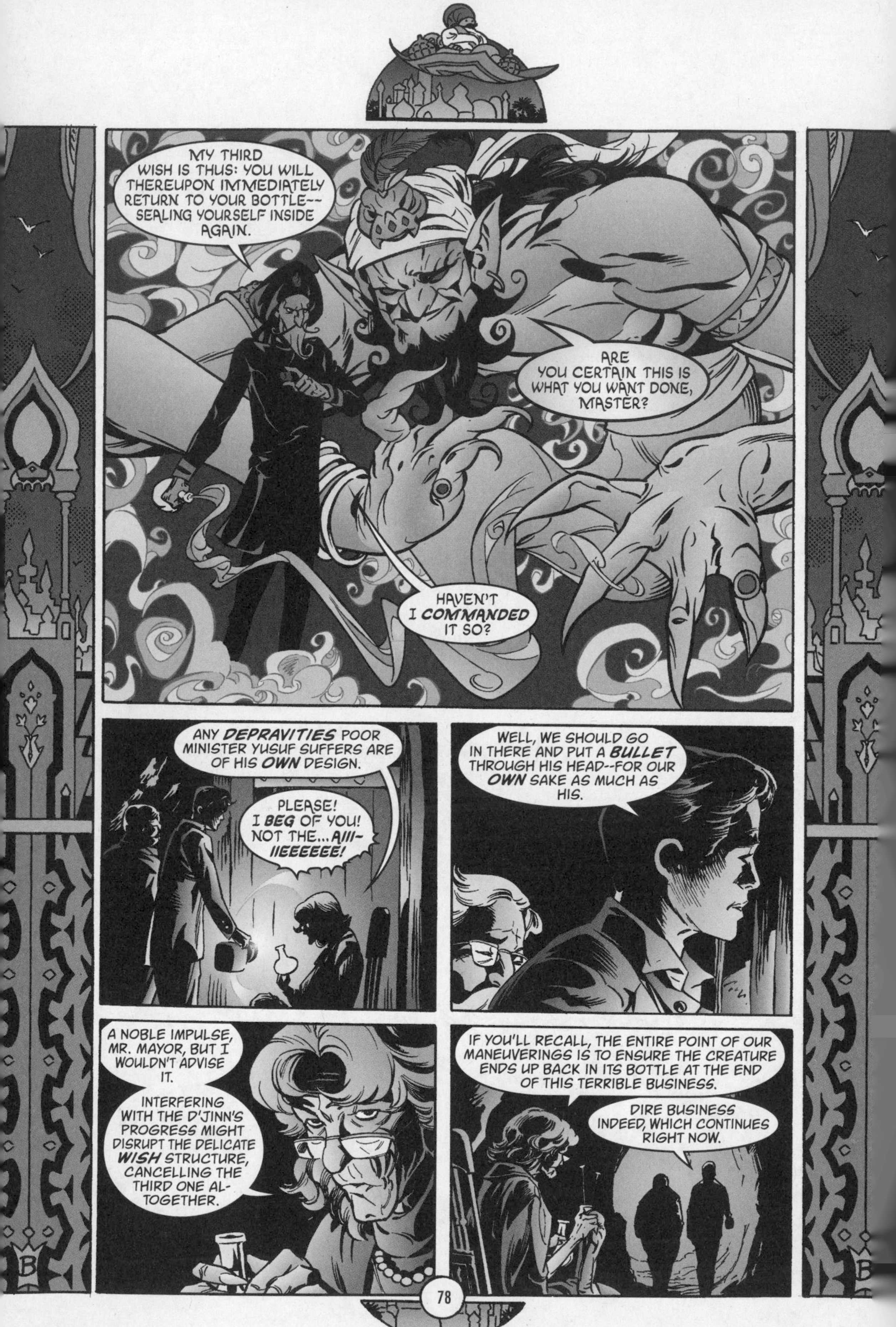
MY THIRD WISH IS THUS: YOU WILL THEREUPON IMMEDIATELY RETURN TO YOUR BOTTLE--SEALING YOURSELF INSIDE AGAIN.
ARE YOU CERTAIN THIS IS WHAT YOU WANT DONE, MASTER?
HAVEN'T I COMMANDED IT SO?
ANY DEPRAVITIES POOR MINISTER YUSUF SUFFERS ARE OF HIS OWN DESIGN.
PLEASE! I BEG OF YOU! NOT THE...AIII-IIEEEEEE!
WELL, WE SHOULD GO IN THERE AND PUT A BULLET THROUGH HIS HEAD--FOR OUR OWN SAKE AS MUCH AS HIS.
A NOBLE IMPULSE, MR. MAYOR, BUT I WOULDN'T ADVISE IT.
INTERFERING WITH THE D'JINN'S PROGRESS MIGHT DISRUPT THE DELICATE WISH STRUCTURE, CANCELLING THE THIRD ONE AL-TOGETHER.
IF YOU'LL RECALL, THE ENTIRE POINT OF OUR MANEUVERINGS IS TO ENSURE THE CREATURE ENDS UP BACK IN ITS BOTTLE AT THE END OF THIS TERRIBLE BUSINESS.
DIRE BUSINESS INDEED, WHICH CONTINUES RIGHT NOW.

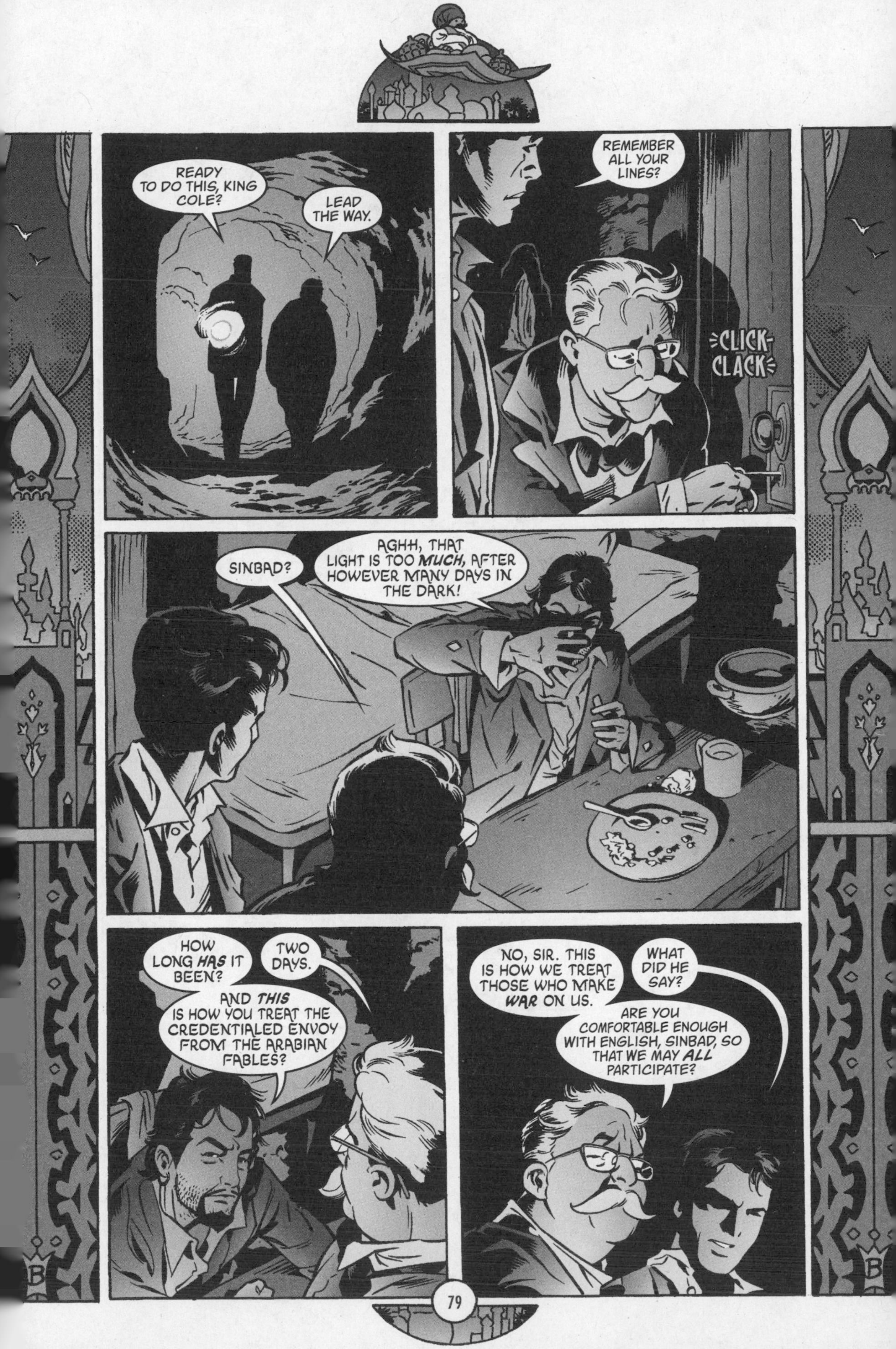
READY TO DO THIS, KING COLE?
LEAD THE WAY.
REMEMBER ALL YOUR LINES?
CLICK-CLACK
SINBAD?
AGHH, THAT LIGHT IS TOO MUCH, AFTER HOWEVER MANY DAYS IN THE DARK!
HOW LONG HAS IT BEEN?
TWO DAYS.
AND THIS IS HOW YOU TREAT THE CREDENTIALED ENVOY FROM THE ARABIAN FABLES?
NO, SIR. THIS IS HOW WE TREAT THOSE WHO MAKE WAR ON US.
WHAT DID HE SAY?
ARE YOU COMFORTABLE ENOUGH WITH ENGLISH, SINBAD, SO THAT WE MAY ALL PARTICIPATE?

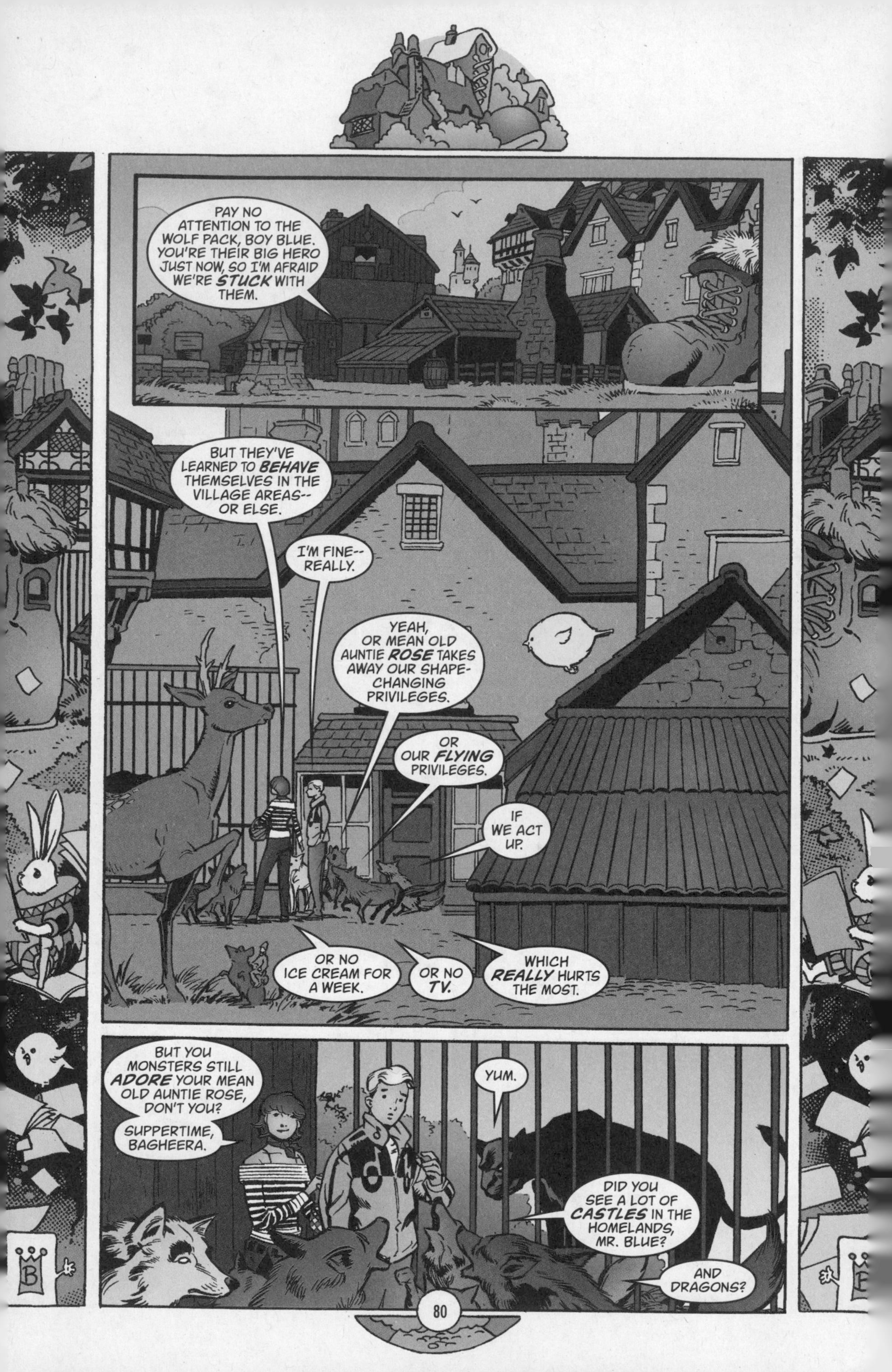
PAY NO ATTENTION TO THE WOLF PACK, BOY BLUE. YOU'RE THEIR BIG HERO JUST NOW, SO I'M AFRAID WE'RE STUCK WITH THEM.
BUT THEY'VE LEARNED TO BEHAVE THEMSELVES IN THE VILLAGE AREAS-- OR ELSE.
I'M FINE-- REALLY.
YEAH, OR MEAN OLD AUNTIE ROSE TAKES AWAY OUR SHAPE-CHANGING PRIVILEGES.
OR OUR FLYING PRIVILEGES.
IF WE ACT UP.
OR NO ICE CREAM FOR A WEEK.
OR NO TV.
WHICH REALLY HURTS THE MOST.
BUT YOU MONSTERS STILL ADORE YOUR MEAN OLD AUNTIE ROSE, DON'T YOU?
SUPPERTIME, BAGHEERA.
YUM.
DID YOU SEE A LOT OF CASTLES IN THE HOMELANDS, MR. BLUE?
AND DRAGONS?

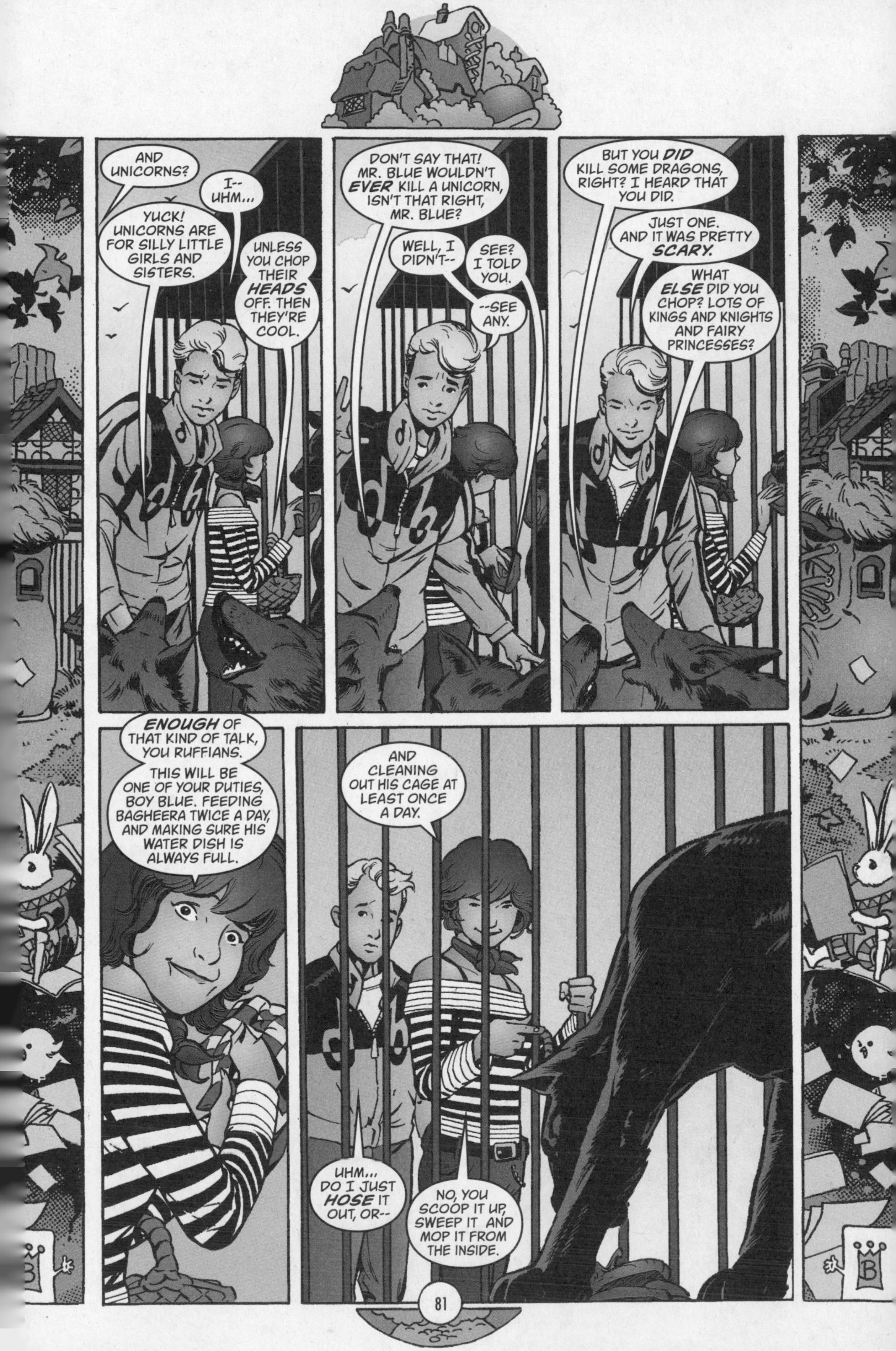

AND UNICORNS?
I-- UHM...
YUCK! UNICORNS ARE FOR SILLY LITTLE GIRLS AND SISTERS.
UNLESS YOU CHOP THEIR HEADS OFF. THEN THEY'RE COOL.
DON'T SAY THAT! MR. BLUE WOULDN'T EVER KILL A UNICORN, ISN'T THAT RIGHT, MR. BLUE?
WELL, I DIDN'T--
SEE? I TOLD YOU.
--SEE ANY.
BUT YOU DID KILL SOME DRAGONS, RIGHT? I HEARD THAT YOU DID.
JUST ONE. AND IT WAS PRETTY SCARY.
WHAT ELSE DID YOU CHOP? LOTS OF KINGS AND KNIGHTS AND FAIRY PRINCESSES?
ENOUGH OF THAT KIND OF TALK, YOU RUFFIANS.
THIS WILL BE ONE OF YOUR DUTIES, BOY BLUE. FEEDING BAGHEERA TWICE A DAY, AND MAKING SURE HIS WATER DISH IS ALWAYS FULL.
AND CLEANING OUT HIS CAGE AT LEAST ONCE A DAY.
UHM... DO I JUST HOSE IT OUT, OR--
NO, YOU SCOOP IT UP, SWEEP IT AND MOP IT FROM THE INSIDE.

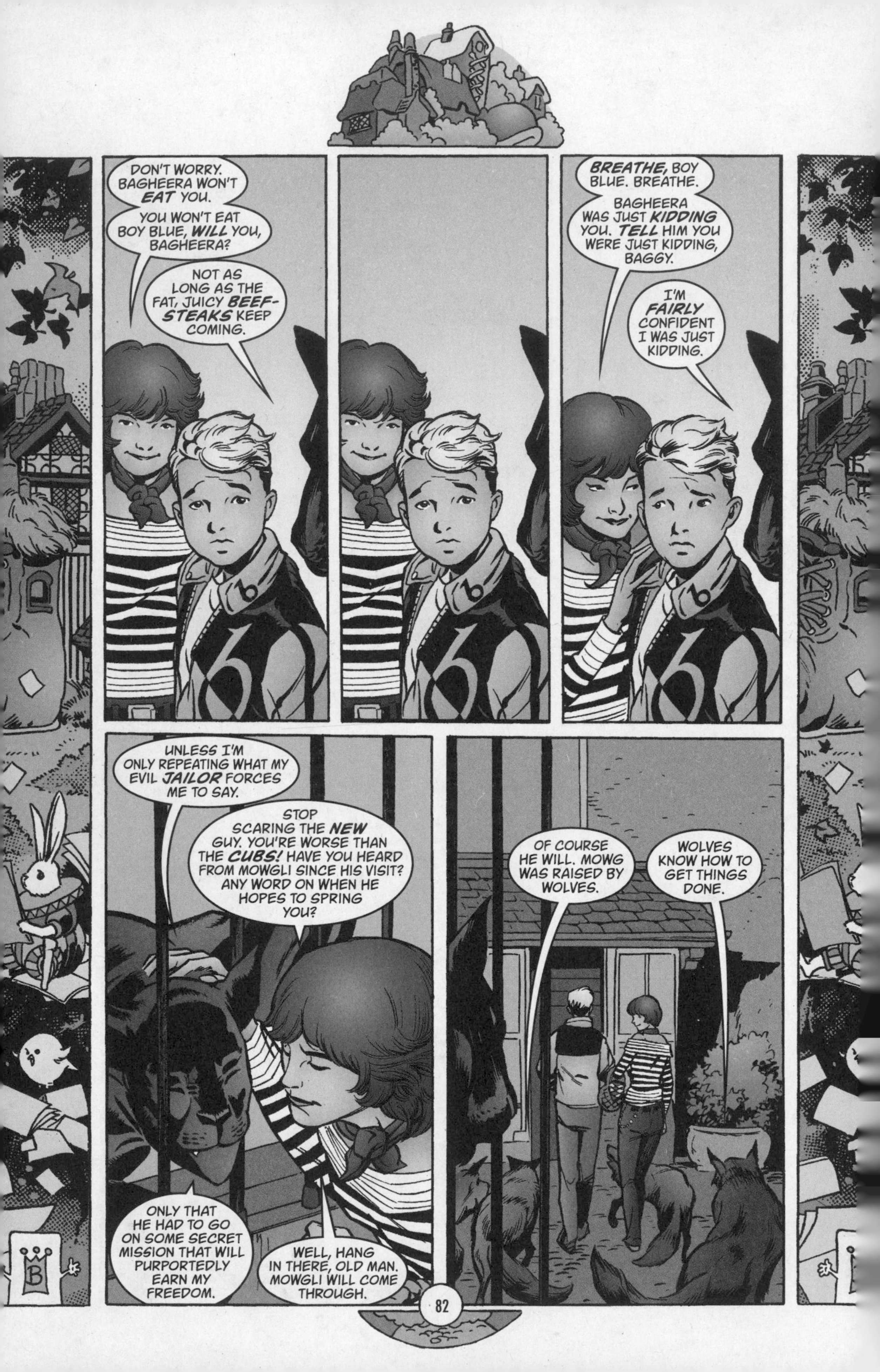
DON'T WORRY. BAGHEERA WON'T EAT YOU.
YOU WON'T EAT BOY BLUE, WILL YOU, BAGHEERA?
NOT AS LONG AS THE FAT, JUICY BEEF-STEAKS KEEP COMING.
BREATHE, BOY BLUE. BREATHE.
BAGHEERA WAS JUST KIDDING YOU. TELL HIM YOU WERE JUST KIDDING, BAGGY.
I'M FAIRLY CONFIDENT I WAS JUST KIDDING.
UNLESS I'M ONLY REPEATING WHAT MY EVIL JAILOR FORCES ME TO SAY.
STOP SCARING THE NEW GUY. YOU'RE WORSE THAN THE CUBS! HAVE YOU HEARD FROM MOWGLI SINCE HIS VISIT? ANY WORD ON WHEN HE HOPES TO SPRING YOU?
ONLY THAT HE HAD TO GO ON SOME SECRET MISSION THAT WILL PURPORTEDLY EARN MY FREEDOM.
WELL, HANG IN THERE, OLD MAN. MOWGLI WILL COME THROUGH.
OF COURSE HE WILL. MOWG WAS RAISED BY WOLVES.
WOLVES KNOW HOW TO GET THINGS DONE.

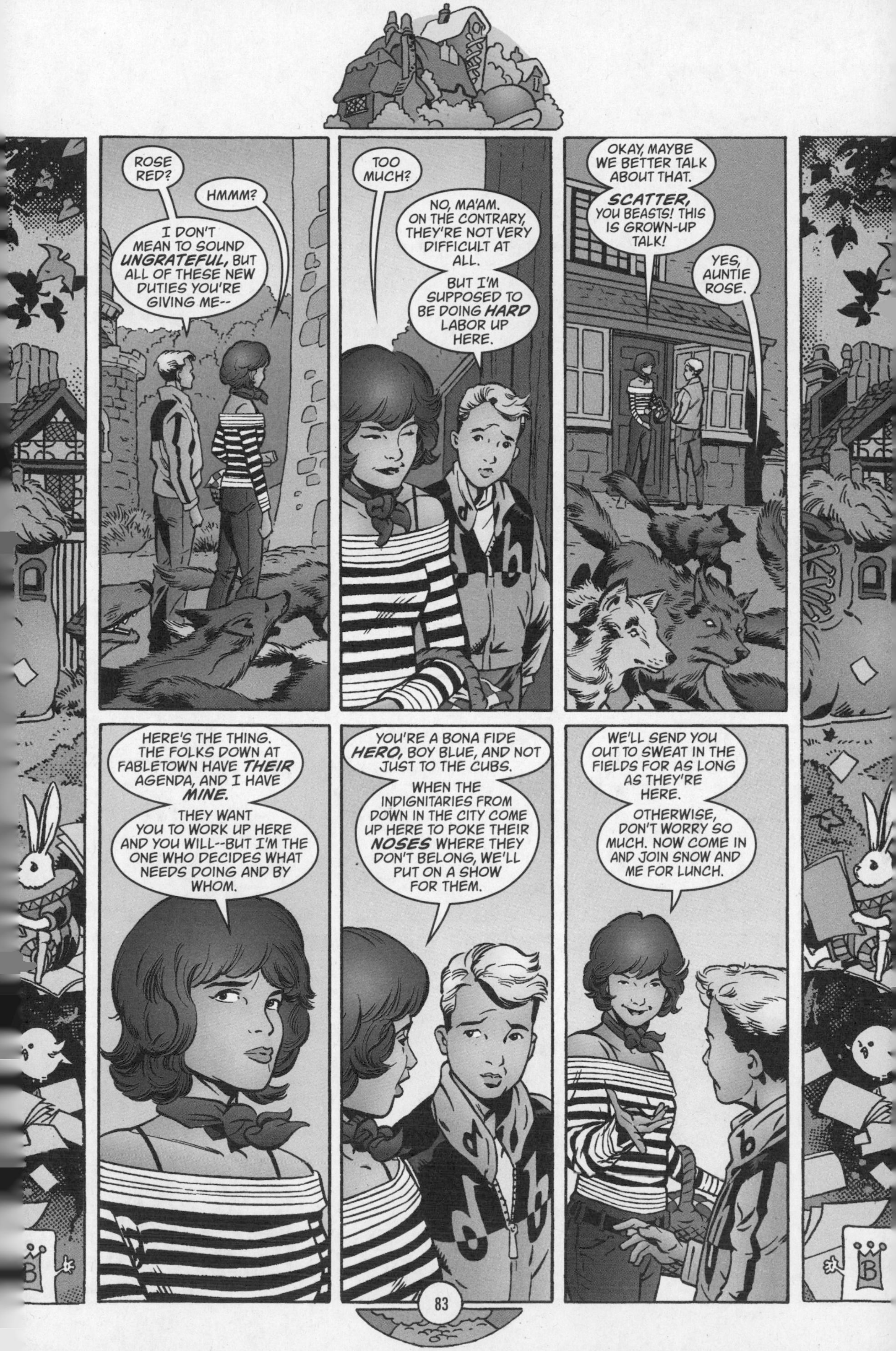

ROSE RED?
HMMM?
I DON'T MEAN TO SOUND UNGRATEFUL, BUT ALL OF THESE NEW DUTIES YOU'RE GIVING ME--
TOO MUCH?
NO, MA'AM. ON THE CONTRARY, THEY'RE NOT VERY DIFFICULT AT ALL.
BUT I'M SUPPOSED TO BE DOING HARD LABOR UP HERE.
OKAY, MAYBE WE BETTER TALK ABOUT THAT.
SCATTER, YOU BEASTS! THIS IS GROWN-UP TALK!
YES, AUNTIE ROSE.
HERE'S THE THING. THE FOLKS DOWN AT FABLETOWN HAVE THEIR AGENDA, AND I HAVE MINE.
THEY WANT YOU TO WORK UP HERE AND YOU WILL--BUT I'M THE ONE WHO DECIDES WHAT NEEDS DOING AND BY WHOM.
YOU'RE A BONA FIDE HERO, BOY BLUE, AND NOT JUST TO THE CUBS.
WHEN THE INDIGNITARIES FROM DOWN IN THE CITY COME UP HERE TO POKE THEIR NOSES WHERE THEY DON'T BELONG, WE'LL PUT ON A SHOW FOR THEM.
WE'LL SEND YOU OUT TO SWEAT IN THE FIELDS FOR AS LONG AS THEY'RE HERE.
OTHERWISE, DON'T WORRY SO MUCH. NOW COME IN AND JOIN SNOW AND ME FOR LUNCH.

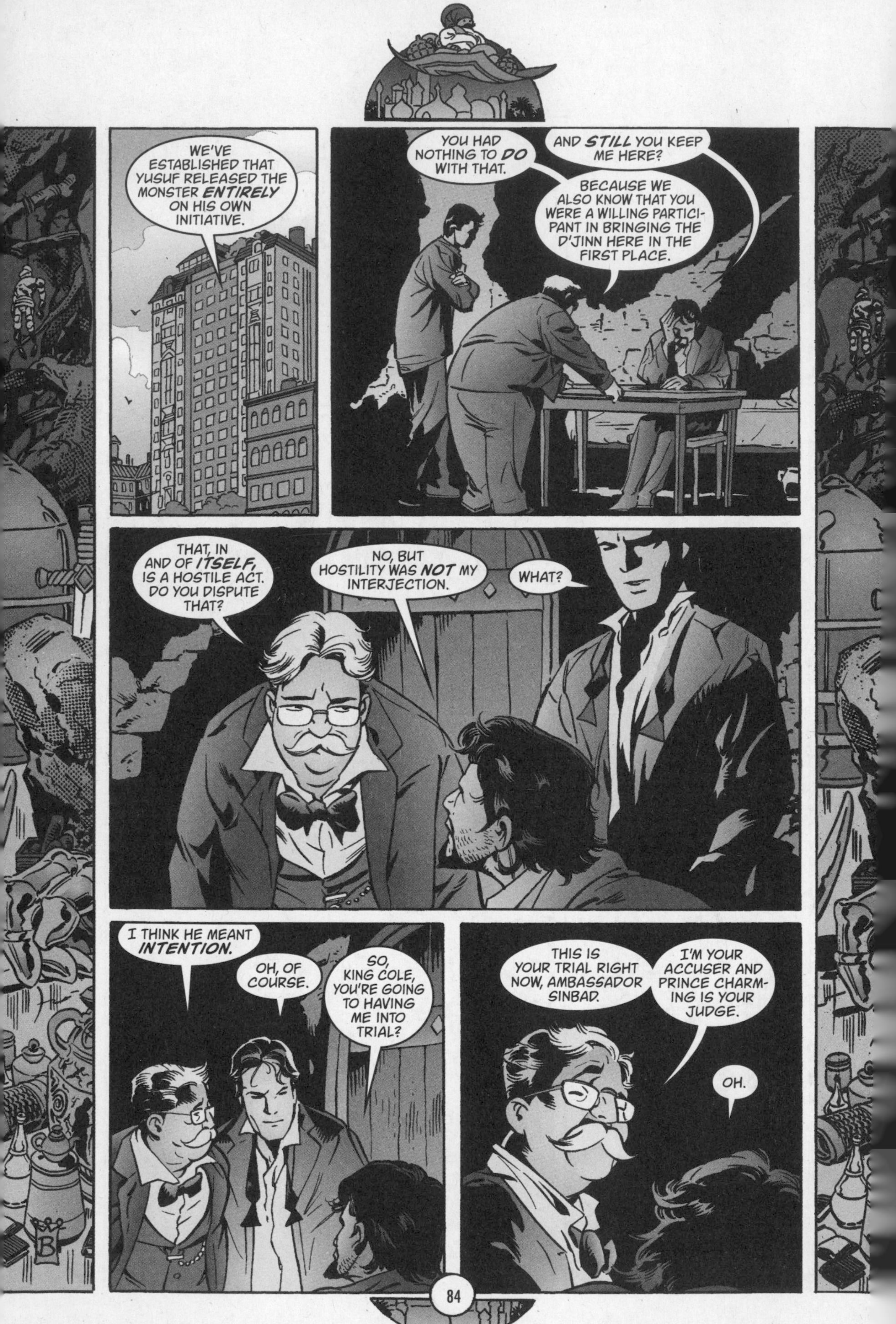

WE'VE ESTABLISHED THAT YUSUF RELEASED THE MONSTER ENTIRELY ON HIS OWN INITIATIVE.
YOU HAD NOTHING TO DO WITH THAT.
AND STILL YOU KEEP ME HERE?
BECAUSE WE ALSO KNOW THAT YOU WERE A WILLING PARTICIPANT IN BRINGING THE D'JINN HERE IN THE FIRST PLACE.
THAT, IN AND OF ITSELF, IS A HOSTILE ACT. DO YOU DISPUTE THAT?
NO, BUT HOSTILITY WAS NOT MY INTERJECTION.
WHAT?
I THINK HE MEANT INTENTION.
OH, OF COURSE.
SO, KING COLE, YOU'RE GOING TO HAVING ME INTO TRIAL?
THIS IS YOUR TRIAL RIGHT NOW, AMBASSADOR SINBAD.
I'M YOUR ACCUSER AND PRINCE CHARMING IS YOUR JUDGE.
OH.

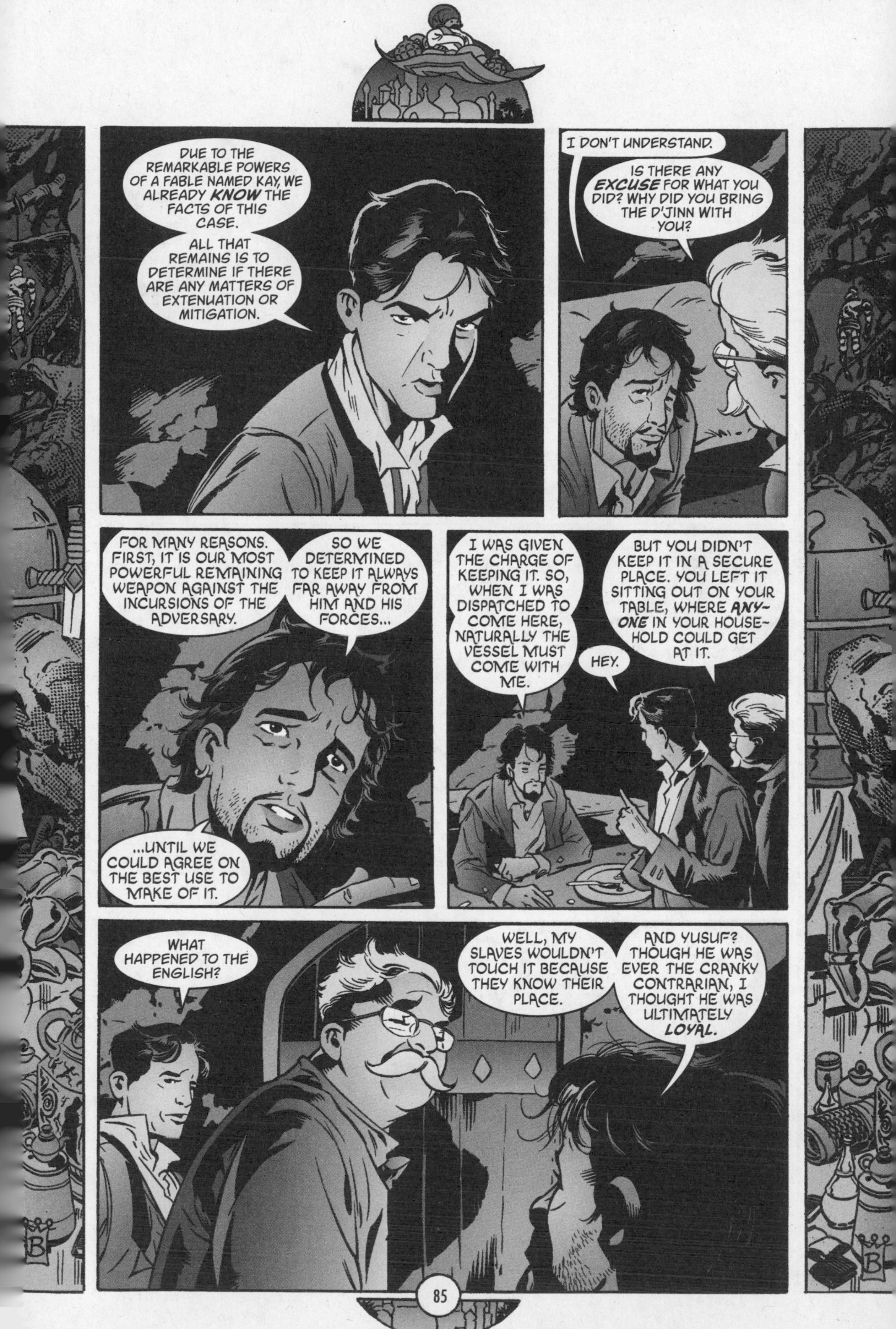
DUE TO THE REMARKABLE POWERS OF A FABLE NAMED KAY, WE ALREADY KNOW THE FACTS OF THIS CASE.
ALL THAT REMAINS IS TO DETERMINE IF THERE ARE ANY MATTERS OF EXTENUATION OR MITIGATION.
I DON'T UNDERSTAND.
IS THERE ANY EXCUSE FOR WHAT YOU DID? WHY DID YOU BRING THE D'JINN WITH YOU?
FOR MANY REASONS. FIRST, IT IS OUR MOST POWERFUL REMAINING WEAPON AGAINST THE INCURSIONS OF THE ADVERSARY.
SO WE DETERMINED TO KEEP IT ALWAYS FAR AWAY FROM HIM AND HIS FORCES...
...UNTIL WE COULD AGREE ON THE BEST USE TO MAKE OF IT.
I WAS GIVEN THE CHARGE OF KEEPING IT. SO, WHEN I WAS DISPATCHED TO COME HERE, NATURALLY THE VESSEL MUST COME WITH ME.
BUT YOU DIDN'T KEEP IT IN A SECURE PLACE. YOU LEFT IT SITTING OUT ON YOUR TABLE, WHERE ANY-ONE IN YOUR HOUSE-HOLD COULD GET AT IT.
HEY.
WHAT HAPPENED TO THE ENGLISH?
WELL, MY SLAVES WOULDN'T TOUCH IT BECAUSE THEY KNOW THEIR PLACE.
AND YUSUF? THOUGH HE WAS EVER THE CRANKY CONTRARIAN, I THOUGHT HE WAS ULTIMATELY LOYAL.

I'M AFRAID THAT'S NOT *GOOD* ENOUGH, SINBAD. EVEN THOUGH I TRUST MY FELLOW CITIZENS OF FABLETOWN, THAT DIDN'T PREVENT ME FROM KEEPING THE BAD STUFF LOCKED AWAY.

ENGLISH!

OH. SORRY. SINBAD, DO YOU HAVE ANYTHING FURTHER TO ADD?

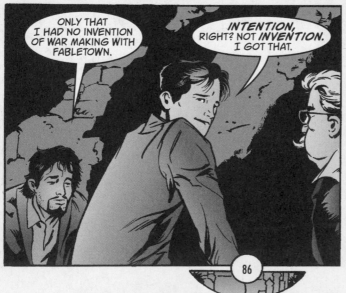

ONLY THAT I HAD NO INVENTION OF WAR MAKING WITH FABLETOWN.

INTENTION, RIGHT? NOT *INVENTION.* I GOT THAT.

THEN, IF YOU'LL *EXCUSE* US, PRINCE CHARMING AND I WILL RETIRE TO CONSIDER YOUR FATE.

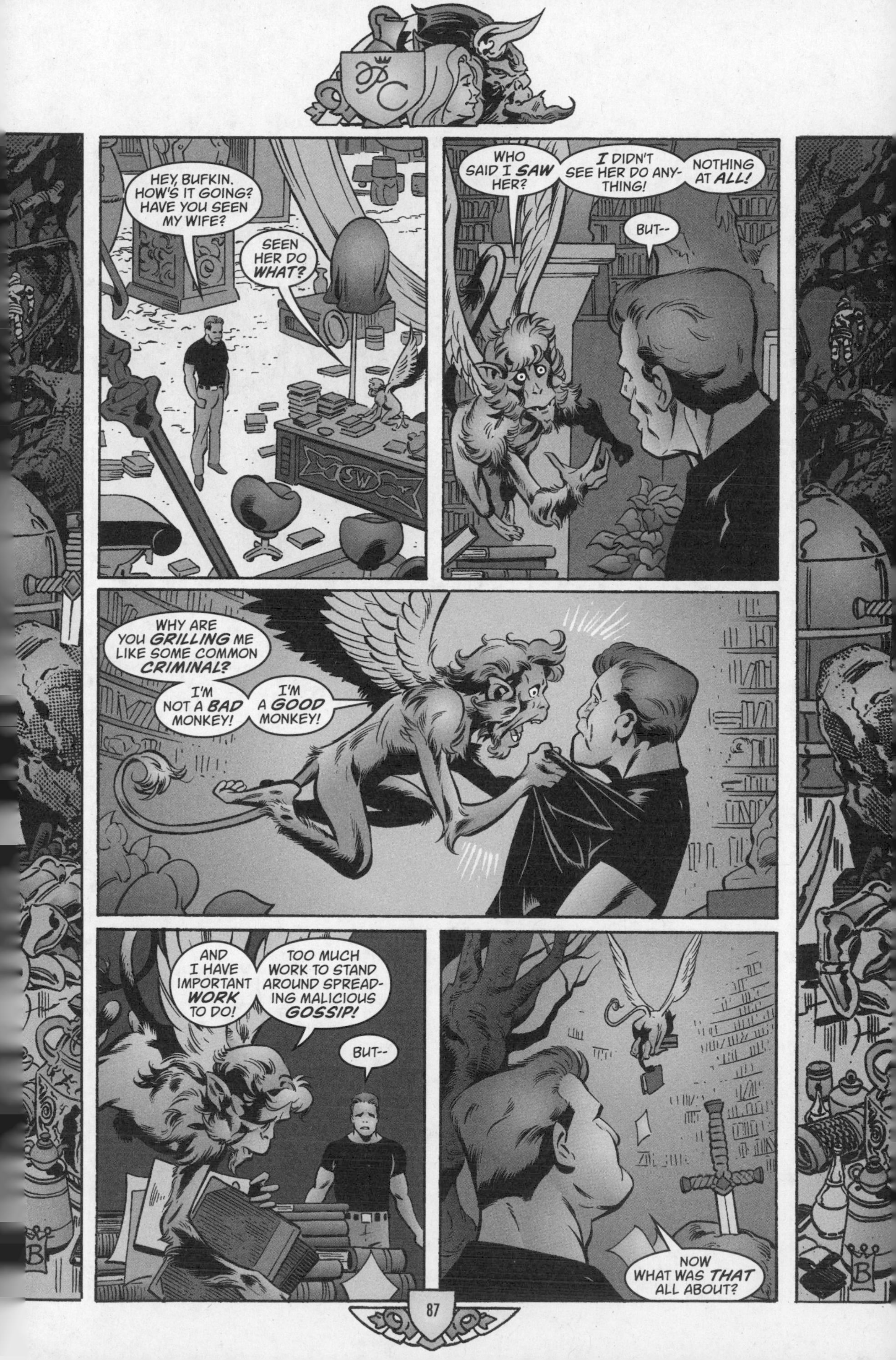
HEY, BUFKIN. HOW'S IT GOING? HAVE YOU SEEN MY WIFE?
SEEN HER DO WHAT?
WHO SAID I SAW HER?
I DIDN'T SEE HER DO ANY-THING!
NOTHING AT ALL!
BUT--
WHY ARE YOU GRILLING ME LIKE SOME COMMON CRIMINAL?
I'M NOT A BAD MONKEY!
I'M A GOOD MONKEY!
AND I HAVE IMPORTANT WORK TO DO!
TOO MUCH WORK TO STAND AROUND SPREAD-ING MALICIOUS GOSSIP!
BUT--
NOW WHAT WAS THAT ALL ABOUT?

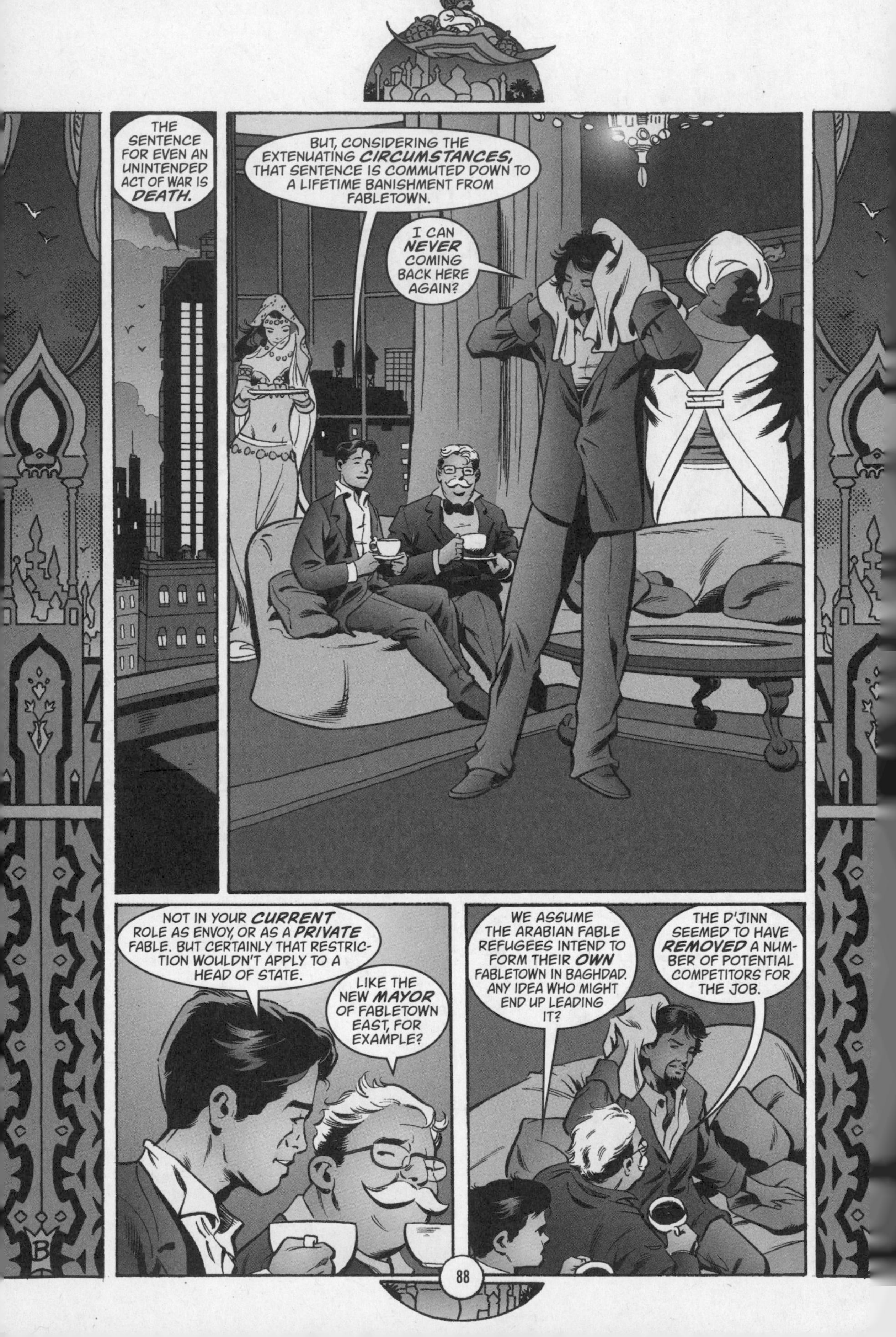
THE SENTENCE FOR EVEN AN UNINTENDED ACT OF WAR IS DEATH.
BUT, CONSIDERING THE EXTENUATING CIRCUMSTANCES, THAT SENTENCE IS COMMUTED DOWN TO A LIFETIME BANISHMENT FROM FABLETOWN.
I CAN NEVER COMING BACK HERE AGAIN?
NOT IN YOUR CURRENT ROLE AS ENVOY, OR AS A PRIVATE FABLE. BUT CERTAINLY THAT RESTRICTION WOULDN'T APPLY TO A HEAD OF STATE.
LIKE THE NEW MAYOR OF FABLETOWN EAST, FOR EXAMPLE?
WE ASSUME THE ARABIAN FABLE REFUGEES INTEND TO FORM THEIR OWN FABLETOWN IN BAGHDAD. ANY IDEA WHO MIGHT END UP LEADING IT?
THE D'JINN SEEMED TO HAVE REMOVED A NUMBER OF POTENTIAL COMPETITORS FOR THE JOB.

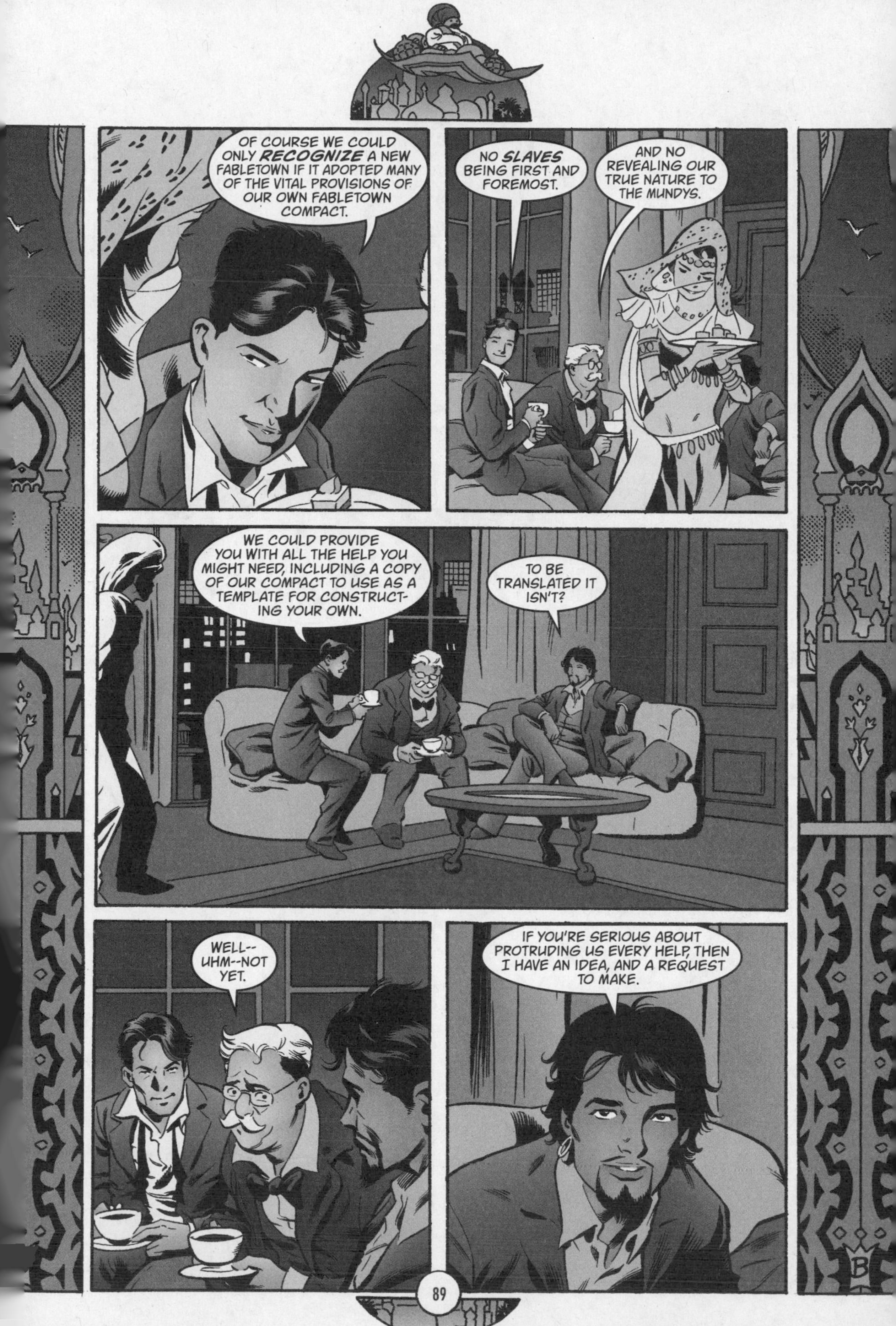
OF COURSE WE COULD ONLY RECOGNIZE A NEW FABLETOWN IF IT ADOPTED MANY OF THE VITAL PROVISIONS OF OUR OWN FABLETOWN COMPACT.
NO SLAVES BEING FIRST AND FOREMOST.
AND NO REVEALING OUR TRUE NATURE TO THE MUNDYS.
WE COULD PROVIDE YOU WITH ALL THE HELP YOU MIGHT NEED, INCLUDING A COPY OF OUR COMPACT TO USE AS A TEMPLATE FOR CONSTRUCTING YOUR OWN.
TO BE TRANSLATED IT ISN'T?
WELL--UHM--NOT YET.
IF YOU'RE SERIOUS ABOUT PROTRUDING US EVERY HELP, THEN I HAVE AN IDEA, AND A REQUEST TO MAKE.

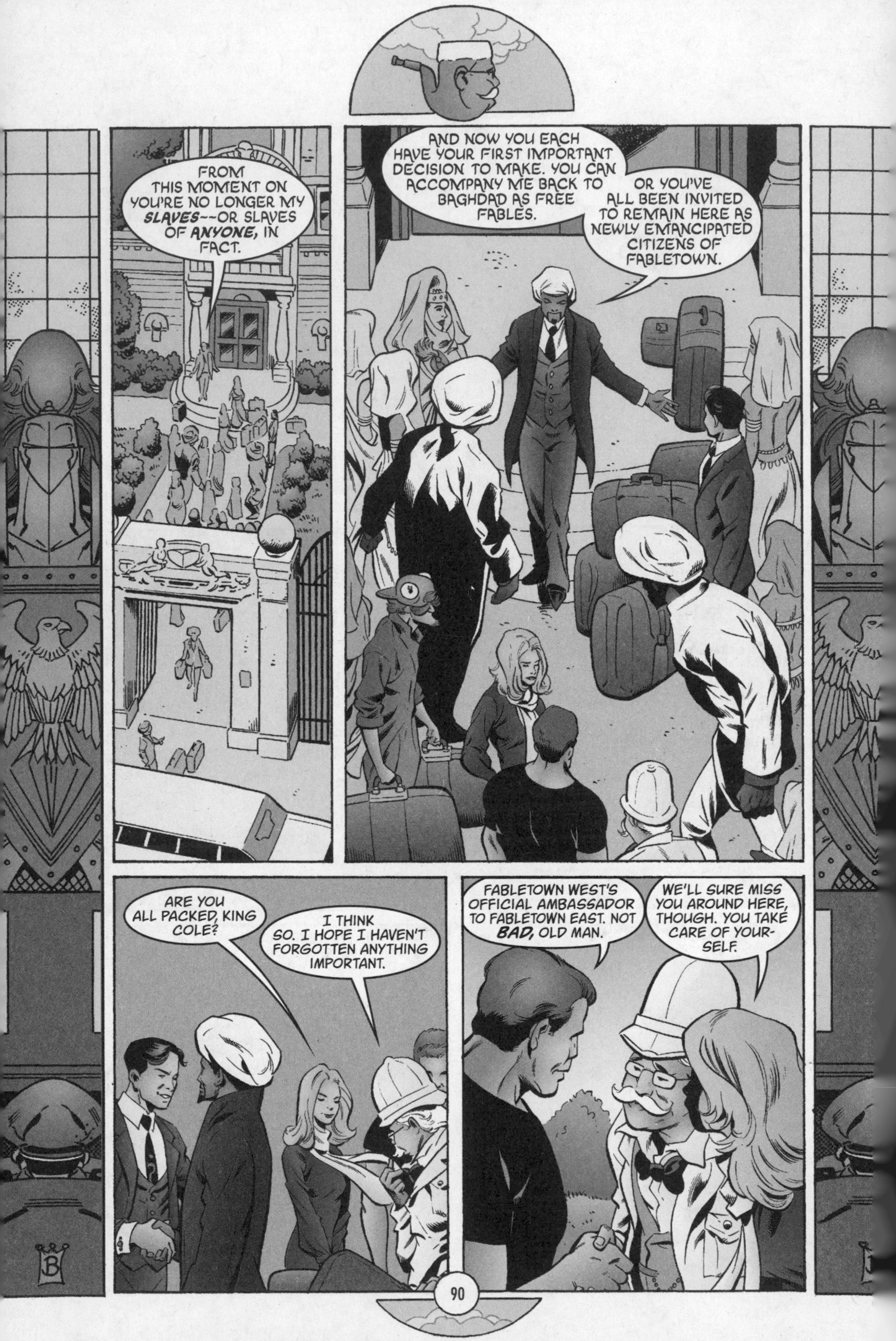

FROM THIS MOMENT ON YOU'RE NO LONGER MY SLAVES--OR SLAVES OF ANYONE, IN FACT.
AND NOW YOU EACH HAVE YOUR FIRST IMPORTANT DECISION TO MAKE. YOU CAN ACCOMPANY ME BACK TO BAGHDAD AS FREE FABLES.
OR YOU'VE ALL BEEN INVITED TO REMAIN HERE AS NEWLY EMANCIPATED CITIZENS OF FABLETOWN.
ARE YOU ALL PACKED, KING COLE?
I THINK SO. I HOPE I HAVEN'T FORGOTTEN ANYTHING IMPORTANT.
FABLETOWN WEST'S OFFICIAL AMBASSADOR TO FABLETOWN EAST. NOT BAD, OLD MAN.
WE'LL SURE MISS YOU AROUND HERE, THOUGH. YOU TAKE CARE OF YOURSELF.

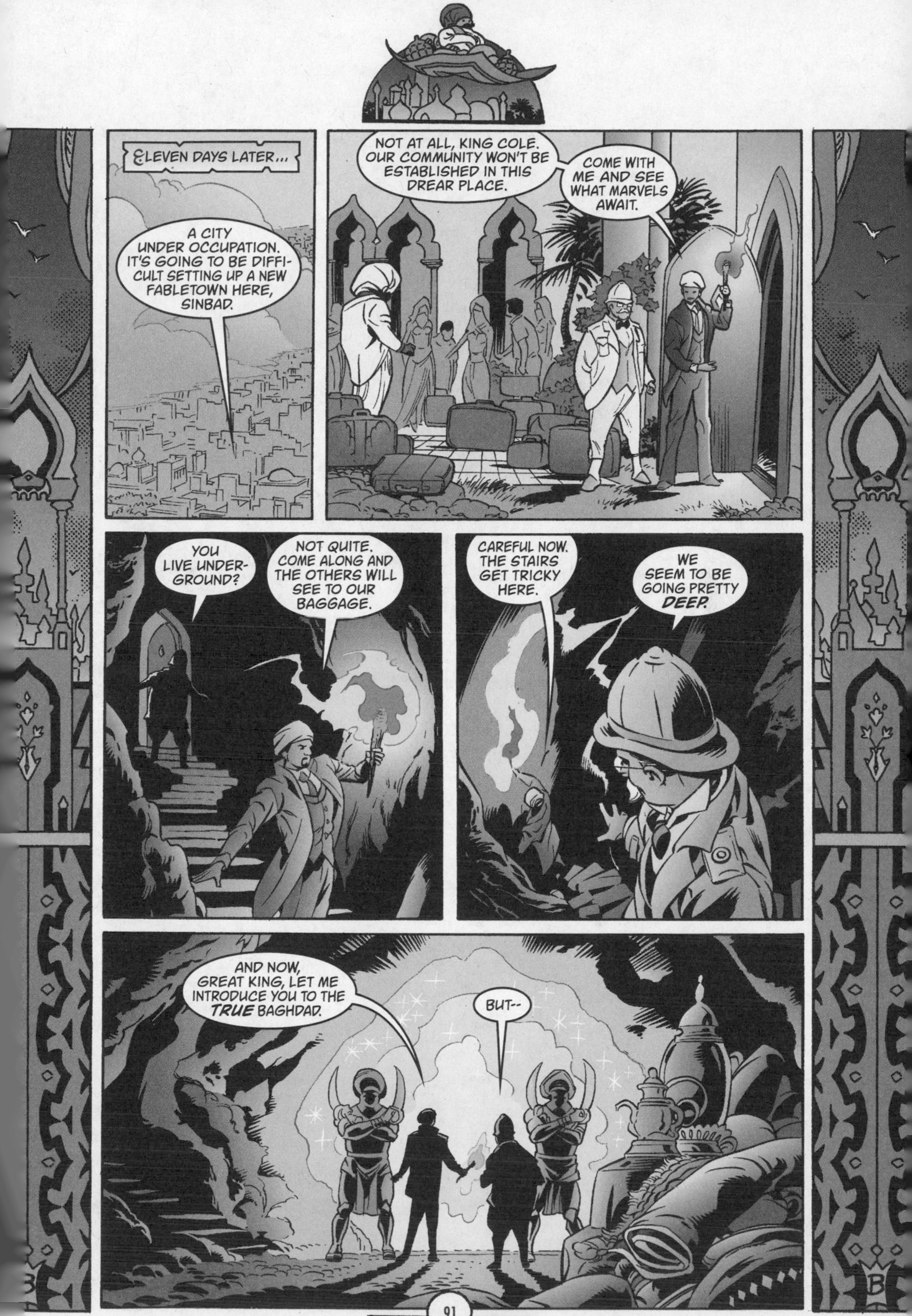
ELEVEN DAYS LATER...
A CITY UNDER OCCUPATION. IT'S GOING TO BE DIFFICULT SETTING UP A NEW FABLETOWN HERE, SINBAD.
NOT AT ALL, KING COLE. OUR COMMUNITY WON'T BE ESTABLISHED IN THIS DREAR PLACE.
COME WITH ME AND SEE WHAT MARVELS AWAIT.
YOU LIVE UNDERGROUND?
NOT QUITE. COME ALONG AND THE OTHERS WILL SEE TO OUR BAGGAGE.
CAREFUL NOW. THE STAIRS GET TRICKY HERE.
WE SEEM TO BE GOING PRETTY DEEP.
AND NOW, GREAT KING, LET ME INTRODUCE YOU TO THE TRUE BAGHDAD.
BUT--

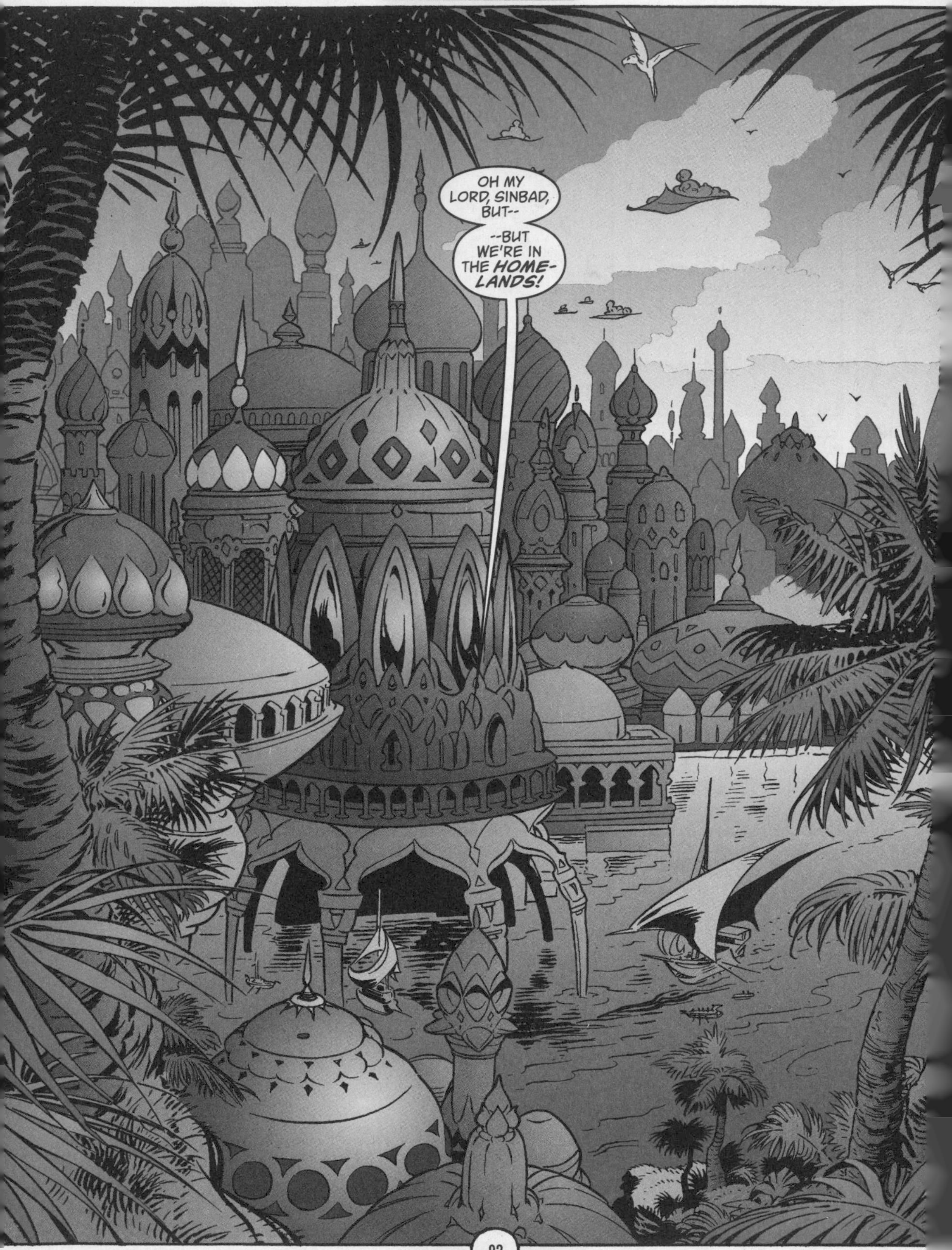
OH MY LORD, SINBAD, BUT--
--BUT WE'RE IN THE HOME-LANDS!

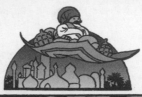

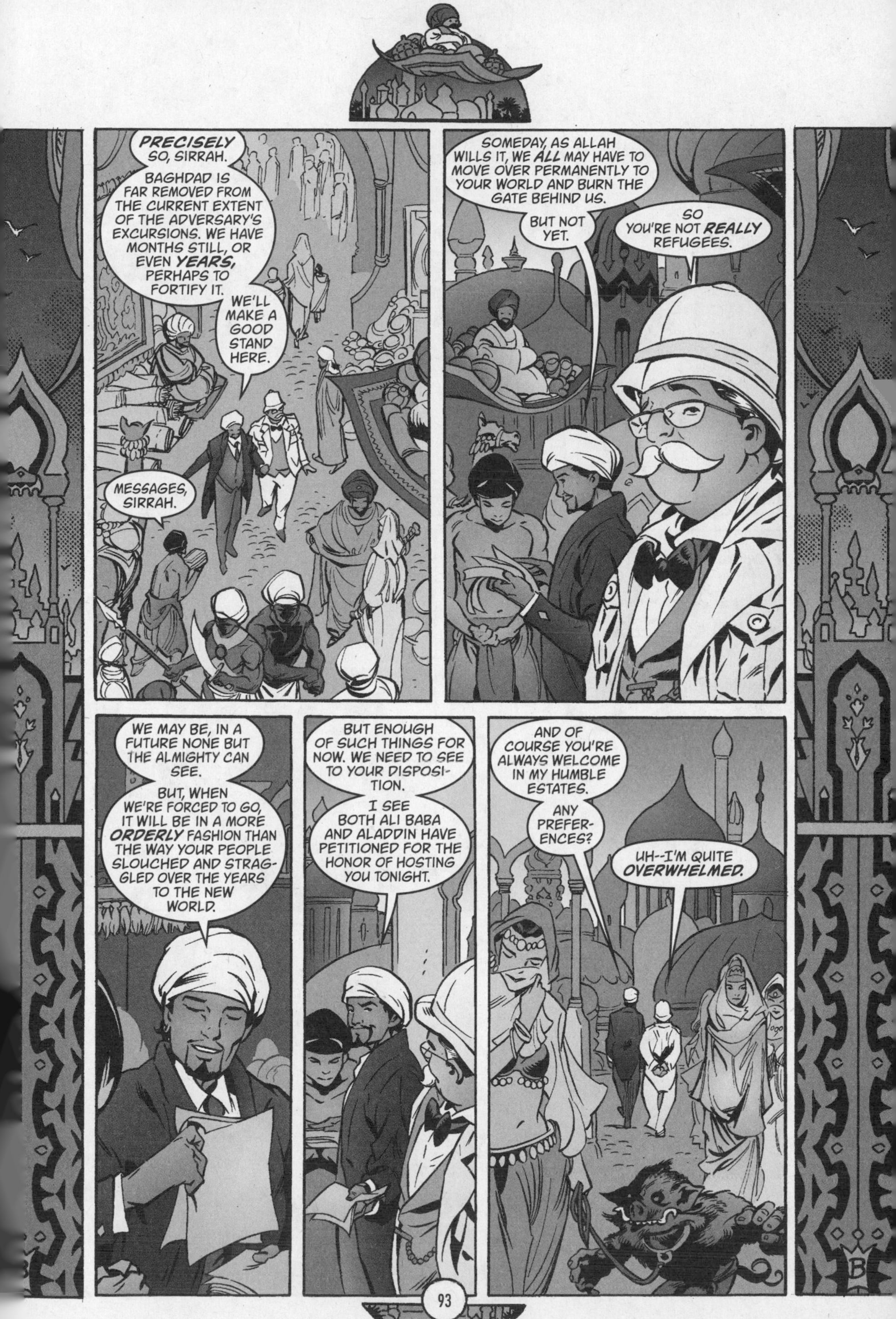

PRECISELY SO, SIRRAH.
BAGHDAD IS FAR REMOVED FROM THE CURRENT EXTENT OF THE ADVERSARY'S EXCURSIONS. WE HAVE MONTHS STILL, OR EVEN YEARS, PERHAPS TO FORTIFY IT.
WE'LL MAKE A GOOD STAND HERE.
MESSAGES, SIRRAH.
SOMEDAY, AS ALLAH WILLS IT, WE ALL MAY HAVE TO MOVE OVER PERMANENTLY TO YOUR WORLD AND BURN THE GATE BEHIND US.
BUT NOT YET.
SO YOU'RE NOT REALLY REFUGEES.
WE MAY BE, IN A FUTURE NONE BUT THE ALMIGHTY CAN SEE.
BUT, WHEN WE'RE FORCED TO GO, IT WILL BE IN A MORE ORDERLY FASHION THAN THE WAY YOUR PEOPLE SLOUCHED AND STRAGGLED OVER THE YEARS TO THE NEW WORLD.
BUT ENOUGH OF SUCH THINGS FOR NOW. WE NEED TO SEE TO YOUR DISPOSITION.
I SEE BOTH ALI BABA AND ALADDIN HAVE PETITIONED FOR THE HONOR OF HOSTING YOU TONIGHT.
AND OF COURSE YOU'RE ALWAYS WELCOME IN MY HUMBLE ESTATES.
ANY PREFERENCES?
UH--I'M QUITE OVERWHELMED.

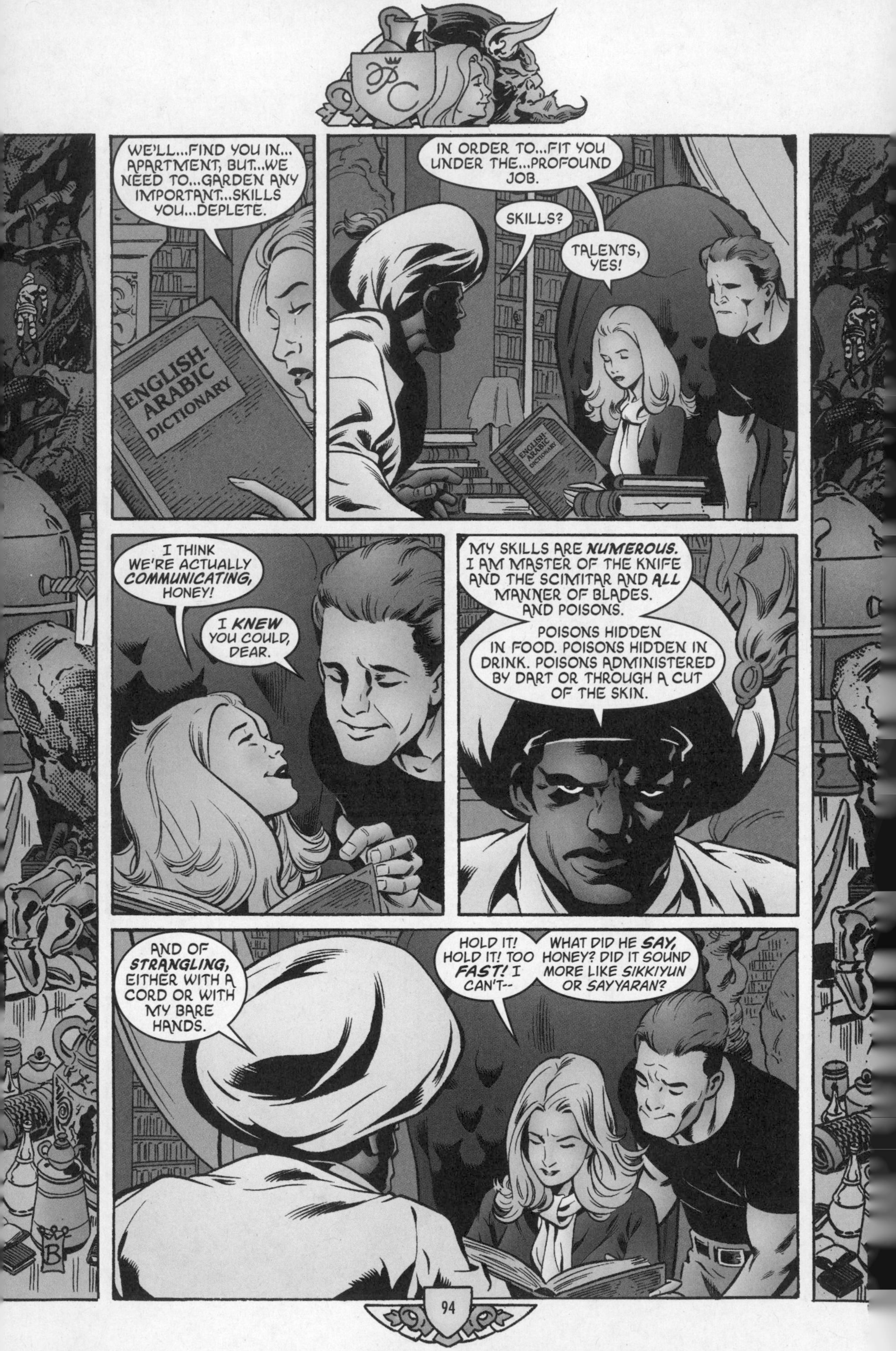
WE'LL...FIND YOU IN... APARTMENT, BUT...WE NEED TO...GARDEN ANY IMPORTANT...SKILLS YOU...DEPLETE.
ENGLISH-ARABIC DICTIONARY
IN ORDER TO...FIT YOU UNDER THE...PROFOUND JOB.
SKILLS?
TALENTS, YES!
ENGLISH-ARABIC DICTIONARY
I THINK WE'RE ACTUALLY COMMUNICATING, HONEY!
I KNEW YOU COULD, DEAR.
MY SKILLS ARE NUMEROUS. I AM MASTER OF THE KNIFE AND THE SCIMITAR AND ALL MANNER OF BLADES. AND POISONS.
POISONS HIDDEN IN FOOD. POISONS HIDDEN IN DRINK. POISONS ADMINISTERED BY DART OR THROUGH A CUT OF THE SKIN.
AND OF STRANGLING, EITHER WITH A CORD OR WITH MY BARE HANDS.
HOLD IT! HOLD IT! TOO FAST! I CAN'T--
WHAT DID HE SAY, HONEY? DID IT SOUND MORE LIKE SIKKIYUN OR SAYYARAN?

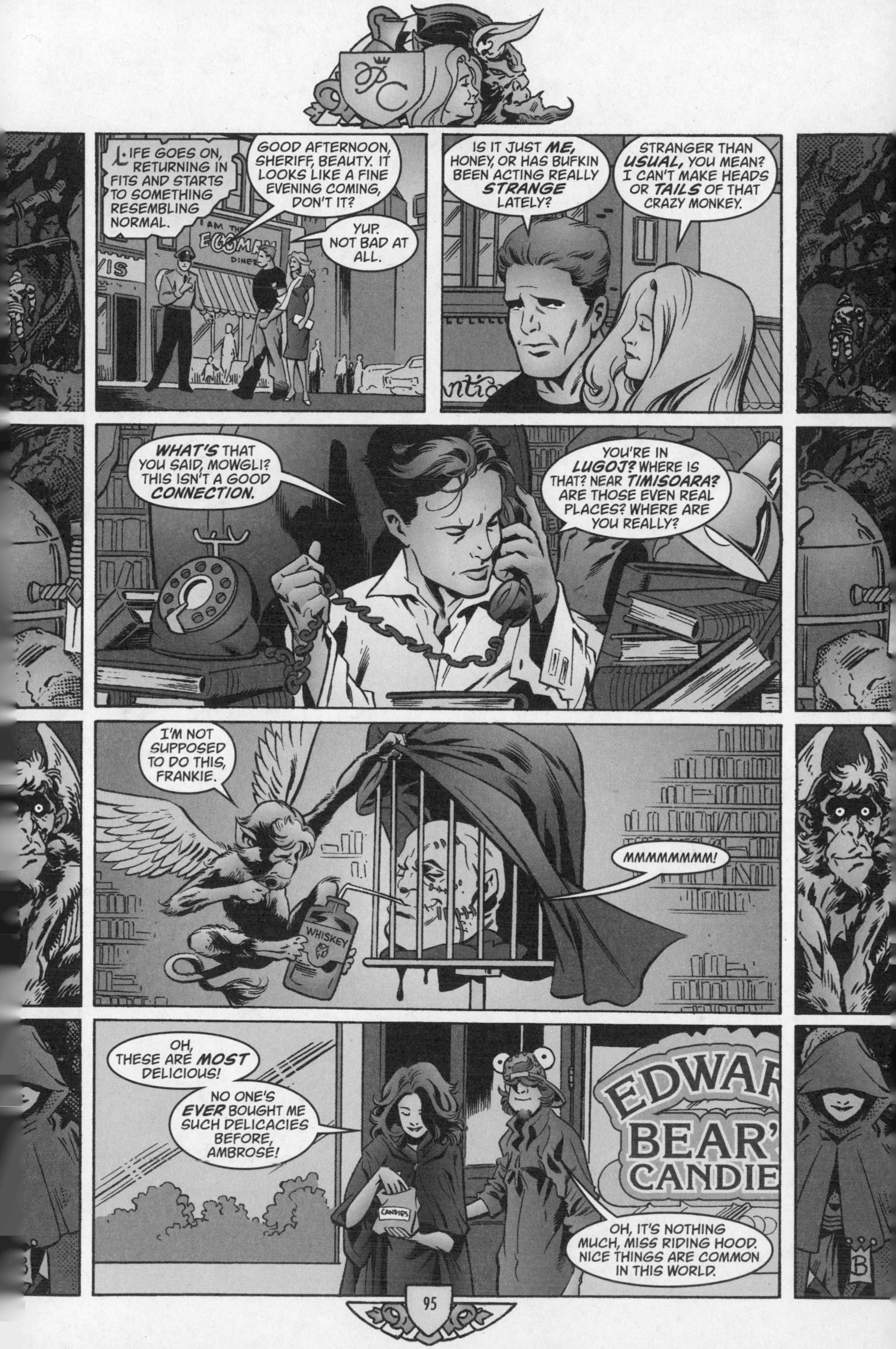
LIFE GOES ON, RETURNING IN FITS AND STARTS TO SOMETHING RESEMBLING NORMAL.
GOOD AFTERNOON, SHERIFF, BEAUTY. IT LOOKS LIKE A FINE EVENING COMING, DON'T IT?
YUP. NOT BAD AT ALL.
IS IT JUST ME, HONEY, OR HAS BUFKIN BEEN ACTING REALLY STRANGE LATELY?
STRANGER THAN USUAL, YOU MEAN? I CAN'T MAKE HEADS OR TAILS OF THAT CRAZY MONKEY.
WHAT'S THAT YOU SAID, MOWGLI? THIS ISN'T A GOOD CONNECTION.
YOU'RE IN LUGOJ? WHERE IS THAT? NEAR TIMISOARA? ARE THOSE EVEN REAL PLACES? WHERE ARE YOU REALLY?
I'M NOT SUPPOSED TO DO THIS, FRANKIE.
WHISKEY
MMMMMMMM!
OH, THESE ARE MOST DELICIOUS!
NO ONE'S EVER BOUGHT ME SUCH DELICACIES BEFORE, AMBROSE!
EDWAR
BEAR'
CANDIE
CANDIES
OH, IT'S NOTHING MUCH, MISS RIDING HOOD. NICE THINGS ARE COMMON IN THIS WORLD.

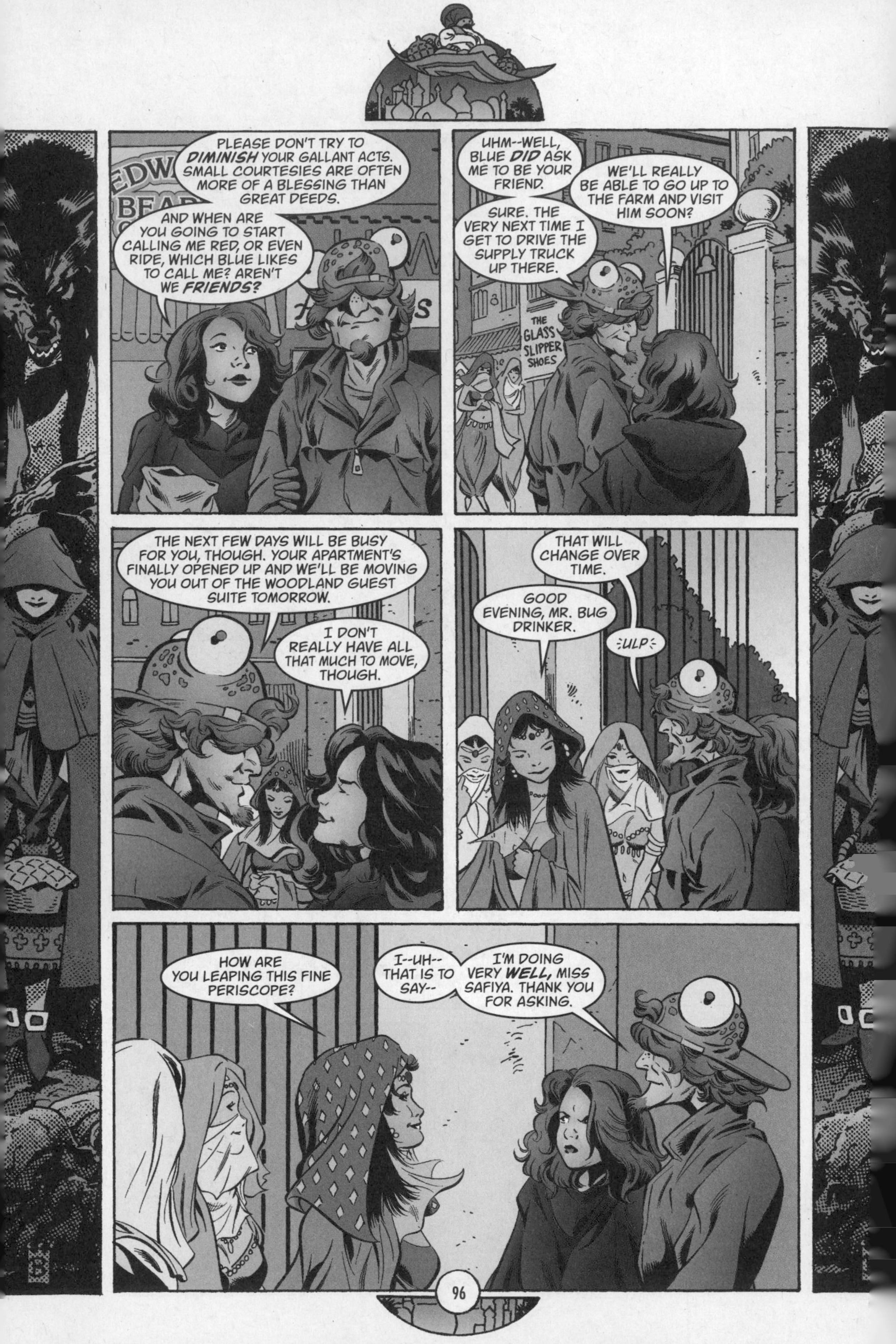
PLEASE DON'T TRY TO DIMINISH YOUR GALLANT ACTS. SMALL COURTESIES ARE OFTEN MORE OF A BLESSING THAN GREAT DEEDS.
AND WHEN ARE YOU GOING TO START CALLING ME RED, OR EVEN RIDE, WHICH BLUE LIKES TO CALL ME? AREN'T WE FRIENDS?
UHM--WELL, BLUE DID ASK ME TO BE YOUR FRIEND.
WE'LL REALLY BE ABLE TO GO UP TO THE FARM AND VISIT HIM SOON?
SURE. THE VERY NEXT TIME I GET TO DRIVE THE SUPPLY TRUCK UP THERE.
THE GLASS SLIPPER SHOES
THE NEXT FEW DAYS WILL BE BUSY FOR YOU, THOUGH. YOUR APARTMENT'S FINALLY OPENED UP AND WE'LL BE MOVING YOU OUT OF THE WOODLAND GUEST SUITE TOMORROW.
I DON'T REALLY HAVE ALL THAT MUCH TO MOVE, THOUGH.
THAT WILL CHANGE OVER TIME.
GOOD EVENING, MR. BUG DRINKER.
ULP
HOW ARE YOU LEAPING THIS FINE PERISCOPE?
I--UH--THAT IS TO SAY--
I'M DOING VERY WELL, MISS SAFIYA. THANK YOU FOR ASKING.

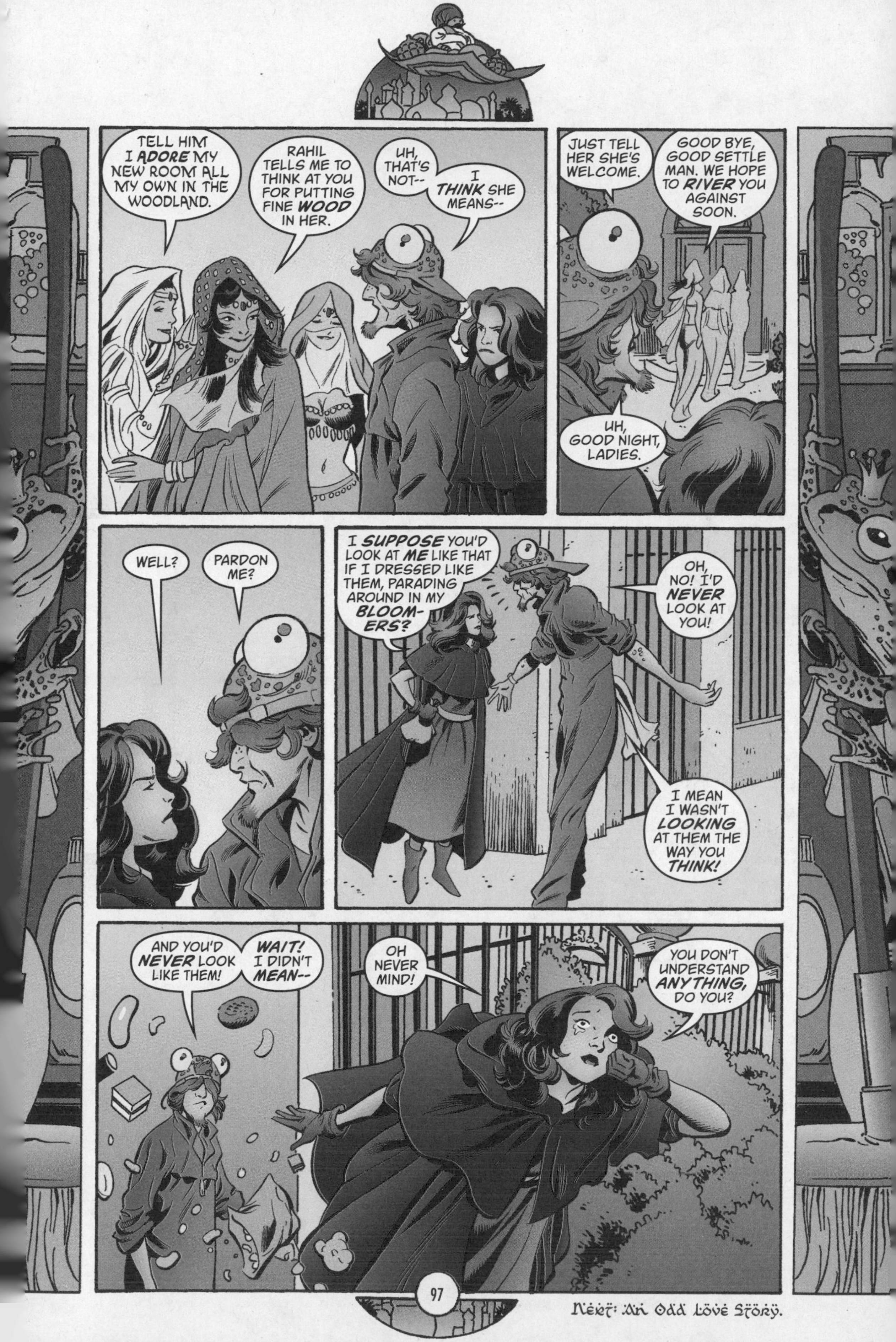
TELL HIM I ADORE MY NEW ROOM ALL MY OWN IN THE WOODLAND.
RAHIL TELLS ME TO THINK AT YOU FOR PUTTING FINE WOOD IN HER.
UH, THAT'S NOT--
I THINK SHE MEANS--
JUST TELL HER SHE'S WELCOME.
GOOD BYE, GOOD SETTLE MAN. WE HOPE TO RIVER YOU AGAINST SOON.
UH, GOOD NIGHT, LADIES.
WELL?
PARDON ME?
I SUPPOSE YOU'D LOOK AT ME LIKE THAT IF I DRESSED LIKE THEM, PARADING AROUND IN MY BLOOMERS?
OH, NO! I'D NEVER LOOK AT YOU!
I MEAN I WASN'T LOOKING AT THEM THE WAY YOU THINK!
AND YOU'D NEVER LOOK LIKE THEM!
WAIT! I DIDN'T MEAN--
OH NEVER MIND!
YOU DON'T UNDERSTAND ANYTHING, DO YOU?

Next: An Odd Love Story.

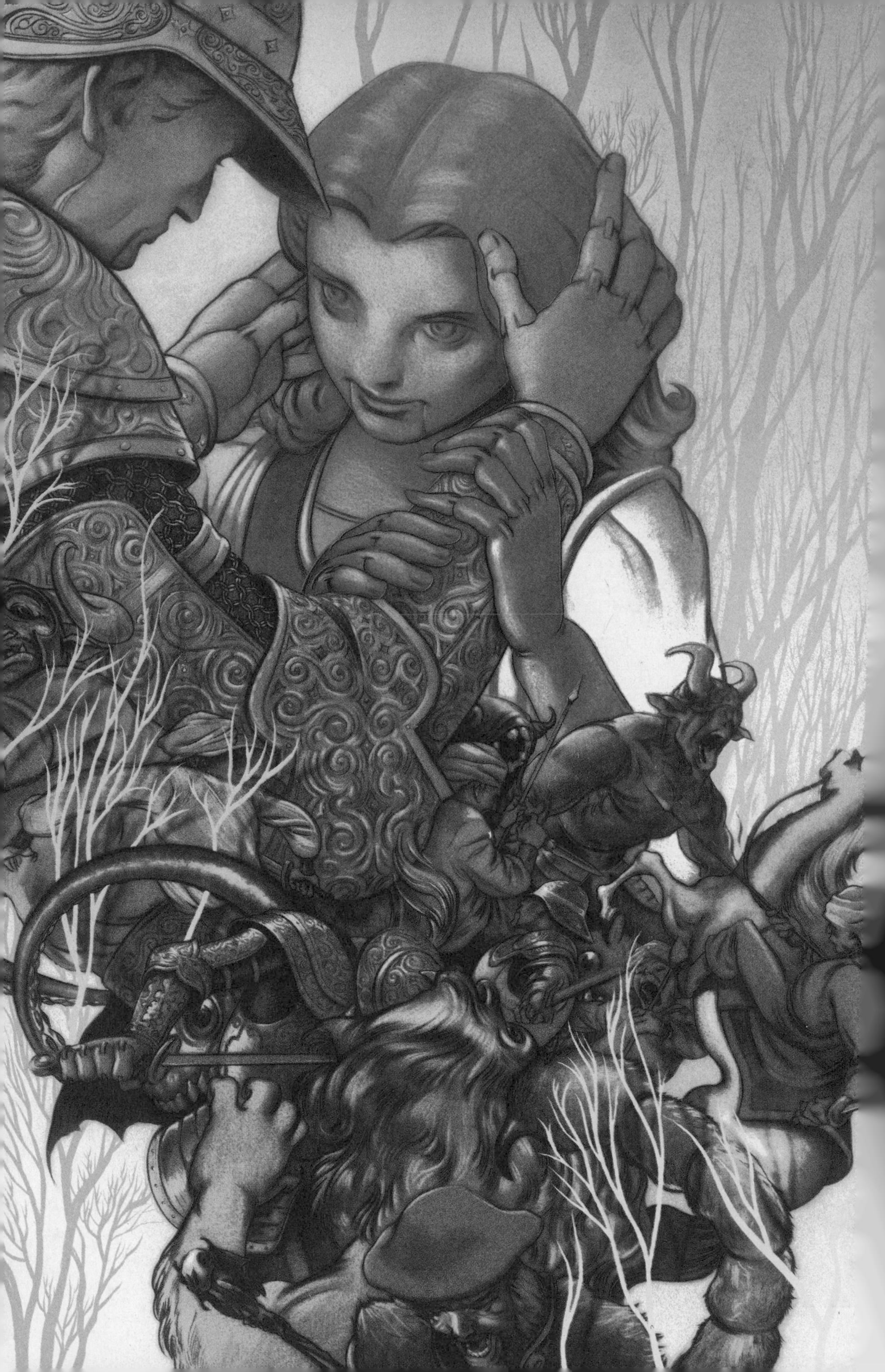

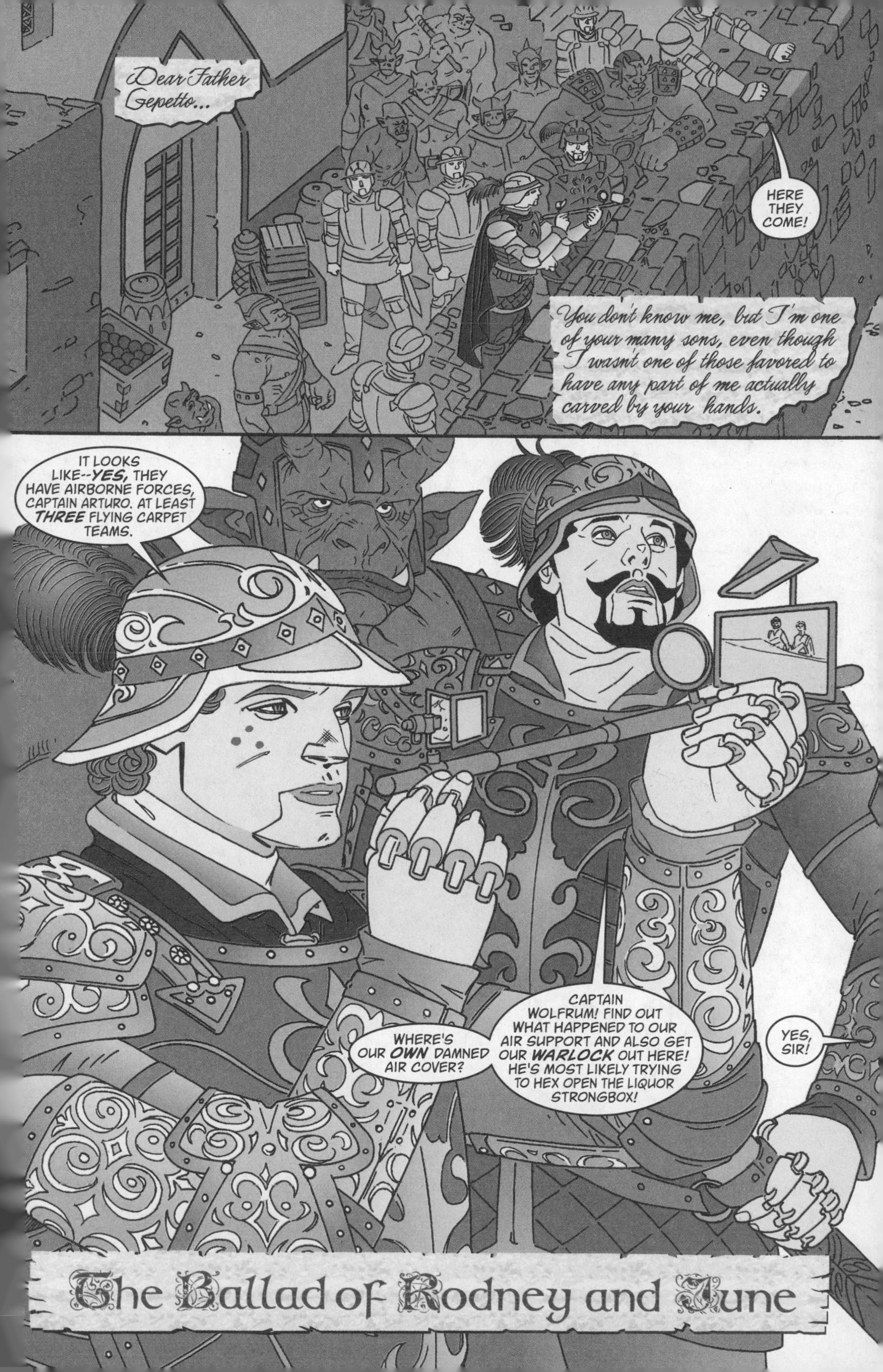
Dear Father Gepetto...
HERE THEY COME!
You don't know me, but I'm one of your many sons, even though I wasn't one of those favored to have any part of me actually carved by your hands.
IT LOOKS LIKE--YES, THEY HAVE AIRBORNE FORCES, CAPTAIN ARTURO. AT LEAST THREE FLYING CARPET TEAMS.
WHERE'S OUR OWN DAMNED AIR COVER?
CAPTAIN WOLFRUM! FIND OUT WHAT HAPPENED TO OUR AIR SUPPORT AND ALSO GET OUR WARLOCK OUT HERE! HE'S MOST LIKELY TRYING TO HEX OPEN THE LIQUOR STRONGBOX!
YES, SIR!
The Ballad of Rodney and June

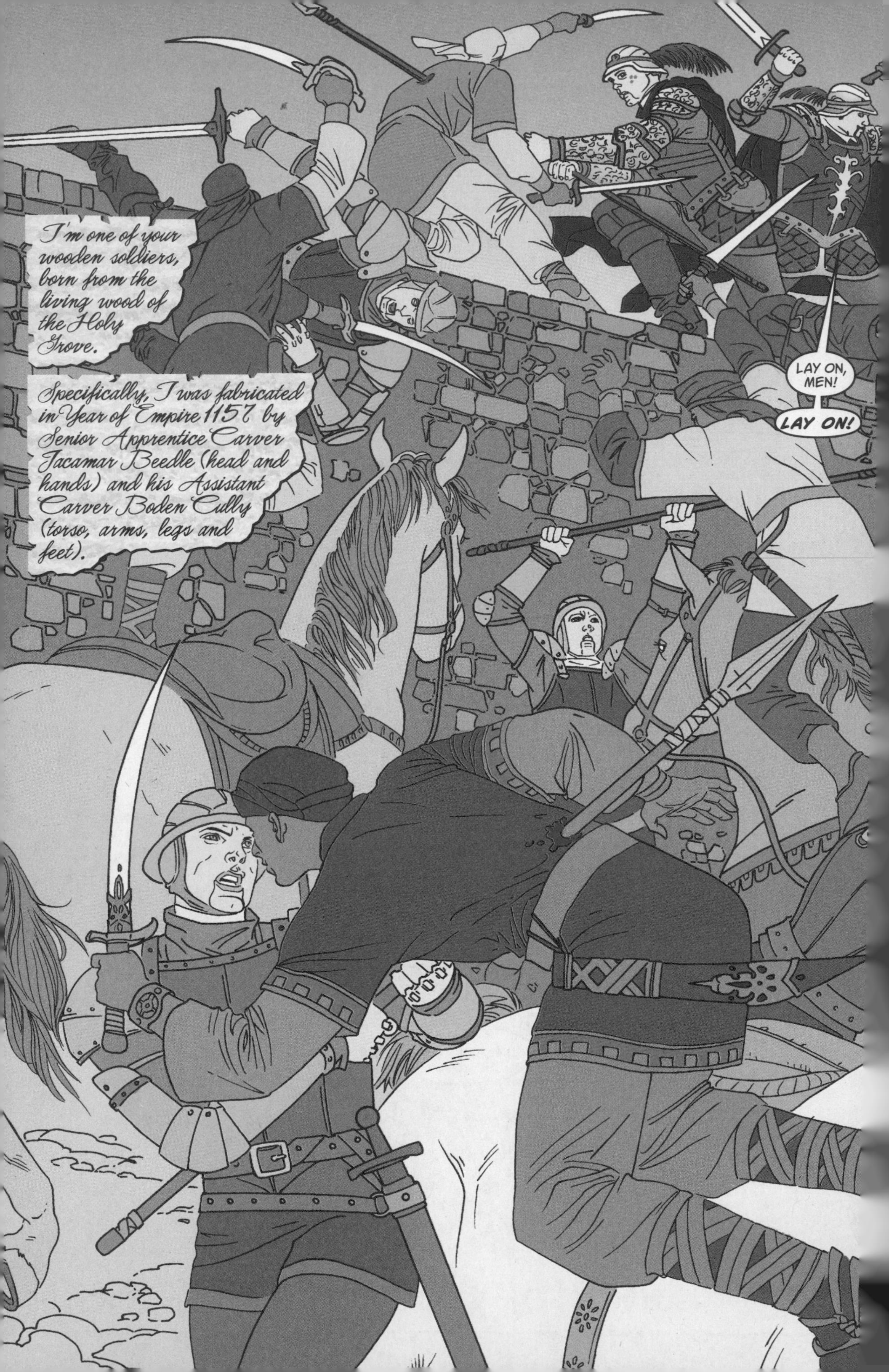
I'm one of your wooden soldiers, born from the living wood of the Holy Grove.
Specifically, I was fabricated in Year of Empire 1157 by Senior Apprentice Carver Jacamar Beedle (head and hands) and his Assistant Carver Boden Cully (torso, arms, legs and feet).
LAY ON, MEN!
LAY ON!

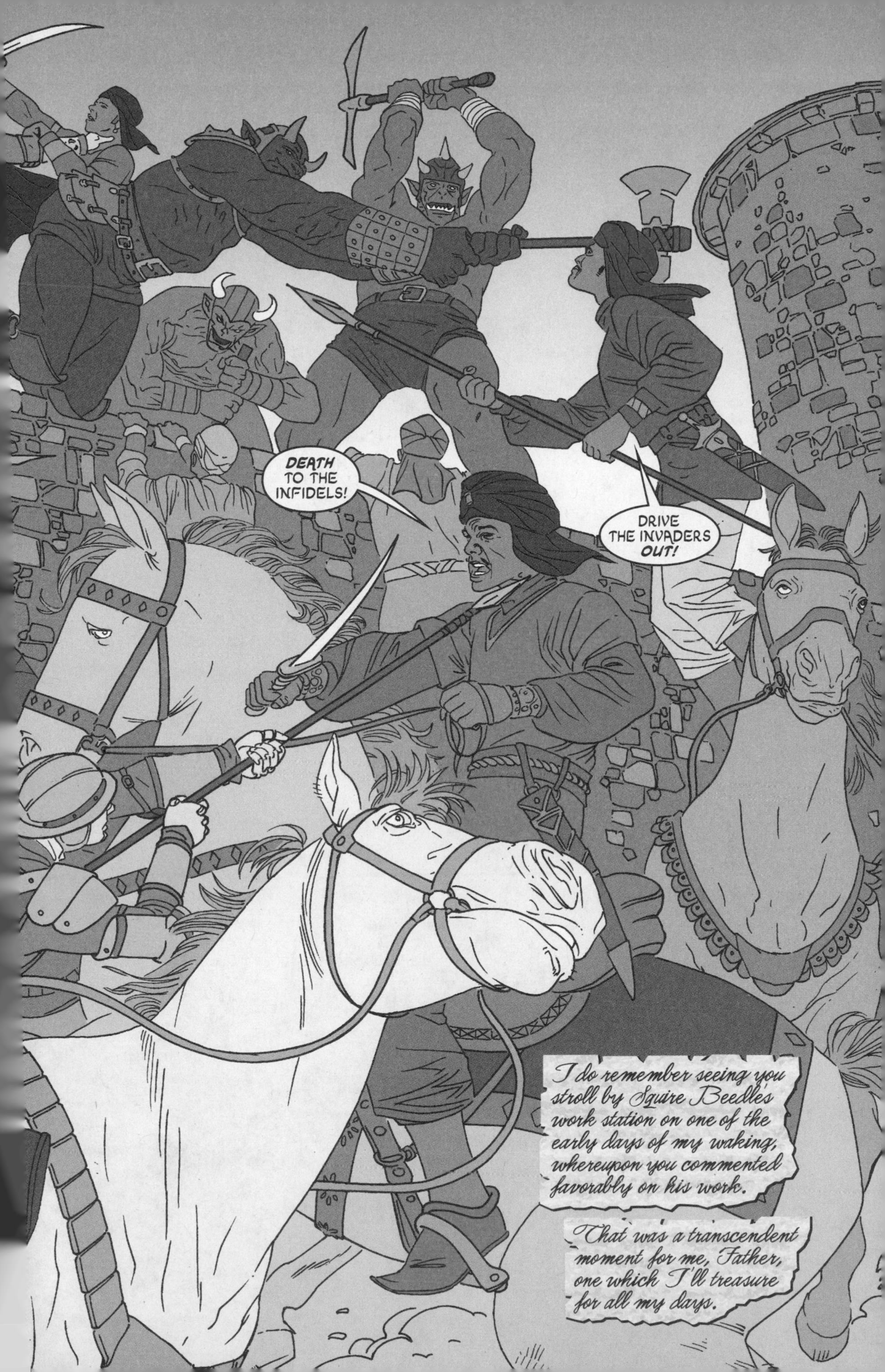
DEATH TO THE INFIDELS!
DRIVE THE INVADERS OUT!
I do remember seeing you stroll by Squire Beedle's work station on one of the early days of my waking, whereupon you commented favorably on his work.
That was a transcendent moment for me, Father, one which I'll treasure for all my days.

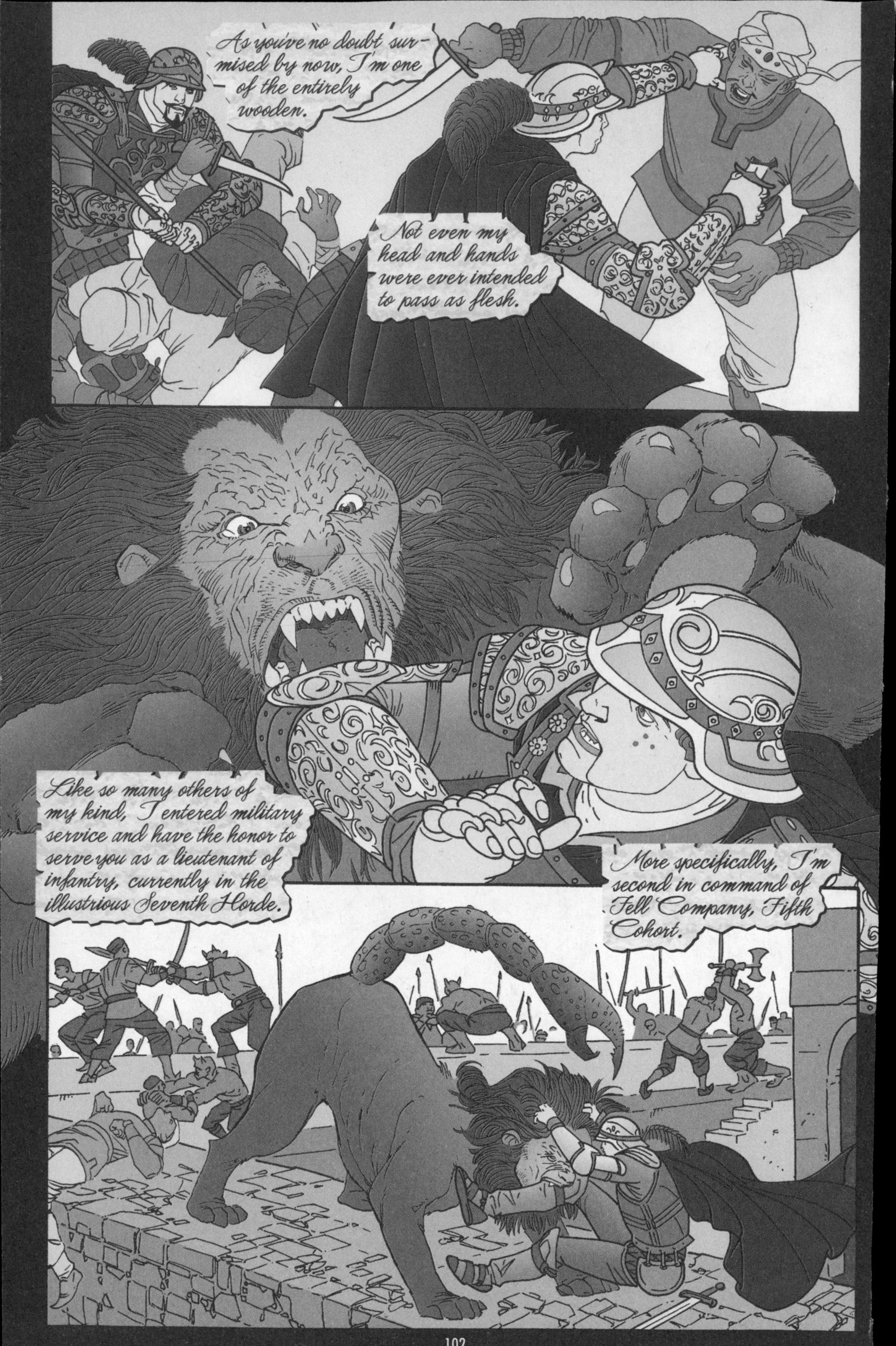
As you've no doubt surmised by now, I'm one of the entirely wooden.
Not even my head and hands were ever intended to pass as flesh.
Like so many others of my kind, I entered military service and have the honor to serve you as a lieutenant of infantry, currently in the illustrious Seventh Horde.
More specifically, I'm second in command of Fell Company, Fifth Cohort.

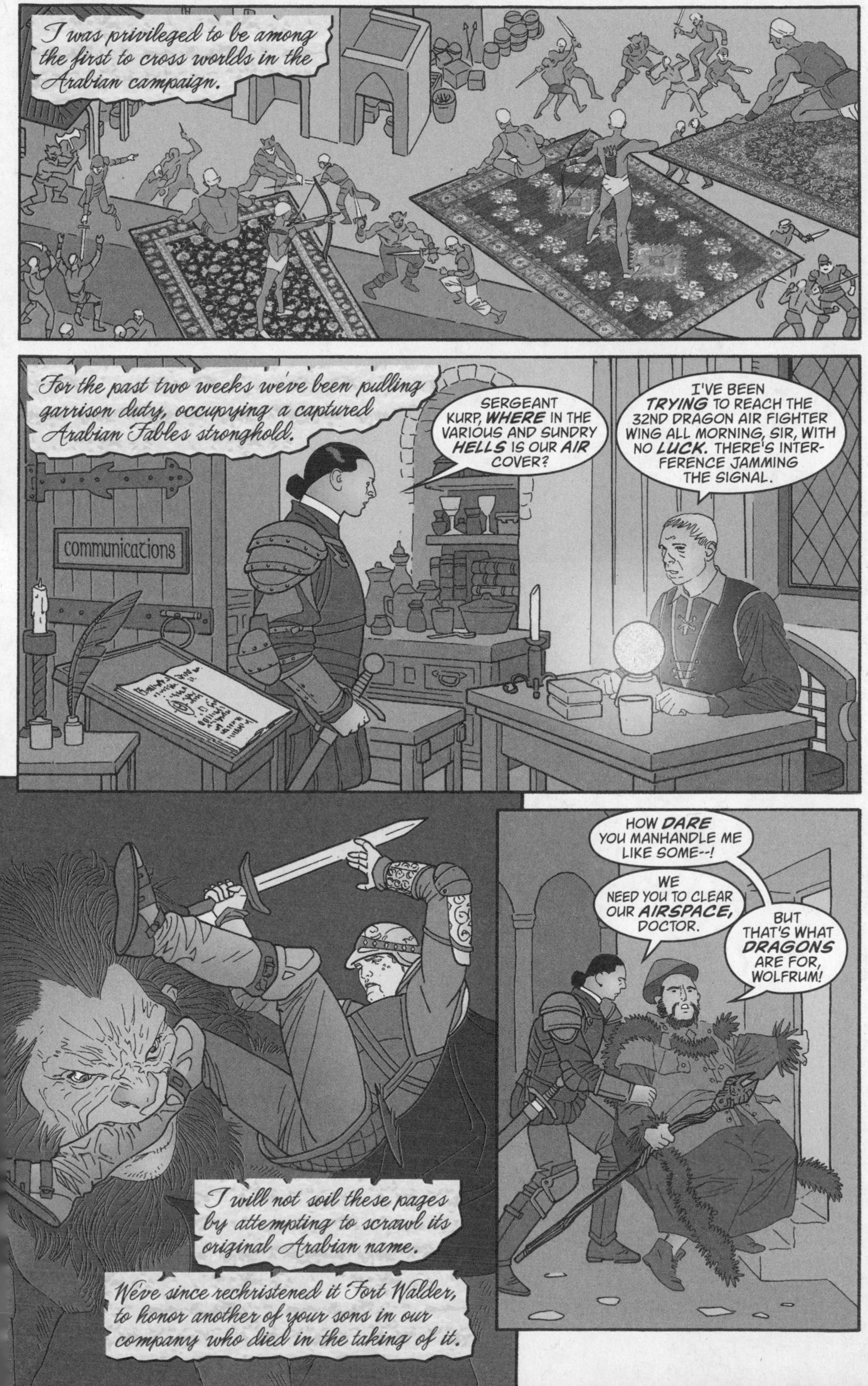

I was privileged to be among the first to cross worlds in the Arabian campaign.
For the past two weeks we've been pulling garrison duty, occupying a captured Arabian Fables stronghold.
SERGEANT KURP, WHERE IN THE VARIOUS AND SUNDRY HELLS IS OUR AIR COVER?
I'VE BEEN TRYING TO REACH THE 32ND DRAGON AIR FIGHTER WING ALL MORNING, SIR, WITH NO LUCK. THERE'S INTERFERENCE JAMMING THE SIGNAL.
communications
I will not soil these pages by attempting to scrawl its original Arabian name.
We've since rechristened it Fort Walder, to honor another of your sons in our company who died in the taking of it.
HOW DARE YOU MANHANDLE ME LIKE SOME--!
WE NEED YOU TO CLEAR OUR AIRSPACE, DOCTOR.
BUT THAT'S WHAT DRAGONS ARE FOR, WOLFRUM!

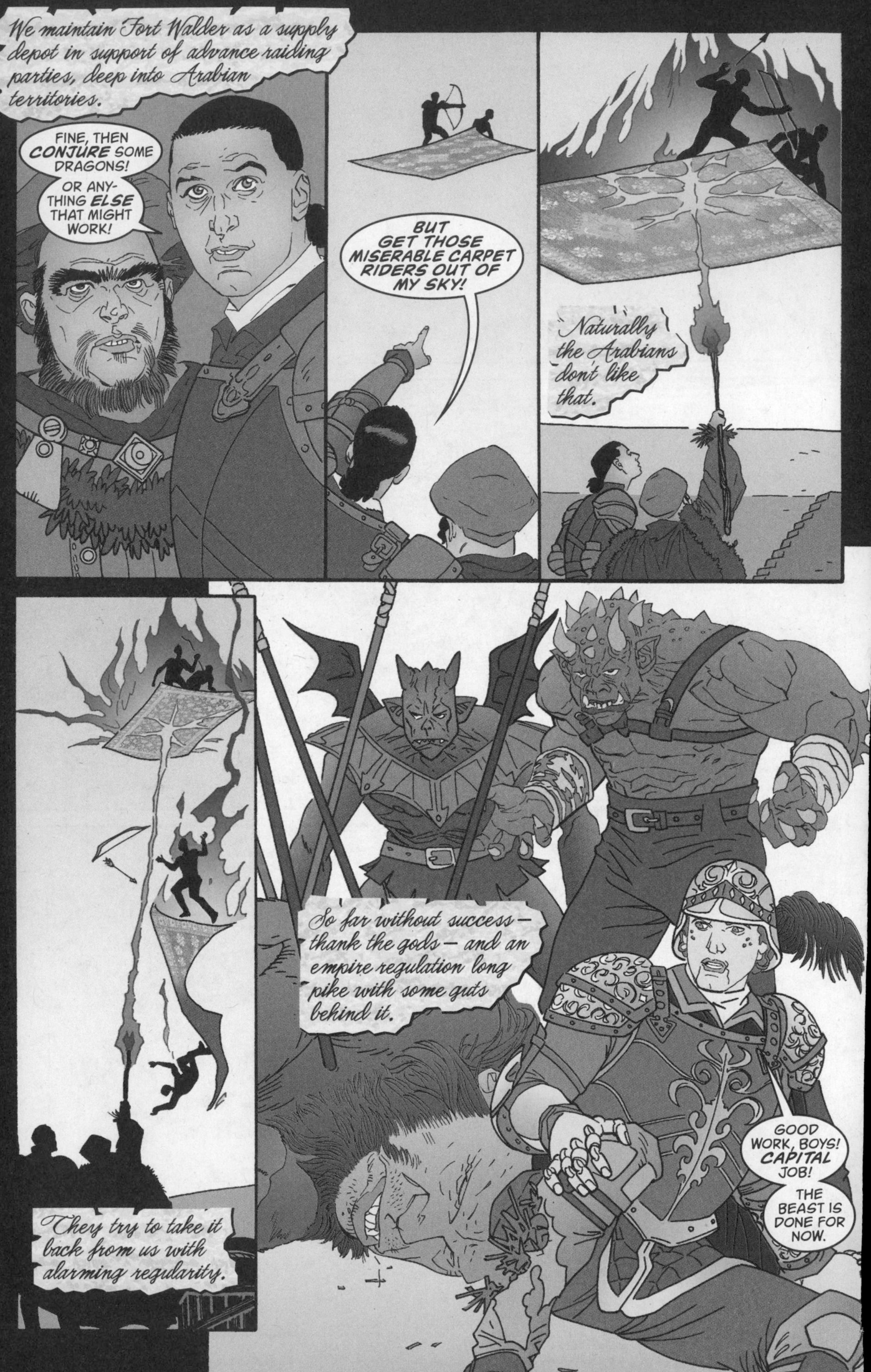
We maintain Fort Walder as a supply depot in support of advance raiding parties, deep into Arabian territories.
FINE, THEN CONJURE SOME DRAGONS!
OR ANYTHING ELSE THAT MIGHT WORK!
BUT GET THOSE MISERABLE CARPET RIDERS OUT OF MY SKY!
Naturally the Arabians don't like that.
They try to take it back from us with alarming regularity.
So far without success— thank the gods— and an empire regulation long pike with some guts behind it.
GOOD WORK, BOYS! CAPITAL JOB!
THE BEAST IS DONE FOR NOW.

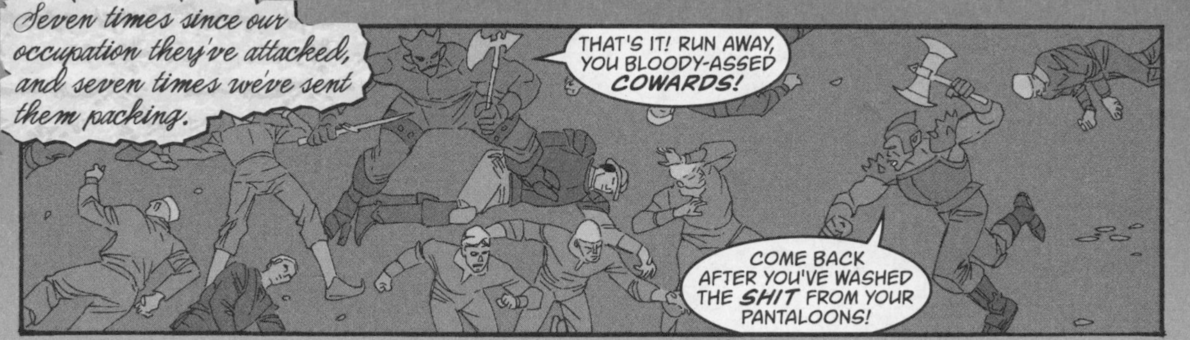
Seven times since our occupation they've attacked, and seven times we've sent them packing.
THAT'S IT! RUN AWAY, YOU BLOODY-ASSED COWARDS!
COME BACK AFTER YOU'VE WASHED THE SHIT FROM YOUR PANTALOONS!

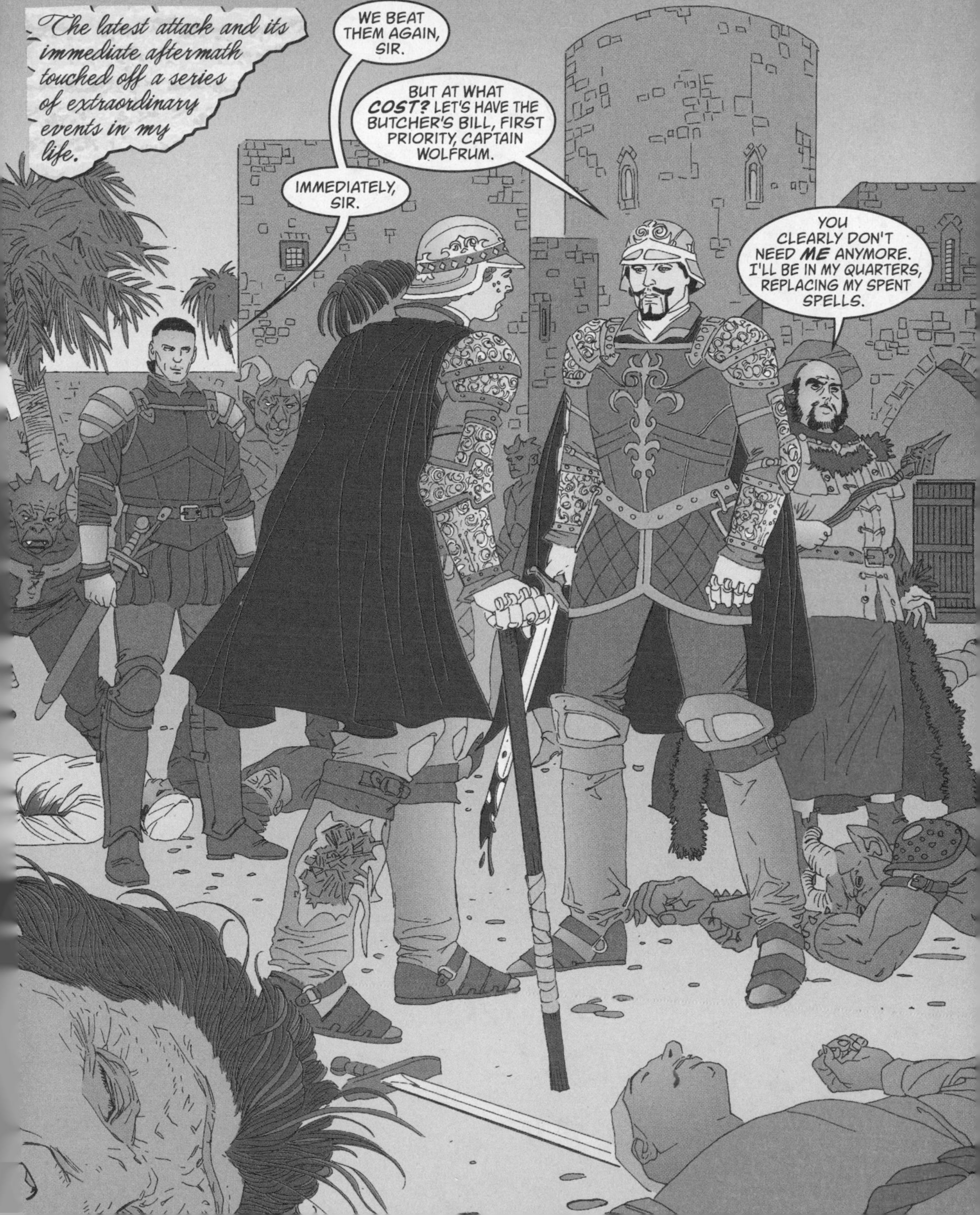
The latest attack and its immediate aftermath touched off a series of extraordinary events in my life.
WE BEAT THEM AGAIN, SIR.
BUT AT WHAT COST? LET'S HAVE THE BUTCHER'S BILL, FIRST PRIORITY, CAPTAIN WOLFRUM.
IMMEDIATELY, SIR.
YOU CLEARLY DON'T NEED ME ANYMORE. I'LL BE IN MY QUARTERS, REPLACING MY SPENT SPELLS.

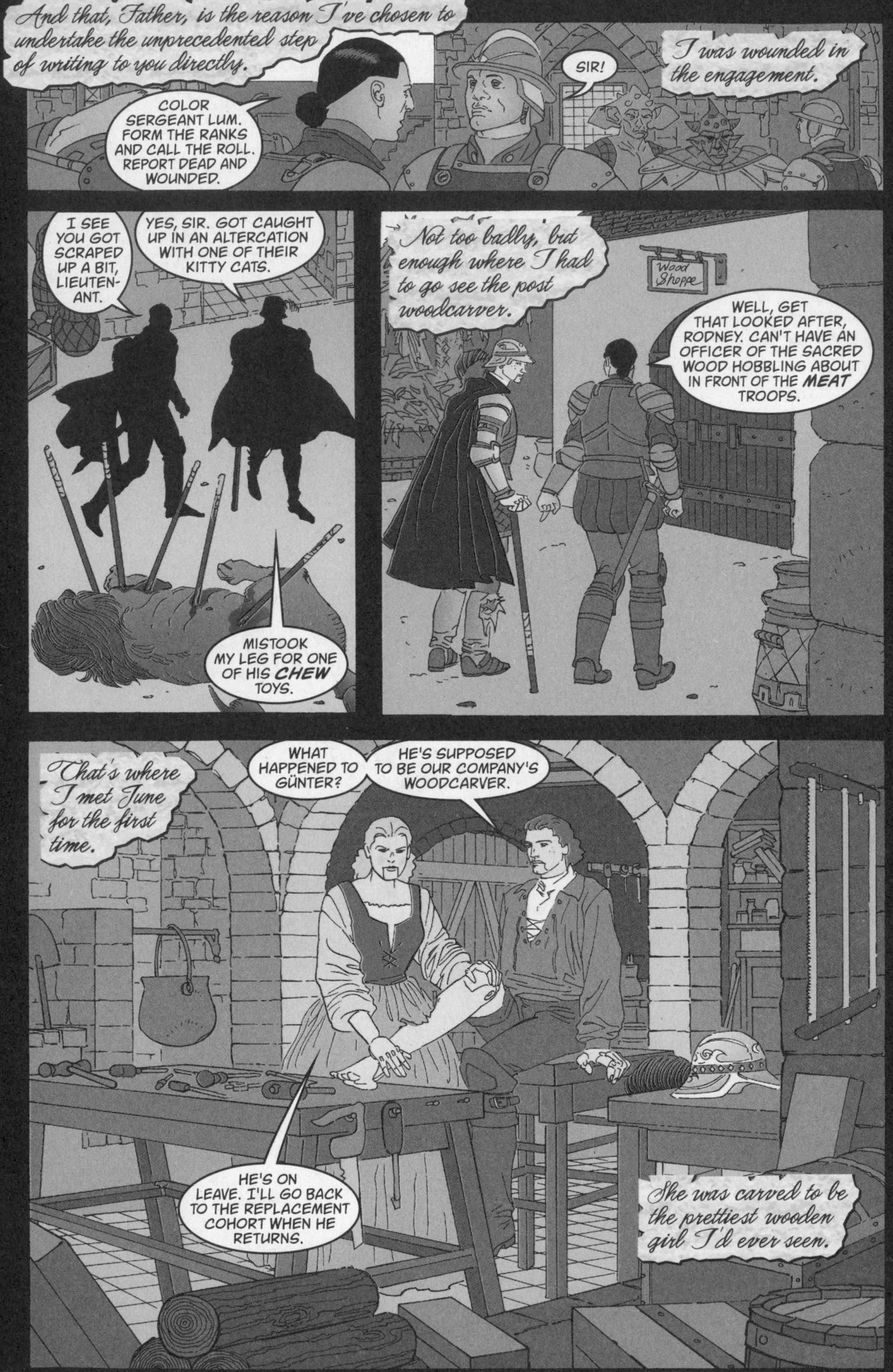
And that, Father, is the reason I've chosen to undertake the unprecedented step of writing to you directly.
COLOR SERGEANT LUM. FORM THE RANKS AND CALL THE ROLL. REPORT DEAD AND WOUNDED.
SIR!
I was wounded in the engagement.
I SEE YOU GOT SCRAPED UP A BIT, LIEUTEN-ANT.
YES, SIR. GOT CAUGHT UP IN AN ALTERCATION WITH ONE OF THEIR KITTY CATS.
MISTOOK MY LEG FOR ONE OF HIS CHEW TOYS.
Not too badly, but enough where I had to go see the post woodcarver.
Wood Shoppe
WELL, GET THAT LOOKED AFTER, RODNEY. CAN'T HAVE AN OFFICER OF THE SACRED WOOD HOBBLING ABOUT IN FRONT OF THE MEAT TROOPS.
That's where I met June for the first time.
WHAT HAPPENED TO GÜNTER?
HE'S SUPPOSED TO BE OUR COMPANY'S WOODCARVER.
HE'S ON LEAVE. I'LL GO BACK TO THE REPLACEMENT COHORT WHEN HE RETURNS.
She was carved to be the prettiest wooden girl I'd ever seen.

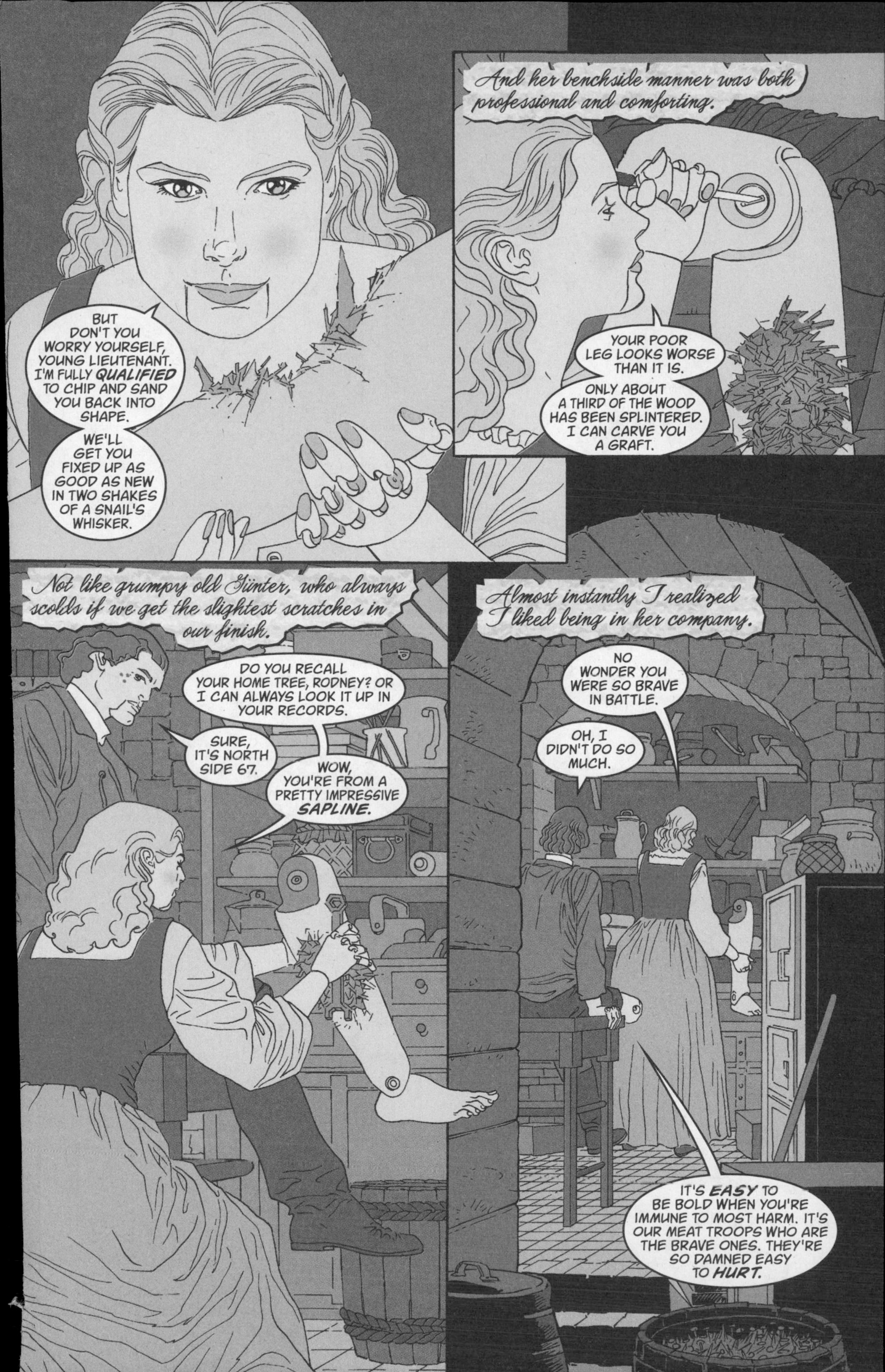
BUT DON'T YOU WORRY YOURSELF, YOUNG LIEUTENANT. I'M FULLY QUALIFIED TO CHIP AND SAND YOU BACK INTO SHAPE.
WE'LL GET YOU FIXED UP AS GOOD AS NEW IN TWO SHAKES OF A SNAIL'S WHISKER.
And her benchside manner was both professional and comforting.
YOUR POOR LEG LOOKS WORSE THAN IT IS.
ONLY ABOUT A THIRD OF THE WOOD HAS BEEN SPLINTERED. I CAN CARVE YOU A GRAFT.
Not like grumpy old Günter, who always scolds if we get the slightest scratches in our finish.
DO YOU RECALL YOUR HOME TREE, RODNEY? OR I CAN ALWAYS LOOK IT UP IN YOUR RECORDS.
SURE, IT'S NORTH SIDE 67.
WOW, YOU'RE FROM A PRETTY IMPRESSIVE SAPLINE.
Almost instantly I realized I liked being in her company.
NO WONDER YOU WERE SO BRAVE IN BATTLE.
OH, I DIDN'T DO SO MUCH.
IT'S EASY TO BE BOLD WHEN YOU'RE IMMUNE TO MOST HARM. IT'S OUR MEAT TROOPS WHO ARE THE BRAVE ONES. THEY'RE SO DAMNED EASY TO HURT.

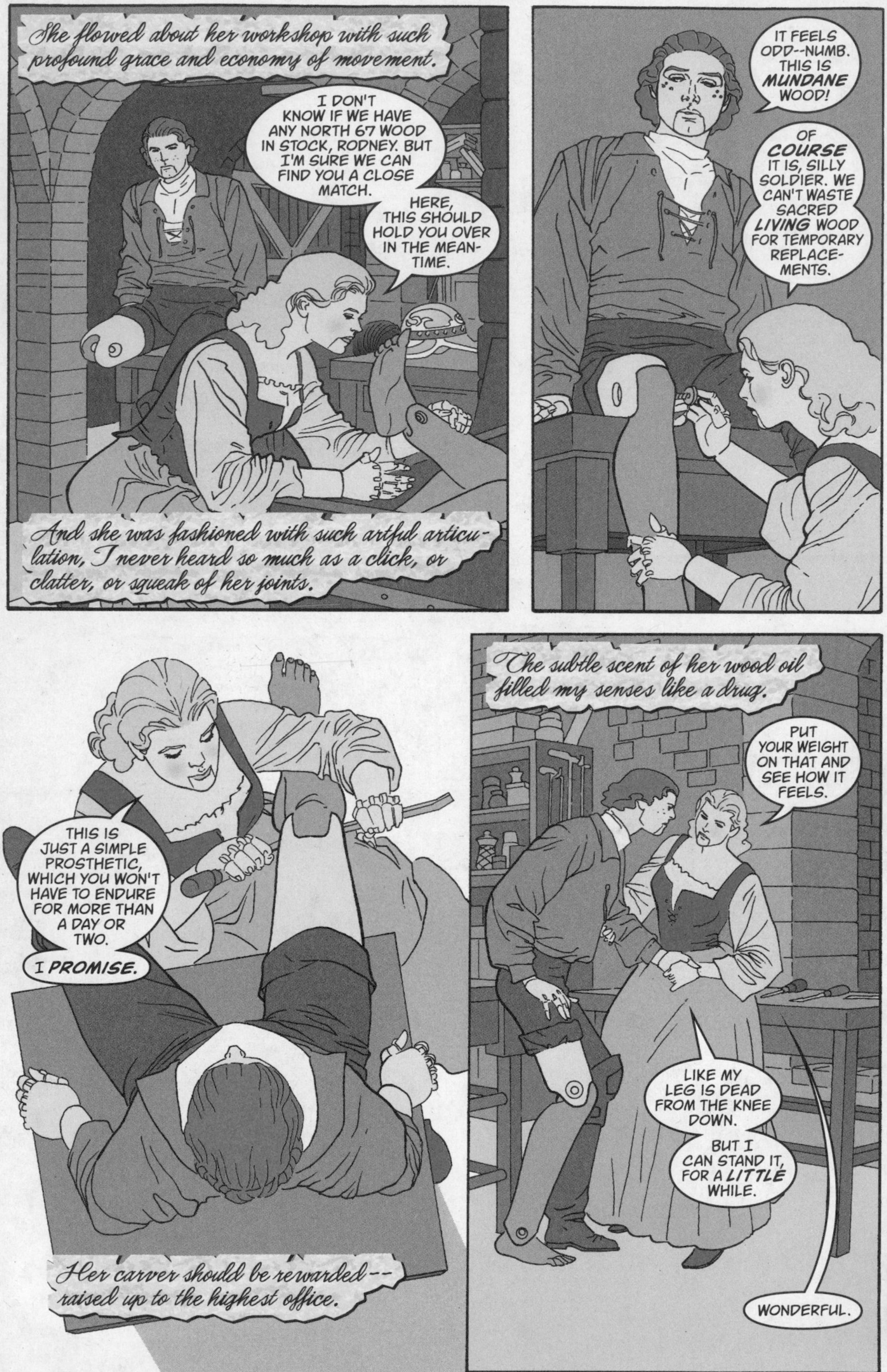
She flowed about her workshop with such profound grace and economy of movement.
I DON'T KNOW IF WE HAVE ANY NORTH 67 WOOD IN STOCK, RODNEY. BUT I'M SURE WE CAN FIND YOU A CLOSE MATCH.
HERE, THIS SHOULD HOLD YOU OVER IN THE MEAN-TIME.
And she was fashioned with such artful articu-lation, I never heard so much as a click, or clatter, or squeak of her joints.
IT FEELS ODD--NUMB. THIS IS MUNDANE WOOD!
OF COURSE IT IS, SILLY SOLDIER. WE CAN'T WASTE SACRED LIVING WOOD FOR TEMPORARY REPLACE-MENTS.
THIS IS JUST A SIMPLE PROSTHETIC, WHICH YOU WON'T HAVE TO ENDURE FOR MORE THAN A DAY OR TWO.
I PROMISE.
Her carver should be rewarded-- raised up to the highest office.
The subtle scent of her wood oil filled my senses like a drug.
PUT YOUR WEIGHT ON THAT AND SEE HOW IT FEELS.
LIKE MY LEG IS DEAD FROM THE KNEE DOWN.
BUT I CAN STAND IT, FOR A LITTLE WHILE.
WONDERFUL.

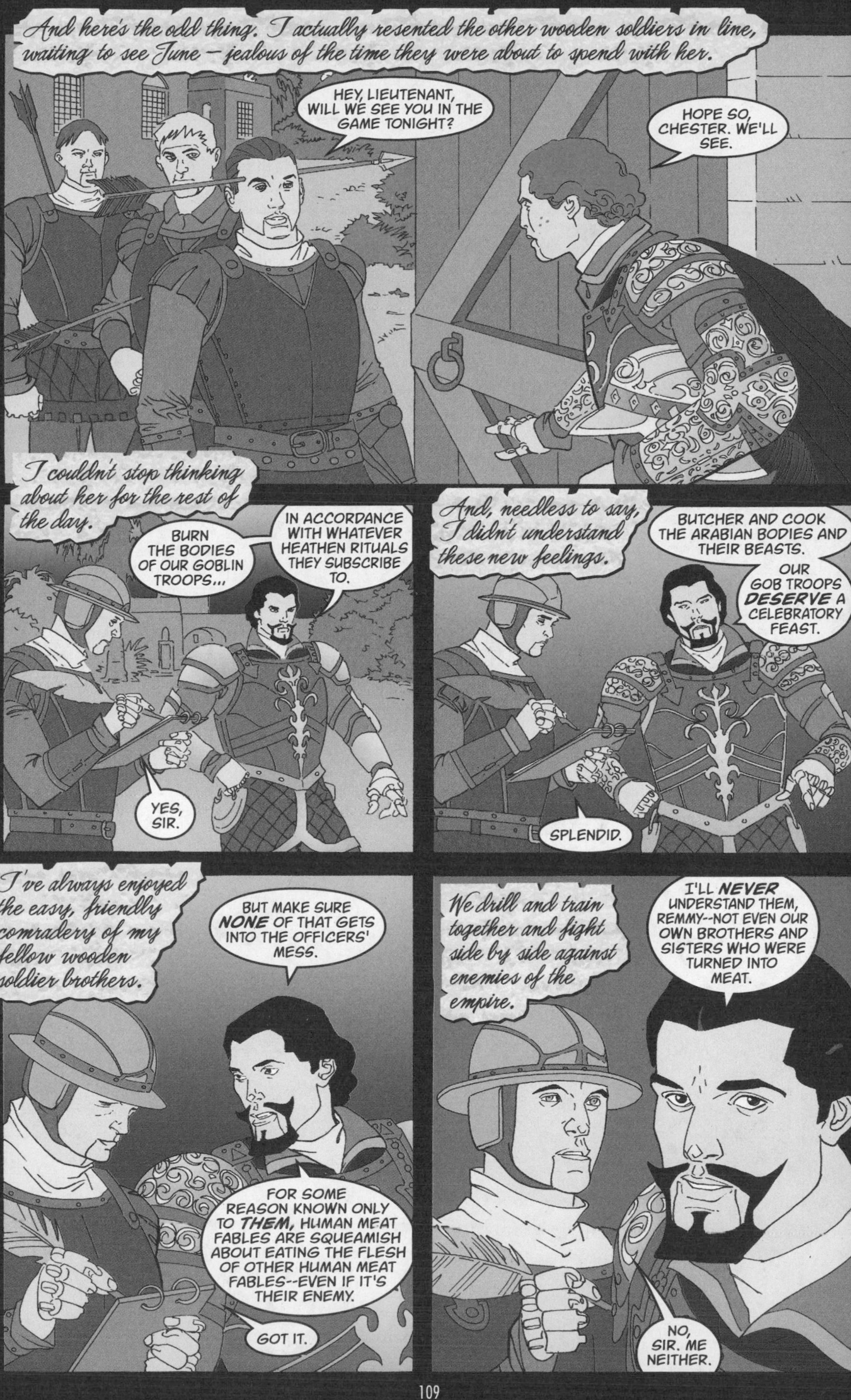
And here's the odd thing. I actually resented the other wooden soldiers in line, waiting to see June — jealous of the time they were about to spend with her.
HEY, LIEUTENANT, WILL WE SEE YOU IN THE GAME TONIGHT?
HOPE SO, CHESTER. WE'LL SEE.
I couldn't stop thinking about her for the rest of the day.
BURN THE BODIES OF OUR GOBLIN TROOPS...
IN ACCORDANCE WITH WHATEVER HEATHEN RITUALS THEY SUBSCRIBE TO.
YES, SIR.
And, needless to say, I didn't understand these new feelings.
BUTCHER AND COOK THE ARABIAN BODIES AND THEIR BEASTS.
OUR GOB TROOPS DESERVE A CELEBRATORY FEAST.
SPLENDID.
I've always enjoyed the easy, friendly comradery of my fellow wooden soldier brothers.
BUT MAKE SURE NONE OF THAT GETS INTO THE OFFICERS' MESS.
FOR SOME REASON KNOWN ONLY TO THEM, HUMAN MEAT FABLES ARE SQUEAMISH ABOUT EATING THE FLESH OF OTHER HUMAN MEAT FABLES--EVEN IF IT'S THEIR ENEMY.
GOT IT.
We drill and train together and fight side by side against enemies of the empire.
I'LL NEVER UNDERSTAND THEM, REMMY--NOT EVEN OUR OWN BROTHERS AND SISTERS WHO WERE TURNED INTO MEAT.
NO, SIR. ME NEITHER.

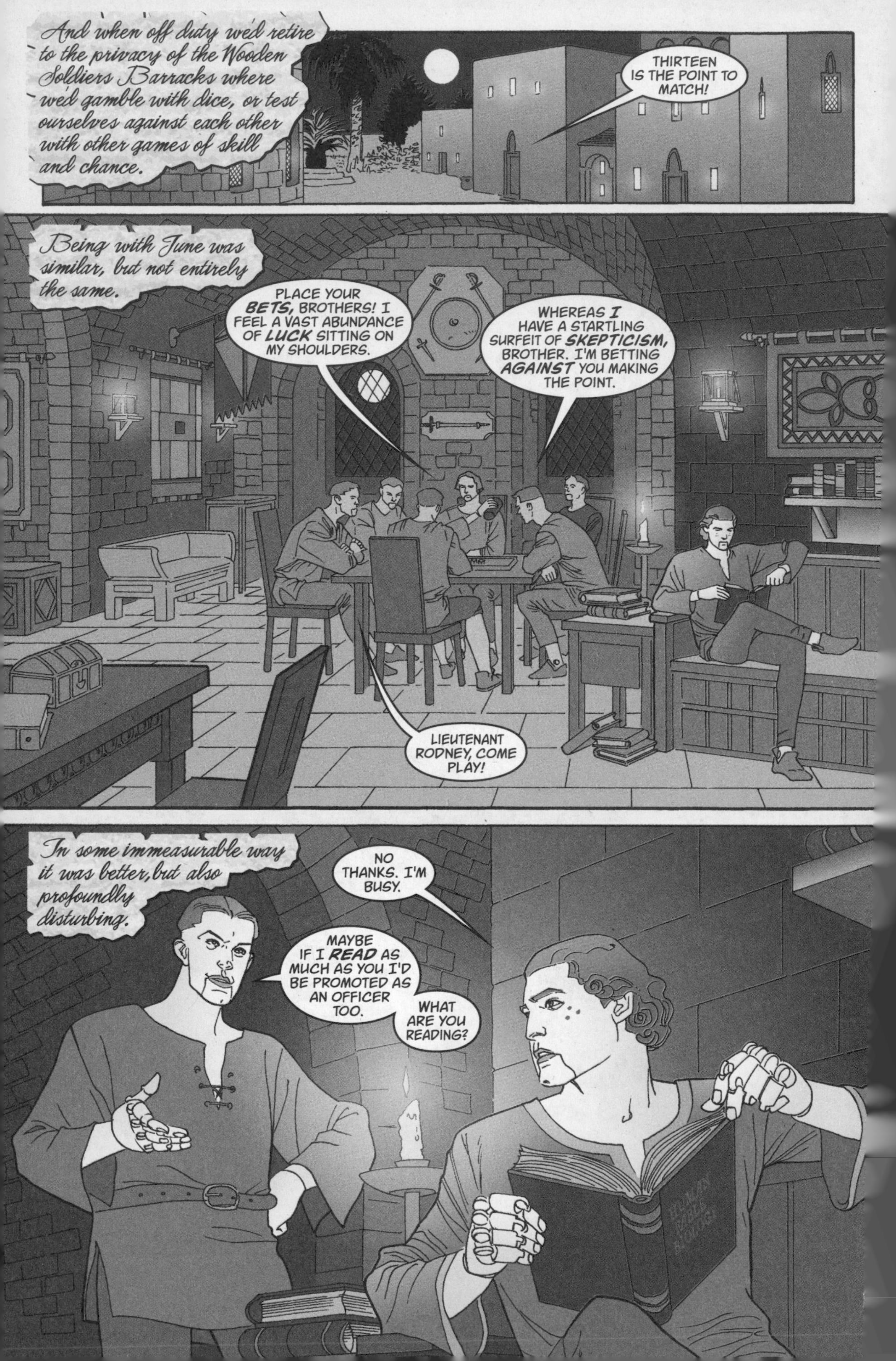
And when off duty we'd retire to the privacy of the Wooden Soldiers Barracks where we'd gamble with dice, or test ourselves against each other with other games of skill and chance.
THIRTEEN IS THE POINT TO MATCH!
Being with June was similar, but not entirely the same.
PLACE YOUR BETS, BROTHERS! I FEEL A VAST ABUNDANCE OF LUCK SITTING ON MY SHOULDERS.
WHEREAS I HAVE A STARTLING SURFEIT OF SKEPTICISM, BROTHER. I'M BETTING AGAINST YOU MAKING THE POINT.
LIEUTENANT RODNEY, COME PLAY!
In some immeasurable way it was better, but also profoundly disturbing.
NO THANKS. I'M BUSY.
MAYBE IF I READ AS MUCH AS YOU I'D BE PROMOTED AS AN OFFICER TOO.
WHAT ARE YOU READING?

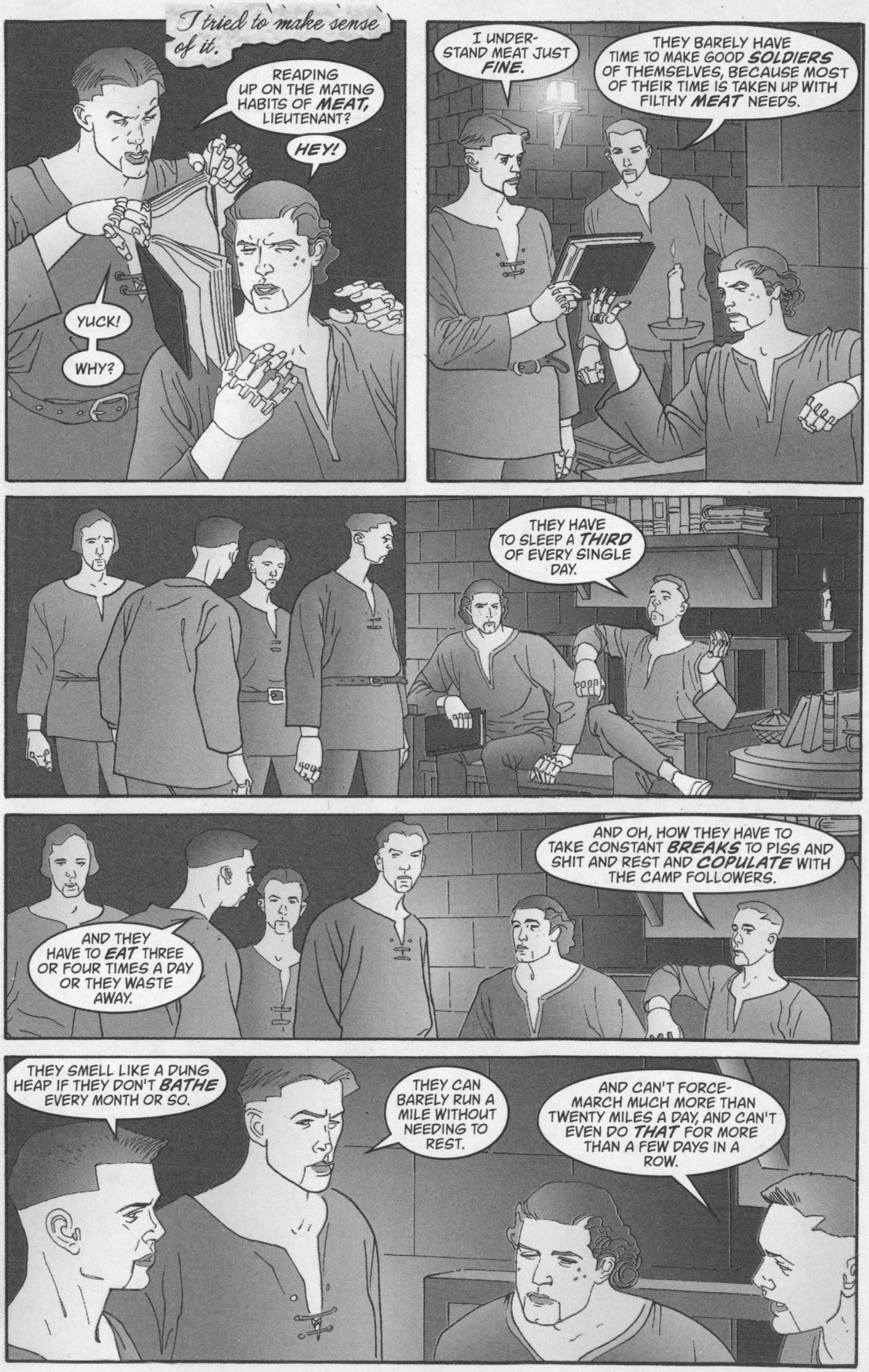
I tried to make sense of it.
READING UP ON THE MATING HABITS OF MEAT, LIEUTENANT?
HEY!
YUCK!
WHY?
I UNDER-STAND MEAT JUST FINE.
THEY BARELY HAVE TIME TO MAKE GOOD SOLDIERS OF THEMSELVES, BECAUSE MOST OF THEIR TIME IS TAKEN UP WITH FILTHY MEAT NEEDS.
THEY HAVE TO SLEEP A THIRD OF EVERY SINGLE DAY.
AND OH, HOW THEY HAVE TO TAKE CONSTANT BREAKS TO PISS AND SHIT AND REST AND COPULATE WITH THE CAMP FOLLOWERS.
AND THEY HAVE TO EAT THREE OR FOUR TIMES A DAY OR THEY WASTE AWAY.
THEY SMELL LIKE A DUNG HEAP IF THEY DON'T BATHE EVERY MONTH OR SO.
THEY CAN BARELY RUN A MILE WITHOUT NEEDING TO REST.
AND CAN'T FORCE-MARCH MUCH MORE THAN TWENTY MILES A DAY, AND CAN'T EVEN DO THAT FOR MORE THAN A FEW DAYS IN A ROW.

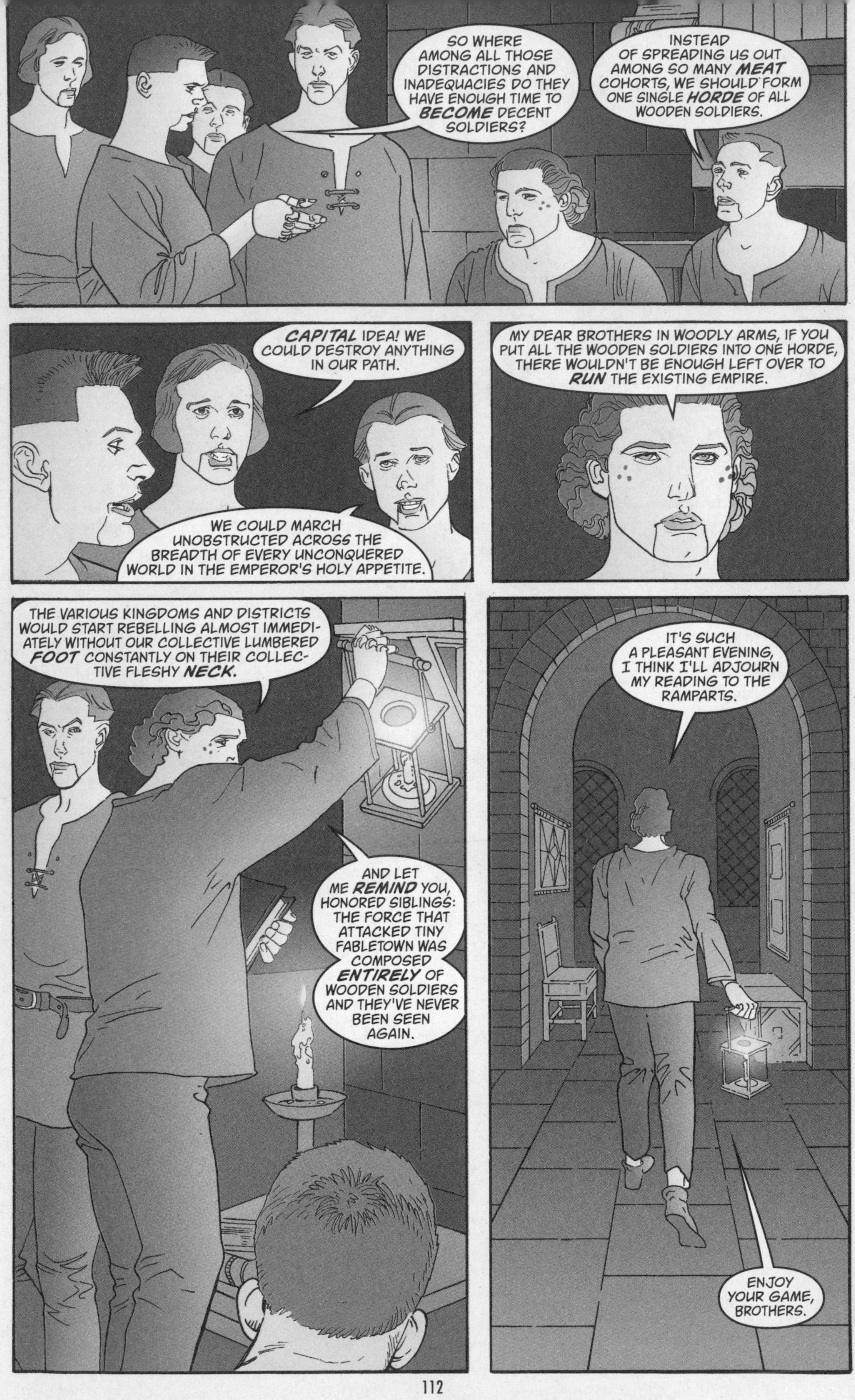
SO WHERE AMONG ALL THOSE DISTRACTIONS AND INADEQUACIES DO THEY HAVE ENOUGH TIME TO BECOME DECENT SOLDIERS?
INSTEAD OF SPREADING US OUT AMONG SO MANY MEAT COHORTS, WE SHOULD FORM ONE SINGLE HORDE OF ALL WOODEN SOLDIERS.
CAPITAL IDEA! WE COULD DESTROY ANYTHING IN OUR PATH.
WE COULD MARCH UNOBSTRUCTED ACROSS THE BREADTH OF EVERY UNCONQUERED WORLD IN THE EMPEROR'S HOLY APPETITE.
MY DEAR BROTHERS IN WOODLY ARMS, IF YOU PUT ALL THE WOODEN SOLDIERS INTO ONE HORDE, THERE WOULDN'T BE ENOUGH LEFT OVER TO RUN THE EXISTING EMPIRE.
THE VARIOUS KINGDOMS AND DISTRICTS WOULD START REBELLING ALMOST IMMEDIATELY WITHOUT OUR COLLECTIVE LUMBERED FOOT CONSTANTLY ON THEIR COLLECTIVE FLESHY NECK.
AND LET ME REMIND YOU, HONORED SIBLINGS: THE FORCE THAT ATTACKED TINY FABLETOWN WAS COMPOSED ENTIRELY OF WOODEN SOLDIERS AND THEY'VE NEVER BEEN SEEN AGAIN.
IT'S SUCH A PLEASANT EVENING, I THINK I'LL ADJOURN MY READING TO THE RAMPARTS.
ENJOY YOUR GAME, BROTHERS.

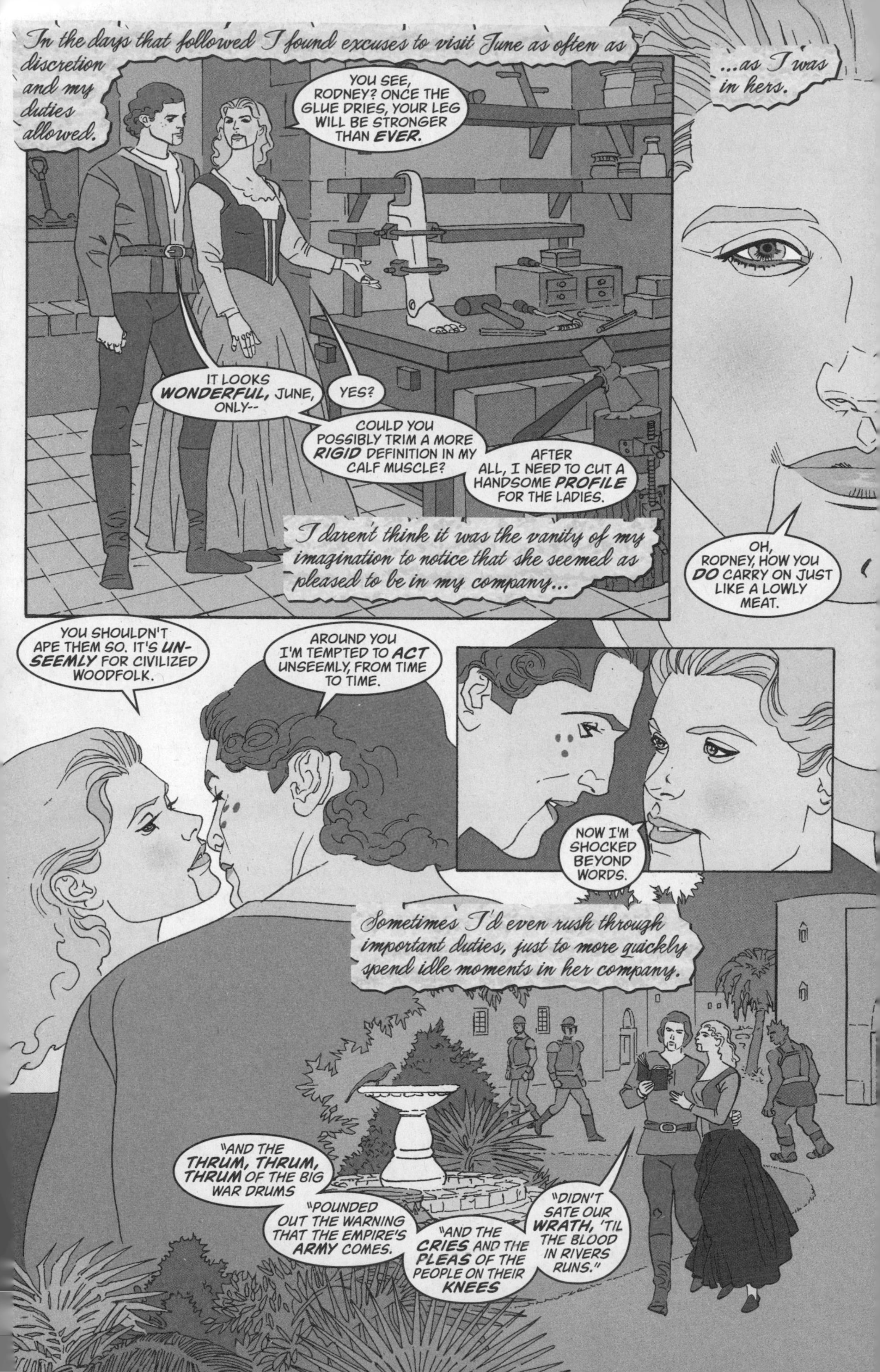

In the days that followed I found excuses to visit June as often as discretion and my duties allowed.
YOU SEE, RODNEY? ONCE THE GLUE DRIES, YOUR LEG WILL BE STRONGER THAN EVER.
IT LOOKS WONDERFUL, JUNE, ONLY--
YES?
COULD YOU POSSIBLY TRIM A MORE RIGID DEFINITION IN MY CALF MUSCLE?
AFTER ALL, I NEED TO CUT A HANDSOME PROFILE FOR THE LADIES.
I daren't think it was the vanity of my imagination to notice that she seemed as pleased to be in my company...
...as I was in hers.
OH, RODNEY, HOW YOU DO CARRY ON JUST LIKE A LOWLY MEAT.
YOU SHOULDN'T APE THEM SO. IT'S UNSEEMLY FOR CIVILIZED WOODFOLK.
AROUND YOU I'M TEMPTED TO ACT UNSEEMLY, FROM TIME TO TIME.
NOW I'M SHOCKED BEYOND WORDS.
Sometimes I'd even rush through important duties, just to more quickly spend idle moments in her company.
"AND THE THRUM, THRUM, THRUM OF THE BIG WAR DRUMS
"POUNDED OUT THE WARNING THAT THE EMPIRE'S ARMY COMES.
"AND THE CRIES AND THE PLEAS OF THE PEOPLE ON THEIR KNEES
"DIDN'T SATE OUR WRATH, 'TIL THE BLOOD IN RIVERS RUNS."

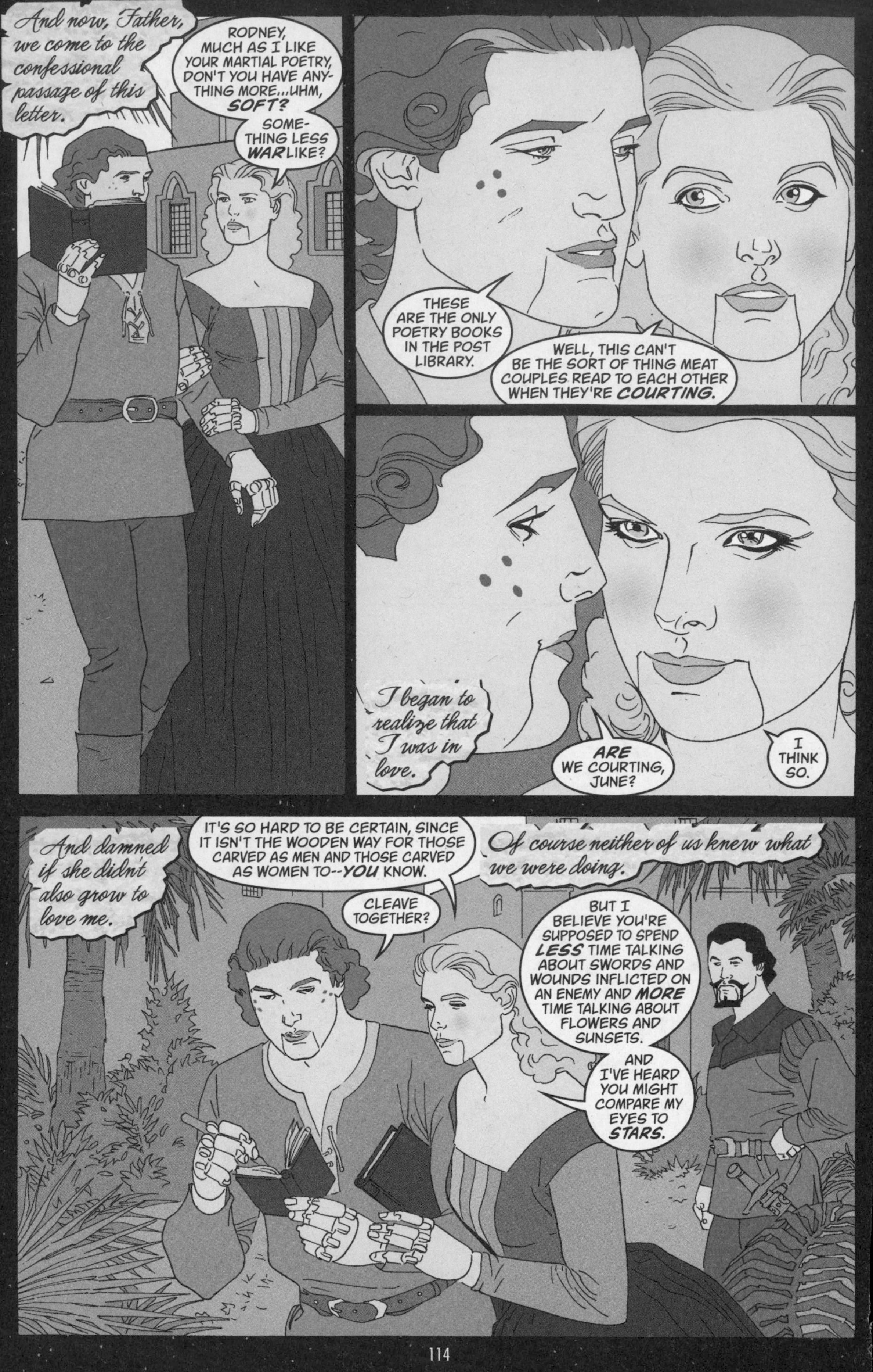
And now, Father, we come to the confessional passage of this letter.
RODNEY, MUCH AS I LIKE YOUR MARTIAL POETRY, DON'T YOU HAVE ANY-THING MORE...UHM, SOFT?
SOME-THING LESS WARLIKE?
THESE ARE THE ONLY POETRY BOOKS IN THE POST LIBRARY.
WELL, THIS CAN'T BE THE SORT OF THING MEAT COUPLES READ TO EACH OTHER WHEN THEY'RE COURTING.
I began to realize that I was in love.
ARE WE COURTING, JUNE?
I THINK SO.
And damned if she didn't also grow to love me.
IT'S SO HARD TO BE CERTAIN, SINCE IT ISN'T THE WOODEN WAY FOR THOSE CARVED AS MEN AND THOSE CARVED AS WOMEN TO--YOU KNOW.
CLEAVE TOGETHER?
Of course neither of us knew what we were doing.
BUT I BELIEVE YOU'RE SUPPOSED TO SPEND LESS TIME TALKING ABOUT SWORDS AND WOUNDS INFLICTED ON AN ENEMY AND MORE TIME TALKING ABOUT FLOWERS AND SUNSETS.
AND I'VE HEARD YOU MIGHT COMPARE MY EYES TO STARS.

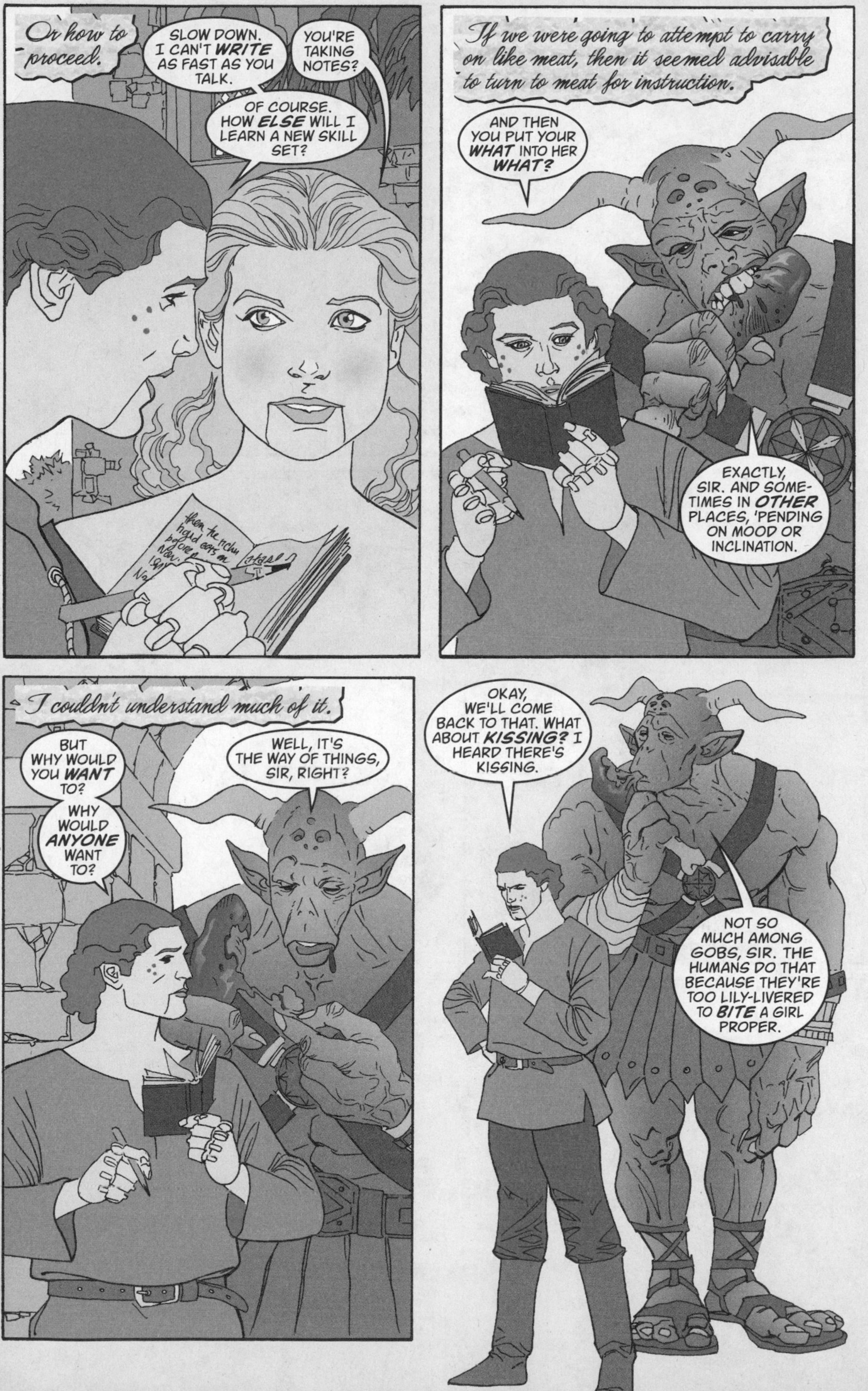

Or how to proceed.
SLOW DOWN. I CAN'T WRITE AS FAST AS YOU TALK.
YOU'RE TAKING NOTES?
OF COURSE. HOW ELSE WILL I LEARN A NEW SKILL SET?
If we were going to attempt to carry on like meat, then it seemed advisable to turn to meat for instruction.
AND THEN YOU PUT YOUR WHAT INTO HER WHAT?
EXACTLY, SIR. AND SOMETIMES IN OTHER PLACES, 'PENDING ON MOOD OR INCLINATION.
I couldn't understand much of it.
BUT WHY WOULD YOU WANT TO?
WHY WOULD ANYONE WANT TO?
WELL, IT'S THE WAY OF THINGS, SIR, RIGHT?
OKAY, WE'LL COME BACK TO THAT. WHAT ABOUT KISSING? I HEARD THERE'S KISSING.
NOT SO MUCH AMONG GOBS, SIR. THE HUMANS DO THAT BECAUSE THEY'RE TOO LILY-LIVERED TO BITE A GIRL PROPER.

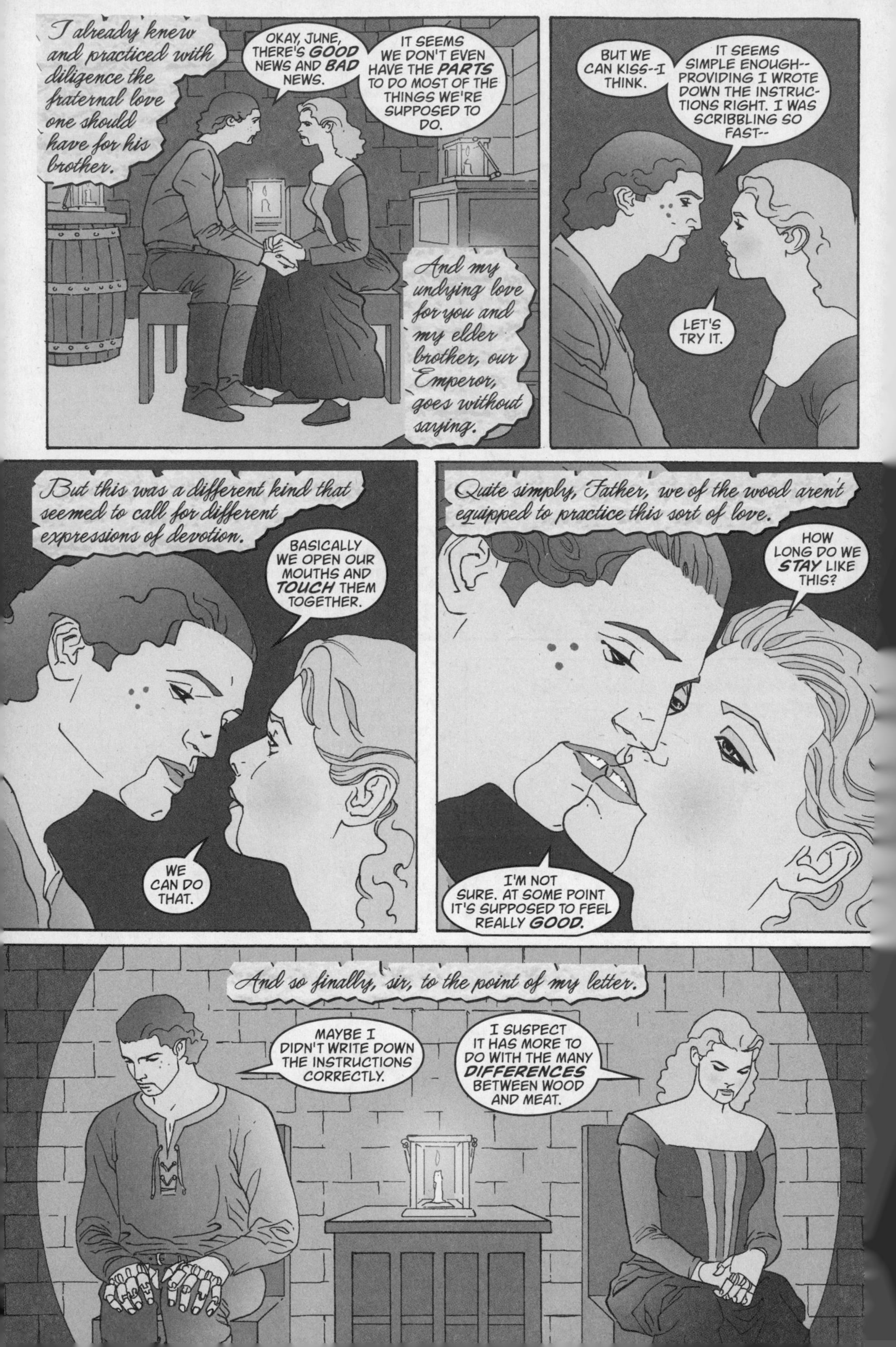
I already knew and practiced with diligence the fraternal love one should have for his brother.
OKAY, JUNE, THERE'S GOOD NEWS AND BAD NEWS.
IT SEEMS WE DON'T EVEN HAVE THE PARTS TO DO MOST OF THE THINGS WE'RE SUPPOSED TO DO.
And my undying love for you and my elder brother, our Emperor, goes without saying.
BUT WE CAN KISS--I THINK.
IT SEEMS SIMPLE ENOUGH--PROVIDING I WROTE DOWN THE INSTRUCTIONS RIGHT. I WAS SCRIBBLING SO FAST--
LET'S TRY IT.
But this was a different kind that seemed to call for different expressions of devotion.
BASICALLY WE OPEN OUR MOUTHS AND TOUCH THEM TOGETHER.
WE CAN DO THAT.
Quite simply, Father, we of the wood aren't equipped to practice this sort of love.
HOW LONG DO WE STAY LIKE THIS?
I'M NOT SURE. AT SOME POINT IT'S SUPPOSED TO FEEL REALLY GOOD.
And so finally, sir, to the point of my letter.
MAYBE I DIDN'T WRITE DOWN THE INSTRUCTIONS CORRECTLY.
I SUSPECT IT HAS MORE TO DO WITH THE MANY DIFFERENCES BETWEEN WOOD AND MEAT.

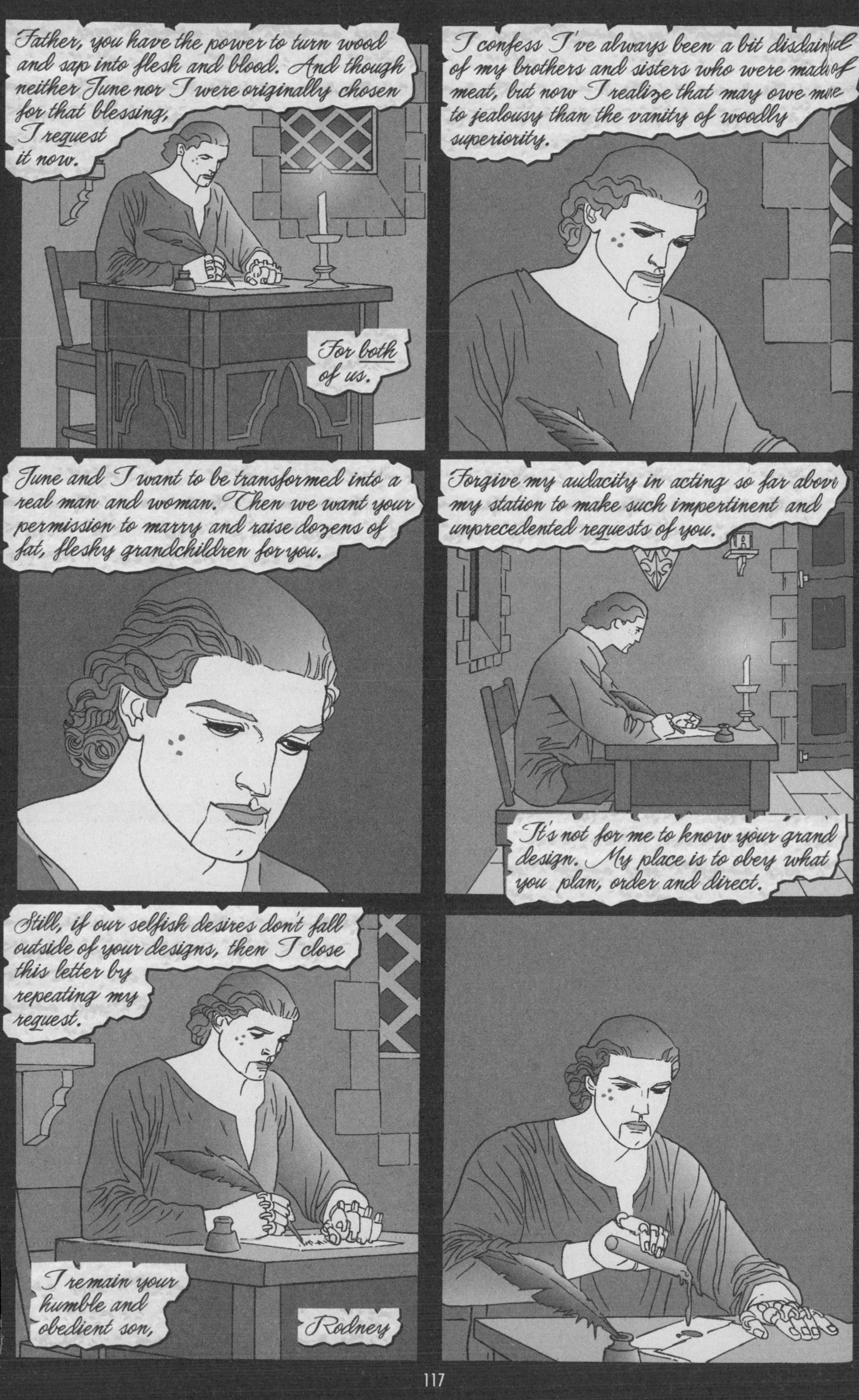

Father, you have the power to turn wood and sap into flesh and blood. And though neither June nor I were originally chosen for that blessing, I request it now.
For both of us.
I confess I've always been a bit disdainful of my brothers and sisters who were made of meat, but now I realize that may owe more to jealousy than the vanity of woodly superiority.
June and I want to be transformed into a real man and woman. Then we want your permission to marry and raise dozens of fat, fleshy grandchildren for you.
Forgive my audacity in acting so far above my station to make such impertinent and unprecedented requests of you.
It's not for me to know your grand design. My place is to obey what you plan, order and direct.
Still, if our selfish desires don't fall outside of your designs, then I close this letter by repeating my request.
I remain your humble and obedient son,
Rodney

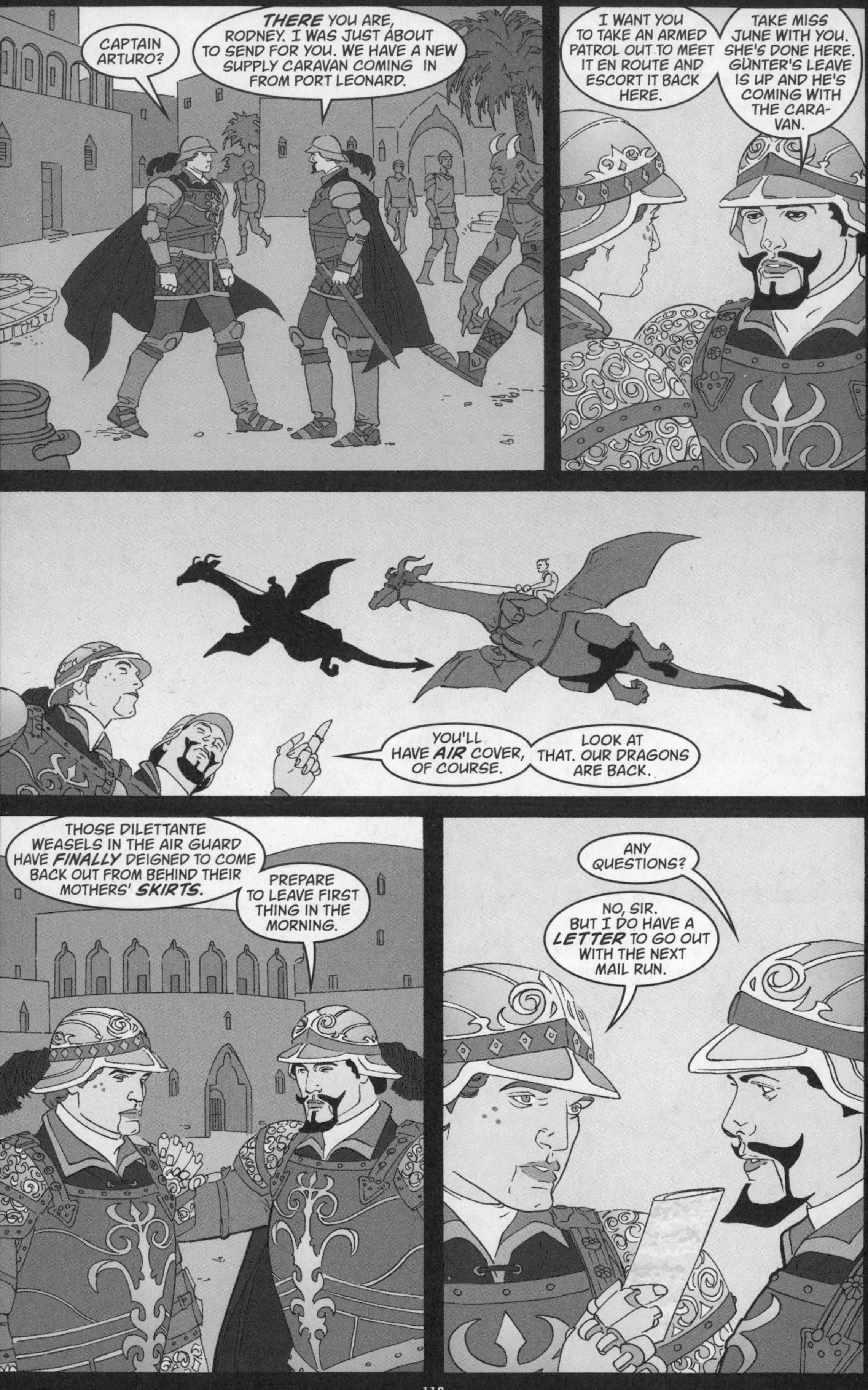
CAPTAIN ARTURO?
THERE YOU ARE, RODNEY. I WAS JUST ABOUT TO SEND FOR YOU. WE HAVE A NEW SUPPLY CARAVAN COMING IN FROM PORT LEONARD.
I WANT YOU TO TAKE AN ARMED PATROL OUT TO MEET IT EN ROUTE AND ESCORT IT BACK HERE.
TAKE MISS JUNE WITH YOU. SHE'S DONE HERE. GÜNTER'S LEAVE IS UP AND HE'S COMING WITH THE CARA-VAN.
LOOK AT THAT. OUR DRAGONS ARE BACK.
YOU'LL HAVE AIR COVER, OF COURSE.
THOSE DILETTANTE WEASELS IN THE AIR GUARD HAVE FINALLY DEIGNED TO COME BACK OUT FROM BEHIND THEIR MOTHERS' SKIRTS.
PREPARE TO LEAVE FIRST THING IN THE MORNING.
ANY QUESTIONS?
NO, SIR. BUT I DO HAVE A LETTER TO GO OUT WITH THE NEXT MAIL RUN.

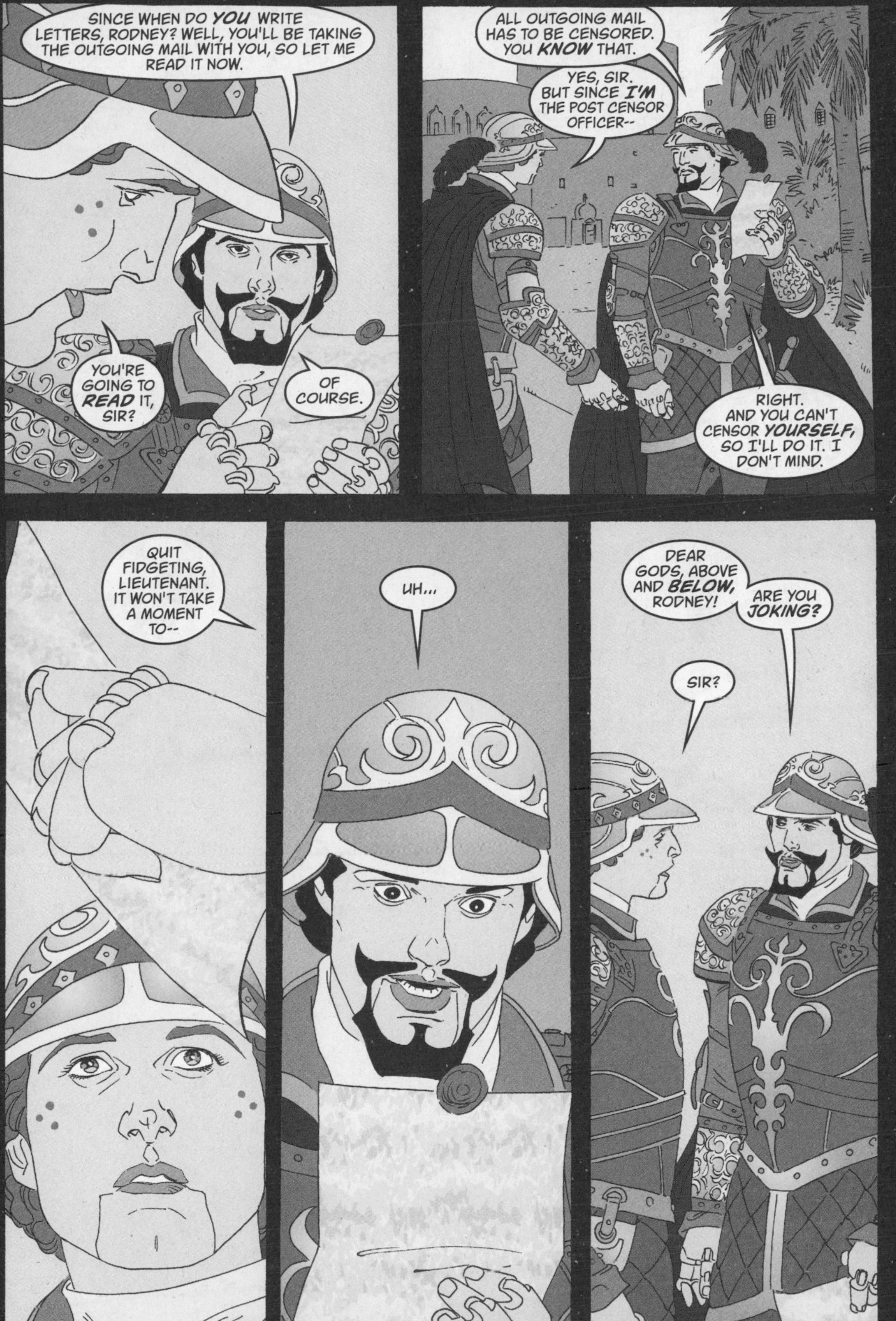

SINCE WHEN DO YOU WRITE LETTERS, RODNEY? WELL, YOU'LL BE TAKING THE OUTGOING MAIL WITH YOU, SO LET ME READ IT NOW.
YOU'RE GOING TO READ IT, SIR?
OF COURSE.
ALL OUTGOING MAIL HAS TO BE CENSORED. YOU KNOW THAT.
YES, SIR. BUT SINCE I'M THE POST CENSOR OFFICER--
RIGHT. AND YOU CAN'T CENSOR YOURSELF, SO I'LL DO IT. I DON'T MIND.
QUIT FIDGETING, LIEUTENANT. IT WON'T TAKE A MOMENT TO--
UH...
DEAR GODS, ABOVE AND BELOW, RODNEY!
ARE YOU JOKING?
SIR?

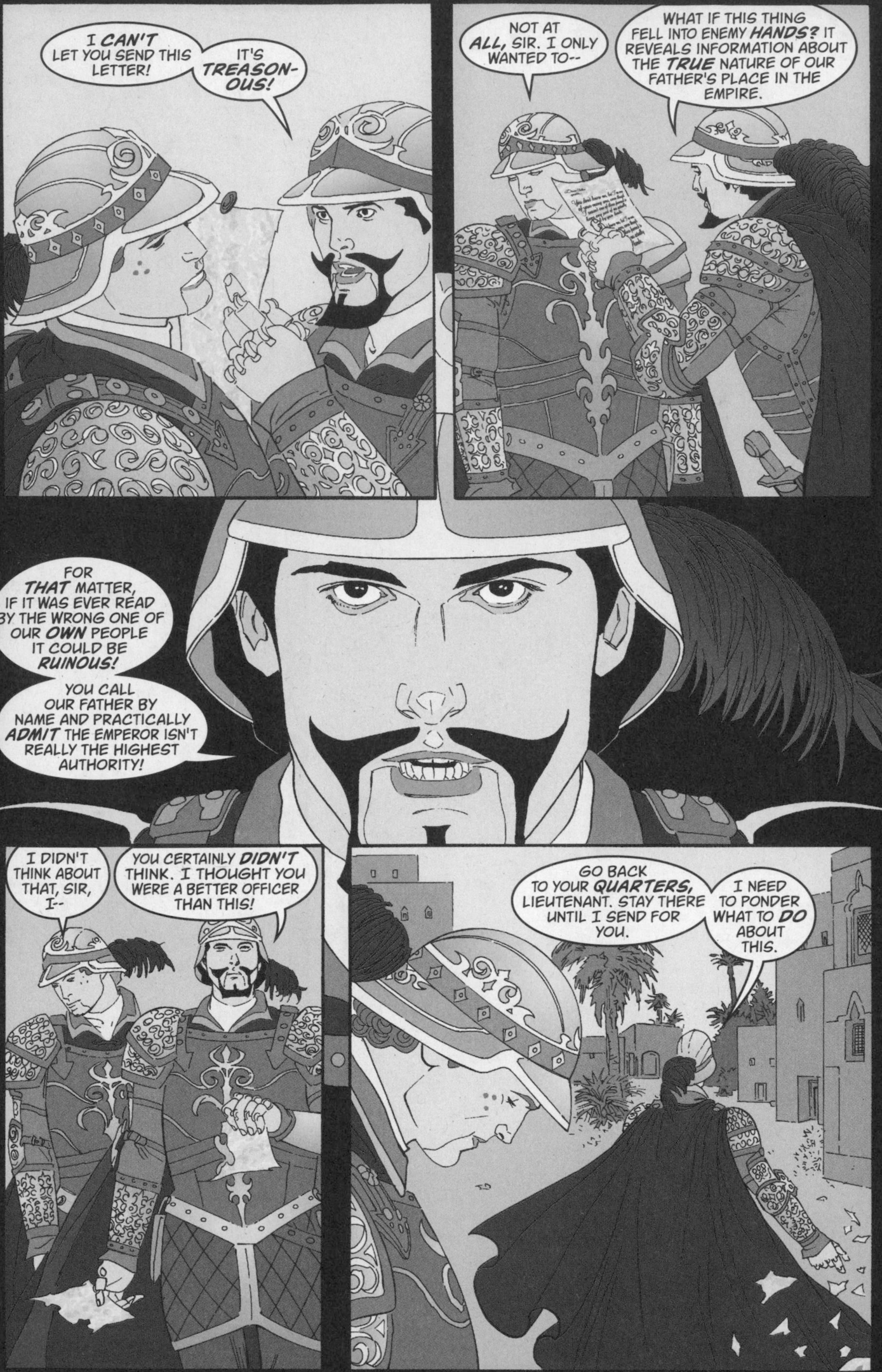
I CAN'T LET YOU SEND THIS LETTER!
IT'S TREASON-OUS!
NOT AT ALL, SIR. I ONLY WANTED TO--
WHAT IF THIS THING FELL INTO ENEMY HANDS? IT REVEALS INFORMATION ABOUT THE TRUE NATURE OF OUR FATHER'S PLACE IN THE EMPIRE.
FOR THAT MATTER, IF IT WAS EVER READ BY THE WRONG ONE OF OUR OWN PEOPLE IT COULD BE RUINOUS!
YOU CALL OUR FATHER BY NAME AND PRACTICALLY ADMIT THE EMPEROR ISN'T REALLY THE HIGHEST AUTHORITY!
I DIDN'T THINK ABOUT THAT, SIR, I--
YOU CERTAINLY DIDN'T THINK. I THOUGHT YOU WERE A BETTER OFFICER THAN THIS!
GO BACK TO YOUR QUARTERS, LIEUTENANT. STAY THERE UNTIL I SEND FOR YOU.
I NEED TO PONDER WHAT TO DO ABOUT THIS.

next: some of the consequences of forbidden love.

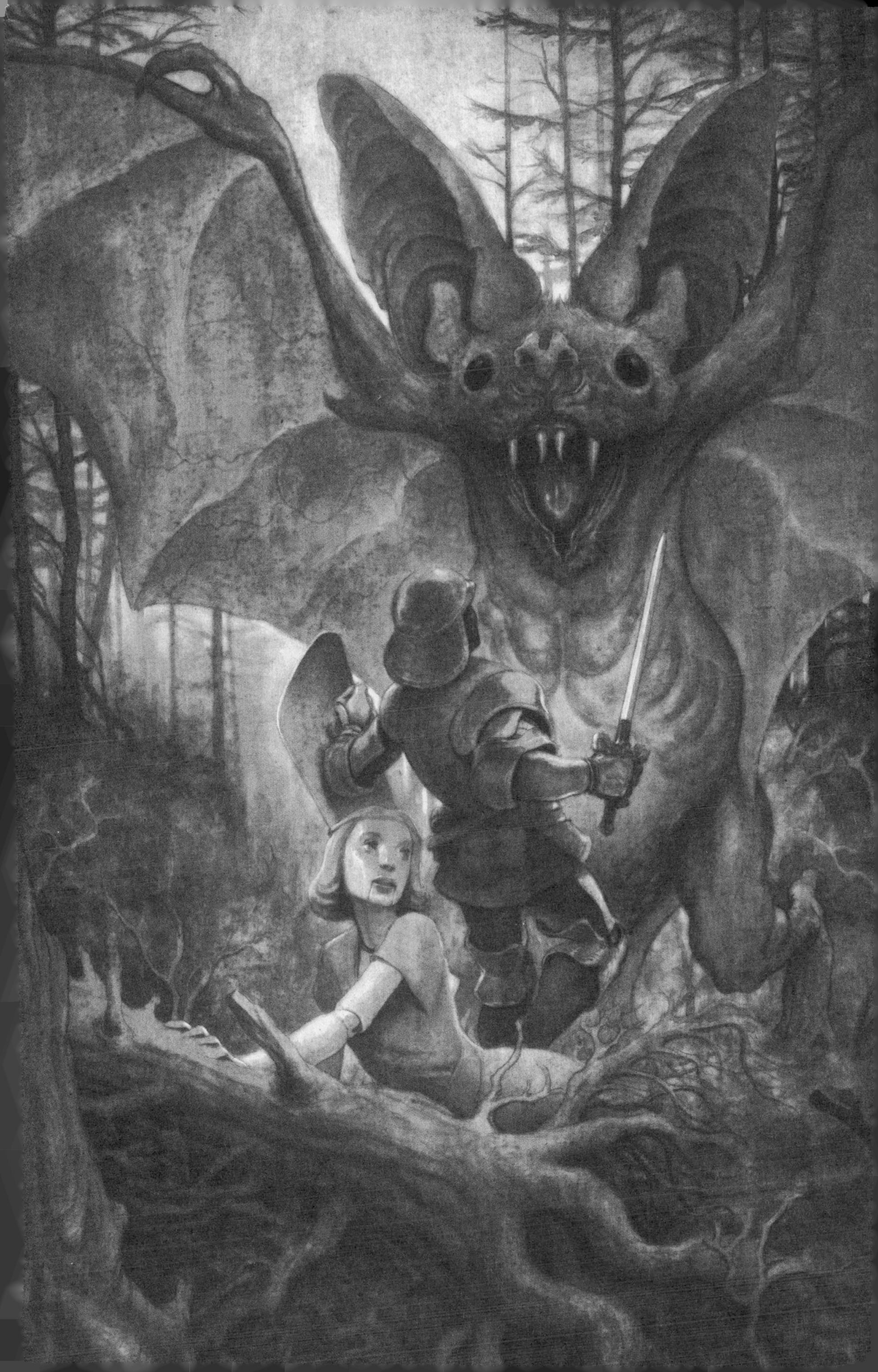

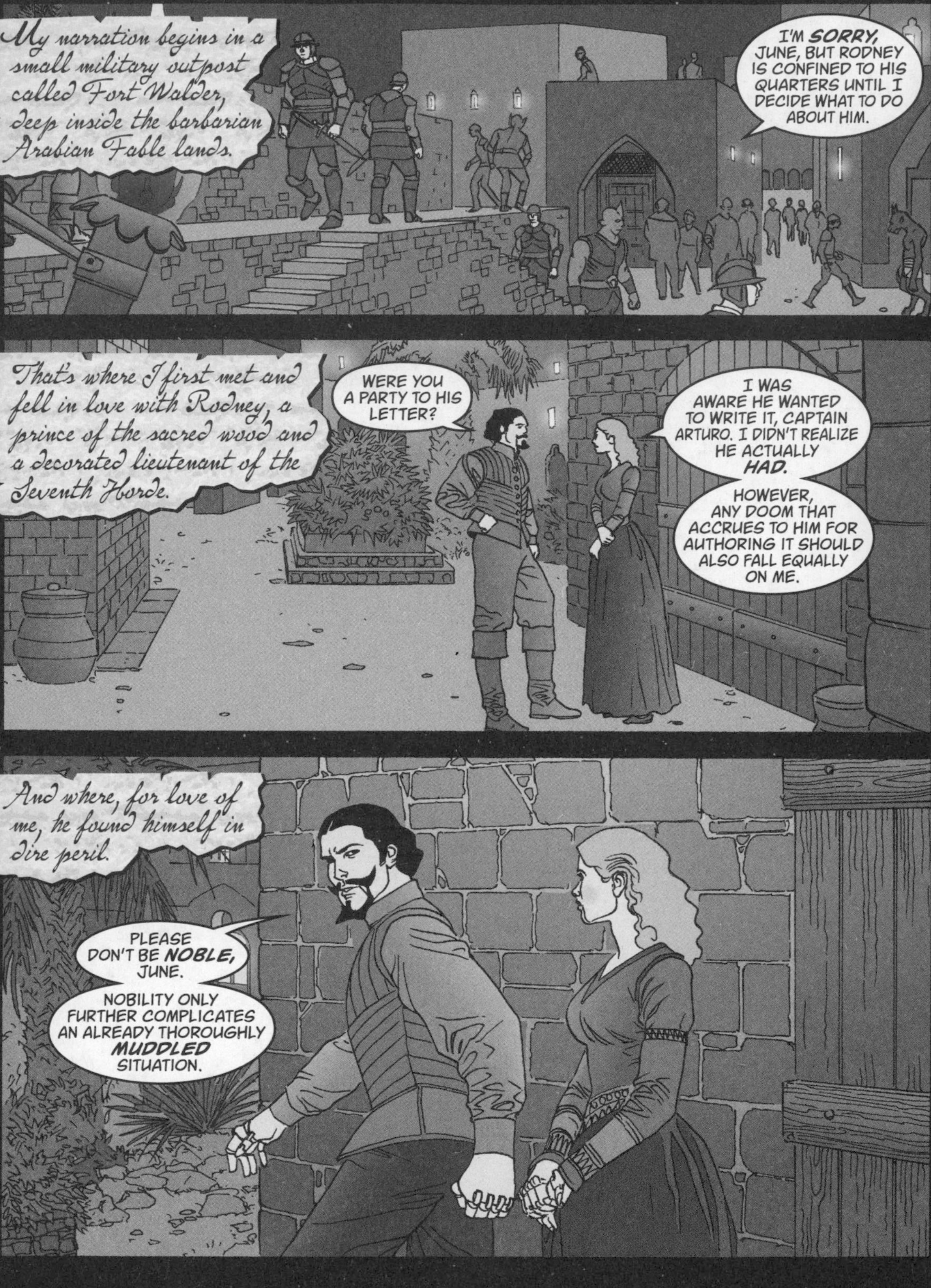
My narration begins in a small military outpost called Fort Walder, deep inside the barbarian Arabian Fable lands.
I'M SORRY, JUNE, BUT RODNEY IS CONFINED TO HIS QUARTERS UNTIL I DECIDE WHAT TO DO ABOUT HIM.
That's where I first met and fell in love with Rodney, a prince of the sacred wood and a decorated lieutenant of the Seventh Horde.
WERE YOU A PARTY TO HIS LETTER?
I WAS AWARE HE WANTED TO WRITE IT, CAPTAIN ARTURO. I DIDN'T REALIZE HE ACTUALLY HAD.
HOWEVER, ANY DOOM THAT ACCRUES TO HIM FOR AUTHORING IT SHOULD ALSO FALL EQUALLY ON ME.
And where, for love of me, he found himself in dire peril.
PLEASE DON'T BE NOBLE, JUNE.
NOBILITY ONLY FURTHER COMPLICATES AN ALREADY THOROUGHLY MUDDLED SITUATION.

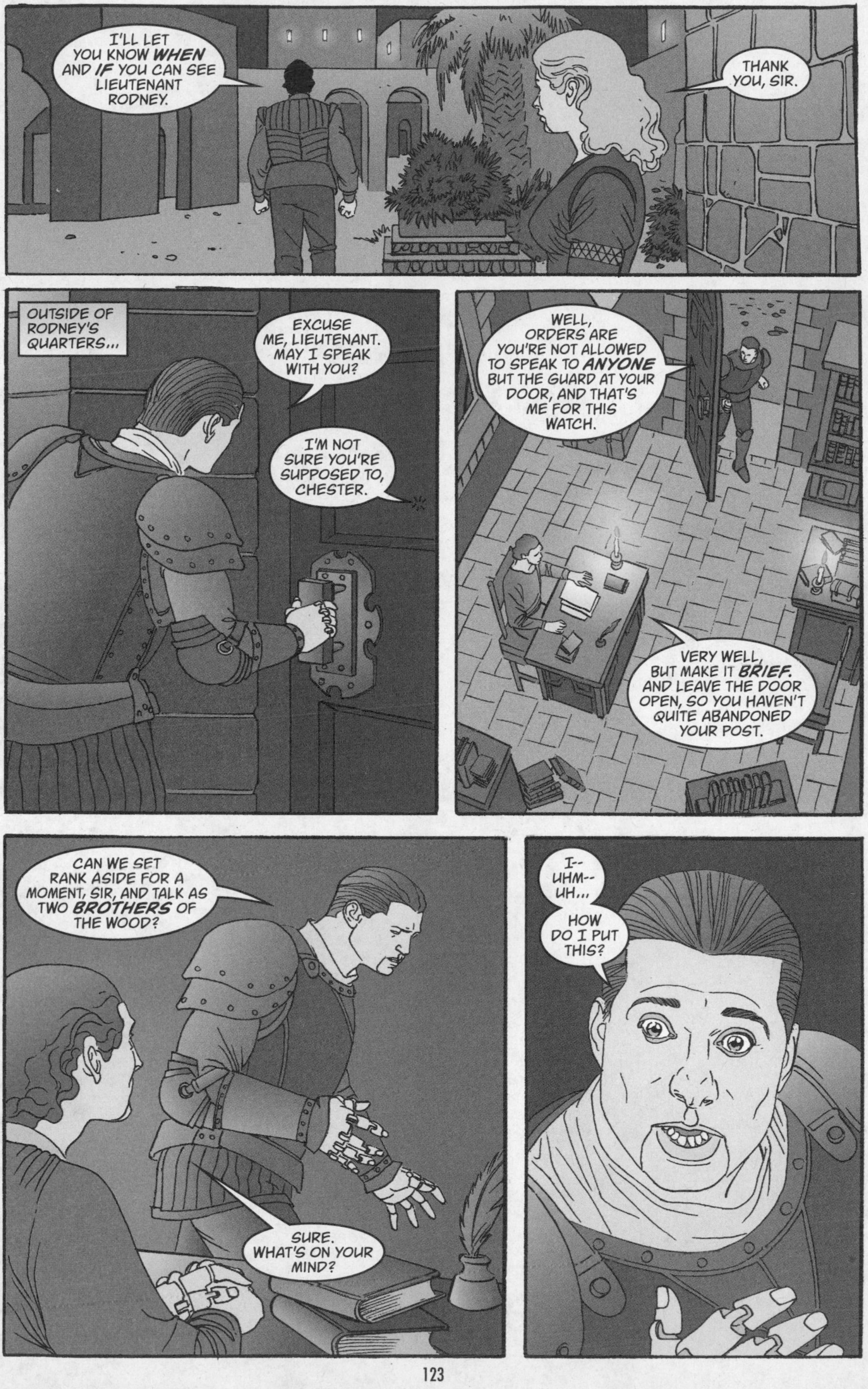
I'LL LET YOU KNOW WHEN AND IF YOU CAN SEE LIEUTENANT RODNEY.
THANK YOU, SIR.
OUTSIDE OF RODNEY'S QUARTERS...
EXCUSE ME, LIEUTENANT. MAY I SPEAK WITH YOU?
I'M NOT SURE YOU'RE SUPPOSED TO, CHESTER.
WELL, ORDERS ARE YOU'RE NOT ALLOWED TO SPEAK TO ANYONE BUT THE GUARD AT YOUR DOOR, AND THAT'S ME FOR THIS WATCH.
VERY WELL, BUT MAKE IT BRIEF. AND LEAVE THE DOOR OPEN, SO YOU HAVEN'T QUITE ABANDONED YOUR POST.
CAN WE SET RANK ASIDE FOR A MOMENT, SIR, AND TALK AS TWO BROTHERS OF THE WOOD?
SURE. WHAT'S ON YOUR MIND?
I-- UHM-- UH...
HOW DO I PUT THIS?

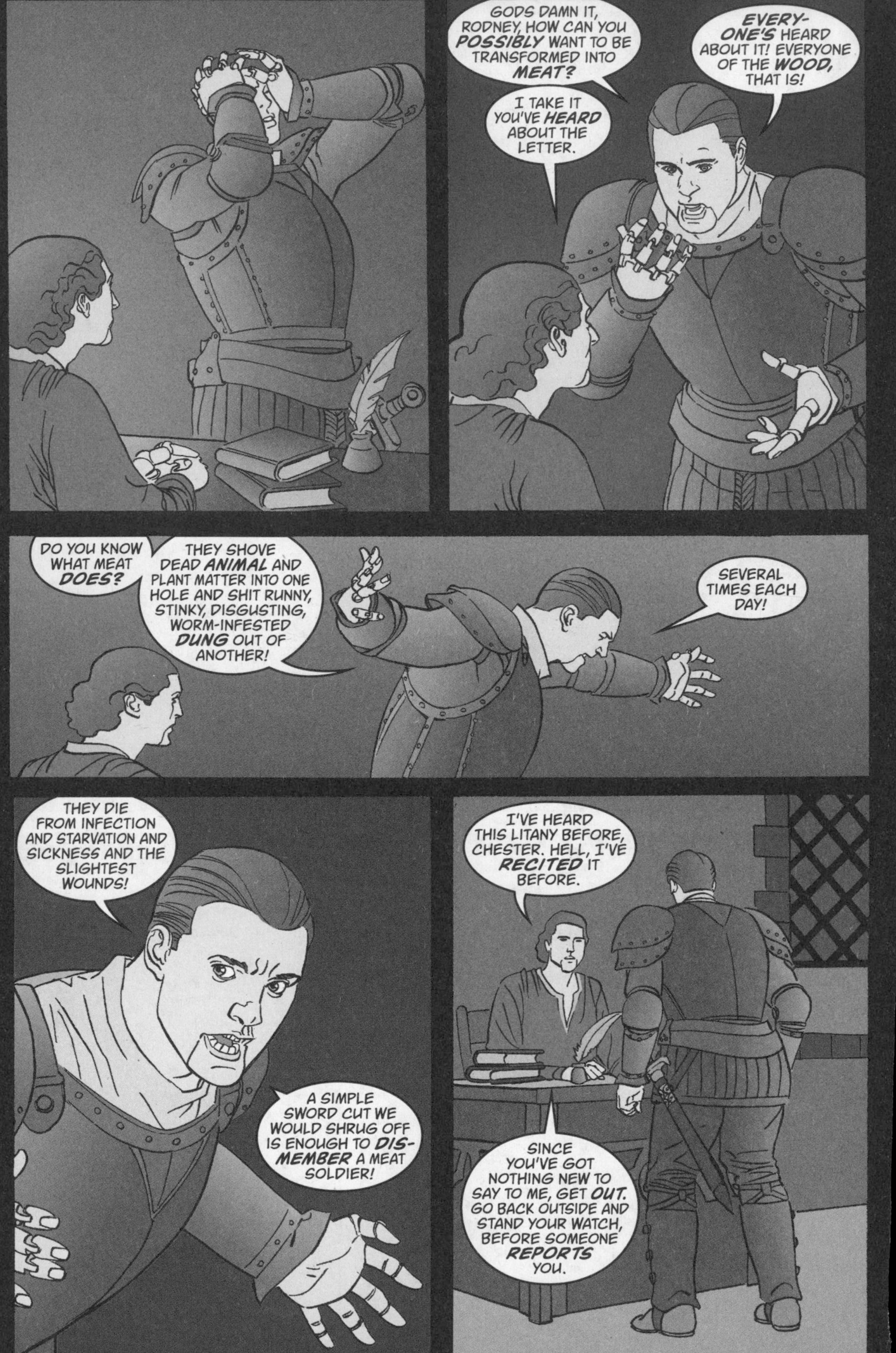

GODS DAMN IT, RODNEY, HOW CAN YOU POSSIBLY WANT TO BE TRANSFORMED INTO MEAT?
I TAKE IT YOU'VE HEARD ABOUT THE LETTER.
EVERY-ONE'S HEARD ABOUT IT! EVERYONE OF THE WOOD, THAT IS!
DO YOU KNOW WHAT MEAT DOES?
THEY SHOVE DEAD ANIMAL AND PLANT MATTER INTO ONE HOLE AND SHIT RUNNY, STINKY, DISGUSTING, WORM-INFESTED DUNG OUT OF ANOTHER!
SEVERAL TIMES EACH DAY!
THEY DIE FROM INFECTION AND STARVATION AND SICKNESS AND THE SLIGHTEST WOUNDS!
A SIMPLE SWORD CUT WE WOULD SHRUG OFF IS ENOUGH TO DIS-MEMBER A MEAT SOLDIER!
I'VE HEARD THIS LITANY BEFORE, CHESTER. HELL, I'VE RECITED IT BEFORE.
SINCE YOU'VE GOT NOTHING NEW TO SAY TO ME, GET OUT. GO BACK OUTSIDE AND STAND YOUR WATCH, BEFORE SOMEONE REPORTS YOU.

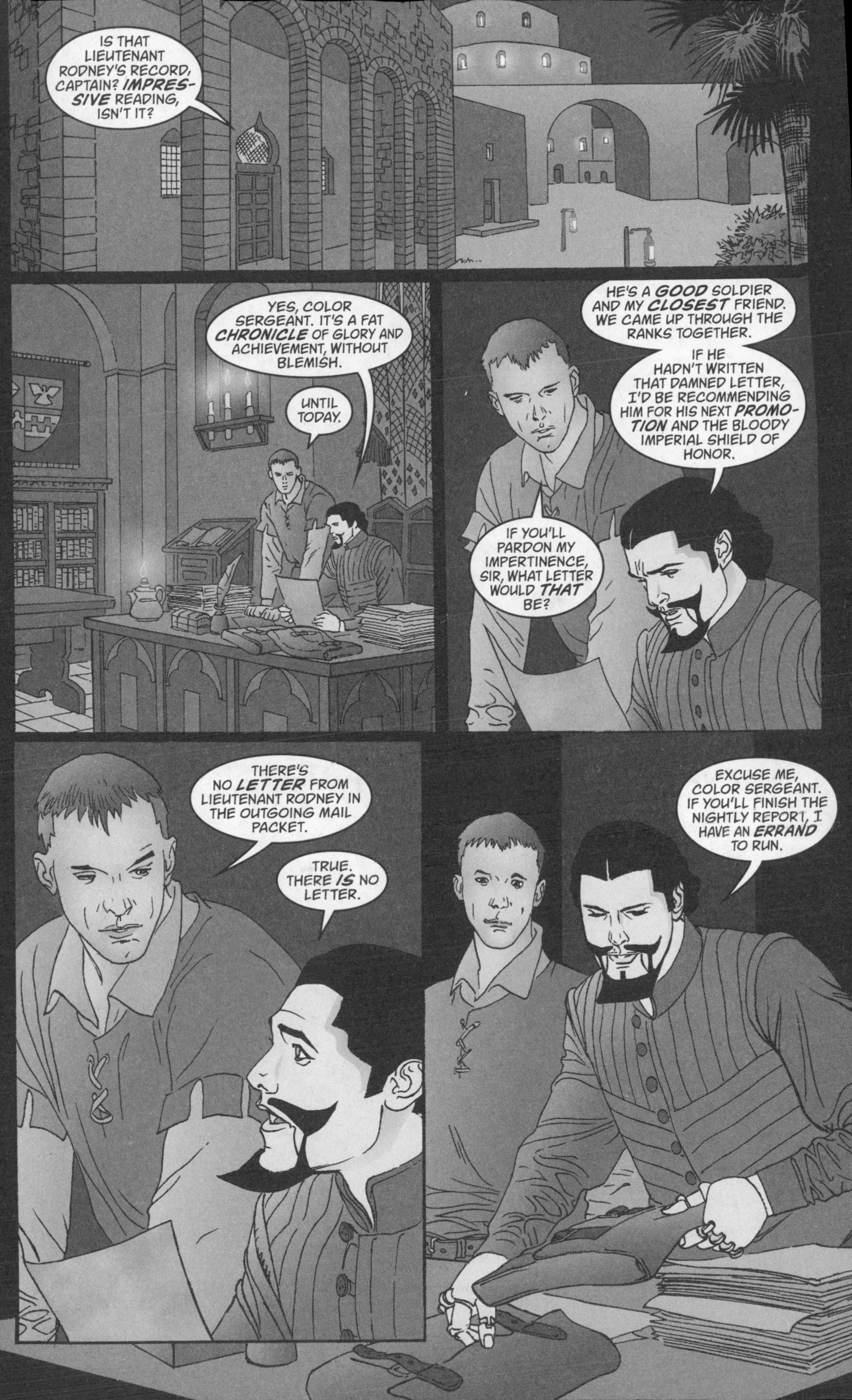
IS THAT LIEUTENANT RODNEY'S RECORD, CAPTAIN? *IMPRESSIVE* READING, ISN'T IT?
YES, COLOR SERGEANT. IT'S A FAT *CHRONICLE* OF GLORY AND ACHIEVEMENT, WITHOUT BLEMISH.
UNTIL TODAY.
HE'S A *GOOD* SOLDIER AND MY *CLOSEST* FRIEND. WE CAME UP THROUGH THE RANKS TOGETHER.
IF HE HADN'T WRITTEN THAT DAMNED LETTER, I'D BE RECOMMENDING HIM FOR HIS NEXT *PROMOTION* AND THE BLOODY IMPERIAL SHIELD OF HONOR.
IF YOU'LL PARDON MY IMPERTINENCE, SIR, WHAT LETTER WOULD *THAT* BE?
THERE'S NO *LETTER* FROM LIEUTENANT RODNEY IN THE OUTGOING MAIL PACKET.
TRUE. THERE *IS* NO LETTER.
EXCUSE ME, COLOR SERGEANT. IF YOU'LL FINISH THE NIGHTLY REPORT, I HAVE AN *ERRAND* TO RUN.

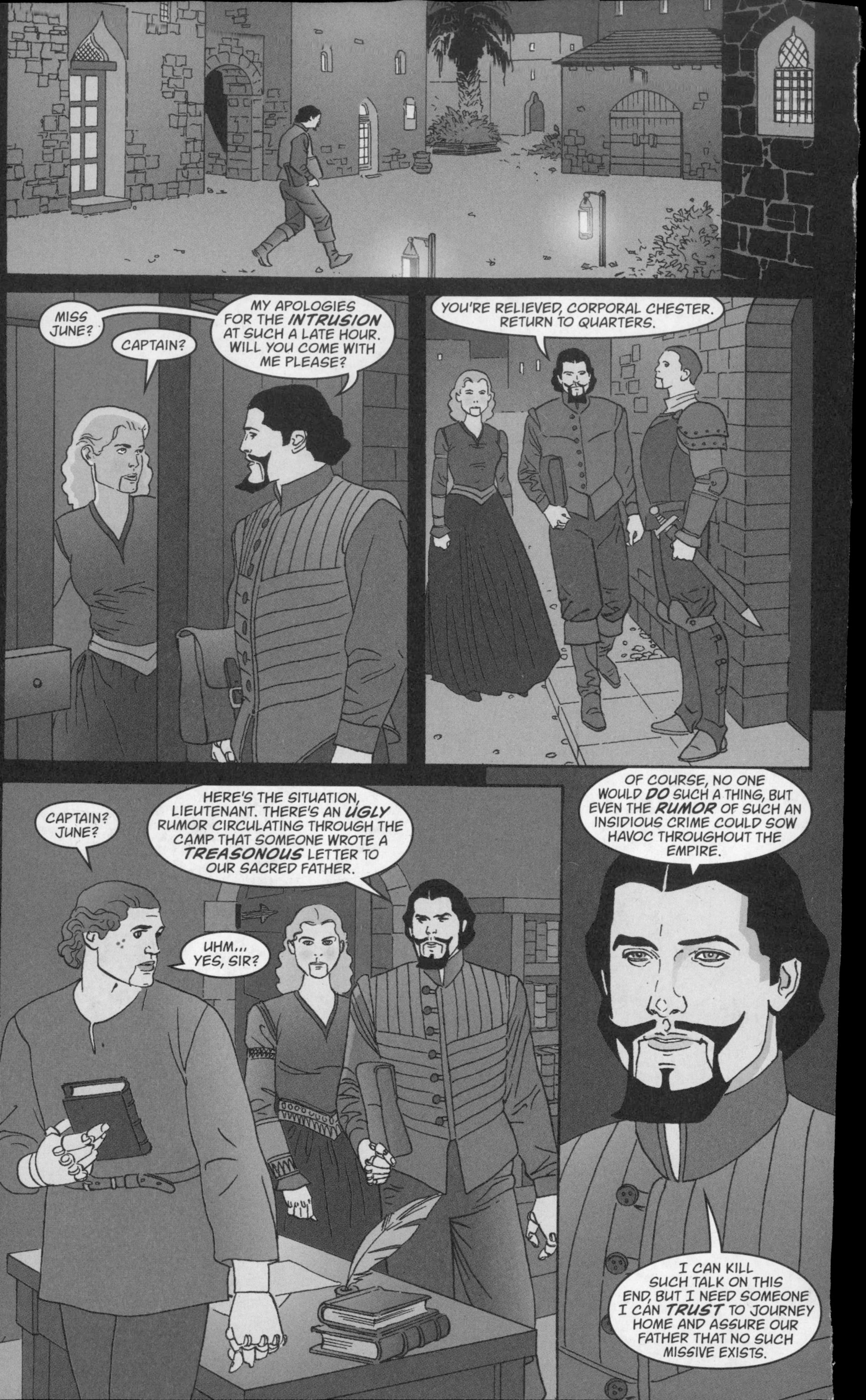
MISS JUNE?
MY APOLOGIES FOR THE INTRUSION AT SUCH A LATE HOUR. WILL YOU COME WITH ME PLEASE?
CAPTAIN?
YOU'RE RELIEVED, CORPORAL CHESTER. RETURN TO QUARTERS.
CAPTAIN? JUNE?
HERE'S THE SITUATION, LIEUTENANT. THERE'S AN UGLY RUMOR CIRCULATING THROUGH THE CAMP THAT SOMEONE WROTE A TREASONOUS LETTER TO OUR SACRED FATHER.
UHM... YES, SIR?
OF COURSE, NO ONE WOULD DO SUCH A THING, BUT EVEN THE RUMOR OF SUCH AN INSIDIOUS CRIME COULD SOW HAVOC THROUGHOUT THE EMPIRE.
I CAN KILL SUCH TALK ON THIS END, BUT I NEED SOMEONE I CAN TRUST TO JOURNEY HOME AND ASSURE OUR FATHER THAT NO SUCH MISSIVE EXISTS.

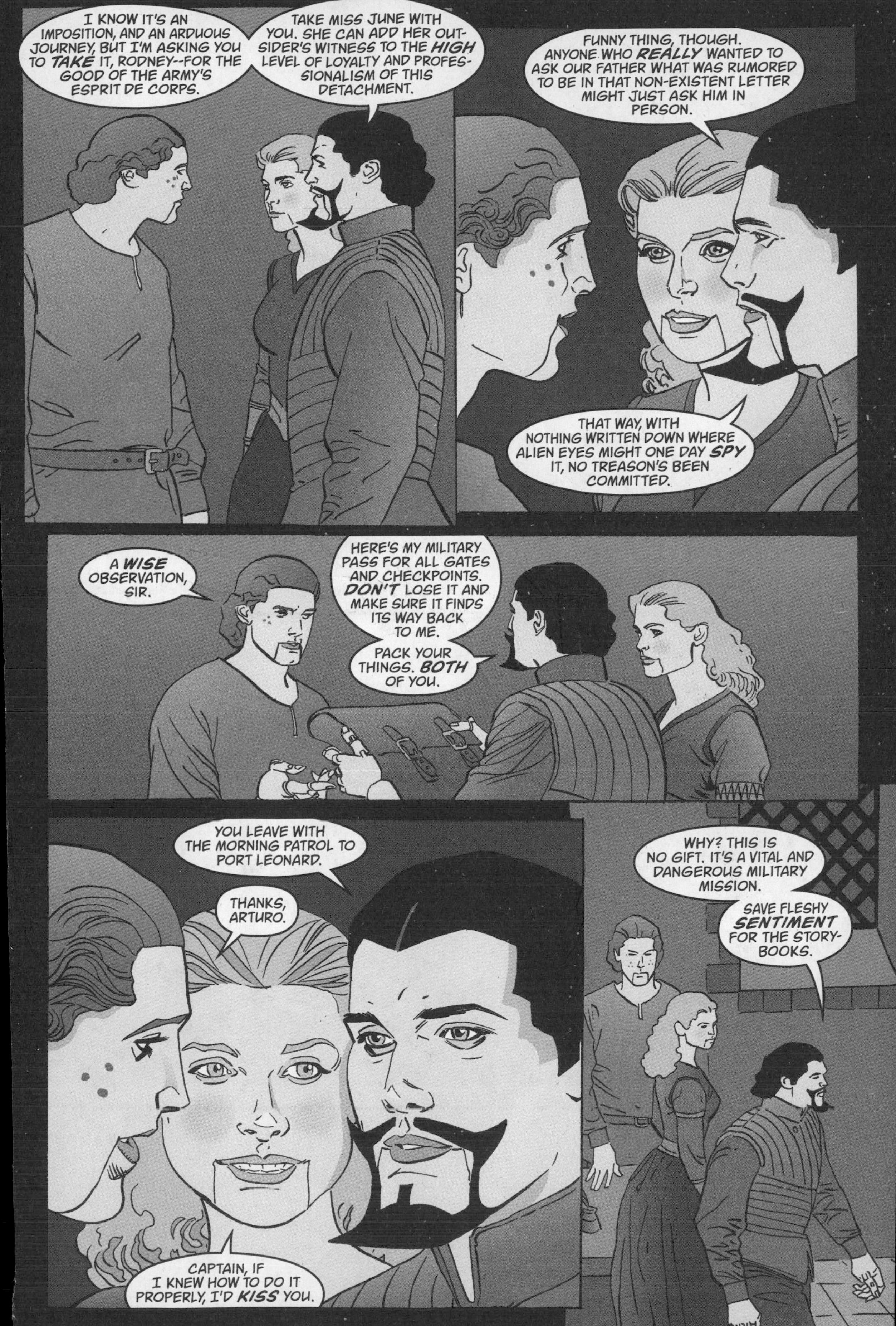
I KNOW IT'S AN IMPOSITION, AND AN ARDUOUS JOURNEY, BUT I'M ASKING YOU TO TAKE IT, RODNEY--FOR THE GOOD OF THE ARMY'S ESPRIT DE CORPS.
TAKE MISS JUNE WITH YOU. SHE CAN ADD HER OUTSIDER'S WITNESS TO THE HIGH LEVEL OF LOYALTY AND PROFESSIONALISM OF THIS DETACHMENT.
FUNNY THING, THOUGH. ANYONE WHO REALLY WANTED TO ASK OUR FATHER WHAT WAS RUMORED TO BE IN THAT NON-EXISTENT LETTER MIGHT JUST ASK HIM IN PERSON.
THAT WAY, WITH NOTHING WRITTEN DOWN WHERE ALIEN EYES MIGHT ONE DAY SPY IT, NO TREASON'S BEEN COMMITTED.
A WISE OBSERVATION, SIR.
HERE'S MY MILITARY PASS FOR ALL GATES AND CHECKPOINTS. DON'T LOSE IT AND MAKE SURE IT FINDS ITS WAY BACK TO ME.
PACK YOUR THINGS. BOTH OF YOU.
YOU LEAVE WITH THE MORNING PATROL TO PORT LEONARD.
THANKS, ARTURO.
CAPTAIN, IF I KNEW HOW TO DO IT PROPERLY, I'D KISS YOU.
WHY? THIS IS NO GIFT. IT'S A VITAL AND DANGEROUS MILITARY MISSION.
SAVE FLESHY SENTIMENT FOR THE STORYBOOKS.

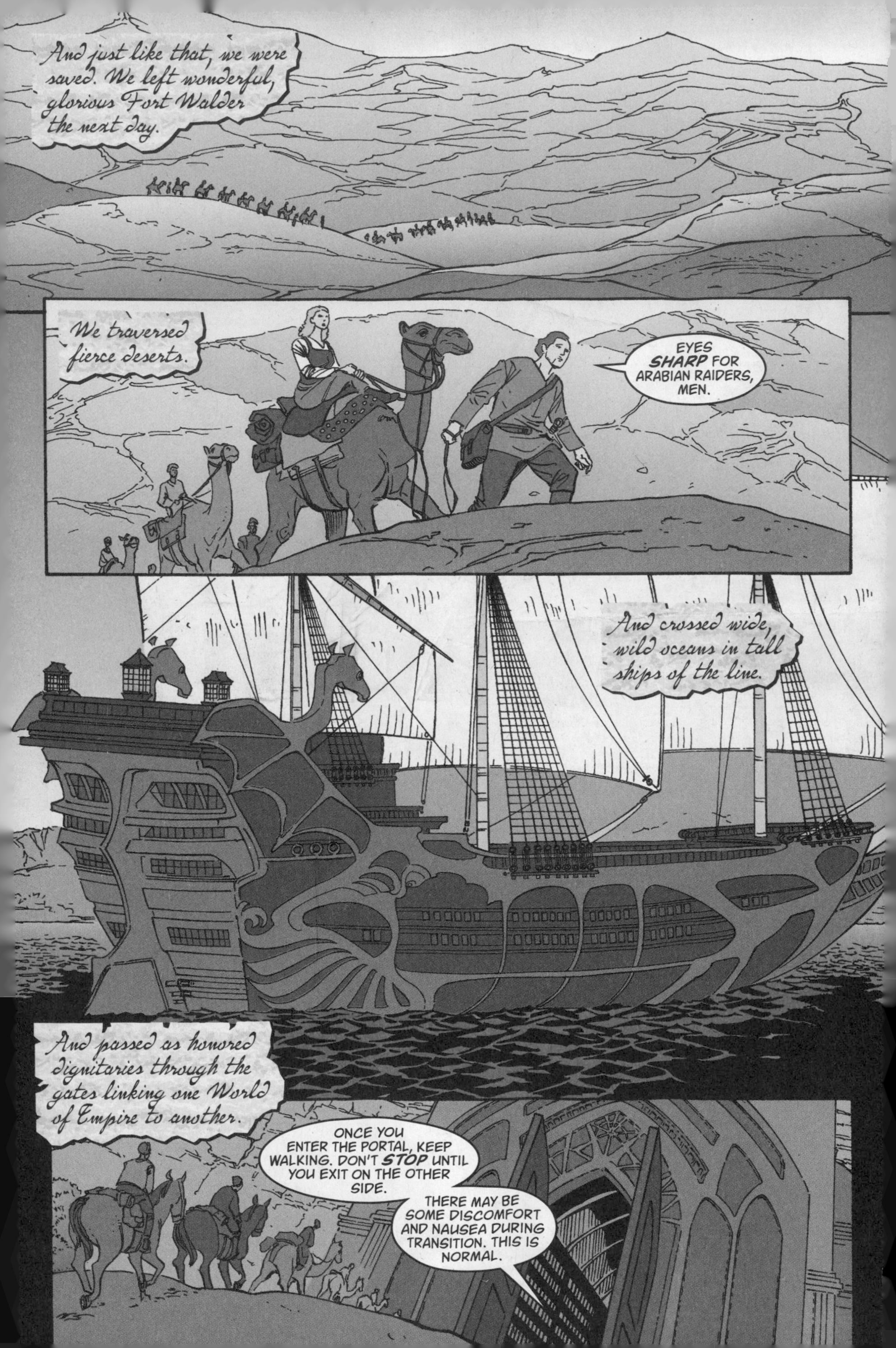
And just like that, we were saved. We left wonderful, glorious Fort Walder the next day.
We traversed fierce deserts.
EYES SHARP FOR ARABIAN RAIDERS, MEN.
And crossed wide, wild oceans in tall ships of the line.
And passed as honored dignitaries through the gates linking one World of Empire to another.
ONCE YOU ENTER THE PORTAL, KEEP WALKING. DON'T STOP UNTIL YOU EXIT ON THE OTHER SIDE.
THERE MAY BE SOME DISCOMFORT AND NAUSEA DURING TRANSITION. THIS IS NORMAL.

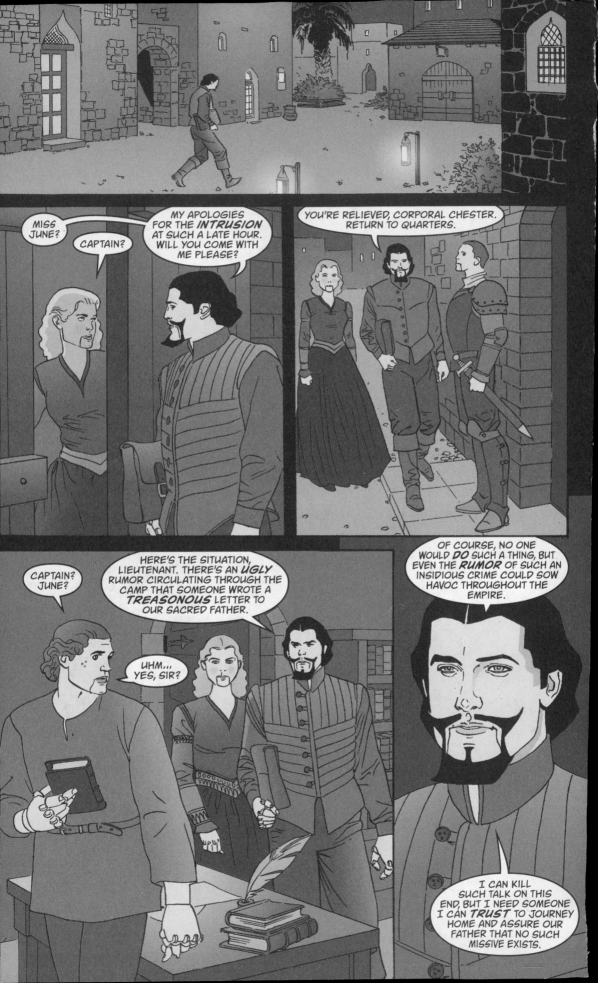

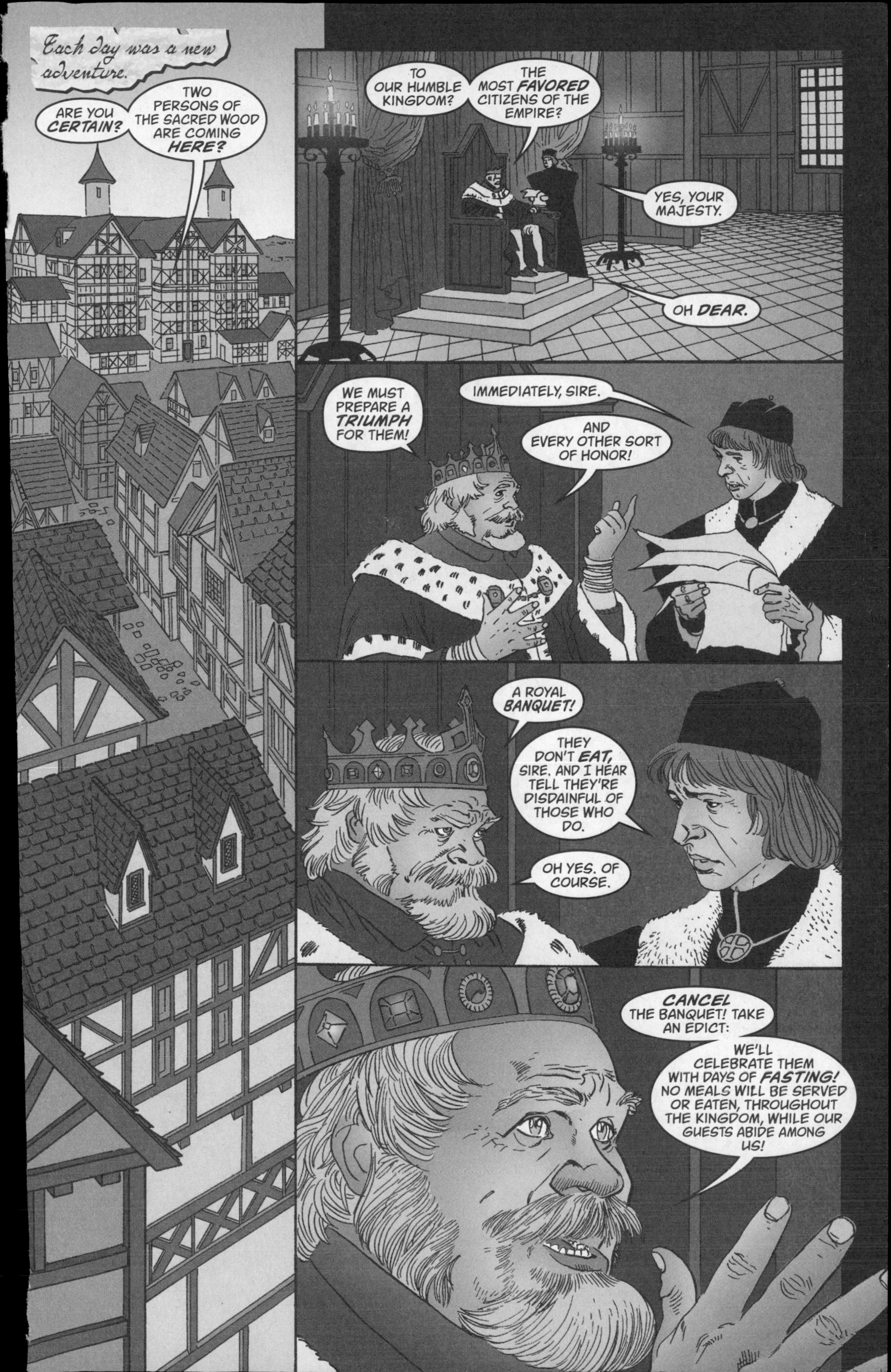
Each day was a new adventure.
ARE YOU CERTAIN?
TWO PERSONS OF THE SACRED WOOD ARE COMING HERE?
TO OUR HUMBLE KINGDOM?
THE MOST FAVORED CITIZENS OF THE EMPIRE?
YES, YOUR MAJESTY.
OH DEAR.
WE MUST PREPARE A TRIUMPH FOR THEM!
IMMEDIATELY, SIRE.
AND EVERY OTHER SORT OF HONOR!
A ROYAL BANQUET!
THEY DON'T EAT, SIRE. AND I HEAR TELL THEY'RE DISDAINFUL OF THOSE WHO DO.
OH YES. OF COURSE.
CANCEL THE BANQUET! TAKE AN EDICT:
WE'LL CELEBRATE THEM WITH DAYS OF FASTING! NO MEALS WILL BE SERVED OR EATEN, THROUGHOUT THE KINGDOM, WHILE OUR GUESTS ABIDE AMONG US!

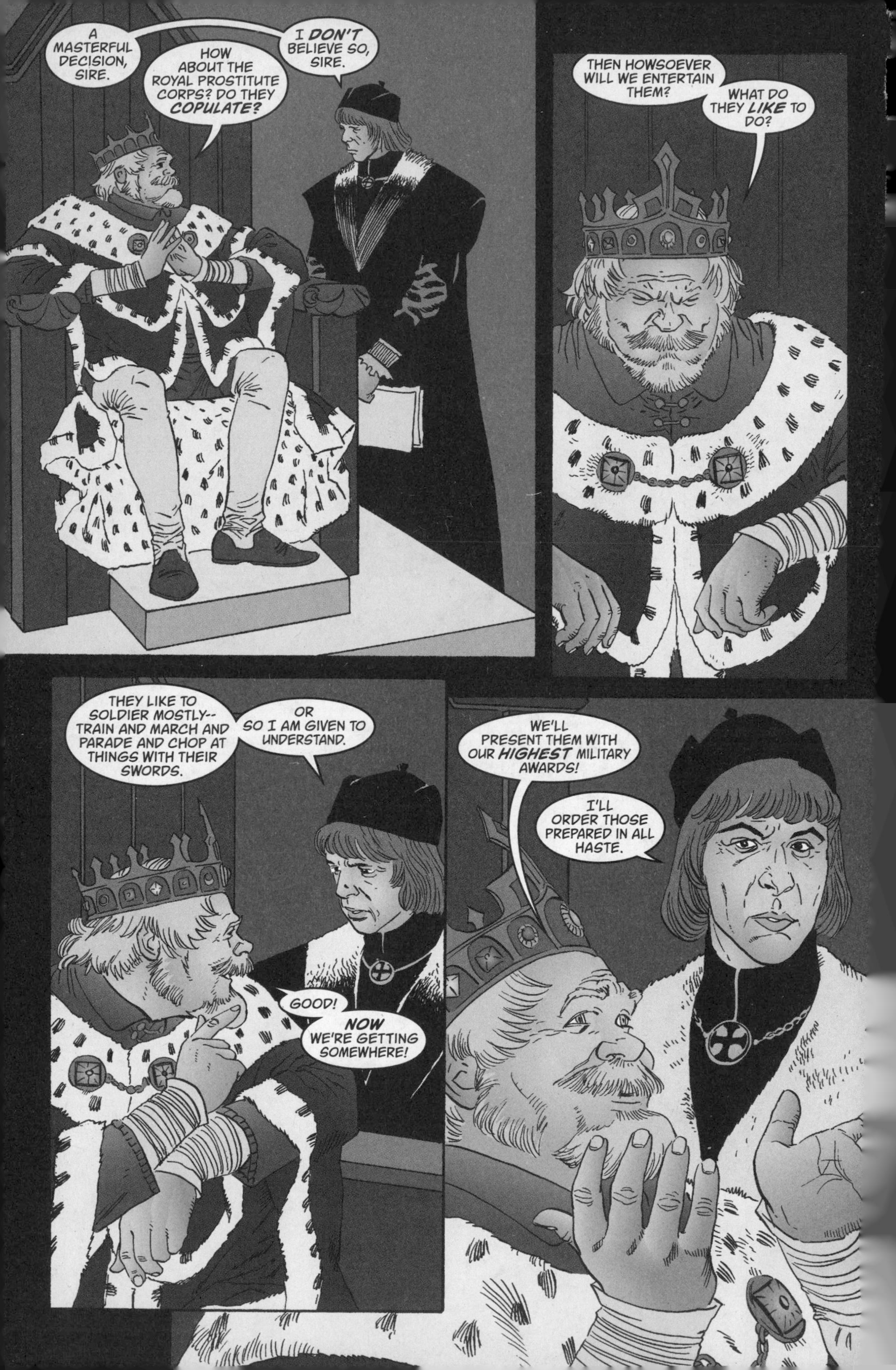
A MASTERFUL DECISION, SIRE.
HOW ABOUT THE ROYAL PROSTITUTE CORPS? DO THEY COPULATE?
I DON'T BELIEVE SO, SIRE.
THEN HOWSOEVER WILL WE ENTERTAIN THEM?
WHAT DO THEY LIKE TO DO?
THEY LIKE TO SOLDIER MOSTLY-- TRAIN AND MARCH AND PARADE AND CHOP AT THINGS WITH THEIR SWORDS.
OR SO I AM GIVEN TO UNDERSTAND.
GOOD!
NOW WE'RE GETTING SOMEWHERE!
WE'LL PRESENT THEM WITH OUR HIGHEST MILITARY AWARDS!
I'LL ORDER THOSE PREPARED IN ALL HASTE.

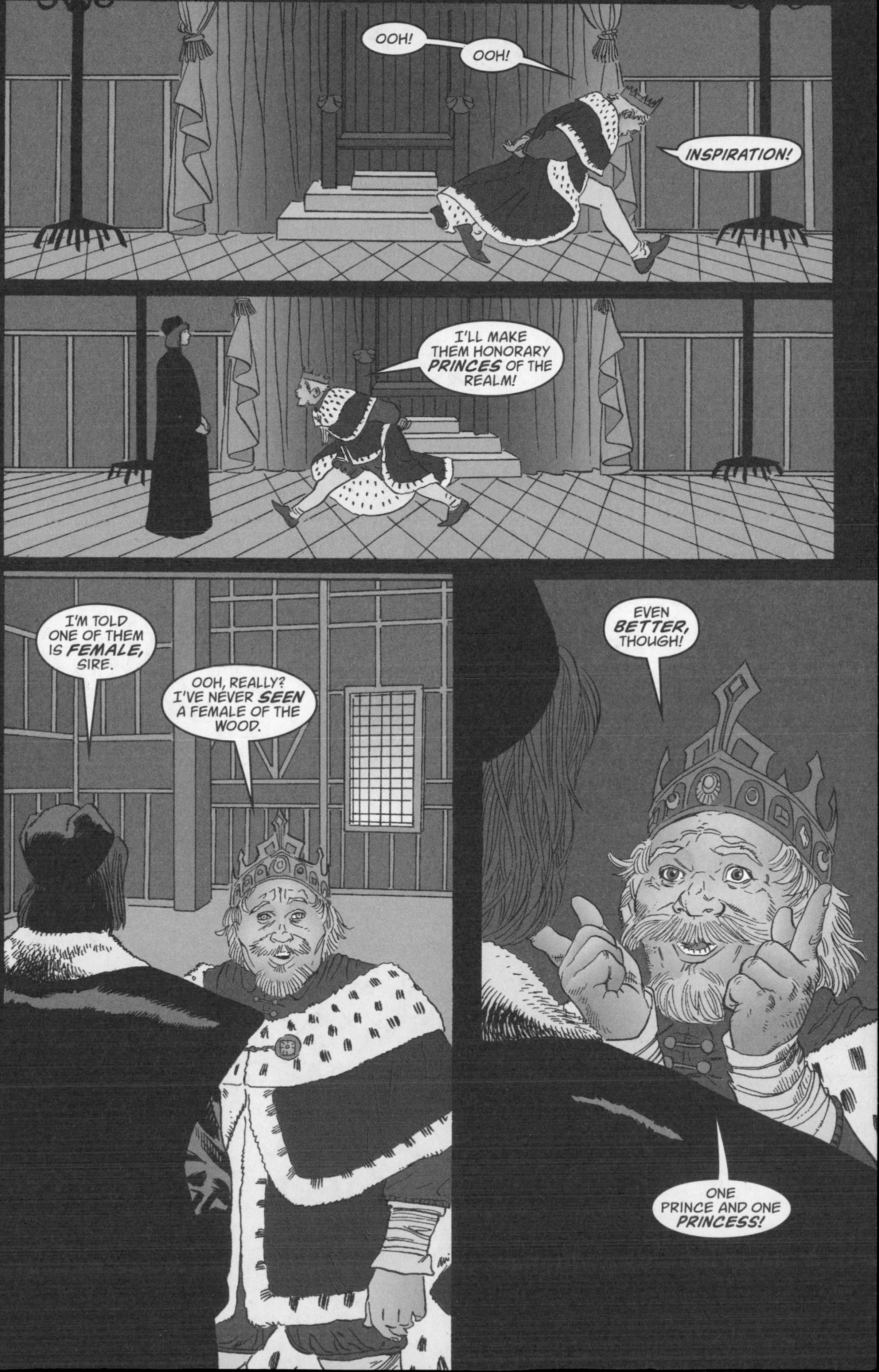
OOH!
OOH!
INSPIRATION!
I'LL MAKE THEM HONORARY PRINCES OF THE REALM!
I'M TOLD ONE OF THEM IS FEMALE, SIRE.
OOH, REALLY? I'VE NEVER SEEN A FEMALE OF THE WOOD.
EVEN BETTER, THOUGH!
ONE PRINCE AND ONE PRINCESS!

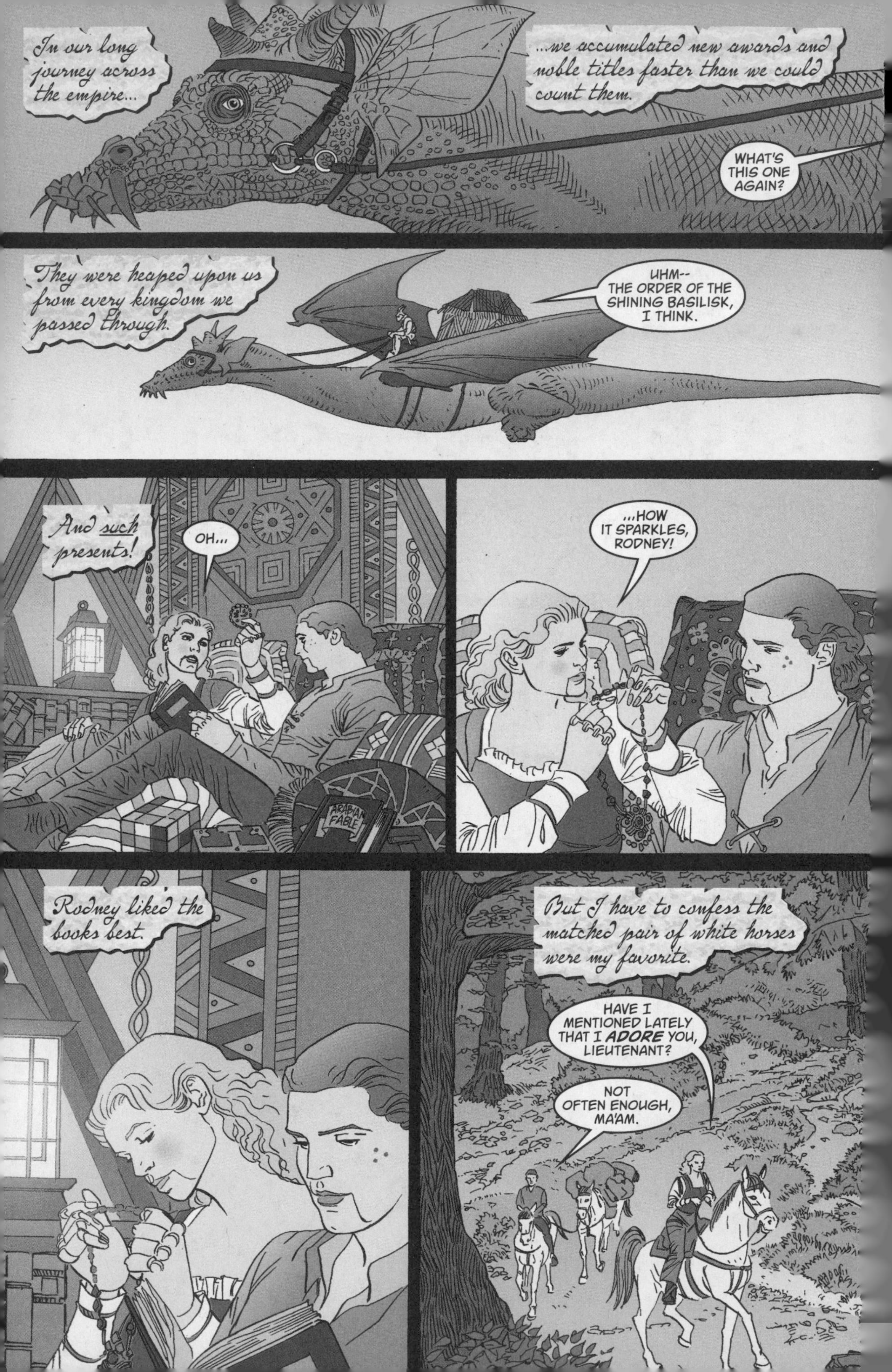
In our long journey across the empire...
...we accumulated new awards and noble titles faster than we could count them.
WHAT'S THIS ONE AGAIN?
They were heaped upon us from every kingdom we passed through.
UHM-- THE ORDER OF THE SHINING BASILISK, I THINK.
And such presents!
OH...
ARABIAN FABLE
...HOW IT SPARKLES, RODNEY!
Rodney liked the books best.
But I have to confess the matched pair of white horses were my favorite.
HAVE I MENTIONED LATELY THAT I ADORE YOU, LIEUTENANT?
NOT OFTEN ENOUGH, MA'AM.

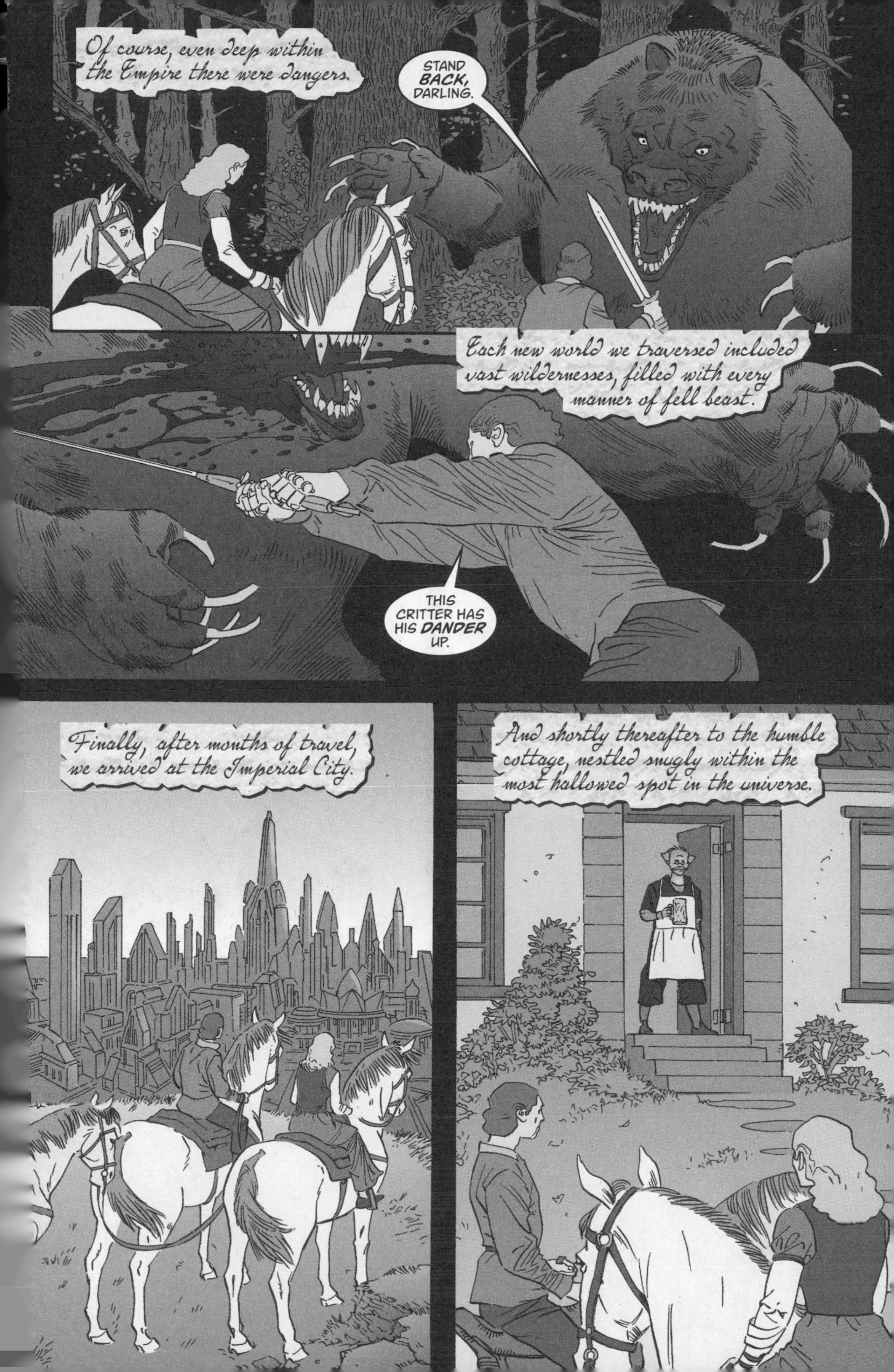
Of course, even deep within the Empire there were dangers.
STAND BACK, DARLING.
Each new world we traversed included vast wildernesses, filled with every manner of fell beast.
THIS CRITTER HAS HIS DANDER UP.
Finally, after months of travel, we arrived at the Imperial City.
And shortly thereafter to the humble cottage, nestled snugly within the most hallowed spot in the universe.

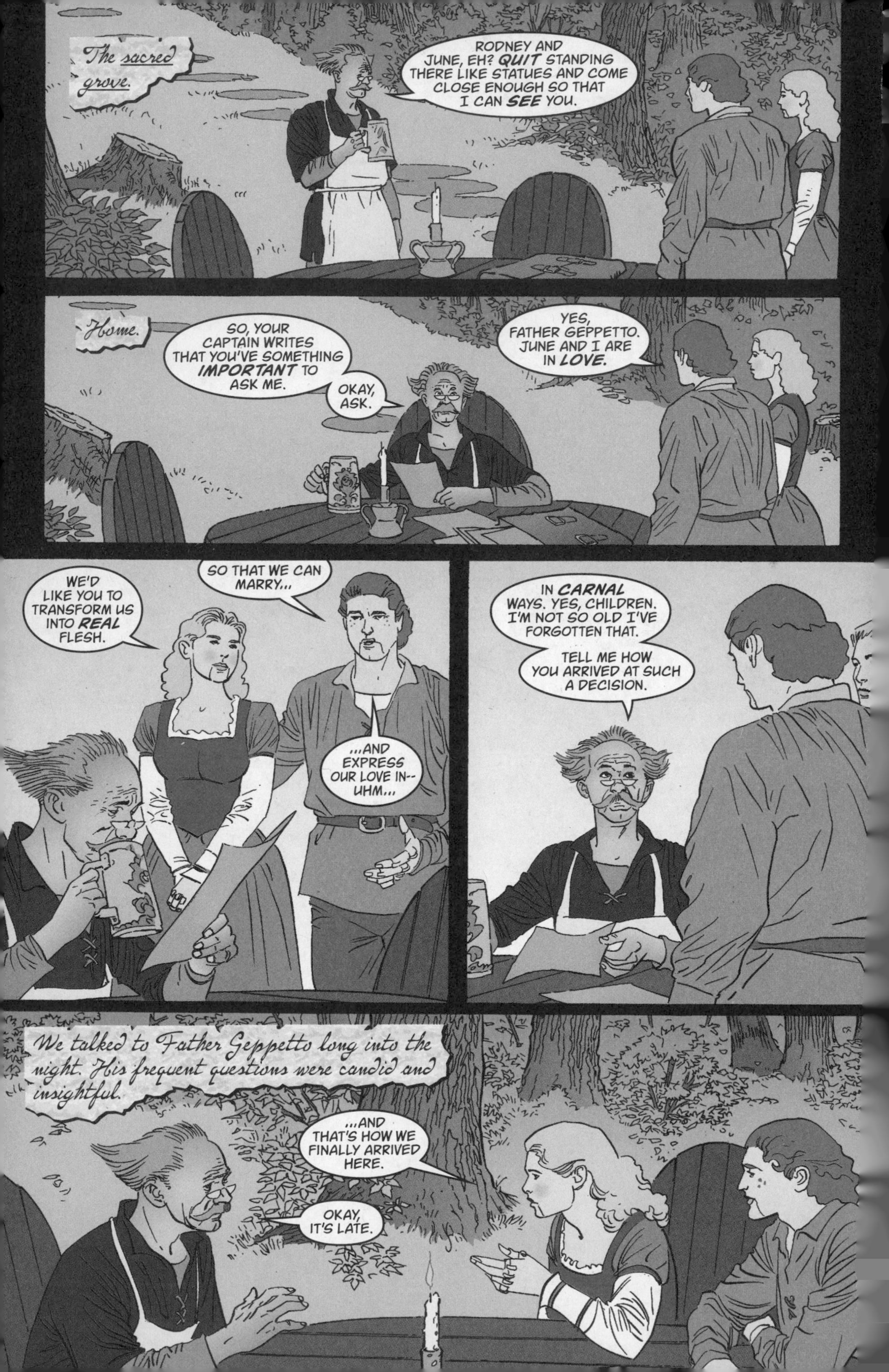

The sacred grove.
RODNEY AND JUNE, EH? QUIT STANDING THERE LIKE STATUES AND COME CLOSE ENOUGH SO THAT I CAN SEE YOU.
Home.
SO, YOUR CAPTAIN WRITES THAT YOU'VE SOMETHING IMPORTANT TO ASK ME.
OKAY, ASK.
YES, FATHER GEPPETTO. JUNE AND I ARE IN LOVE.
WE'D LIKE YOU TO TRANSFORM US INTO REAL FLESH.
SO THAT WE CAN MARRY...
...AND EXPRESS OUR LOVE IN-- UHM...
IN CARNAL WAYS. YES, CHILDREN. I'M NOT SO OLD I'VE FORGOTTEN THAT.
TELL ME HOW YOU ARRIVED AT SUCH A DECISION.
We talked to Father Geppetto long into the night. His frequent questions were candid and insightful.
...AND THAT'S HOW WE FINALLY ARRIVED HERE.
OKAY, IT'S LATE.

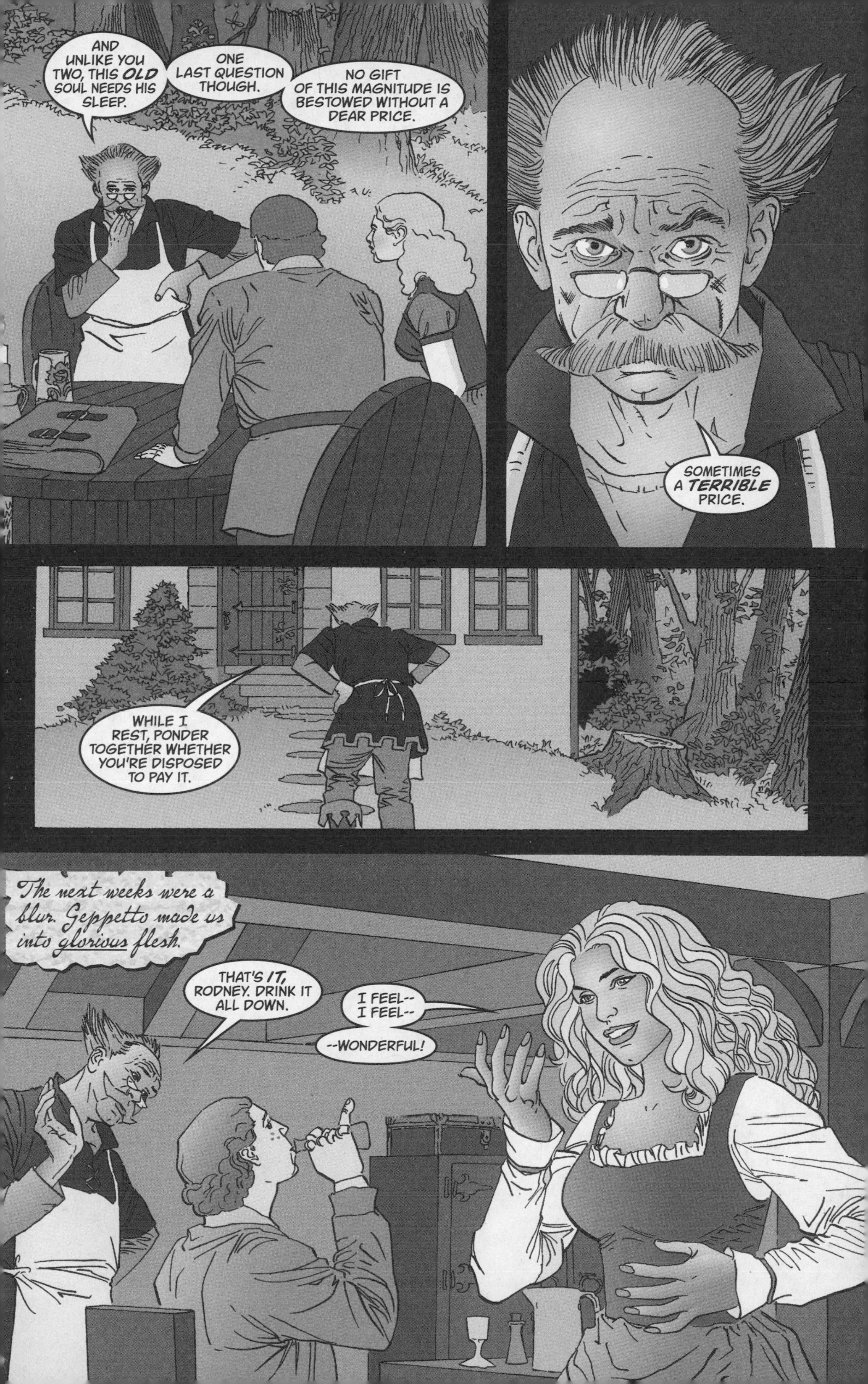
AND UNLIKE YOU TWO, THIS OLD SOUL NEEDS HIS SLEEP.
ONE LAST QUESTION THOUGH.
NO GIFT OF THIS MAGNITUDE IS BESTOWED WITHOUT A DEAR PRICE.
SOMETIMES A TERRIBLE PRICE.
WHILE I REST, PONDER TOGETHER WHETHER YOU'RE DISPOSED TO PAY IT.
The next weeks were a blur. Geppetto made us into glorious flesh.
THAT'S IT, RODNEY. DRINK IT ALL DOWN.
I FEEL-- I FEEL--
--WONDERFUL!

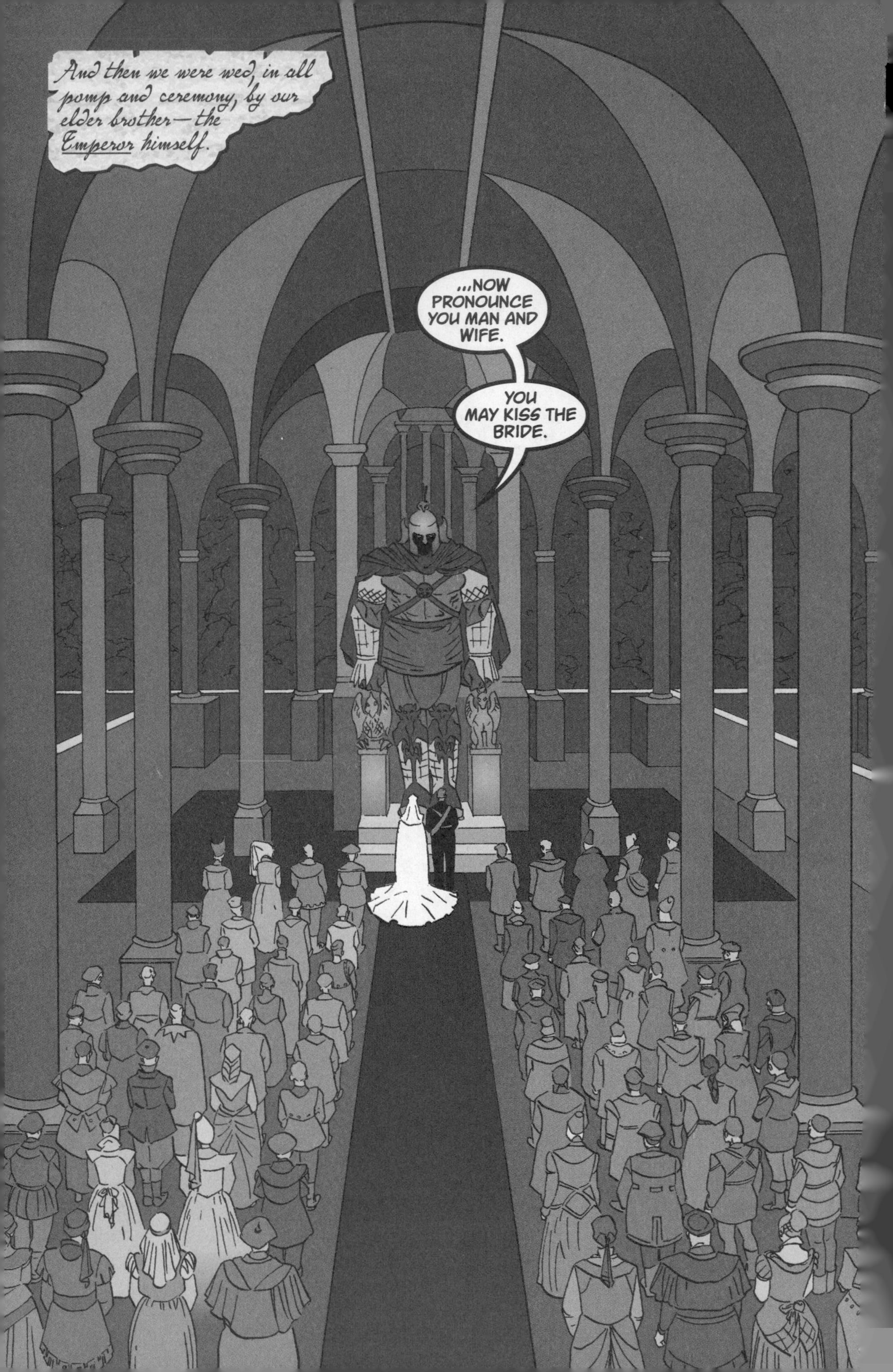
And then we were wed, in all pomp and ceremony, by our elder brother—the Emperor himself.
...NOW PRONOUNCE YOU MAN AND WIFE.
YOU MAY KISS THE BRIDE.

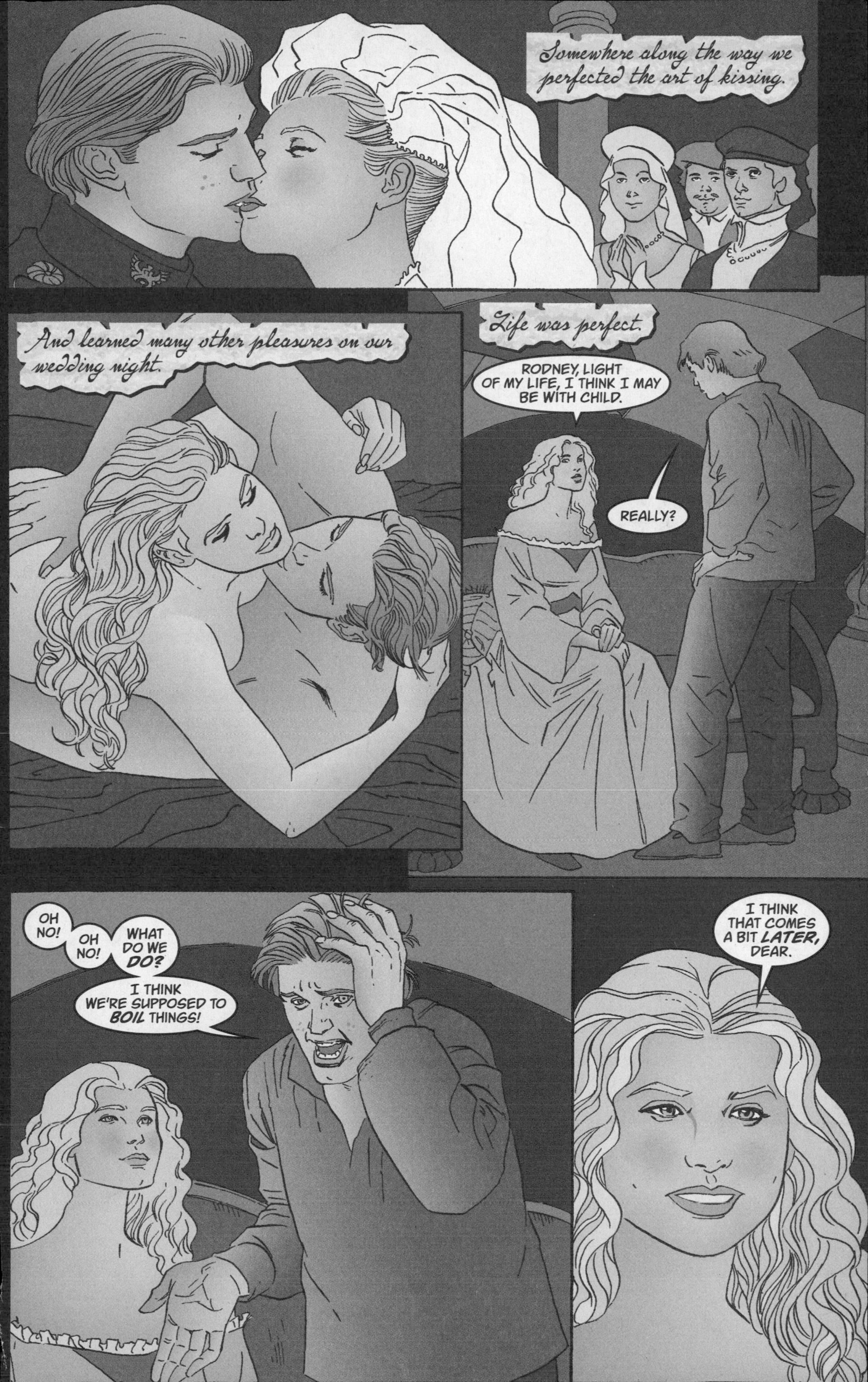
Somewhere along the way we perfected the art of kissing.
And learned many other pleasures on our wedding night.
Life was perfect.
RODNEY, LIGHT OF MY LIFE, I THINK I MAY BE WITH CHILD.
REALLY?
OH NO!
OH NO!
WHAT DO WE DO?
I THINK WE'RE SUPPOSED TO BOIL THINGS!
I THINK THAT COMES A BIT LATER, DEAR.

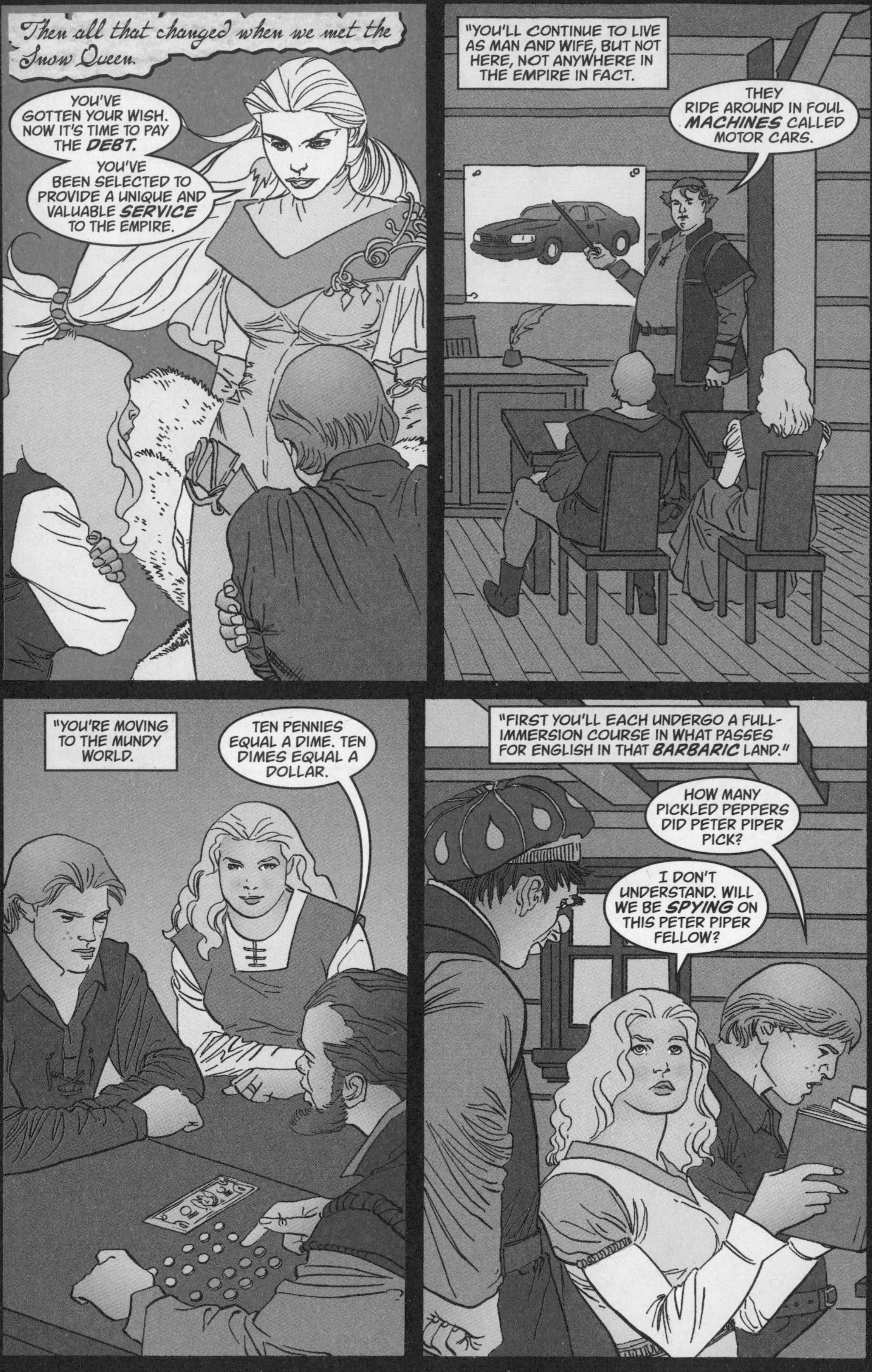
Then all that changed when we met the Snow Queen.
YOU'VE GOTTEN YOUR WISH. NOW IT'S TIME TO PAY THE DEBT.
YOU'VE BEEN SELECTED TO PROVIDE A UNIQUE AND VALUABLE SERVICE TO THE EMPIRE.
"YOU'LL CONTINUE TO LIVE AS MAN AND WIFE, BUT NOT HERE, NOT ANYWHERE IN THE EMPIRE IN FACT.
THEY RIDE AROUND IN FOUL MACHINES CALLED MOTOR CARS.
"YOU'RE MOVING TO THE MUNDY WORLD.
TEN PENNIES EQUAL A DIME. TEN DIMES EQUAL A DOLLAR.
"FIRST YOU'LL EACH UNDERGO A FULL-IMMERSION COURSE IN WHAT PASSES FOR ENGLISH IN THAT BARBARIC LAND."
HOW MANY PICKLED PEPPERS DID PETER PIPER PICK?
I DON'T UNDERSTAND. WILL WE BE SPYING ON THIS PETER PIPER FELLOW?

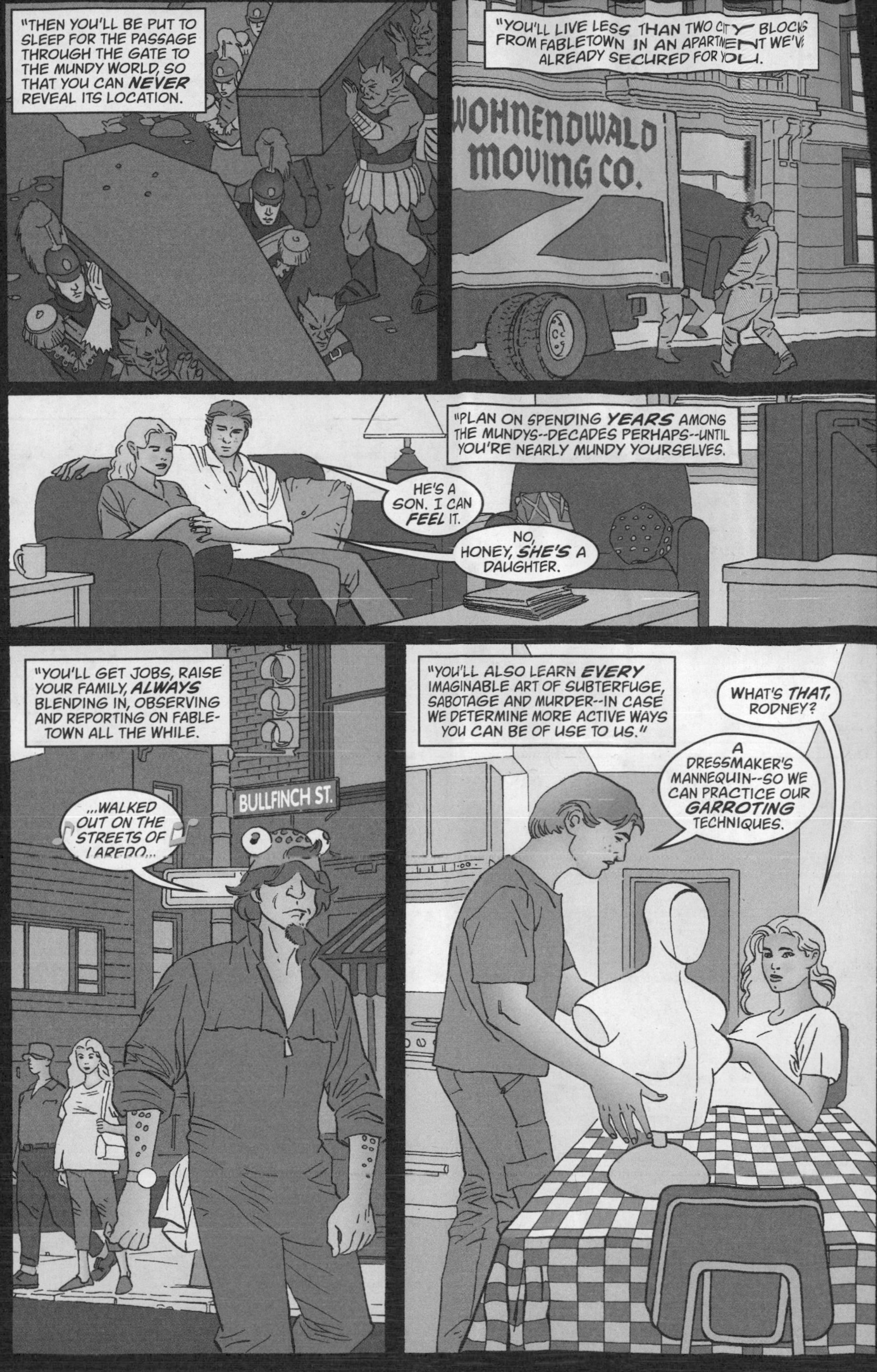
"THEN YOU'LL BE PUT TO SLEEP FOR THE PASSAGE THROUGH THE GATE TO THE MUNDY WORLD, SO THAT YOU CAN NEVER REVEAL ITS LOCATION.
"YOU'LL LIVE LESS THAN TWO CITY BLOCKS FROM FABLETOWN IN AN APARTMENT WE'VE ALREADY SECURED FOR YOU.
WOHNENDWALD MOVING CO.
"PLAN ON SPENDING YEARS AMONG THE MUNDYS--DECADES PERHAPS--UNTIL YOU'RE NEARLY MUNDY YOURSELVES.
HE'S A SON. I CAN FEEL IT.
NO, HONEY, SHE'S A DAUGHTER.
"YOU'LL GET JOBS, RAISE YOUR FAMILY, ALWAYS BLENDING IN, OBSERVING AND REPORTING ON FABLETOWN ALL THE WHILE.
BULLFINCH ST.
...WALKED OUT ON THE STREETS OF LAREDO...
"YOU'LL ALSO LEARN EVERY IMAGINABLE ART OF SUBTERFUGE, SABOTAGE AND MURDER--IN CASE WE DETERMINE MORE ACTIVE WAYS YOU CAN BE OF USE TO US."
WHAT'S THAT, RODNEY?
A DRESSMAKER'S MANNEQUIN--SO WE CAN PRACTICE OUR GARROTING TECHNIQUES.

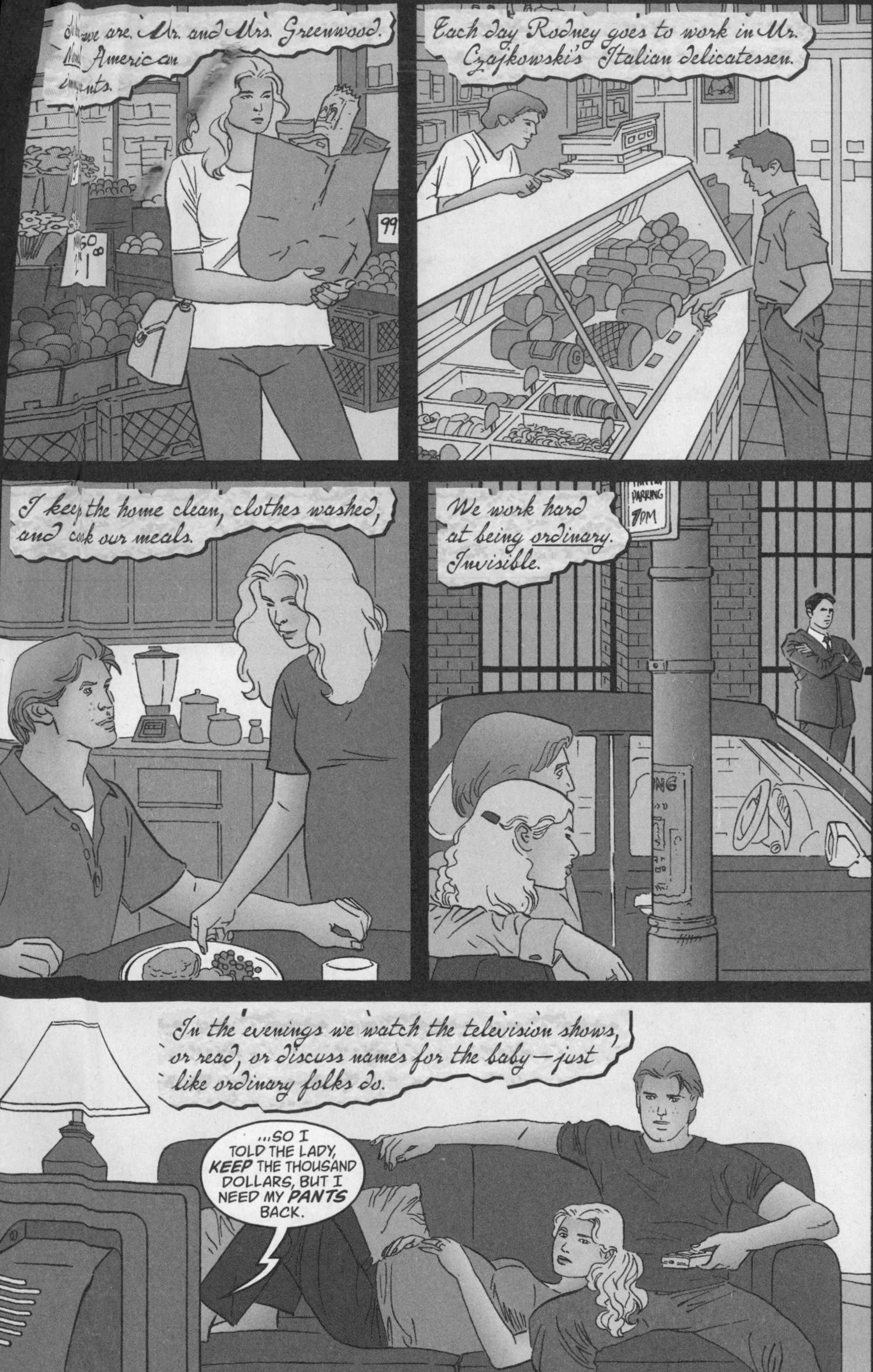
we are. Mr. and Mrs. Greenwood.
American
Each day Rodney goes to work in Mr. Czajkowski's Italian delicatessen.
I keep the home clean, clothes washed, and cook our meals.
We work hard at being ordinary. Invisible.
In the evenings we watch the television shows, or read, or discuss names for the baby—just like ordinary folks do.
...SO I TOLD THE LADY, KEEP THE THOUSAND DOLLARS, BUT I NEED MY PANTS BACK.

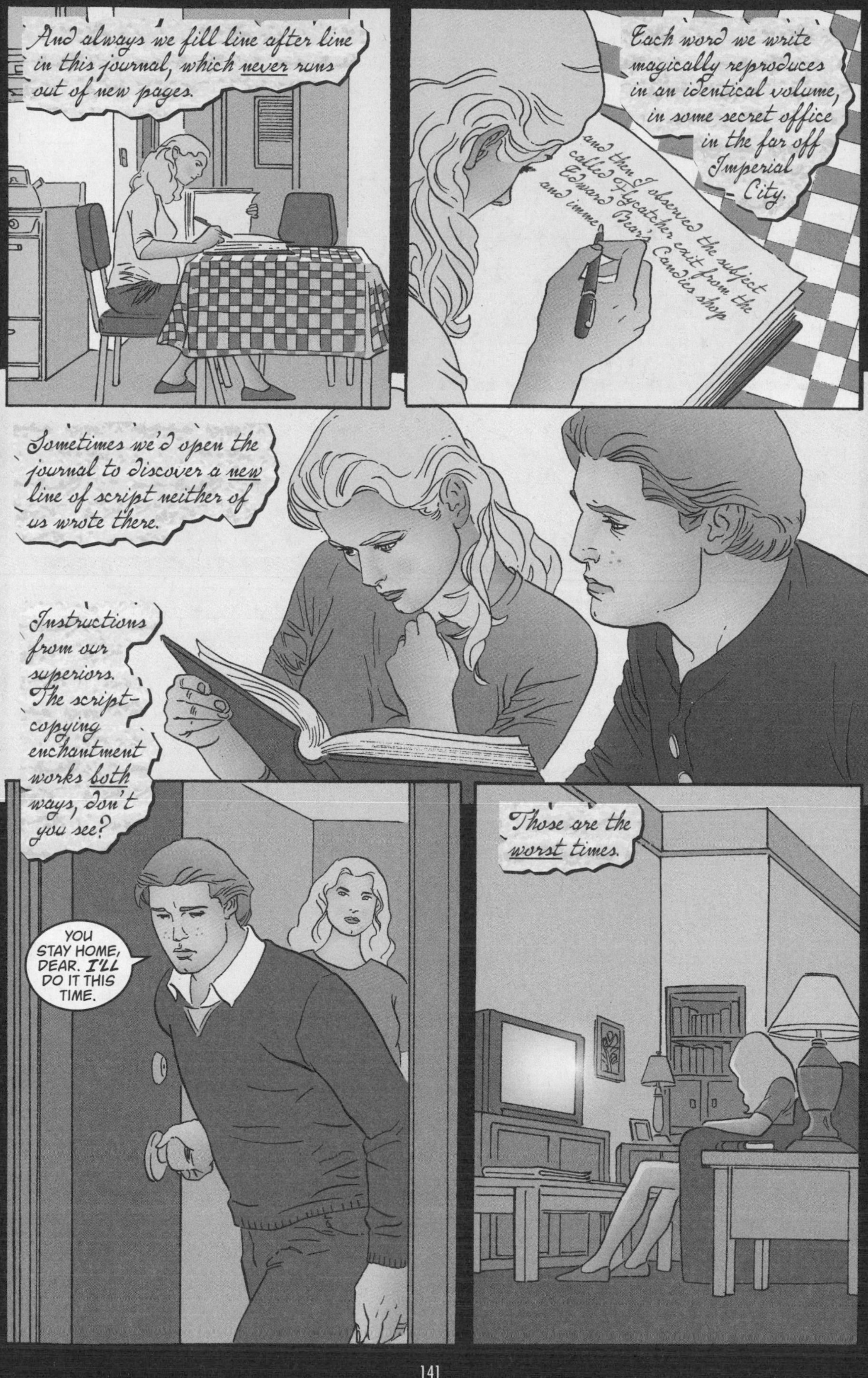
And always we fill line after line in this journal, which never runs out of new pages.
Each word we write magically reproduces in an identical volume, in some secret office in the far off Imperial City.
and then I observed the subject called Flycatcher exit from the Edward Bear's Candies shop and imme
Sometimes we'd open the journal to discover a new line of script neither of us wrote there.
Instructions from our superiors. The script-copying enchantment works both ways, don't you see?
YOU STAY HOME, DEAR. I'LL DO IT THIS TIME.
Those are the worst times.

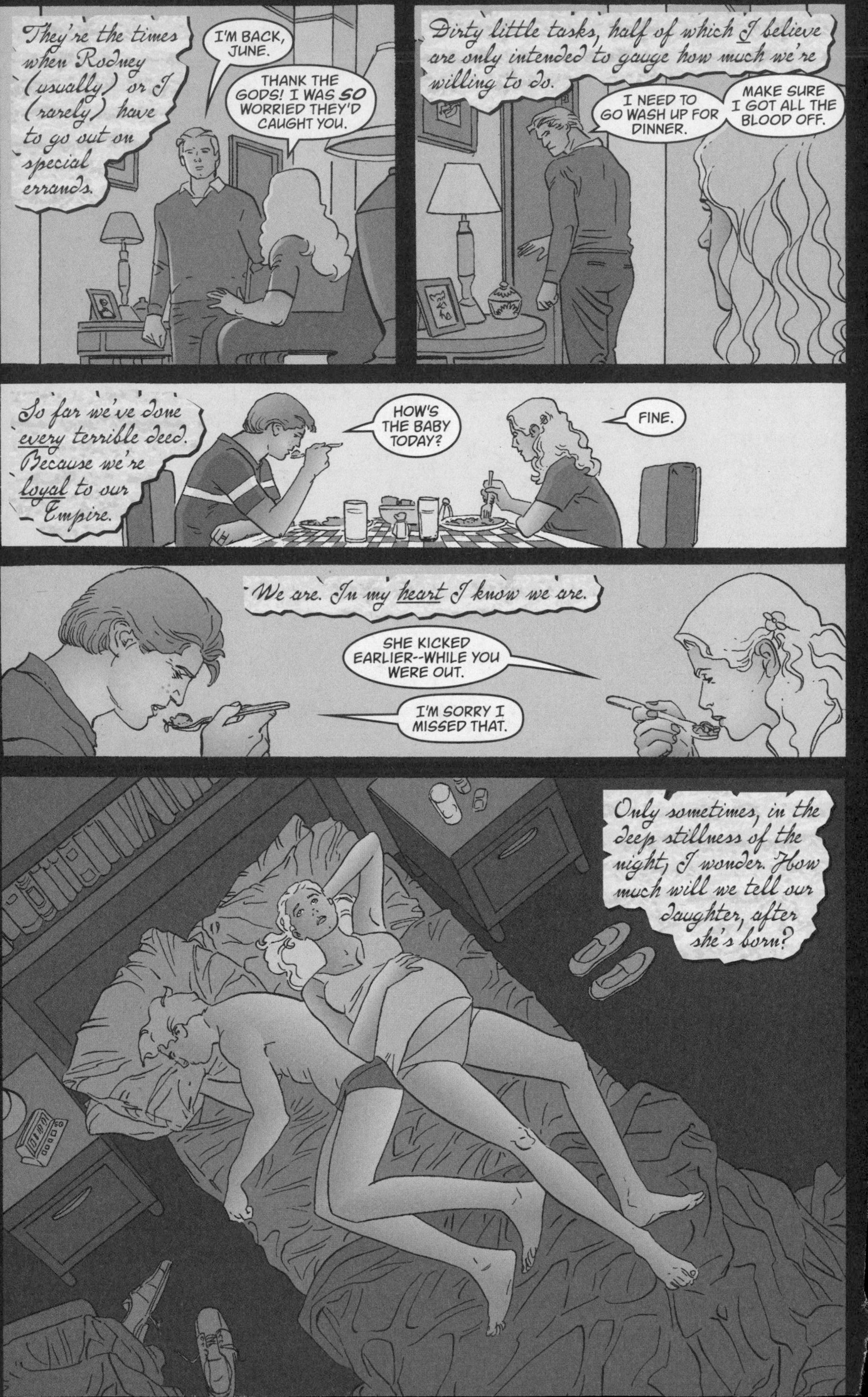
They're the times when Rodney (usually) or I (rarely) have to go out on special errands.
I'M BACK, JUNE.
THANK THE GODS! I WAS SO WORRIED THEY'D CAUGHT YOU.
Dirty little tasks, half of which I believe are only intended to gauge how much we're willing to do.
I NEED TO GO WASH UP FOR DINNER.
MAKE SURE I GOT ALL THE BLOOD OFF.
So far we've done every terrible deed. Because we're loyal to our Empire.
HOW'S THE BABY TODAY?
FINE.
We are. In my heart I know we are.
SHE KICKED EARLIER--WHILE YOU WERE OUT.
I'M SORRY I MISSED THAT.
Only sometimes, in the deep stillness of the night, I wonder. How much will we tell our daughter, after she's born?

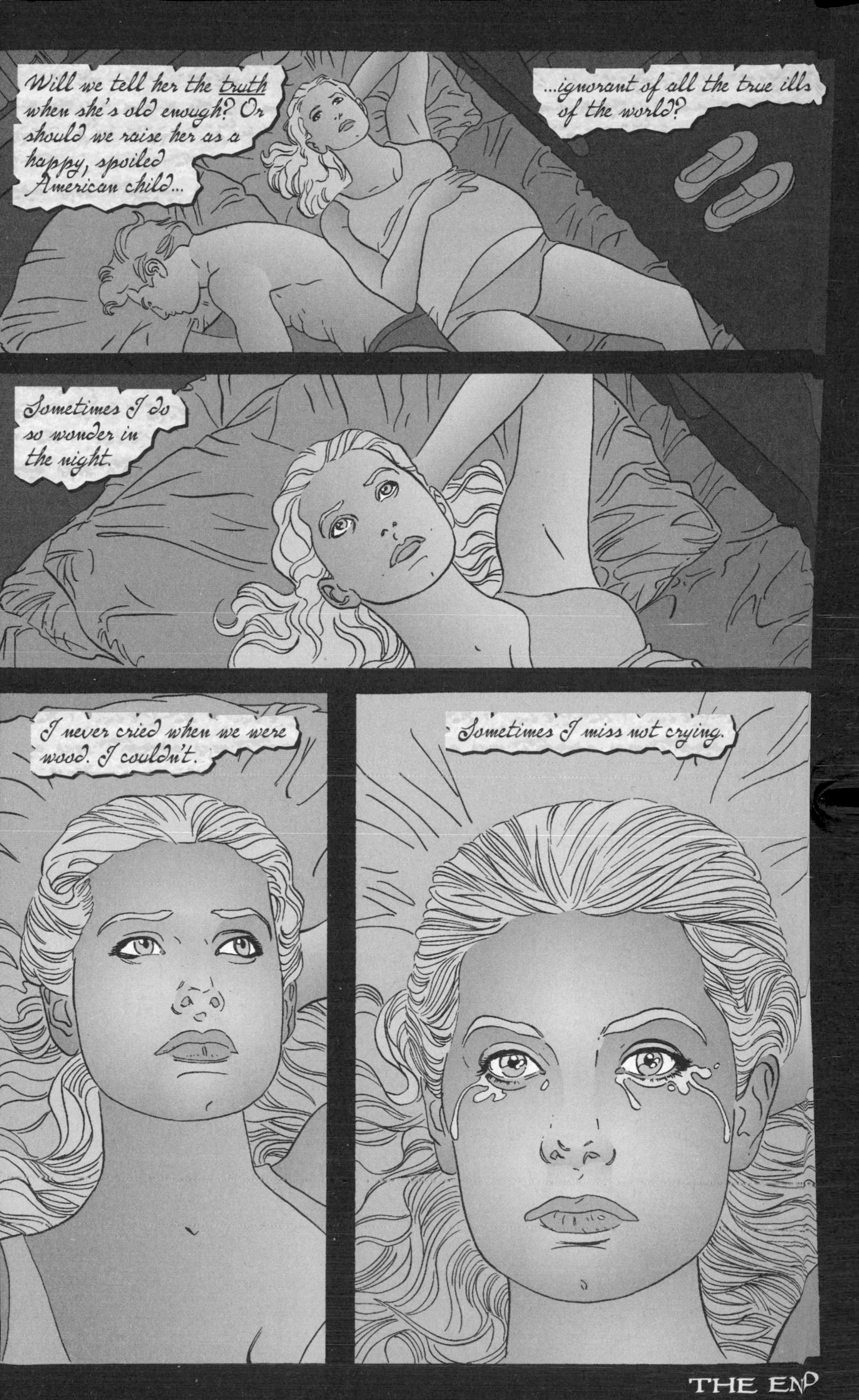
Will we tell her the truth when she's old enough? Or should we raise her as a happy, spoiled American child...
...ignorant of all the true ills of the world?
Sometimes I do so wonder in the night.
I never cried when we were wood. I couldn't.
Sometimes I miss not crying.
THE END